THE DYNAMICS OF
MIDDLE EAST NUCLEAR PROLIFERATION

THE DYNAMICS OF
MIDDLE EAST NUCLEAR PROLIFERATION

Edited by

Steven L. Spiegel
Jennifer D. Kibbe
and
Elizabeth G. Matthews

Symposium Series
Volume 66

The Edwin Mellen Press
Lewiston•Queenston•Lampeter

Library of Congress Cataloging-in-Publication Data

The dynamics of Middle East nuclear proliferation / edited by Steven L. Spiegel, Jennifer D. Kibbe, and Elizabeth G. Matthews.
     p. cm. -- (Symposium series ; v. 66)
  Includes bibliographical references and index.
  ISBN 0-7734-7959-7
  1. Nuclear weapons--Middle East. 2. Nuclear arms control--Middle East. 3. Nuclear nonproliferation. 4. Middle East--Military policy. I. Spiegel, Steven L. II. Kibbe, Jennifer D. III. Matthews, Elizabeth G. IV. Symposium series (Edwin Mellen Press) ; v. 66.

UA832 .D96 2001
327.1'747'0956--dc21

                          2001044478

This is volume 66 in the continuing series
Symposium Series
Volume 66 ISBN 0-7734-7959-7
SS Series ISBN 0-88946-989-X

A CIP catalog record for this book is available from the British Library.

The Edwin Mellen Press
Box 450
Lewiston, New York
USA 14092-0450

The Edwin Mellen Press
Box 67
Queenston, Ontario
CANADA L0S 1L0

The Edwin Mellen Press, Ltd.
Lampeter, Ceredigion, Wales
UNITED KINGDOM SA48 8LT

Printed in the United States of America

This book is part of the BCIR Book Series, "Studies in International Relations" of the Burkle Center for International Relations at UCLA.

Table of Contents

Abbreviations Used in This Work

ABM	Anti-ballistic Missile
ACDA	Arms Control and Disarmament Agency
ACRS	Arms Control and Regional Security
AEB	Atomic Energy Board – South Africa
AEC	Atomic Energy Corporation – South Africa
AEE	Atomic Energy Establishment
ANC	African National Conference
ARMSCOR	South African Armaments Corporation
BJP	Bharatiya Janata Party
BW	biological weapons
CBM	Confidence Building Measures
CD	Conference on Disarmament
CEA	French Atomic Energy Commission
CERN	European Center for Nuclear Research
CIA	Central Intelligence Agency
CSBM	Confidence and Security Building Measures
CTBT	Comprehensive Test Ban Treaty
CW	chemical weapons
CWC	Chemical Weapons Convention
EBAE	Egyptian Board of Atomic Energy
EMIS	electromagnetic isotope separation
FMCT	Fissile Material Cut-Off Treaty
GCC	Gulf Cooperation Council
HEU	highly-enriched uranium
IAEA	International Atomic Energy Agency
IAEC	Israel Atomic Energy Committee
ICBM	intercontinental ballistic missile
ICJ	International Court of Justice
INF	Intermediate Nuclear Treaty
MRBM	medium-range ballistic missile
MTCR	Missile Technology Control Regime
NAM	Non-Aligned Movement
NATO	North Atlantic Treaty Organization
NPT	Nuclear Non-proliferation Treaty

NPTREC	Nuclear Non-Proliferation Treaty Review and Extension Conference
NWFZ	nuclear weapons-free zone
NWFZN	nuclear weapons-free zone, Nordic Area
NWS	Nuclear Weapons States
OMV	ongoing monitoring and verification process
PLO	Palestine Liberation Organization
SRBM	Short-range ballistic missile
UAR	United Arab Republic
UN	United Nations
UNIVOC	United Nations Monitoring, Verification and Inspection Commission
UNSCOM	United Nations Special Commission on Iraq
WMD	weapons of mass destruction
WMDFZ	weapons of mass destruction free zone

Preface

At the dawn of the 21st century, clearly one of the world's great problems is the proliferation of weapons of mass destruction, including nuclear, biological, and chemical weapons, as well as the missiles to deliver them. Areas of particular concern are the Far East, especially regarding the two Koreas, South Asia, and the Middle East. This volume focuses on the last region and attempts to deal with the most likely cases of proliferation and their ramifications. The emphasis is on nuclear weapons, and particularly on those states which have or could have them in the not-too-distant future, which necessarily concentrates the spotlight on Israel, Iran and Iraq.

The prospects for controlling proliferation in the Middle East are grim indeed. In 1995 the situation did not seem quite as serious as it does today, but the clouds of trouble were beginning to gather. At that time, a group of specialists from the region, the United States and Europe were invited by UCLA's Burkle Center for International Relations to discuss the issue of nuclear proliferation. In particular, the group was asked to examine lessons on how decisions to go nuclear are made, some lessons from other regions which might inform how decisions not to proliferate evolve, and lessons on how proliferation decisions might be reversed.

The conference was held in Limassol, Cyprus, in August 1995. A long series of discussions and evaluations followed. In the process, the conference became an annual event and the subject broadened to issues of regional security and arms control. The papers for the original conference were refined and evaluated. Some papers were added from other conferences; others of the original papers became less

i

relevant to the subject at hand. Finally, those working on this project decided that the papers included here were ready for publication, leading to the present volume.

It begins with three papers that examine the broad picture of Middle East proliferation. In the first chapter, Steven Spiegel sets the context for the ensuing discussions by assessing each state's current weapons of mass destruction (WMD) capability and then predicting what the region will look like in 2015. His conclusion that WMD proliferation in the region is inevitable, no matter what happens in the peace process, only serves to highlight the necessity of this volume. The second chapter, by Lawrence Scheinman, addresses the definition of arms control and the purpose of the process. Scheinman argues that "arms control overlaps diplomacy in defense policy, at times involving formal negotiations, at other times employing informal arrangements and unilateral actions." The third chapter, by Professor Janice Stein, uses Israel and Egypt as case studies and finds that the perspectives of strategic leaders are critical not only to decisions of whether or not to proliferate, but also to restraint and reversal on this issue.

These three chapters are followed by a set of six, two each on the crucial cases of Iraq, Iran and Israel. Some chapters have been largely rewritten since their 1995 presentations; others are accompanied by updates and amendments. Following the six case studies of the three countries, we move to another six chapters with three Israeli views of regional proliferation followed by three Arab perspectives. The book concludes with two examples of countries which ultimately rejected the nuclear option. South Africa secretly developed nuclear weapons and then publicly announced that it was renouncing the option and disassembling its nuclear force. Sweden could have developed a nuclear force but chose not to. Both David Albright on South Africa and Jan Prawitz on Sweden provide considerable detail on how the decisions of each country were made. It is possible that South Africa and Sweden and countries like them who have renounced nuclear weapons could serve as a model for the Middle East but, unfortunately, Mideast states are more likely to emulate those countries which continue to have nuclear weapons or maintain an active option.

Dealing with the resolution of this challenge is beyond the scope of this volume. Rather, the essays which follow set out the background and parameters of the issues before us. They are intended to orient the reader to the nature of the proliferation question as it is developing in the region in the belief that this is the first step toward seeking the resolutions which will be essential if disaster is to be averted.

The Burkle Center for International Relations wishes to thank the many people who have contributed to the publication of this volume. First, the first two conferences, from which most of the chapters contained in these pages were taken, were funded by Sandia National Laboratories on behalf of the Department of Energy, the Arms Control and Disarmament Agency, the Ploughshares Foundation, and the Swedish Foreign Ministry. Second, the Center wishes to express its gratitude to Dr. Michael Yaffe of the U.S. Department of State for his guidance and support throughout the long gestation process in the preparation of this book. Last, but by no means least, we would like to thank the two assistants who aided in the hard, fundamental work that formed the basis for this volume and without whom the task could not have been completed. We are most grateful to Elizabeth Matthews and Jennifer D. Kibbe for their determined perseverance and their critical acumen. In addition, Michael Blakley worked in the early stages to move the project forward. All of us who toiled in putting together this manuscript over several years offer it to our readers in the hopes that it will sharpen and refine discussions of the future of the Middle East.

Steven L. Spiegel
Los Angeles, January 2001

Foreword

This book on the proliferation of weapons of mass destruction in the Middle East could not be more timely. There have been several recent developments in the Middle East which are causes of great concern. The decline of the Arab-Israeli peace process, the return of the Palestinian intifada, and the increase in terrorism and violence endanger the long-term security of the entire Middle East region. One possible result is that of stimulating incentives for states in the region to acquire weapons of mass destruction, including nuclear, chemical, and biological/ bacteriological weapons. The spread of such weapons, particularly nuclear weapons, in the broader Middle East region, including states of the Gulf and the Mahgreb, could lead to a regional qualitative arms race in the development of these weapons. The world could well witness in the region a repeat of the chains of proliferation that have become familiar for nuclear weapons worldwide. In the case of nuclear weapons, the initial development of these weapons by the United States in 1945, stimulated in part by fear of their development in Nazi Germany, led in turn to their development by the Soviet Union in 1949, the United Kingdom in 1952, and France in 1960. This led to their development by China in 1964, which, in turn led to their development by India in 1972 and, eventually, to Pakistan in 1998. These type of proliferation links could repeat in the Middle East. Israel undoubtedly possesses nuclear weapons; Iraq and Iran may soon acquire them. This latest proliferation would jeopardize existing deterrence relations and could even lead to the use of such weapons in a future Middle East conflict, with devastating effects that would go well beyond those of the chemical weapons that have already been used in the region.

Professor Steven L. Spiegel, my colleague in both the UCLA Department of Political Science and the Burkle Center for International Relations at UCLA, has organized a very important book on this topic of weapons of mass destruction in the Middle East region. It includes case studies, analyses, and prognoses dealing with Israel, Iran, Iraq, with important treatments of the denuclearization of South Africa and the decision by Sweden to forego nuclear weapons development. Its authors are experts from universities, think tanks, and governments in the United States, Sweden, and Canada as well as the region itself. The book should be of wide interest to everyone concerned with security in this important region.

Michael D. Intriligator
Professor of Economics, Political Science, and Policy Studies
Director, Burkle Center for International Relations, UCLA

Chapter 1

The Middle East and WMDs in 2015

Steven L. Spiegel

This article analyzes regional trends in proliferation and arms control in an effort to predict what the Middle East will look like in 2015. If you compare the Middle East of today with what the region looked like 15 years ago, it is clear that much has changed. In the mid-1980s, Israel and the PLO were bitter enemies trying to destroy each other. The United States was tilting towards Iraq in the Iran-Iraq War, the Cold War was very much alive, and Mikhail Gorbachev had just come to power. Anyone who would have predicted in 1985 that within five years the Cold War would be over and within six years the Soviet Union would have collapsed, would have had their sanity questioned. So these kinds of prognostications should always be taken with more than one grain of salt.

The changes brought about in the region by the end of the Cold War have been both good and bad. On the one hand, without the United States and the Soviet Union exercising their competition in the Middle East, there has been an opportunity to move towards general peace accords, which, with the exception of the Egyptian-Israeli accord, had long been blocked by the superpower competition. Certainly the Madrid and Oslo processes were in part generated by the end of the Cold War. On the other hand, however, just as the superpowers are no longer limiting cooperation in the region, they are also no longer limiting conflict. During the Cold War, although the superpowers allowed plenty of conflict, and even encouraged it, they did not allow one state to destroy its opponent (or itself); either the United States or the Soviet Union would step in to prevent this final, destabilizing step. If the Cold War had continued, it is doubtful that we would be as concerned about the proliferation of weapons of mass destruction (WMD)[1] as we are today.

The conventional wisdom has been to view these two aspects, the peace process and weapons of mass destruction, as somehow congruent; the assumption is that if there is progress in one, there will be progress in the other. If the peace process is successful, there will be concurrent advances in limiting the danger of weapons of mass destruction, and by contrast, if the peace process collapses, then weapons of mass destruction will proliferate.

The major argument I want to set forth in this article is that the peace process cannot and will not prevent further proliferation, which I believe to be inevitable. The peace process can, however, help to manage that proliferation. Moreover, this is just the most significant example of a fundamental error that Americans are making in their approach to the peace process: it is not just a question of settling particular issues but also one of creating the potential for the United States to be able to deal with other concerns that deeply affect American interests, the threat of WMD proliferation most prominent among them. In other words, the peace process is not the entire house, it is just the gate – the entry point for trying to manage further problems.

It has been said that Hollywood is incapable of dealing with marriage. It is good at the romance and getting people to the altar, but it doesn't know how to portray the normalcy of marriage. In a sense, the Arabs and Israelis, as well as the Americans in their Middle East policy, are very similar. They are focused on peace treaties as the end game, and there is very little thinking about life after the peace

---

[1] Weapons of mass destruction as defined here include nuclear, chemical and biological weapons, as well as their delivery systems.

treaties are signed. The United States is going to be critical to the post-peace period, and especially so to any effort to manage the problem of weapons of mass destruction. That said, stemming the proliferation of weapons of mass destruction is something that cannot wait until the peace process concludes.

Why WMDs in the Middle East?

Why would Middle Eastern states turn to weapons of mass destruction? The first, and most basic, reason is simple security. They may be afraid of somebody. However, their very act of acquiring a WMD, even if they intend it only for protection, may well threaten the state they were trying to protect themselves from, causing that state to seek out WMDs as well, a dynamic known as the security dilemma. And one of the particular difficulties in the Middle East is the additional characteristic of overlapping problems, which tends to multiply the security dilemma. If a country takes actions *vis-à-vis* another country that it is concerned about, it may open up a Pandora's Box in relation to several other countries. Thus, Iran may make moves in response to its principal worry, Iraq, but the Gulf states, Israel, Egypt, and others are concerned about what Iran does. Similarly, although Pakistan and India's recent proliferation moves were clearly aimed at each other, they also worried Tehran. And Israel may be concerned about a situation in Lebanon, but how it responds may pose problems for other Arab states in the region. Thus, because there are so many overlapping power balances in the Middle East involving Arabs, Persians, Israelis, Turks, the Gulf states, and the countries of the Eastern Mediterranean and the Maghreb, it is not just protective weapons which proliferate, but the security dilemma itself.

Second, WMDs, particularly chemical and biological weapons, are cheaper than a large arsenal of conventional weapons. Despite the recent rise of oil prices, the oil bonanza is over for many of these states. Middle East states have less money and thus are buying fewer conventional weapons. WMDs, therefore, represent an easy way to shore up their security while staying on a budget. It is not accidental that biological and chemical weapons are called the "poor man's nuke." Moreover, not only are they cheaper, but they are also easier and less technologically sophisticated to produce. And in the irony that is WMD logic, many proposed forms of counter-proliferation (i.e., defenses against WMDs), can act as incentives for states to develop biological weapons (which, to date, cannot be defended against) and use unconventional means of delivery.

For several states, WMDs actually serve a deterrent function. Some states see the value of WMDs in being able to use them to prevent the United States or a regional power from exercising coercive diplomacy or from taking particular actions. For example, would the United States have acted the way it did in the Persian Gulf War or in the Kosovo crisis if it had known then what we know now about Iraq's WMD capabilities, or if Yugoslavia had had WMDs? To some states, then, this category of weapons may represent an affordable, feasible way to at least partially even out the balance of power, even when they have no thought of actually using them.

Finally, there are also several non-security-related reasons for acquiring WMDs. Nuclear weapons in particular have long been seen as a sure-fire way of gaining national prestige. As a Bharatiya Janata Party (BJP) spokesperson put it in 1993, "[n]uclear weapons will give us prestige, power, standing. An Indian will talk straight and walk straight when we have the bomb."[2] And for many of the Middle Eastern states, the prestige afforded by WMDs is critical in the all-important task of keeping up with Israel. The drive to acquire a WMD capability has also been fueled by the ambition of scientists trying to prove their ability, and by the need of leaders

---

[2] Quoted in George Perkovich, "Nuclear Proliferation," *Foreign Policy* (Fall 1998), 14.

to score points or create distractions in domestic political battles.[3] All three of these elements were certainly factors in Iraq's WMD development, and to some extent in Iran as well.

WMD Capabilities in 2015

In trying to make any kind of prediction about the Middle East in 2015, the next thing to consider is which states will have WMD capability by then. Because I am taking this long lead time and am looking at 2015 rather than 2005 or 2010, my task is easier. Many of the recent debates in Washington, particularly about Iran, have been about when, not whether, it would acquire nuclear capability, and the question has been phrased in terms of three, five or seven years. Looking at a 15 year period, it is not difficult to predict that Iran will have a viable WMD force. In its August 2000 semiannual report to Congress on foreign countries' efforts to acquire WMD-related technology, the Central Intelligence Agency (CIA) declared that Iran "remains one of the most active countries seeking to acquire WMD . . . technology from abroad," and noted that it is developing production capabilities in every WMD category: nuclear, chemical and biological, as well as missiles.[4]

Iran continues to seek missile development assistance from China, North Korea, and Russia.[5] In addition to already being able to produce its own Scud short-range ballistic missiles (SRBM), in July 2000, Tehran conducted its first successful test of the Shahab 3 medium-range ballistic missile (MRBM). The Shahab 3, based on North Korea's No-Dong MRBM upgraded with Russian technology, has a range

---

[3] Perkovich; Scott D. Sagan, "Why Do States Build Nuclear Weapons?" *International Security* 21:3 (Winter 1996-97).

[4] "Unclassified Report to Congress on the Acquisition of Technology Relating to Weapons of Mass Destruction and Advanced Conventional Munitions, 1 July Through 31 December 1999," Central Intelligence Agency, August 2000.

[5] Anthony H. Cordesman, "Weapons of Mass Destruction in the Middle East," Center for Strategic and International Studies, July 2000, 41-51.

of 1,300-1,500 km (810-940 m) and thus gives Iran the ability to hit both Israel and Saudi Arabia.[6] Both Israeli and American officials have expressed concern that the successful Shahab 3 test means that Iran will move on to completing the Shahab 4, expected to have a range of 2,000 km (1250 m), and the Shahab 5, estimated to have an intercontinental range of 5,500 km (3,400 m). Experts differ in their estimates of when Iran will be ready to test its first ICBM capable of hitting the United States. Israeli officials estimate that the Shahab 5 will be ready in 2005;[7] the CIA's 1999 National Intelligence Estimate estimated that Iran could test a missile capable of hitting the U.S. by 2010; and other experts have said Iran has less than an even chance of testing such a missile by 2015.[8]

Iran has made limited progress in the nuclear area. Despite its claims that it is solely interested in nuclear technology to strengthen its civilian energy program, there is little doubt among intelligence analysts that Iran is trying to develop a nuclear weapons capability. It is trying to negotiate with several sources, particularly in Russia, for the purchase of whole facilities, such as a uranium conversion facility, which could be used to produce the fissile material needed for a nuclear weapon. Moreover, according to the CIA, in addition to its efforts to complete several new nuclear reactors, ostensibly for civilian use, "Tehran continues to seek fissile material and technology for weapons development and has set up an elaborate system of military and civilian organizations to support its effort."[9] Iran ratified the Non-Proliferation Treaty in 1970, and the International Atomic Energy Agency (IAEA) has reported that it has found no evidence of weapons development in declared

---

[6] Andrew Koch and Steve Rodan, "Concern as test boosts Iranian missile development," *Jane's Defence Weekly*, July 26, 2000; Barry Rubin, "Shihab 3 test: The Iranian nuclear threat should not be overestimated," *Jerusalem Post*, July 17, 2000.
[7] Koch and Rodan.
[8] Cordesman, 64, and 51, respectively.
[9] "Unclassified Report to Congress"; Cordesman, 57-64.

facilities in Iran. However, the IAEA only inspects Iran's small research reactors, and conducts only informal walk-throughs of its other sites.[10] In addition, as many skeptics readily point out, the IAEA never found anything awry in Iraq before 1990 either. The United States has attempted to restrain Iran's efforts through supporting a near international consensus against nuclear cooperation with Iran. The U.S. has also put pressure on Russia, the only nuclear supplier assisting Iran, by focusing on specific Russian firms engaged in missile and nuclear development cooperation with Iran. So far, however, these efforts have met with only limited success.

Iran has had an active chemical weapons program since being the victim of several Iraqi chemical attacks early in the Iran-Iraq war and is thought to have increased its efforts to build a self-supporting CW infrastructure in the early 1990s when the UN discovered substantial Iraqi progress with advanced agents such as VX gas. Iran is estimated to have an inventory of several thousand tons of various agents, including blister, blood and choking agents, and its production capacity is estimated at as much as 1,000 tons a year. Although Iran ratified the Chemical Weapons Convention, under which it will be obligated to eliminate its chemical weapons program over a period of years, the CIA has noted that Tehran continues to seek production technology, training, expertise and chemicals that could be used as precursor agents from both Russia and China, indicating its plans to maintain and improve its CW capability.[11]

Iran also began a biological warfare (BW) program during the Iran-Iraq war, which is now believed to be in the advanced research and development phase. Although there is little confirmed information on Iran's BW program, it is believed to have weaponized both live agents and toxins for artillery and bombs. Iran is also

---

[10] Cordesman, 57.
[11] "Unclassified Report to Congress"; "Iran: Chemical Weapons," Federation of American Scientists report, September 24, 2000: http://www.fas.org; Cordesman, 51-54.

judged to be able to support an independent BW program with little foreign assistance (although it is receiving some foreign expertise, especially from Russia). Again, Iran has ratified the Biological Weapons Convention, but "continues to seek considerable dual-use biotechnical materials, equipment, and expertise from abroad ... ostensibly for civilian uses."[12] In sum, then, it seems clear that Iran will have at least a minimal force, nuclear as well as biological and chemical, by 2015.

What about Iraq? Even before the UN inspectors left Iraq in December 1998, the information they had been able to gather about Iraq's WMD capabilities was incomplete at best. Now that there have been no inspections at all since then, most analysts assume that Iraq is developing whatever it can. It is known that Iraq has rebuilt many of its key chemical facilities since 1991, albeit in the inspection-acceptable guise of industrial and commercial uses. However, as with its various biotechnical research facilities, much of the technology is dual-use and could be converted for weapons development relatively quickly. Moreover, Iraqi scientists still have the knowledge they did before, and Iraq's leader, Saddam Hussein, is thought to retain a wide range of precursor chemicals, production equipment, filled munitions and program documentation. For example, according to Iraq's own production figures, the equipment it is known to possess could produce 350 liters of weapons-grade anthrax per week.[13] In addition, an Iraqi Air Force document found by UNSCOM in July 1998 but later seized by Baghdad indicated that Iraq had not consumed as many chemical weapons during the Iran-Iraq war as it had claimed, raising the possibility that as many as 6,000 CW munitions remain hidden.[14]

---

[12] Cordesman, 54-55; "Iran: Biological Weapons, " Federation of American Scientists report, September 24, 2000: http://www.fas.org.
[13] "Iraq: Biological Weapons – Current Capabilities," Federation of American Scientists report, September 24, 2000: http://www.fas.org.
[14] "Unclassified Report to Congress"; Cordesman, 72.

On the missile front, the U.S. State Department reported in September 1999 that Iraq has refused to credibly account for over 40 Scud biological and conventional warheads, seven Iraqi-produced Scuds, and truckloads of Scud components. Moreover, Iraq continues to work on the short-range missiles that it is allowed to possess. It completed a set of eight tests of its Al Samoud ballistic missile in June 2000. Although the Samoud's range is less than 150 km (95 miles), and thus does not violate restrictions imposed by the UN, experts have pointed out that it nonetheless provides Iraq with valuable practice in ballistic missile technology, which could be adapted to longer-range missiles as soon as sanctions are lifted.[15]

Even on the nuclear issue, not all information is known. UN inspections found evidence of two potential weapons designs, a neutron initiator, explosives and triggering technology, plutonium processing technology, centrifuge technology, Calutron enrichment technology, and experiments with chemical separation technology. What remains unknown is whether Baghdad managed to conceal a high speed centrifuge program, whether it made any progress on a radiological weapon, whether it is continuing to develop a missile warhead capable of carrying a nuclear device, and the whereabouts of a "substantial number" of nuclear weapons components and research equipment which Iraq declared to the UN but which were never recovered. Thus, although the UN believes that Iraq's nuclear program has been largely disabled, it warns that Iraq retains substantial technology as well as a clandestine purchasing network that it has used since 1990 to import prohibited weapons components. U.S. experts believe that, despite the sanctions regime, Iraq has an ongoing research and development nuclear program.[16]

---

[15] Steven Lee Myers, "Flight Tests Show Iraq has Resumed a Missile Program," *New York Times*, July 1, 2000, A1.
[16] Cordesman, 77-78.

It is clear, therefore, that in fifteen years, Iraq will have some form of WMD capability, if not a full complement. Looking at the political side of the equation, fifteen years ago Saddam Hussein was in power. It is not inconceivable that fifteen years from now Hussein will still be in power in Iraq. Unless he is replaced at some point by a government with a different strategy, the safe assumption is that Iraq will have a stronger force than it possesses today, and that it will still be a significant threat to its neighbors.

Libya remains a significant proliferation concern, particularly in the area of chemical weapons. Libya is known to have been producing small amounts of chemical weapons since the early 1980s, and even though its main plant at Rabta has not been operating at full strength, it has nonetheless produced at least 100 metric tons of blister and nerve agents. Even greater concern has been raised by the ongoing construction of a major new underground chemical weapons plant near Tarhunah, and the speed with which Tripoli renewed its contacts with sources of expertise, parts and precursor chemicals in Western Europe as soon as the UN lifted its sanctions against the country in April 1999. Although Libya's ability to deliver any chemical weapon so far remains limited to its aging Scud B missiles (with a range of 310 km or 196 miles), it has engaged in continuous efforts to obtain ballistic missile-related equipment, technology, materials and expertise from foreign sources.[17] Libya is not likely to obtain a WMD capability without substantial foreign assistance.

Syria has also focused primarily on missiles and chemical weapons and is considerably further along than Libya in both categories. Syria is believed to have around 200 Scud B missiles, possibly with chemical warheads. It has also deployed, however, the longer-range North Korean Scud C missiles, which have ranges of up to 600 km (374 miles), thus rendering Syria capable of reaching targets throughout

---

[17] "Unclassified Report to Congress"; Cordesman, 16-18.

Israel from much deeper within its own territory. Syria is estimated to have 50-80 Scud C missiles, and is now able to build both the entire Scud B and Scud C. Syria has been developing its chemical weapons arsenal since the 1970s, and is currently estimated to be capable of producing several hundred tons of CW agents per year. Its current stockpiles have been estimated at "several thousand aerial bombs, filled mostly with sarin," and between 50 to 100 ballistic missile warheads. Intelligence analysts also believe that Syria is actively seeking to manufacture the more powerful VX gas.[18]

For the sake of argument, I am assuming that it will be easier to control the Syrian and Libyan capabilities than the Iranian and Iraqi capabilities because of their location and size, and because of some indications that both countries are moving in a somewhat more moderate direction.

Israel clearly possesses the most advanced WMDs in the region. Israel is estimated to have 50 Jericho I missiles (with a range of up to 640 km, or 400 m) deployed, and to have developed the Jericho II, with an increased range of up to 1440km, or 900 m, enabling it to reach almost the entire Arab world (although it is unclear how many are deployed). Israel has also been working on stretching the Jericho II's range to 2000 km, and on developing submarine-launched cruise missiles, which would give it a second-strike capability. There have been reports that Israel carried out its first test launches of Popeye Turbo cruise missiles (capable of carrying nuclear warheads), from its *Dolphin*-class submarines in May 2000.[19] In terms of biological and chemical weapons, specific information is scarce, but U.S. experts do include Israel on the list of nations with stocks of both. As for nuclear weapons,

---

[18] "Syria - Special Weapons," Federation of American Scientists report, September 24, 2000: http://www.fas.org; Cordesman, 35-41.

[19] "Israel," Federation of American Scientists report, September 24, 2000: http://www.fas.org.

estimates of Israel's arsenal vary widely, from 60 to 300, with most falling somewhere between 100 and 200.[20]

If Israel is to retain its position of perceived superiority given developments elsewhere in the Middle East, these forces will have to improve, even with an effective peace process since, as I am arguing here, WMDs will continue to proliferate even with the successful conclusion of peace treaties. Unless Israel's security can be assured by outside powers, particularly the U.S., Israel is likely to believe that its WMDs are even more central to its security after it has returned additional territory. And maintaining a deterrent against WMDs will be complex; not only will Israel be trying to deter several potential aggressors in a multipolar situation, but with WMDs, there is less room for error than with conventional weapons. Pursuing advantages such as a second strike capability, whether in the form of submarine-launched missiles, anti-missile defense or other new technology, is extremely expensive, leading me to predict that although Israel will be stronger in absolute terms in fifteen years than it is now, it could actually be more vulnerable than it is today, in terms of both its military security and its economic stability, relative to weapons developments elsewhere in the region.

The wild card in all of these calculations is Egypt. Egypt was the first country in the Middle East to obtain chemical weapons training and materiel, and was also the first to use chemical weapons (in the Yemeni civil war in the early 1960s).[21] Cairo is thought to have a current stockpile of mustard gas and phosgene (the agents it used in Yemen), and to be producing VX gas. Egypt also has a long-running relationship of ballistic missile cooperation with North Korea, has

---

[20] Cordesman, 23-30; "Israel - Special Weapons," Federation of American Scientists report, September 24, 2000: http://www.fas.org.

[21] E. J. Hogendoorn, "A Chemical Weapons Atlas," *Bulletin of the Atomic Scientists* 53:5 (Sept.-Oct. 1997), 35.

approximately 100 Scud B missiles, and is thought to be working on the medium-range Scud C.[22]

However, in the area of nuclear weapons, Cairo has not been a player militarily, having chosen instead to try to affect the nuclear balance in the region through diplomatic means. It has called for a nuclear-free zone in the Middle East since 1974, urging all countries to sign the Nuclear Non-proliferation Treaty (NPT). It added to this effort in April 1990, calling for the Middle East to be free of all WMDs, and in April 1996, hosted the conference for the signing of the declaration of the African nuclear weapons-free zone.[23]

If all conditions remain the same, however, particularly with Israel's presumed capabilities or if Israel obtains a true long-range nuclear strike capability, it is questionable whether Cairo will be content to stay in this moderately passive role over the next 15 years. But, because of its unconventional approach, Egypt is the most difficult country to predict in terms of its WMD capacity and the most uncertain and problematic. It is still entirely possible that Cairo will be content to voice major diplomatic protests but then do very little, although doing little, may work against Egypt's desire to be a lead state in the region.

Factors For and Against Proliferation

First, although the peace process will not solve the proliferation problem, it is one of the factors that can help stem it by defusing incentives for conflict and increasing the possibility of cooperation between regional states to help manage new perils. Accommodations between states would also enable the U.S. to exercise greater leadership in attempting to thwart the effects of proliferation.

---

[22] Cordesman, 19-22.
[23] Cordesman, 21.

Second, there is the possibility of moderation, coup, or revolution in Iraq and Iran which might limit the danger from either. Clearly there are forces already at work in Iran in favor of moderation, reinforced by the 70% of the population under 30 where President Khatami's support is strongest. The Iranian radicals have a biological problem in the sense that they will die before the moderates. Gradually, and quite possibly by 2015, the Iranian WMD problem may be solved through a change of government there. In Iraq, the only possibility of internal change is by overthrowing the government somehow, a prospect which is dim indeed as long as Hussein is around to maintain his iron grip on any dissent. Iraq is therefore a more dangerous proliferation prospect because it lacks the possibility of a long term positive trend which is at least present in Iran.

Unfortunately, there are a larger number of potential factors fueling WMD proliferation in the Middle East. One of the most potent factors pointing towards further proliferation stems from the very nature of technological advances – that they always inevitably trickle down to less advanced powers. So improvements in satellite targeting and weather models, cheap cruise missiles, drones and aircraft conversions will all have a potentially lethal impact by increasing every state's destructive capability. On the missile level, hardened or mobile launch facilities, large numbers of spur systems, and the ability to launch rapidly with minimal warning indicators, will all contribute to the declining prospects for control of WMDs. On all levels, the situation will be further exacerbated by advanced computer modeling and simulation technology, reduced testing requirements, and the availability of strike aircraft with some stealth features.

The next generation of chemical weapons will not just be more effective, but also likely to be more stable than those Iraq used before 1990 – giving states increased confidence in working with them. In the biological weapons arena, every major power in the Middle East will have the required technology base to rapidly manufacture advanced biological weapons by 2010. There are likely to be the most dramatic improvements in such areas as genetic engineering, weaponizing infectious agents like Ebola, and the ability to rapidly convert civilian pharmaceutical fermentation and other facilities. As the American experience with Sudan suggests, it is very difficult to distinguish pharmaceutical plants from those involved in weapons production. The U.S. bombardment of a suspect Sudanese pharmaceutical plant in 1998 in retaliation for the terrorist attacks on the U.S. embassies in Kenya and Tanzania is still being debated, with many experts claiming that it was an innocent installation. Finally, there will be more sophisticated covert delivery systems and possible terrorist devices.

Beyond the risks of technological advancements, the factors favoring increasing proliferation include: the availability of outside technical assistance; rising regional rivalries and military insecurities; lessening U.S. involvement and political/economic assistance in the region as well as military disengagement; the rising belief that the United States cannot safeguard the security and stability in the region; the inability to contain Iran's and Iraq's competing WMD ambitions; the political fallout from the Indian and Pakistani nuclear tests; and the perception of an increasing Israeli WMD capability. A breakdown in the Arab-Israeli peace process would only accelerate these trends. Indeed, if one looks at the last five years, most of the developments have been in the wrong direction.

What Will Rampant WMD Proliferation in the Middle East Be Like?

So these technological developments, and the clear possibility of many more, convince me that we will have a WMD Middle East in 2015, even with the successful completion of agreements on all outstanding issues between the Arabs and Israelis. What would this WMD Middle East be like? Some political scientists argue that countries that acquire WMDs become more cautious. The ultimate logic of this position is that we should be giving them out like prophylactics.[24] In the case of India and Pakistan, for example, some analysts have argued that India and Pakistan were deterred from war in the Kashmir crisis of 1990 by each side's knowledge that the other was nuclear weapon-capable.[25] Given the history and complexity of both South Asia and the Middle East, however, it would seem reckless indeed to simply assume that hostilities will end and that a new-found caution will ensue just because these states have acquired WMDs.

In addition, there is the problem of overlapping concerns. For example, Israel alone could be engaged in a variety of confrontations by 2015 with countries that possess WMDs, including Iran, Iraq, Syria, and possibly even Libya. This is one situation where the peace process is critical because it could remove the spark to the conflict and limit the intensity and diversity of these confrontations. And complicating the situation even further is the possibility that these overlapping interests will induce new countries to acquire WMDs. In the Gulf, for example, with Iran and Iraq both developing their WMD capabilities, Saudi Arabia may also feel impelled to enter the WMD competition.

Predictions are also complicated by the proclivity of Middle East states for switching alliances. Libya and Iran were both once close to the U.S. and Britain. Before 1973, Egypt was a major Soviet client. During the 1980's, Iraqi relations with the U.S. improved dramatically only to collapse after the invasion of Kuwait. The PLO, once Israel's most bitter foe, is now a tense partner with Jerusalem in

---

[24] Kenneth N. Waltz, "More May Be Better," in Scott D. Sagan and Kenneth N. Waltz, The Spread of Nuclear Weapons: A Debate (New York: W. W. Norton, 1995); John J. Weltman, "Nuclear Devolution and World Order," *World Politics* 32: 2 (January 1980), 169-193; John J. Mearsheimer, "The Case for a Ukrainian Nuclear Deterrent," *Foreign Affairs* 72: 3 (Summer 1993), 50-66.
[25] Devin T. Hagerty, "Nuclear Deterrence in South Asia: The 1990 Indo-Pakistani Crisis," *International Security* 20:3 (Winter 1995-96): 79-114.

peacemaking. In trying to predict what the WMD balance will look like in 2015, we must consider the revolving door nature of relations in the Middle East.

Concluding, from the above, that Iraq, Iran, and Israel will all have a full complement of WMDs, and that several other key states, particularly Egypt, Libya, Syria, and Algeria, will have smaller arsenals of biological and/or chemical weapons, this could be a highly unstable, multipolar system, an international relations theorist's nightmare. The countries of the area would have to prepare for several adversaries at once. To make matters worse, although Israel will probably have a second strike capability by then, it is difficult to believe that any of the other states would be able to develop the stabilizing sort of second strike capability that characterized the Cold War. Yet another problem that states in the region will have to deal with is that of collateral damage. The Palestinians and Jordanians, for instance, warn that if an adversary decided to attack Israel, it could inadvertently hit Jordan or Palestine instead because of poor targeting, weapons failure, or poor weather.

One way to alleviate the multipolar problem is for the United States to provide some sort of guarantee to potential target states which would help deter potential aggressors from employing these weapons. For the United States to contribute to the region's stability in this way, however, Americans would have to confront the implications of accepting this new responsibility.

Even though in general it is true that nuclear weapons are more useful to states for deterrence, prestige or political bargaining purposes rather than for their actual war fighting capability (because of the potential for mutual destruction if they are employed), there still could be an incentive to use them in a clandestine fashion. Indeed, the issue of WMD terrorism is the greatest threat we face from the proliferation of these weapons. The capability already exists to make biological and chemical weapons which can be delivered in a suitcase. However ineptly handled, the Tokyo subway bombing by the *Aum Shinrikyo* sect in March 1995 demonstrated that a WMD attack against a civilian installation was possible. These weapons can be delivered by ship, truck, or plane. We already have transnational terrorists such as Osama Bin Laden who operate globally out of several different places. Because of this global as well as regional threat, by 2015 the United States will be critical to stability in the area, by promoting the status quo and enforcing a disincentive to acquiring and using WMDs. Washington may not be able to prevent countries from acquiring WMDs but it is likely to become a major factor in the new deterrence equation in the area. Therefore, countries or groups would have an incentive to frighten the United States off or at least to encourage isolationists in the Pat Buchanan vein to question why the United States was risking its own people and territory by playing a role in the Middle East. During the 2000 U.S. presidential campaign, Buchanan argued that the U.S. should drop its sanctions against both Iran and Iraq and let each sell as much oil as they want because "[n]one of these Gulf regimes is worth another war." [26]   This kind of thinking would certainly grow if Americans thought that the United States would be particularly vulnerable to a terrorist attack because of its role in the Middle East.

However, while the terrorist use of WMDs may well increase as a threat to the U.S. by 2015, in the Middle East this threat is likely to be even greater. An extremist group or a dissatisfied government could use a clandestine weapon to inflict serious damage on the population of a perceived enemy. The leaders of Iran or Iraq might conclude that they could devastate the other party, for example, or someone might seek to destroy Israel. The perpetrator of the attack could well remain anonymous because there would be so many candidates; either several possible governments or independent non-governmental terrorist "operators." Neither advanced anti-missile systems nor or a second strike capacity would be

---

[26] Jill Zuckman, "Campaign 2000: End Oil Limits, Buchanan Urges," *Boston Globe*, April 1, 2000.

effective against this kind of hidden threat. Therefore, in terms of regional trends, the danger of a WMD terrorist attack is likely to be the greatest peril the Middle East would face by 2015.

To effectively confront the Mideast proliferation problem, then, we must take account of the following factors: 1) there is no present prospect that any combination of arms control, deterrence, and active or passive counter-proliferation can fully secure the region, any state in the region, or Western power projection forces; 2) theater missile defense will be meaningless without radical improvements in defense against air attacks, cruise missiles, and unconventional means of delivery; and 3) there is no present prospect that any combination of measures will be able to defend against biological warfare.

These are severe problems and no easy answers are in sight. But the terrible challenges posed by Middle East proliferation will be even greater if the Arab-Israeli peace process fails and the attention of the parties remains diverted onto specific territorial and emotional issues in dispute.

The proliferation challenge will also be greater if no regional security system is developed, if the multilateral arms control process known as ACRS (Arms Control and Regional Security) suspended since 1995 is not resurrected, if Iran remains outside the regional diplomatic context, if Iraq remains a pariah under Saddam Hussein, and if the international efforts to prevent WMD acquisition by countries of proliferation concern break down. If, however, there is success on some or certainly all of these matters, then the way may well be found for a cooperative security context for dealing with a horrifying problem that is a threat to all countries in the area. Despite current headlines to the contrary, it will be the relative success of these endeavors which will be the most important in determining the future of the Middle East in the next half-century.

✳

Chapter 2

Nuclear Weapons and Peace in the Middle East

Lawrence Scheinman

Introduction

The conference from which this volume emerged is another link in the chain of informal and formal endeavors, events, and negotiations that collectively aim at and contribute to realizing the objective of the Middle East Peace Process. If it is difficult to imagine a more demanding challenge, it is even more difficult to contemplate living under the cloud of continuing if not increasing tension, insecurity and instability that inevitably would flow from a failure to keep the process going. My contribution to this enterprise is to offer a perspective on how arms control and confidence building measures can serve national security interests, be factored into diplomacy and defense policy, facilitate the reduction of tension, and promote national security and regional stability. The conference agenda, covered various factors in detail – threat perception, strategies of response, and practical near-term measures addresses – my comments will be more general, but hopefully of some value.

The United States has an extensive experience in the development of arms control concepts and principles, in bilateral and multilateral arms control negotiations, in negotiating strategies and techniques, and in verification approaches and technologies. The Arms Control and Disarmament Agency was itself established in 1961 to deal with the problem of reduction and control of armaments. It was authorized by statute to prepare for and manage U.S. participation in negotiations in the arms control and disarmament field and to serve as an advocate of positive arms control in support of national security interests. After an agreement to that effect by Secretary of State Madeleine Albright and Senate Foreign Relations Committee Chairman Jesse Helms, it ceased to exist in 1999 and was folded into the State Department.

One of the Arms Control and Disarmament Agency's (ACDA) primary mission beyond practical involvement in fashioning arms control and disarmament policies, and negotiating arrangements and agreements that support those ends, was to be a lead constituent of the U.S. Government in imparting our national experience and in providing arms control education to other nations. We of course recognize that our experience cannot be directly transcribed, or in all cases even applied, but also note that apparently unique situations more often than not have some similarities with other ostensibly unique situations thus opening the door to applying lessons learned in one environment to another. ACDA's former role has now been absorbed into relevant agencies, some newly created, by the State Department.

Purpose of Arms Control

Arms control in the abstract can produce high-sounding rhetoric, but for governments contemplating concrete measures, the purpose of arms control must be to further the achievement of their nation's security. In *Necessity for Choice*, Henry Kissinger noted that to be meaningful, arms control cannot be conceived "in a fit of moral indignation. Effective schemes require careful, detailed, dispassionate studies and the willingness to engage in patient, highly technical negotiations. Otherwise, arms control may increase rather than diminish insecurity." Arms control, from the policy perspective, is not the practice of idealism, but the promoting of national security.

That is the spirit in which we as a nation have pursued arms control. The United States has never viewed arms control simply as an end in itself, as a moral good to be pursued for its own sake. Rather, arms control is an integral part of our overall national strategy. It is a policy tool used to enhance our national security, and cannot be seen in isolation from other aspects of foreign and defense policy. In this sense it may be said that an overriding purpose of arms control has been to limit the military forces or activities of an adversary while retaining maximum possible freedom of action for oneself. But, as my following remarks are intended to convey, this is only part of the story.

Arms control complements national defense in the pursuit of national security; it is a diplomatic component serving the same end as do military components. Accidents of history and politics have led some to the mistaken conclusion that arms control and defense are somehow opposites. In so doing, they are confusing a difference in means - the diplomatic versus the military - with a difference in ends.

The fundamental purpose of arms control and defense are, in fact, exactly the same – to make us safer. As the head of ACDA, John Holum, once noted, defense deters, or if need be defeats threats to national security while arms control works to remove those threats in the first instance. Former Secretary of Defense Perry put it most succinctly in saying that arms control is defense by other means. If the Cold War taught us anything, it taught us the need for both military might and arms control. Arms control may lessen the need for defenses, but it does not take their place. As we examine the very difficult and intertwined security problems in the world today, arms control stands out as a concept which holds promise for lessening tensions and enhancing the security of all states.

At its heart, arms control is a gradual, long term, incremental political process; it is about making choices, often difficult ones. Arms control is a process which can lead to a strengthening of security through reciprocal measures that can be achieved by direct negotiation or, by unilateral or, perhaps, coordinated steps such as mutual restraint.

It has been said that arms control is impossible to achieve under conditions of hostility, and unnecessary to pursue where friendship and cooperation prevail. This assertion does not stand up to scrutiny. At the height of the Cold War, under conditions verging on open warfare, when the United States and the Soviet Union had thousands of nuclear warheads poised to be launched at each other, extending to overflights of sovereign territory and even shoot downs, arms control negotiations took place. Under conditions of great tension in which our very existence was threatened, meaningful agreements – the Hot Line, the Limited Nuclear Test Ban Treaty, the Anti-Ballistic Missile Treaty, and the first Strategic Offensive Arms Treaty (SALT I Interim Agreement) – were reached. Even where progress was slow, or nonexistent, the dialogue was significant and helped to prepare the way for rapid agreement when the political climate changed. During this period, two important purposes for arms control crystallized:

- first, arms control can be used to reduce the risks of war;
- second, and less obvious, arms control can help to transform political relations in a manner conducive to creating cooperative security.

These observations are sufficiently important and potentially generalizable to deserve some further elaboration. They underscore a paradox, namely that during the most tense periods of the Cold War, the two superpowers found that cooperation in the most sensitive area of national sovereignty – the military area – was virtually the only issue they could agree to discuss. During the worst of times, arms control negotiations often seemed the only form of communication between East and West on security issues and underscored the interest of the United States and the Soviet Union to keep their confrontation from leading to Armageddon.

Admittedly, SALT I and II did not place meaningful limits on the number of strategic nuclear warheads that the U.S. and Soviet Union could build and direct at each other. But for their times they represented an order of magnitude leap in the willingness of Washington and Moscow to talk about the leading edge of their military technology and their deterrent forces.

Changes did not account for the sudden acceleration in the rate at which the U.S. and the Soviet Union were able to produce major arms control accords; it was changes in the political circumstances in both countries, in the political and economic context in which arms control negotiations were carried on that allowed arms control negotiations to begin to really take off. To be more specific, even in situations where technical matters seemed to facilitate arms limitation agreements, it was really the state of political relationships that determined the extent to which such accords were possible. Arms control agreements in the final analysis have been the product of favorable political circumstances.

But in saying this we should not overlook that they also can be important catalysts for change. Former ACDA Director Ron Lehman, for example, has pointed out that the 1986 Stockholm Confidence and Security Building Measures (CSBM) agreement, in placing western inspectors in Eastern Europe led to reducing the coercive influence of the Soviet Union and to giving the Warsaw Pact greater freedom of action. It opened the door to monitoring and transparency, subsequently strengthened in the Intermediate Nuclear Treaty (INF), and it reinforced political glasnost.

Also, and very importantly, arms control discussions even during periods of tension and danger kept communication channels open; offered a vision of cooperation as an alternative to confrontation; and built an organizational infrastructure in which more serious arms control programs could proceed when the time came. Continuing dialogue during the long periods of deadlock had a crucial parenthetical advantage – it helped to educate Soviet security officials about concepts of stability and sufficiency and contributed to fresh thinking and influenced a new generation of foreign policy and security experts that emerged after the demise of the Soviet Union. This socialization process cannot and should not be underestimated.

While recognizing that lessons from one situation are not directly transferable to another, there is something to be gained from examining past experience, even if it is not one's own. And arguably, Europe in the 1960s and the Middle East in the 1990s may not be all that dissimilar. In both situations there are fear and mistrust; there is a concern with the risk of sudden attack; sizable military forces are maintained in a high state of readiness and so on. From the U.S.-Soviet experience we can draw some insights:

- major progress in arms control should not be expected except in the presence of a political atmosphere that makes cooperation between adversaries seem to outweigh the advantages of a purely confrontational stance;

- the process of talking with an adversary about arms control, even when prospects for progress are bleak, can serve to clarify the nature of the principal issues at stake, and in doing so help to create a dynamic that facilitates moving to concrete measures that offer solutions to specific problems;

- contrary to what some claim, there is no evidence that the process of arms control discussion have caused any of the participants to be lulled into a false sense of security; there is far more talk about slippery slopes than confirmation of their existence.

- arms control agreements cannot and should not be expected to automatically lead to uninterrupted improvement in relationships between adversaries, or to alone stabilize those relationships; it is not easily argued, for example, that the formal U.S.-Soviet negotiations to limit or regulate armaments had a controlling effect on the vicissitudes of the Cold War over the years that it dominated international politics. Or, to take a more classical situation out of the history of the interwar period earlier this century, the Washington Naval Conference of 1922 while stabilizing Anglo-American relations, which were marked by only superficial tensions, was unable to achieve the same in regard to the U.S.-Japanese relationship where underlying tensions were substantial and fundamental.

- on the other hand, the process of negotiating agreements can, and in the case of the U.S. and Soviet Union did, reinforce the idea that there was an alternative to unremitting confrontation; by influencing how state actors thought about their security situations and relations with one another, it contributed to altering the political atmosphere that was itself necessary to bring about political change;

- experience suggests that limited and circumscribed steps are the most realistic objectives in the initial phases of breaking down long-standing hostile relationships. At this stage, measures involving massive intrusions into state sovereignty such as open skies or short notice on-site inspection with no right of refusal as found in the Stockholm Document of 1986 do not work, but smaller and more limited steps such as the Limited Nuclear Test Ban Treaty or modest first steps in increasing openness and transparency as were done in the Helsinki Final Act of 1975, do.

To tie this to our opening theme, arms control is not something separate from national security strategy, but rather an integral part of it. Countries do not need to – and should not – wait until peace and friendship have been secured to engage in it. Conceptually, arms control has several goals:

- it can be used to reduce incentives for surprise attack or to alter force structures, either qualitatively or quantitatively, that could trigger war. This is usually referred to as the goal of "crisis stability;"

- it may be used to curtail military developments that could trigger a military build-up by one's adversaries. This is the goal of "arms race stability;"

- it can reduce or limit weapons or weapon systems and thus reduce the economic and social burdens of defense – another way of expressing this is to say that every weapon we can take or keep out of the hands of our potential adversaries is a weapon we do not have to spend more to defend against, thus reducing the pressure on resources that could be deployed in support of other social goals;

- it can have as its objective the improvement of political relations among states by creating, through intensive dialogue and routine cooperation, a set of principles, norms and rules that govern the military dimension of interstate relations, that is to say the instituting, of regimes. This is the goal of cooperative security and is normally associated with confidence building measures.

The United States has pursued all of these arms control goals as part of its broader foreign policy and national security policies.

Arms Control Broadly Defined

Often, when people think of arms control, they envision formal, highly structured negotiations aimed at objectives such as banning weapons of mass destruction or reducing other weapons systems. They tend to think of negotiations in Geneva as a model, either the multilateral Conference on Disarmament (CD) or the bilateral negotiations between the U.S. and the former Soviet Union which were a dominant feature of the Cold War, especially during the '70s and '80s. No doubt this is a pervasive and surely highly publicized aspect of arms control.

But in reality, arms control encompasses a far broader range of security measures such as acts of unilateral restraint, reciprocal unilateral measures, negotiated confidence building measures, as well as the formal bilateral and multilateral agreements to reduce or limit specific weapon systems. There is a debate whether arms control and confidence building measures are separate and distinct or whether they are points on a continuum moving from less to more formal politically and legally binding arrangements which is where I come out on the matter.

Arms control achievements do not emerge full-grown; they require practical, step-by-step preparation and attention or, as some say, tender, loving care. In our experience, arms control agreements work best when they address practical issues. Broad declaratory statements on intent are important and can help set goals. In key areas, however, they cannot substitute for the enactment or negotiation of specific measures designed to strengthen security.

The more demanding the objectives of a particular negotiation, the greater the need for rigorous definitions, agreed terms, and specific limitations and undertakings in order to avoid ambiguities and minimize later disagreements over the meaning of commitments. Anyone who has been involved in the negotiation of the technical details of an arms control agreement fully appreciates that the "devil is in the details."

Furthermore, due consideration must be given to measures for enhancing confidence in the security benefits of arms control. These measures must fit the nature of the commitments. For example, far reaching arms control agreements limiting the numbers of specific objects such as tanks or missiles require very intrusive verification measures, while other arms control agreements such as the Limited Nuclear Test Ban Treaty have not required such intrusive verification measures in order to have confidence in compliance. Thus, verification can involve measures ranging from openness and transparency to national technical means and on-site inspections. The key point is that verification measures and arms control commitments must match.

Finally, the work of arms control does not end when a negotiation is concluded, the agreement is signed and enters into force. Implementation provisions, including institutions such as the numerous arms control commissions, are particularly important to ensure that commitments are fulfilled by all parties to the agreement. In the end, compliance with agreements serves as an important gauge of political progress and intentions.

In the Middle East, the Arms Control and Regional Security (ACRS) Working Group provided a formal venue for regional discussions and negotiations on security issues within the framework of the Middle East Peace Process, until the talks were suspended in 1998. Supplementing this official and formal track, however, is an array of non-official workshops and seminars, such as the meeting in which we are now participating. These Track II activities are playing a valuable role in supporting the official diplomatic track. They provide informal settings where regional participants can explore, in off-the-record discussions, new issues to be pursued as well as opportunities for government officials to exchange views with nongovernmental parties. Track II workshops on threat perceptions, confidence building measures and arms control hold a very real potential for generating ideas that can be carried back to the formal tracks.

Conclusion

To summarize: Arms control overlaps diplomacy and defense policy, at times involving formal negotiations, at other times employing informal arrangements or even unilateral actions. The realm of arms control includes, but is not limited to, treaty negotiation, implementation of agreements, non-proliferation, verification and compliance, confidence and security building measures and even defense conversion.

Whatever their specific character, in order to be successful, arms control measures must be practical. In their aggregate they must balance all of the parties' security interests. Measures must be well designed. Confidence and verification provisions must fit the nature of the commitments, and implementation provisions are important in order to help ensure that the security benefits of arms control are in fact realized by the parties to the agreement.

At its heart, as commented earlier, arms control is a gradual, step-by-step, incremental political process: it involves making choices, often difficult ones. Still, arms control is a process which can lead over time to the strengthening of security through negotiation rather than confrontation, to the building of regional cooperative security measures, to increased stability and security for all of the involved parties. History has demonstrated the benefits that can accrue from the arms control process, and how the latter can help build toward a more secure and stable order.

The history of the Middle East is that of tension, confrontation, and conflict. Acquisition of weapons systems and related resources has been seen as the principal means to enhance national security and the political realities of the region have made diplomatic solutions to regional security concerns elusive. However, progress is being made in bringing peace to the region. And the peace process that is in place offers an opportunity to start down the long but dynamic road of arms control and regional security. Regional discussions on arms control, confidence building and other security measures are in and of themselves important confidence building measures. They are vital first steps and sometimes all that is possible for a while. But such discussions and dialogues can, if the parties are willing, lead to fresh thinking. Middle East states have much to gain by being open to such dialogue.

The Middle East is also a region where positive political developments affecting many parties have occurred after long and arduous negotiations. States in the region know how to take the 'long view.' The process of arms control requires such a long view, as well as patience, persistence and a commitment to exploring all avenues available to strengthen national security. With venues such as this in which to carry out this task, a long prospect is not all that bad a thing to contemplate.

Chapter 3

Proliferation, Non-proliferation, and Anti-proliferation: Egypt and Israel in the Middle East

Janice Gross Stein

Abstention, Proliferation and Penitence

If we take past predictions seriously, the Middle East should have far more nuclear weapons states than it does today. Widespread proliferation has been predicted for at least the last two decades, but the Middle East today has only one state, Israel, with an ambiguous nuclear posture. Admittedly, Iraq tried – and failed under very special circumstances – and Iran, as well as Syria, Libya, and Algeria, continues to worry the international community. Nevertheless, proliferation has not accelerated as expected in the last decade.

Estimates were off in large part because we have no good theory of nuclear proliferation. Existing theories predict that in a zone of intense, protracted conflict like the Middle East, the probability of proliferation is high.[1] In the absence of good theory which explains who will choose to develop nuclear weapons, when, and under what conditions, we cannot explain why states choose not to develop nuclear weapons. A good theory of proliferation is the mirror image of a theory of non-proliferation. Closely related but analytically distinct, we have no theory which explains why threshold proliferators repent and reverse course. Until we understand

---

[1]See T.V.Paul, *Power Versus Norms: Why Nations Forbear Nuclear Weapons*, unpublished paper.

what separates proliferators from non-proliferators, we will have difficulty designing appropriate strategies to encourage non-proliferation and anti-proliferation.

The absence of theory is in part, but only in part, a function of the small number of cases of proliferators. Only eight states are known or believed to be nuclear weapons capable: the original five, plus India, Pakistan, and Israel. South Africa, Ukraine, Belarus, and Kazakhstan are anti-proliferators who have voluntarily given up nuclear weapons, while Brazil, Argentina, Taiwan, and South Korea can be considered threshold proliferators who reversed course. Canada, Sweden, Italy, Australia, and Egypt, among others, considered but did not develop or acquire nuclear weapons.[2]

I propose to examine only two of the critical choices along the road to proliferation: the decision to develop or not to develop a military nuclear capability; then, among those who developed, the choice to either move to a nuclear weapons posture, – covertly through ambiguity or overtly through minimal deterrence – or to create some kind of arms control regime – non-weaponized deterrence, controlled proliferation, or a nuclear weapons free zone.[3] States with a developed nuclear military capability that sign the NPT or create an even more rigorous arms control regime can be considered as penitents, as proliferators who have reversed course.

Drawing on available case material, I will look primarily at Egyptian and Israeli decisions, with the subtext of Indian and Pakistani decisions woven into the comparison. I pay particular attention to the variation in Egyptian and Pakistani responses after they suspected that their adversarial neighbor was developing nuclear weapons. The latter chose to develop a military nuclear capability, while the former

---

[2]There are many other potential states, but we do not have careful enough studies and good enough data to create a comprehensive list.

[3]For a closely related but distinct analysis, see Etel Solingen, "The Domestic Sources of Regional Regimes: The Evolution of Nuclear Ambiguity in the Middle East," *International Studies Quarterly* 38 (1994), 305-337. Solingen is principally interested in the determinants of regime creation.

did not. This kind of controlled comparison should allow us to discriminate among states who are locked into serious rivalries, and who face important threats to their security, but who nevertheless vary significantly in their responses.

To Develop or Not to Develop Nuclear Weapons
System-level Explanations.

At least five theoretical approaches, formulated at different levels of analysis, attempt to explain or predict nuclear proliferation. At the systemic level, neo-realism, neo-liberal institutionalism, and world sociology generate competing explanations and predictions. I can treat these quickly, since none satisfactorily explains the variation in decisions to abstain or proliferate.

Neo-realism would predict widespread proliferation in the wake of the end of the bipolar system.[4] With the exception of Iraq, an arrested rather than a penitent proliferator, such proliferation has not occurred. Neo-liberal institutionalism would expect that with the creation and strengthening of the non-proliferation regime, proliferation would diminish. Pakistan – and Iraq – do not fit this expectation.[5] Sociological approaches to global change predict that, over time, the diffusion of the global norm of non-proliferation and global learning would diminish proliferation; again, there are two important exceptions to this expectation.[6]

---

[4]Kenneth Waltz, *Theory of International Relations* (Reading, Mass.: Addison-Wesley, 1979), and "The Spread of Nuclear Weapons: More May be Better," *Adelphi Papers* 171 (London: 1981); John Mearsheimer, "Back to the Future: Instability in Europe After the Cold War," *International Security*, 15 (1990), 5-56.

[5]Robert Keohane, "International Institutions: Two Approaches," *International Studies Quarterly*, 32(1988), 379-396.

[6]See, for example, George M. Thomas, John W. Meyer, Francisco O. Ramirez, and John Boli, eds. *Institutional Structure: Constituting State, Society, and the Individual* (Newbury Park, CA: Sage Publications, 1987), and Albert Bergesen, ed. *Studies of the Modern World System* (New York: Academic Press, 1980).

State-level Explanations.

Analyses at the state level are more promising candidate explanations of the variation. Realists posit nuclear weapons as a fundamental component of the deterrence of an adversary who is likely to launch a conventional attack. Analysts of mutual deterrence have argued that nuclear deterrence promotes stability, prevents escalation, and avoids miscalculation that can culminate in war.[7] I consider the merits of this argument later, but the empirical evidence indicates that, unlike their counterparts in Europe and North America, states in the Middle East have not accepted explicit nuclear deterrence as either the foundation or the scaffolding of security.

Analysts have also examined the malignant impact of the security dilemma, where the defensive actions of one appear offensive to another, and provoke escalation.[8] The security dilemma seems to provide a convincing explanation of Pakistan's development of a nuclear military capability. It was after India's self-proclaimed peaceful nuclear explosion in 1974 that Pakistan began seriously to develop a military nuclear capability, although it did not announce its capability until 1987.[9] If this analysis is correct, it warns of the escalating consequences of proliferation by even one member of a regional system, when that member is locked into one or more enduring conflicts.

The Egyptian experience, however, as well as that of South Korea and Taiwan, raise serious doubts about the security dilemma as a single variable

---

[7]This argument was frequently made during the Cold War. For its application to the Middle East, see Shai Feldman, *Israeli Nuclear Deterrence* (New York: Columbia University Press, 1982). For a countervailing argument, see Yair Evron, *Israel's Nuclear Dilemma* (Ithaca: Cornell University Press, 1995).

[8]Robert Jervis, *Perception and Misperception in International Politics* (Princeton: Princeton University Press, 1976).

[9]See Mitchell Reiss, *Bridled Ambition: Why Countries Constrain Their Nuclear Capabilities* (Washington: Woodrow Wilson Center Press, 1995), p.187.

explanation of proliferation. Israel had publicly acknowledged its facility at Dimona in 1960 and Egypt went through a critical period from 1960 until the war in 1967 when the development of a nuclear military capability was under consideration. Yet Egypt did not develop nuclear weapons, even though Egyptian officials strongly suspected that Israel was doing so. A security dilemma may be a necessary condition, but it is clearly an insufficient explanation of proliferation.

The general search for prestige and status, which nuclear weapons allegedly confer, is ubiquitously cited by analysts of proliferation.[10] This explanation is even less satisfactory. If prestige-seeking were a powerful explanation, the incidence of nuclear proliferation would be far higher than it currently is. Nor can Egypt's decision not to develop nuclear weapons be accommodated. President Nasser was the leader of the pan-Arab movement and during the years from 1960-1967, heavily engaged in asserting his leadership against rival contenders. Israel's refusal to acknowledge its nuclear status also runs counter to this generalized expectation.[11] A generalized quest for status and prestige is far too undifferentiated to account satisfactorily for the variation between those who proliferate and those who abstain.

An intriguing proposition is, that states with identities that are not secure, with formative principles that are challenged or rejected at home or abroad, are more likely to seek absolute security in nuclear capabilities.[12] This kind of conflict is about "deep" security, an existential conflict that transcends disputes over territory,

---

[10]See, for example, Brahma Chellaney, "Regional Proliferation: Issues and Challenges," in Stephen P. Cohen, ed. *Nuclear Proliferation in South Asia: The Prospects for Arms Control* (Boulder, Colorado: Westview Press, 1991), p.312; and Richard Betts, "Paranoids, Pygmies, Pariahs, and Non-proliferation Revisited," in Zachary Davis and Benjamin Frankel, eds. *The Proliferation Puzzle* (London: Frank Cass, 1993), 100-126.

[11]Peter Lavoy, "Nuclear Myths and the Causes of Nuclear Proliferation," in Davis and Frankel,, 192-212, also makes this argument. See p.196.

[12]For a general examination of the concept of identity in an anarchic system, see Alexander Wendt, "Collective Identity Formation and the International State," *American Political Science Review* 88, 2(June 1994), pp. 384-396. Wendt deals with the construction of identity, but not with its contestation.

resources, or other strategic assets. Leaders of states with identities that are fragile or contested may believe, appropriately or inappropriately, that they can guarantee the survival of their states only through absolute military capabilities.

Israel's identity has been repeatedly challenged by outsiders and Pakistan's identity has been challenged by insiders as well as outsiders. Iraq, with arbitrary borders created by colonial powers after World War I, a Sunni leadership ruling a Shi'a majority, and its secularist policies under challenge by its neighbor, may have had similar needs. Egypt, long secure in its Pharonic, Arab, and Muslim identity, with no imperative to reconstruct and reshape its foundations, may have had less need for weapons that promised absolute security.

On closer examination, however, the fit with the available data is not perfect. States such as Canada, Taiwan, and South Korea, with fluctuating and contested identities, considered nuclear weapons and rejected the option. Brazil and Argentina, both with long established and secure identities, traveled some distance down the road to a military nuclear capability before pulling back. Contested or fragile identities are neither necessary nor sufficient conditions; they do not discriminate adequately between abstainers and proliferators.

Domestic Politics and Decision-Making.

The demands of the international environment have a differential impact on the interests and politics of important domestic players; it is they who interpret and mediate the impact of security issues in the shaping of policy.[13] Political institutions, however, affect which coalitions of interests prevail when and how.[14]

---

[13]See Peter Gourevitch, "The Second Image Reversed: The International Sources of Domestic Politics," *International Organization* 32, 4(Autumn 1978), 881-922; Robert Putnam, "Diplomacy and Domestic Politics," *International Organization* 42 (1988), 427-459; Richard Rosecrance and Arthur A. Stein, eds. *The Domestic Bases of Grand Strategy* (Ithaca: Cornell University Press, 1993).

[14]Peter Gourevitch, *Politics in Hard Times: Comparative Responses to International Economic Crises* (Ithaca: Cornell University Press, 1986).

Two analytically distinct explanations of the impact of domestic politics on nuclear weapons policy are particularly relevant. The first is a political economy argument. It suggests that ruling coalitions pursuing economic liberalization are less likely to develop a military nuclear capability than governments that are committed to statist control of the economy; the latter are less interested in global markets and global institutions and consequently less susceptible to pressure from the international community.[15] Governments of this type who also pursue nationalist or revolutionary goals are especially likely candidates.

The second is a more traditional interest-based explanation. It argues that coalitions of interest, inside or outside government, are differentially affected by the response to security issues. Development of a military nuclear capability or abstention can consequently be understood as the result of domestic interests mediated through coalition politics.[16] These two explanations are not necessarily consistent, and can generate quite different predictions.

The political economy of Israel's immediate post-independence years fits nicely with a policy of nuclear weapons development. Prime Minister Ben Gurion was committed to the strengthening of the state against society and the weakening of parallel pre-state economic and political institutions. Statism was combined with a strategy of import substitution, limited reliance on foreign capital, and a deep distrust of international institutions.[17] However, as I shall argue later, the Egyptian experience speaks directly to the contrary. Moreover, coalition politics in Israel worked against a policy to develop nuclear weapons.

---

[15]See Etel Solingen, "The Political Economy of Nuclear Restraint," *International Security* 19, 2(Autumn 1994), 126-169, p.127. Solingen makes this argument somewhat differently; she relates variance in the two types of economic agendas to the propensity to join arms control regimes.
[16]Solingen, "The Domestic Sources of Regional Regimes," makes this argument.
[17]Michael Barnett, *Confronting the Costs of War: Military Power, State, and Society in Egypt and Israel* (Princeton: Princeton University Press, 1992), p.231.

Coalition politics does offer a convincing explanation of why Israel developed the kind of nuclear program that it did. The internal debate about developing a nuclear military capability took place in the early-1960s, at the highest levels of the policy elite, largely insulated from domestic interests.[18] Prime Minister Ben Gurion, a supporter of a nuclear deterrent, faced strong opposition within his own party and within the governing coalition.[19] Leading members of *Mapai*, the pivotal party in the governing coalition,– Levi Eshkol and Abba Eban – worried that the program would not succeed, and that if it did succeed, its costs would be unaffordable. Golda Meir, then the foreign minister, was concerned about the consequences for Israel's relationship with the United States and proposed to her colleagues in the ministry that Israel inform the United States explicitly of its intentions.[20] Israel's nuclear military capability remained "ambiguous" rather than overt in part as a function of the compromises generically produced by coalition politics.[21] Coalition politics was not, however, the most significant constraint; President Kennedy's strong commitment to non-proliferation weighed most heavily with Israel's prime minister.

---

[18]See Avner Cohen, *Israel and the Bomb* (New York: Columbia University Press, 1998), especially pp. 137-53.

[19]Solingen,"The Domestic Sources of Regional Regimes," p.321; Evron, *Israel's Nuclear Dilemma*; Steven Rosen, "Nuclearization and Stability in the Middle East," *Jerusalem Journal of International Relations* 1(1976); Avner Cohen, "Nuclear Weapons, Opacity, and Israeli Democracy," in Avner Yaniv, ed. *National Security and Democracy in Israel* (Boulder, Colorado: Lynn Rienner, 1993); and Alan Dowty, "Nuclear Proliferation: The Israeli Case," *International Studies Quarterly* 22 (1978), 70-120.

[20]See Avner Cohen, "Most Favored Nation," *Bulletin of the Atomic Scientists* (January/February 1995), 44-53; "Stumbling into Opacity: The United States, Israel, and the Atom,"*Security Studies* 4, 2(Winter 1994/95), 195-241; and "The Untold Kennedy-Eshkol Dimona Correspondence," paper prepared for the IGCC Conference on Non-Proliferation, Limassol, Cyprus, August 1995.

[21]Yigal Allon rejected an overt nuclear deterrent that could provoke Arab antagonists as well as the Soviet Union. Allon was among the most influential strategic thinkers, and an important political leader in *Ahdut Ha'avodah*, a coalition partner of *Mapai*. His views, however, became important in 1965, after the critical debate of 1962.

Coalition politics does not explain, however, why a nuclear program began at all, why Israel was not an abstainer. Given the coalition of interests opposed to a nuclear military capability, such a program should not have begun. Yet it did. Almost immediately after the war in 1948, Ben Gurion began his search for a nuclear military capability.[22] Ben Gurion, informing the cabinet, set up the Israel Atomic Energy Commission in 1952, chaired by Ernst Bergmann, a leading scientist and a strong champion of the nuclear option.[23] In 1956, in the wake of the war in the Sinai, Shimon Peres found the opportunity to get the nuclear assistance Ben Gurion had sought so eagerly. In a secret agreement, France undertook to supply Israel with a large 24-megawatt reactor as well as technical help.

When Ben Gurion informed the Cabinet about the reactor, many Cabinet members worried about the expense and the diplomatic and political risks. Seven of the eight members of the Israel Atomic Energy Committee (IAEC) resigned in protest over the process used to make decisions, but Bergmann remained to chair the Commission and supervise the project. In 1957, Peres set up a new secret intelligence agency, later called Lakam, to supervise nuclear security.[24]

Ben Gurion was able, through the unique personal authority he still enjoyed at the time, to prevail over the hesitancy among Cabinet members and to ride out opposition from the scientific community. He changed the terms of the political and domestic debate about nuclear weapons. There was little debate about whether Israel would have a nuclear military capability. The debate was about the far narrower topic of whether it would be overt or covert.

---

[22] As early as 20 December 1948, Ben Gurion invited Maurice Surdin, whom he described in his diary as "the builder of the French atomic oven," to meet with him in Israel. Dan Raviv and Yossi Melman, *Every Spy a Prince* (Boston: Houghton Mifflin, 1990), p.66.

[23] Cohen, *Israel and the Bomb*, pp.1-57.

[24] Raviv and Melman, *Every Spy a Prince*, p.70.

The explanation of why Israel chose to develop a nuclear military capability lies in the strategic beliefs of the prime minister and the young men around him. Ben Gurion, deeply worried that Israel could not withstand a combined attack by all Arab armies, was convinced that nuclear weapons would provide the ultimate guarantee of the survival of the state.[25] The prime minister enjoyed unique authority and was able clandestinely to pursue every opportunity to develop the capability. His deeply-held belief in the value of nuclear weapons and his unique authority were the critical variables.

After the existence of Dimona was announced by the prime minister to Israel's Knesset in December 1960, Egypt was a logical "chain" proliferator. Although Ben Gurion had asserted that the reactor at Dimona was for peaceful purposes only, there was widespread suspicion in the Arab world that Israel was building a military capability. Indeed, President Nasser reacted with outrage to the announcement, threatened preventive war if Israel developed nuclear weapons, and warned publicly that Egypt would be forced to acquire nuclear weapons.[26] Strategic logic, regional system dynamics, and Egypt's political economy all favored proliferation.[27]

President Nasser headed a revolutionary and statist regime, committed to fundamental change at home and the export of Pan-Arabism abroad. In these years, the Egyptian state was extracting large and increasing resources from society;

---

[25] Cohen, "Stumbling into Opacity," p. 198, and interview, Shalheveth Freier, Washington, D.C., May 1990.

[26] In a speech at Port Said, President Nasser warned that if the United Arab Republic became convinced that Israel was making an atomic bomb, Egypt would take preemptive military action and acquire nuclear weapons from other sources. *New York Times*, 24 December 1960, A1.

[27] Stephen M. Meyer, *The Dynamics of Nuclear Proliferation* (Chicago: University of Chicago Press, 1984), 108-109, developed a model of nuclear proliferators and identified Egypt as the single most important anomaly in his results.

economic constraints were not a decisive obstacle to a putative nuclear program.[28]
Nasser's statist strategy of import substitution and economic development generated
little pressure for involvement in global markets and global institutions. This kind
of statist, revolutionary, regime is considered the "ideal type" proliferator.[29]

Yet Egypt did not commit its resources to the development of a nuclear
military capability, even though it had fledgling nuclear research capability. The
Atomic Energy Establishment (AEE) and its supervisory agency, the Egyptian Board
of Atomic Energy (EBAE) were created in 1955.[30] The following year, Egypt signed
a nuclear cooperation agreement with the Soviet Union for the construction of a
small 2 megawatt research reactor in Inchas and, in 1957, concluded an agreement
with India to send Egyptian scientists for training.[31]

---

[28]Mohammed Haykal, *Al-Ahram*, 23 November 1973, as well as many academic analysts, explained
the Egyptian failure to upgrade the Egyptian nuclear program as a consequence of lack of adequate
financial resources and to deficiencies in management. This argument is not persuasive.

Jim Walsh, "Nuclear Threats, Resource Constraints, and State Behavior: Egypt's Nuclear
Program, 1955-1992," paper presented to the Western Political Science Association Meeting,
Albuquerque, New Mexico, 10 March 1994, demonstrates persuasively that resource constraints
provide a very weak explanation. In the early 1960s, Egypt was experiencing its highest levels of
economic growth, had significant extractive capacity, and the option did exist to redirect resources
away from other discretionary expenditures.

Growth of Egypt's GNP was 2.9% from 1954-1958, but 6.2% between 1959 and 1963.
National per capita income in Egypt increased approximately 3% from 1960-1965, a rate of increase
not attained again until 1979. John Waterbury, *The Egypt of Nasser and Sadat: The Political Economy
of Two Regimes* (Princeton: Princeton University Press, 1983), p. 210. During this period, Egypt
spent heavily on discretionary military expenditures. By 1965, for example, the cost of Egypt's
program to produce jet fighter aircraft was approximately $80.6 million annually. See John H.
Hoagland and John B. Teeple, "Regional Stability and Weapons Transfer: The Middle Eastern Case,"
Orbis 9,3(1965), p.471. Walsh (p.9) concludes that the funds spent on any one of the major non-
nuclear programs - enlarging the ground forces, a jet program, a missile program - would have been
enough for Egypt to have upgraded its nuclear infrastructure.

[29]Solingen, "The Domestic Sources of Regional Regimes," p.325; Lewis A. Dunn, *Controlling the
Bomb-Nuclear Proliferation in the 1980s* (New Haven, Conn.:Yale University Press, 1982); Roger
F. Pajak, *Nuclear Proliferation in the Middle East* (Washington, D.C.: National Defense University
Press, 1982).

[30]This summary of Egyptian activities draws heavily on Jim Walsh, "History of Egyptian Nuclear
Efforts, 1955-1992," March 1994, unpublished paper.

[31]Shyam Bhatia, *Nuclear Rivals in the Middle East* (London: Routledge, 1988), p.59.

After the announcement of the Dimona reactor, Egypt intensified its efforts to develop its nuclear capabilities.[32] Salah Hedayat, a leading proponent of nuclear weapons and closely connected to Field Marshall Amer, was appointed the Director of Inchas in 1960, and a year later he was also Chair of the Board of Atomic Energy, Director General of AEE, and Minister of Scientific Research. The Egyptian nuclear program had a strong and powerful advocate.

In July of 1961, the Soviet-built reactor at Inchas was fired up and, in the next two years, Egypt signed nuclear cooperation agreements with India and Yugoslavia.[33] In 1964, Egypt began negotiations with Siemens of West Germany for the construction of a 200MW nuclear desalinization plant and asked the Soviet Union to help in the construction of a radio chemistry center where Egyptian scientists would learn reprocessing and the handling of nuclear waste.[34] In 1965, agreements were signed with China and with France. That same year, however, Egypt canceled its agreement with Siemens and Hedayat resigned his directorship and left the government.[35] When the Egyptian program stalled, Nasser allegedly asked the Soviet Union in December 1965 for assistance to broaden Egypt's small nuclear infrastructure, but the Soviet Union refused.[36] In 1966, Egyptian leaders occasionally

---

[32]Bhatia, *Nuclear Rivals in the Middle East*, p. 54, pp.108-109.

[33]Bhatia, *Nuclear Rivals in the Middle East*, pp.50-59.

[34]Bhatia, *Nuclear Rivals in the Middle East*, p. 55.

[35]Hedayat remained as Nasser's science advisor but abandoned administrative responsibility for Egypt's nuclear program. He apparently resigned as a result of intense rivalry between the civilian and military wings of the program. Walsh, "History of Egyptian Nuclear Efforts, 1955-1992," p. 11, note 21, and Bhatia, *Nuclear Rivalries in the Middle East*, p.53-58, 65-66.

[36]Walsh, "History of Egyptian Nuclear Efforts, 1955-1992," p.12; Evron, *Israel's Nuclear Dilemma*, p. 22; and Paul Jabber, *Not by War Alone: Security and Arms Control in the Middle East* (Berkeley, CA.: University of California Press, 1981), p.38, n.62. Nasser reportedly asked to buy atomic bombs in the event that Israel acquired a nuclear weapon. The Soviet Union reportedly refused but offered a guarantee of nuclear protection which Nasser allegedly rejected. Solingen, "The Domestic Sources of Regional Regimes," p. 324, argues that Soviet opposition to the development of an Egyptian nuclear program was critical; Egypt needed Soviet economic support to maintain domestic legitimacy for their comprehensive revolutionary objectives. The external constraint of Soviet opposition to proliferation conceivably could have been managed, however, through a strategy of ambiguity similar

warned of preemptive action, but routinely belittled Israel's capacity to develop a nuclear weapon, or dismissed the usefulness of nuclear weapons in the Middle East. Despite all the activity from 1960-1965, Egypt had not acquired a large research reactor and a reprocessing facility capable of producing fissile material. Without this capability, Egypt could not develop a nuclear weapons program. Resources, as we have seen, were not a determining constraint in Egypt's failure to push ahead with a substantial research reactor and a reprocessing facility. Insofar as resource constraints are not a convincing explanation, Egypt's abstention is a puzzle for existing theories of the political economy of proliferation. It is also puzzling for realists who would expect balancing behavior and for those who would expect the security dilemma to provoke a response.

Evidence is still very slim on Egyptian decision making about the nuclear program in the critical years from 1960 to 1967, the period in which Egypt was most likely to have decided to build a military nuclear capability.[37] There were influential Egyptians, close to President Nasser, who were strong proponents of nuclear weapons: Mohammed Hassan Heikal, the influential editor of *Al-Ahram*, and a close friend of the president; General Mohammed Sadek, Chief of Special Services and later Chief of Staff; and Salah Hedayat.

In other contexts, influential advisers of senior leaders have been instrumental in pushing nuclear programs forward.[38] In India, for example, Homi Bhabba, a leading atomic physicist, played an extraordinary role in persuading Prime Minister

---

to Israel's. It would have been very difficult for the Soviet leadership to oppose, given Israel's announcement.

[37] I identify these as the critical years because after 1967, Egypt was engaged in a massive economic, political, and military struggle to regain the Sinai. After 1973, under President Sadat, Egypt changed its political, economic, and military strategy in ways that made the creation of an independent nuclear deterrent far more difficult.

[38] See Peter Lavoy, "Nuclear Myths and the Causes of Nuclear Proliferation," in Davis and Frankel, *The Proliferation Puzzle*, 192-212.

Shastri to develop India's nuclear capability. Yet proponents of a nuclear deterrent, closely connected to the president, did not prevail in Egypt.

The most convincing explanation of Egypt's abstention is President Nasser's skepticism of the value of nuclear weapons and their usefulness in any conflict with Israel.[39] President Nasser did not believe that nuclear weapons were "useful," that they could be effectively deployed to achieve Egyptian objectives to change the status quo. Moreover, the president was convinced that the superpowers would never allow either Israel or Egypt to deploy nuclear weapons.[40] Nasser was also consumed by other priorities; in an inversion of the "dove's dilemma," the president was anxious to increase Egypt's military capability, particularly that of the air force and was deeply committed to the jet program.[41] Without a driving commitment – the kind of personal commitment that Ben Gurion demonstrated – Egypt abstained almost by default and did not move forward with a nuclear program that could ultimately lead to a nuclear deterrent.

This analysis suggests that even when the international and the domestic environments are conducive to nuclear proliferation, as they were in Egypt in the early 1960s, beliefs about the value of a nuclear deterrent by the most senior leadership were the critical intervening variable. The strategic beliefs of senior leaders mattered both in Egypt and in Israel. If they matter on proliferation, by extension they should matter in decisions about the usefulness of a military nuclear program once it is in place.

---

[39]Mustaffa Saif, "Egyptian Attitudes Toward Non-Proliferation," Conference on Non-Proliferation, Limassol, Cyprus, August 1995, and Interview, Major-General Ahmed Abdel Halim, August 1995.
[40]Author's interview, Mohammed Hassan Heikal, Cairo, April 1990.
[41]Walsh, "Nuclear Threats, Resource Constraints, and State Behavior: Egypt's Nuclear Program, 1955-1992," p. 15, characterizes the Egyptian nuclear program as low priority in these years. Saif, "Egyptian Attitudes Toward Non-Proliferation," argues that, in addition to the military programs, President Nasser was preoccupied by the war with Yemen and evinced little interest in the development of a nuclear capability.

Proliferation or Penance?

From almost all theoretical perspectives, the moment is ripe now - or riper than it ever has been - for the creation of an arms control regime in the Middle East that caps and eventually reverses proliferation. An effective arms control regime must include chemical and biological as well as nuclear capabilities and must have intrusive and effective monitoring and detection mechanisms. The regime must be comprehensive not only in the scope of its mandate and procedures, but also in its membership.[42] An arms control regime can be created only in tandem with a comprehensive settlement of the Arab-Israel conflict and the participation of Iraq and Iran in the regime.[43] Despite these demanding requirements, a thread of optimism runs through much contemporary analysis: systemic and domestic conditions favor progress both in the resolution of the Arab-Israel conflict and the creation of a regime.[44]

I wish to sound a strong word of caution. Just as environmental conditions were not determining of choices about developing a nuclear weapons capability, they will not be determining of a reversal of course. I first outline the favorable environment, but then, drawing on the earlier analysis, identify several important obstacles to anti-proliferation: strategic beliefs, the endowment and certainty effects, and loss aversion.

---

[42]Peter Jones, *Towards a Regional Security Regime for the Middle East: Issues and Options* (Stockholm: SIPRI, 1998).

[43]Mitchell Reiss, *Bridled Ambition*, p.68, observes that the Brazilian and Argentinian success in reversing early steps toward proliferation depended on their ability to resolve outstanding political issues. "The neuralgic Rio de la Plata dispute had to be settled amicably before the two parties could make real progress in the nuclear sphere, just as Brazilian concerns over Argentine behavior leading up to and during the Falklands-Malvinas war needed to subside before the nuclear dialogue could get back on track....The same reasoning applies to the prospects for arms control agreements in the Middle East between Israel and its Arab neighbors; the pace of progress in this area will be tied to the overall peace process."

[44]Solingen, "The Domestic Sources of Regional Regimes," p.328.

System-level Explanations.

From almost all theoretical perspectives, the international and the regional systems are far more conducive to the creation of an arms control regime than they have been in the past. Only neo-realists argue that the breakdown of bipolarity and an emerging multipolar international system favor the proliferation of nuclear weapons. Neo-liberal institutionalists would point to the strengthening of the global arms control regime in recent years and analysts of global change would emphasize the broad diffusion of norms of non-proliferation and the considerable successes in reversing threshold proliferators.

State-level Explanations.

The security dilemma has been significantly ameliorated by the creation of an arms control regime in the Sinai and the significant progress towards peace made by Israel, Jordan, and the Palestine National Authority. Although serious issues remain outstanding and the process is not yet fully comprehensive, progress has been substantial. In the process, the severity of identity conflicts has been significantly reduced. The proliferation of ballistic missile systems and chemical and biological weapons programs has, however, introduced newly volatile elements into the traditional security dilemma.[45]

Domestic Politics.

It is difficult to predict with precision the constellation of interests, but the broad outline is clear. The military in Arab states is an important constituency. Only in Iraq is there a significant nuclear establishment which could lobby for a nuclear weapons capability, but lobbying is not an effective form of political activity in Saddam Hussein's Iraq. The size of the nuclear establishment in Israel is not known, but it is not considered to be large. The military generally, although there are always

---

[45]Geoffrey Kemp, *The Control of the Middle East Arms Race* (Washington, D.C. Carnegie Endowment for International Peace, 1991), pp.74-86.

important exceptions, tend to worry about the resources that creating a nuclear weapons capability would drain from the conventional forces.

Many important economic and political interests in the "opening" regimes are now engaged in global markets and far more sensitive to international norms. Statist policies have been superseded in Egypt and Israel by an interest in global markets, capital, investment, and technology, and a corresponding openness to international institutions.[46] The Syrian government, though not an "opening" regime, has nevertheless diminished rent-seeking by state enterprises. The Gulf states have long had these kinds of export-driven economic strategies. Only Libya, Iran, and Iraq are the obvious and important exceptions. The political and economic costs of proliferation are far greater for "open" economies and their domestic coalitions than they are for statist regimes.

This quick sweep of the international and domestic landscape suggests that conditions are "riper" now for restraint than they ever have been. Arms control was discussed in the first half of the 1990s in the multilateral working group that grew out of the Madrid Conference and Israel has indicated that it would be prepared to discuss a nuclear free zone after a comprehensive peace settlement, which must include Iran and Iraq, has been reached.

If the Middle East is to be free of weapons of mass destruction, even through non-weaponized deterrence, Israel must at some point in the future agree to build down and eventually eliminate its nuclear weapons. Reversal, however, is far harder than restraint. It is far harder not only because of domestic interests, coalition

---

[46]The opening of Egypt's economy under President Sadat was an important precursor of the peace process with Israel. See my "The Political Economy of Strategic Agreements: The Linked Costs of Failure at Camp David," in Peter Evans, Harold Jacobsen, and Robert Putnam, eds. *Double-Edged Diplomacy: International Bargaining and Domestic Politics* (Berkeley: University of California Press, 1993), pp.77-103.

exigencies, or the security dilemma, but also because of deep psychological processes that are common to all leaderships.

Loss Aversion, the Endowment and Certainty Effects: Framing the Problem
Loss aversion.

Research in the laboratory has demonstrated that people generally pay far more attention to losses than they do to gains.[47] This generalization holds across cultures and contexts. People are loss averse in large part because pain is more urgent than pleasure. Consequently, in framing their choices, people weigh losses more heavily than they do gains. Decisions to cooperate, like all decisions, should reflect this generalized tendency to loss aversion.[48]

The endowment effect.

Psychologists and economists have identified processes that systematically bias people in favor of the status quo. The endowment effect suggests that people frequently demand much more to give up an object than they would be willing to pay to acquire the same object.[49] The principal effect of endowment is not to enhance the attractiveness of what one owns, but rather the pain of giving it up; foregone gains

---

[47]Loss aversion implies that the same difference between two options will be given much greater weight if it is viewed as a difference between two disadvantages, relative to a reference point, than if it is viewed as a difference between two advantages.

[48]While decisions to cooperate internationally should reflect this tendency to loss aversion, estimates of expected losses are far more difficult to analyze systematically outside the confines of the laboratory. It is often very difficult to measure differences in estimated losses when formal measures of equivalence do not exist. This is part of the more generalized problem of measuring "balanced" exchanges which is common to all rational models of bargaining.

[49]Daniel Kahneman, Jack L. Knetsch and Richard H. Thaler, "Anomalies: The Endowment Effect, Loss Aversion, and the Status Quo Bias," *Journal of Economic Perspectives* 5, 1(Winter 1991), 193-206; Richard Thaler, "Toward a Positive Theory of Consumer Choice," *Journal of Economic Behavior and Organization* 1, 1(1980), pp.39-60; Jack L. Knetsch and John A.Sinden, "Willingness to Pay and Compensation Demanded: Experimental Evidence of an Unexpected Disparity in Measures of Value," *Quarterly Journal of Economics* 99, 3(August 1984) 507-21; and Jack L. Knetsch, "The Endowment Effect and Evidence of Nonreversible Indifference Curves," *American Economic Review* 79, 5(December 1989), 1277-84.

are less painful than perceived losses. In addition, people normalize more quickly for gains than they do for losses in part because of the endowment effect. Individuals therefore have a strong tendency to remain at the status quo, because the disadvantages of movement loom larger than the advantages.

Framing the problem.

Prospect theory, developed by cognitive psychologists working within the tradition of behavioral decision theory, asserts that the way people frame a decision determines in part how they see the consequences of choice. People first choose a reference point and then assess gains or losses of options from that point.[50] Outcomes that are above the reference point are treated as gains and those that fall below are considered as losses. Because people are generally averse to loss, whether an outcome is treated as a gain or loss has a significant impact on the choice they make. Most striking, when identical outcomes are reframed as a loss rather than as a gain, people reverse their preferences and make a different choice.[51]

In international politics, there is almost always more than one obvious reference point for leaders facing a problem. Consequently, a given decision problem can often be framed in more than one way and leaders disagree amongst

---

[50]Unlike subjective expected utility models, prospect theory assumes that changes in value rather than final assets are critical to peoples' calculations. Daniel Kahneman and Amos Tversky, "Prospect Theory: An Analysis of Decision Under Risk," *Econometrica* 47, 2(March 1979), 263-291.

[51]Amos Tversky and Daniel Kahneman, "The Framing of Decisions and the Psychology of Choice," *Science* 211, 4481 (30 January 1981), 453-458. Tversky and Kahneman obtained systematic reversal of preferences by varying the description of the reference point. Preference orderings depend on frames.

A personal example nicely illustrates the impact of a reference point on the assessment of gains and losses. If I had expected to write ten pages of this article today but wrote only five, what matters is the "loss" of the five pages, rather than the "gain" of five pages or the total length of the manuscript I had completed. My reference point was my expectation. Rather than consider how much I had accomplished, or my net gain, I estimated loss from the reference point I had chosen. I did not consider my total assets but rather the deviation from my reference point. Similarly, if I had expected to write only two pages, what would matter is the "gain" of three pages from my reference point, rather than the total length.

themselves about the appropriate frame.[52] They can identify personal and political as well as international gains and losses which can cut different ways and leaders may weigh them differently under different conditions.[53]

When prospect theory is applied to foreign policy decisions, it cannot predict the reference point that leaders are likely to select. Prospect theory does, however, provide an explanation of how people choose among competing options once the problem is framed. This process of evaluation differs from rational models in several important respects. First, people are generally risk-averse with respect to gains and risk-acceptant with respect to losses they identify from the reference point they have chosen. They are more willing to take risks to avoid losses than they are to make gains, in large part because losses loom far larger than gains. Framing is critical because of loss aversion; whether an outcome is framed as a gain or as a loss changes the choices people are likely to make.

The certainty effect.

Finally, people generally tend to weigh too heavily certain outcomes in comparison to those that are merely probable. Very likely but uncertain outcomes also are often treated as if they were certain.[54] Certainty magnifies the impact of risk-

---

[52]Amos Tversky and Daniel Kahneman, "Rational Choice and the Framing of Decisions," *Journal of Business* 59, 4(October 1986, Part 2), 251-278. In laboratory experiments, significant changes in preference occurred simply by changing the labeling of the outcomes from positive to negative. The framing of decisions depends on the language of presentation, on the context of choice, and on the reference point that is selected. See also Paul Slovic and Sarah Lichtenstein, "Preference Reversals: A Broader Perspective," *American Economic Review* 73, 4(September 1983), 596-605.

[53]Arthur Stein suggests that the context in which decisions are made, whether a state's position has been deteriorating and the kinds of future leaders can look forward to, also matters. *Why Nations Cooperate*, 110.

[54]Kahneman and Tversky describe the former as the "certainty effect" and the latter as the "pseudocertainty effect." See "Prospect Theory: An Analysis of Decision Under Risk," 282-283, and "Rational Choice and the Framing off Decisions," S268. See also George A. Quattrone and Amos Tversky, "Contrasting Rational and Psychological Analyses of Political Choice," *American Political Science Review* 82, 3(September 1988), 719-36, 730. People also tend to overweigh small probabilities and underweigh moderate and high probabilities.

aversion with respect to gains and risk-seeking with respect to losses. Prospect theory predicts that people will choose a sure gain rather than take a chance on a larger gain that is probable, even if the latter promises higher expected utility. They will also choose to take a chance on a larger loss that is merely probable rather than face a smaller loss that is certain, even when the certain option would minimize expected loss. Both these predictions contradict the expectations of standard models of rational choice.

Scholars who have examined loss-aversion and the endowment and certainty effects suggest that each alone and the three together can impede international cooperation. If both sides in a bargaining situation treat their own concessions as losses and the other's as gains, then each side will overvalue its own concessions relative to those of its negotiating partner. The bargaining space is thereby reduced and trades that are "rational" are missed.[55] I have argued, consistent with the expectations of prospect theory, that cooperation is also likely when leaders identify immediate and certain losses from the status quo, even when they identify larger but uncertain losses from cooperation.[56]

Where is the Leverage?

I argued earlier that leaders' strategic beliefs are the critical intervening variable in abstention and proliferation. There is every reason to expect, therefore,

---

[55]See Jack L. Knetsch and John A. Sinden, "Willingness to Pay and Compensation Demanded: Experimental Evidence of an Unexpected Disparity in Measures of Value," *Quarterly Journal of Economics* 99, 3(August 1984), 507-21, and Jack L. Knetsch, "The Endowment Effect and Evidence of Nonreversible Indifference Curves," *American Economic Review* 79, 5(December 1989), 1277-84. Jervis, "The Political Implications of Loss Aversion," applies these arguments to the prospects of peace.
[56]Janice Gross Stein and Louis Pauly, eds. *Choosing to Cooperate: How States Avoid Loss* (Baltimore: Johns Hopkins University Press, 1993).

that they will also be critical in restraint and reversal. The way leaders frame the problem will matter in the future as it has mattered in the past. The implications of framing effects for restraint and reversal in the Middle East are clear and not encouraging.

Israel, with an undeclared nuclear weapons capability, is likely to use the status quo as the reference point in framing the problem. By now, Israel's leaders have normalized for the "gain" of nuclear capability. Any movement below the status quo will be considered a loss and the loss will be overvalued relative to the gains the concessions of others constitute. The endowment effect will magnify the pain of moving from the status quo, and the certainty effect will amplify the pain even further. The loss is immediate and certain, while the risks of wider proliferation are uncertain, though potentially larger. Leaders generally take "irrational" risks to avoid immediate and certain losses.

Arab leaders will naturally frame the problem at the reference point of a nuclear free Middle East, their aspiration level. To create a regime, they will have to give up their chemical and biological weapons capability and accept some form of conventional arms control. Quite naturally again, they will undervalue the concession Israel makes, and overvalue the "loss" of their own capabilities. If the problem is framed this way, a trade that can be considered "rational" in the present environment will most likely be missed.

Where, then, is the leverage? How can the problem be framed differently? In principle, the answer is clear: the losses of a nuclear status quo must become clearer and more salient to Israel's leaders and the value of an Israeli concession must be upgraded by Arab leaders.[57] In practice, two closely related obstacles work against

---

[57]It was their estimates of the immediate and certain losses of the status quo that have allowed the parties to move forward in political negotiations over the last two decades. See "The Political Economy of Linked Agreements."

reframing. Strategies to make the losses of the nuclear status quo more apparent to Israel work at cross purposes with those designed to increase the value of any concession Israel makes to Arab states; it is difficult to degrade and upgrade the value of nuclear weapons simultaneously. Second, reframing is difficult because of the range of interpretations in Israel of the value of the nuclear status quo.

Notwithstanding Israel's declared policy of willingness to create a nuclear weapons free zone - which predates most of the important domestic and international changes that make the environment "riper" for an arms control regime - the dominant strategic discourse in Israel is between proponents of an overt nuclear deterrent and the defenders of an ambiguous nuclear posture.[58] The debate is intense and I will not attempt to join it here – of interest here is the scope of the discourse rather than its substantive merits. What is relevant is that the debate takes place presently largely within these boundaries. Both these options preclude an arms control regime that effectively limits weapons of mass destruction.

There are, however, countervailing tendencies. Probably the most important is the prospect of proliferation of nuclear weapons in the Middle East. The attempt by Iraq, underestimated by every major intelligence agency, including those in Israel, and aborted only by the war in the Gulf, made proliferation a far more obvious and immediate problem. Iran's nuclear intentions are the subject of considerable controversy. Israel's leaders, irrespective of their political differences, have long regarded a nuclearized Middle East as a strategic threat to Israel; they differ only in the strategies they advocate to prevent proliferation. There is a widely shared consensus, however, that the losses of proliferation would be certain and large. A prominent proponent of nuclear ambiguity recently concluded, for example, that in

---

[58]Exemplars are Feldman, *Israel's Nuclear Deterrent*, and Evron, *Israel's Nuclear Dilemma*. Israel supported a resolution favoring a nuclear weapons free zone at the United Nations' General Assembly in 1975.

a situation where the alternatives are either a nuclearized Middle East or a Middle East in which no state (including Israel) has nuclear capability, the latter is preferable.[59] Some concession on Israel's nuclear capability if it promises to prevent another serious loss - proliferation of ballistic missiles as well as nuclear weapons - may make the loss tolerable. As the likelihood and costs of proliferation loom larger, evaluation of options that depart from the status quo will shift.

Closely related are the strategic beliefs of Israel's current leadership. Although no leader speaks openly of Israel's nuclear weapons capability, the late Prime Minister Yitzhak Rabin long ago expressed skepticism about the value of nuclear weapons. Rising through the army, skilled in conventional force operations, a former chief of staff, Rabin differed sharply from Ben Gurion, who actively promoted a nuclear military capability. In 1974, Rabin described nuclear weapons as "mystical."[60] In his first speech to the Knesset after becoming prime minister in 1992, Rabin identified the threat of nuclear proliferation as one of the principal urgencies to accelerate and broaden the peace process, a view which was echoed by Prime Minister Ehud Barak.[61] In the immediate wake of the Gulf War, that urgency was in part responsible for political concessions. Israel's Likud leadership under Prime Minister Benjamin Netanyahu expressed no such skepticism about the value of nuclear weapons, but was openly concerned about the prospect of nuclear proliferation in the Gulf. It is possible that this concern may drive some concession on Israel's nuclear weapons capability.

---

[59]Evron, *Israel's Nuclear Dilemma*, p. 272.

[60]Cited in Ephraim Inbar, "Israel and Nuclear Weapons since October 1973," in Louis R.Beres, ed. *Security or Armageddon* (Lexington, Mass.: Lexington Books, 1986), p.64, and Solingen, "The Domestic Sources of Regional Regimes," p. 320.

[61]*Divrei Haknesset*, First Session of 13th Knesset, 13 July 1992, pp.9-10, cited by Evron, *Israel's Nuclear Dilemma*, p.266.

What kind of concession? A freeze on Israel's production of fissionable material was proposed as part of a more comprehensive arms control regime by the UN Secretary-General and by President Bush in May 1991, and was discussed again informally in the run-up to the renewal of the Non-Proliferation Treaty.[62] A freeze or a "cap" is especially attractive when we consider again the impact of the loss aversion, the endowment effect, and framing effects on decision making. A cap requires no immediate and obvious loss from the status quo; it does not entail the sacrifice of endowment. Rather, it requires Israel's leadership to forego future "gains," but foregone gains are far less painful than present losses.[63] This analysis suggests that a cap may overcome some of the deep psychological obstacles that otherwise could well lead to "market failure" and a missed opportunity.

Even a freeze is not unproblematic.[64] It would have to be part of a package of reciprocal measures on ballistic missile systems and chemical and biological weapons. If a reciprocal package of freezes could be negotiated, it would begin to unlock the arms control process and start the long slow process toward a more comprehensive arms control regime.[65]

More generally, the promotion and diffusion of knowledge about the costs of nuclear weapons acquisition and use is an essential condition of progress toward

---

[62]See also the Report of the United Nations Secretary General, *Establishment of a Nuclear-Weapons Free Zone in the Region of the Middle East* (A/45/435, 10 October 1990) and Avner Cohen and Marvin Miller, "Facing the Unavoidable: Israel's Nuclear Monopoly Revisited."

[63]Robert Jervis, "Political Implications of Loss Aversion," *Political Psychology* 13, 2(June 1992), pp. 187-204.

[64]Evron, *Israel's Nuclear Dilemma*, p. 273, astutely observes that a freeze would violate Israel's official policy of ambiguity, with potential escalatory consequences. Since Israel's ambiguous nuclear posture has been significantly compromised since the revelations of Mordechai Vanunu, the costs would be considerably less if the freeze were part of an arms control package.

[65]In informal discussions over the last few years, there is a growing consensus, even by Egyptian officials, that Israel's nuclear capability can only be dealt with gradually over time. See Lewis Dunn, "Arms Control and Regional Security," in Fred Wehling, ed. *Promoting Regional Cooperation in the Middle East* (Los Angeles: Institute on Global Conflict and Cooperation, University of California, Policy paper 14, June 1995), pp. 7-15.

arms control. The risks of nuclearization – loss of control, miscalculation, accident, – are becoming increasingly obvious, as are the high environmental and economic costs and the opportunity costs of nuclear weapons programs. The very limited political utility of nuclear weapons for the kinds of problems the Middle East is likely to confront in the next decades is only beginning to be appreciated.

Chapter 4

The Iraqi Nuclear Program:
Past, Present and Future?

Marvin M. Miller

Introduction

The aim of this chapter is to review the salient literature on the above topic, and add some observations of my own. This literature can be roughly divided into four categories: (1) the history of the Iraqi program, its operating methods, and what had been accomplished technically before the beginning of Operation Desert Storm, as revealed by the ongoing inspections carried out by the International Atomic Energy Agency (IAEA) working in collaboration with the United Nations Special Commission on Iraq (UNSCOM); (2) assessments of why interested national intelligence services as well as the IAEA failed to detect key aspects of what was a very large nuclear program; (3) speculations on the course of events if it became known either before or after the invasion of Kuwait that Iraq possessed nuclear weapons; and (4) the prospects for preventing or dissuading Iraq from getting nuclear weapons in the future. This last category includes discussions of the efforts by the IAEA and UNSCOM to implement a system of ongoing monitoring and verification in Iraq; assessments of the efficacy of military action to deny nuclear weapons to a state such as Iraq if the standard non-proliferation tools fail; and the prospects for dissuading Iraq from trying to reactivate their nuclear program if Saddam Hussein is replaced.

Obviously, the above covers a lot of ground, not all of which will be explored in the following. I also note that some of the analyses of the above issues involve information which is considered sensitive by the U.S. and other states who take an interest in such matters; thus, in theory at least, such work is available only to individuals who have the required level of security clearance. In addition, the IAEA also limits the distribution of certain safeguards information. In my view, much, but certainly not all, of what is classified should be in the public domain since the benefits of fostering a more public debate outweigh the risks involved in its disclosure. Moreover, as is well known, supposedly classified information is often deliberately leaked to journalists and others in support of official or personal ends. However, in the following, I only make reference to the unclassified literature.

Context

Chemical & Biological Weapons

Although this chapter focuses on the Iraqi nuclear program, Iraq also made major efforts to develop a chemical and a biological weapons capability as well as long-range ballistic missiles and the "supergun" as alternatives to aircraft for delivery of unconventional weapons. UNSCOM, pursuant to UN Security Council Resolution 687 (April 1991), has made a major effort to discover, and subsequently destroy, remove, or render harmless all such weapons and delivery systems as well as facilities and materials related to them, in parallel with similar actions with regard to the nuclear program. (The division of labor mandated by Resolution 687 is that the IAEA should take the lead in the nuclear area, while UNSCOM has the responsibility for dealing with all the other programs.) Although there is still the possibility that key aspects of all the weapons of mass destruction and missile programs in Iraq remain unknown, the greatest current concern of UNSCOM is with regard to their development of biological weapons. In addition, events outside Iraq, particularly the spread of poison gas in the Tokyo subway system in March 1995, have underscored both the potential destructiveness of chemical and biological weapons, especially when released in urban areas, and their relative ease of manufacture, by sub-national groups as well as states, compared to nuclear weapons. For these reasons, I include here several comments with regard to chemical and biological weapons before moving on to a discussion of nuclear weapons in general, and the nuclear program in Iraq in particular.

The much greater lethality of biological weapons as compared with chemical weapons under similar conditions relating to delivery means and weather is a direct consequence of the fact that the quantities of material needed to infect are typically several orders of magnitude smaller than those needed to poison. Indeed, against unprotected populations in situations where weather conditions as well as delivery systems are favorable to biological weapon agent dissemination, biological weapons have the potential for inflicting casualties of the same magnitude as a nuclear explosive containing a comparable amount of weapons material. (See Figure 1, from a report by the U.S. Office of Technology Assessment[1].)

Thus, under conditions favorable to their use, biological weapons are truly weapons of mass destruction, while chemical weapons would require massive amounts of material under similar conditions to have comparable lethality. In this sense, chemical weapons are truly "the poor man's [nuclear] bomb," both in terms of their greater ease of acquisition, and the fact that their impact, while potentially devastating against ill-prepared troops and civilian populations, is much smaller than that of nuclear and biological weapons.

The widespread notion that both chemical and biological weapons are "beyond the pale" of civilized behavior will help the U.S. and other like-minded

---

[1]*Proliferation of Weapons of Mass Destruction: Assessing the Risks*, U.S. Office of Technology Assessment, Washington, D.C., Report # OTA-ISC-559, August 1993, p. 53.

countries promote international norms, such as the Chemical Weapons Convention (CWC) and the Biological and Toxins Weapons Convention (BTWC), which ban such weapons. However, other states may perceive that U.S. disavowal of such weapons is not only a matter of their inhumanity but of a judgement that as long as the U.S. retains a qualitative edge in advanced conventional weaponry, as well as a powerful nuclear arsenal, global elimination of chemical and biological weapons serves U.S. security interests. In contrast, states lacking both "smart" conventional and nuclear weapons may attempt to acquire the latter, or may view membership in the CWC and the BTWC as a luxury they cannot afford.

Nuclear Weapons

The technology involved in making simple fission weapons has not changed in 50 years, but other factors have. For example, some of the old technology has been declassified, and, inevitably, more will be;[2] new technology simplifies the task; needed dual-use commodities are more available; there are additional countries that can supply the technology; there are more people with the relevant scientific knowledge and technological skills, including growing numbers in developing countries; and there are more possibilities to acquire secret design information.

In large measure, the above is also true for more advanced weapons, including those that utilize the process of nuclear fusion as well as fission, that is, boosted and thermonuclear weapons. However, proliferation of such advanced weapons - which require testing at full yield in order to validate the design - is not the primary concern of the non-proliferation community. Rather, it is the development of pure fission

---

[2] A pertinent example was the publication in Russia in 1992 of espionage documents related to the Manhattan Project, including detailed descriptions of the "Fat Man" Nagasaki bomb, which were supplied by the KGB to the Russian Institute for the History of Science and Technology. The Institute published them in an issue of its journal, *Problems in the History of Science and Technology*. Before the issue had been completely distributed, the Russian government required that it be withdrawn from circulation on the grounds that the two documents with descriptions of the Fat Man bomb abetted nuclear proliferation. However, "the genie was already out of the bottle."

bombs that can be delivered by Scud-type ballistic missiles with ranges on the order of a thousand kilometers. Unfortunately, the development of such warheads – which might weigh on the order of a tonne and have yields in the range of a few to tens of kilotons – by many potential proliferates is credible without any full-yield testing.

Obtaining the required amounts of nuclear material for fission weapons by indigenous production – either plutonium or highly-enriched uranium – remains in general a greater barrier than indigenous weapons design and fabrication. (Of course, if sufficient bomb material can be bought, stolen, or diverted from peaceful use, the calculus changes.) The material of choice for countries seeking to acquire a nuclear "option" in the 1950s and 1960s, e.g., India and Israel, was plutonium. There were several reasons for this. First, the only technology available at that time to enrich uranium – the gaseous diffusion process – was closely held, in contrast to the reprocessing technology used to separate plutonium from irradiated nuclear fuel which was declassified at the first UN Atoms for Peace conference in 1955. Second, the process is expensive to implement and to operate. Finally, it is readily detectable unless special care is taken to disguise its large appetite for electric power. Thus, the plutonium route was chosen, even though the materials-handling and weapons-design problems involved in producing plutonium and then fabricating it into a weapon are more severe, and the reactor and reprocessing plant needed to produce it have signatures which are more difficult to hide.

The invention and subsequent development of the modem gas centrifuge starting in the late 1950s has made the uranium enrichment route to weapons much more attractive. Both the electric power demands and the physical plant required for the centrifuge are much smaller than those required for gaseous diffusion for the same level of enrichment capability. Thus, clandestine construction and operation of such plants is more difficult to detect than in the case of the gaseous diffusion process. To a certain extent, the difficulty involved in finding a clandestine centrifuge plant has been balanced in the past by the need of states such as Pakistan and Iraq to import much of the required technology, mostly from sources in Western Europe. Even with the use of multiple suppliers, front companies, and misdirection as to end-use, efforts to obtain the technology in a clandestine manner have eventually been detected, at least in part. However, with the ongoing development of the relevant indigenous skills detection will become more difficult. Moreover, the experience in Iraq demonstrates the utility of surprise and deception in hiding even large-scale clandestine activities such as the electromagnetic enrichment program; even "obvious" signatures will be missed if no one is looking for them and substantive efforts are made to minimize the risk of chance detection.

The Iraqi Nuclear Program

Sources of Information

Until we have access to the Iraqi version of the "Smyth Report,"[3] if one exists, the most reliable source of information about the plans, technical accomplishments and modi operandi of the Iraqi nuclear program are the cache of documents seized during the sixth IAEA/UNSCOM inspection in August 1991, the 45,000 odd pages which were spirited out of Iraq during and after the famous "parking lot" confrontation between the inspectors and Iraqi officials.[4] This material

---

[3]In August 12, 1945, the U.S. War Department released a report on the Manhattan Project written by Princeton University physicist Henry D. Smyth entitled, *General Account of the Development of Methods of Using Atomic Energy for Military Purposes*. The document, which quickly became known as the Smyth Report, discussed the problems the Manhattan Project had encountered in uranium enrichment, plutonium production, and designing the bomb, and identified the most effective solutions.

[4]However, there is always the possibility that new information may change our perspective. In particular, following the defection to Jordan, on August 8, 1995, of Lieutenant-General Hussein Al Majid, the former Minister of Industry and Military Industrialization in Iraq, the Director General of the IAEA was invited to send an IAEA delegation to Iraq to acquire new information concerning the Iraqi nuclear program, purported to have been withheld at the instruction of General Hussein Kamel. An IAEA delegation went to Baghdad from 17-20 August 1995 for talks with Iraqi authorities who made several new disclosures concerning their nuclear program. The most newsworthy of these was

is regarded as sensitive by both the governments which have copies as well as IAEA/UNSCOM, and thus has had only limited and selective distribution. The only windows on it in the open literature are those provided in articles written by former inspectors such as David Kay,[5] enterprising journalists such as Jeffry Smith and Glenn Frankel, who were briefed by inspectors and other knowledgeable individuals,[6] and security analysts, in particular, David Albright, who in collaboration with the

---

a statement that soon after the invasion of Kuwait, a crash program had been initiated under the direction of General Hussein Kamal aimed at producing a nuclear weapon by using the highly-enriched uranium contained in the safeguarded fuel of the Russian and French-supplied research reactors at the Tuwaitha site. The deadline for completion of the first phase of this effort, namely the recovery of the highly-enriched uranium from the reactor fuel - some of which had been previously irradiated - and its conversion into metallic forms suitable for nuclear weapons, was stated to be April 1991. The possibility of such a crash program was raised during the debate in the U.S. during the fall of 1990 about whether the threat that Iraq might acquire nuclear weapons provided a sufficient rationale for confronting Iraq over its invasion of Kuwait. The position of the Bush administration that the nuclear threat was serious was dismissed as "hype" by most non-proliferation analysts, a notable exception being Paul Leventhal, president of the Nuclear Control Institute. Calculations on how many weapons of what type might be produced by Iraq from the highly-enriched uranium in the safeguarded fuel were made by Avner Cohen and the author in *Nuclear Shadows in the Middle East: Prospects for Arms Control in the Wake of the Gulf Crisis*, Defense and Arms Control Studies Program, MIT, Cambridge, MA, December 1990, and, in more detail, by J. Carson Mark, in *Some Remarks on Iraq's Possible Nuclear Weapons Capability*, Nuclear Control Institute, Washington, D.C., May 1991.

In addition to the disclosures about the crash program, the Iraqi authorities also gave an oral description of the progress made by the Al Atheer project team, who were responsible for the design and fabrication of nuclear weapons. To help substantiate these statements, a 198-page progress report of the project team, covering the period from 1 June 1990 to 7 June 1991, was made available to the IAEA, and is now being translated.

Finally, as the IAEA team and the UNSCOM team, which were simultaneously invited to Baghdad to learn more about Iraq's other weapons of mass destruction and missile programs, were preparing to leave the country, they were led to a farm, purportedly owned by the family of General Hussein Kamel, and shown more than 100 metal trunks and boxes containing documentation relating to all the weapons programs as well as ton quantities of metals in various forms. These documents and materials have been removed to the Monitoring and Verification Center established by the IAEA and UNSCOM in Baghdad where they will be inventoried and analyzed.

[5]See, in particular, David A. Kay, "Denial and Deception Practices of WMD Proliferators: Iraq and Beyond," *The Washington Quarterly*, Vol 18, No. 1, Winter 1995, pp. 85-106.

[6]See, in particular, R. Jeffrey Smith and Glenn Frankel, "Saddam's Nuclear-Weapons Dream: A Lingering Nightmare," The Washington Post, October 13, 1991, p. Al.

journalist Mark Hibbs has published a series of articles on the Iraqi nuclear program based on similar sources.[7]

Smith and Frankel also report on statements made to the inspectors and Western officials by one of the key scientists involved in the Iraqi nuclear effort, Jaffar Dhia Jaffar, and some of his colleagues. The information in the seized documents and the statements by Jaffar et al. are complemented and at least partially corroborated by the observations of the IAEA/UNSCOM inspection teams who detail their findings in reports issued by the IAEA to the UN Security Council which are publicly available. (To date, reports on 27 such inspections carried out under the mandate of Security Council Resolution 687, as well as 7 semi-annual inspections which are part of the ongoing monitoring and verification (OMV) process mandated by Security Council Resolution 715, have been issued.) Finally, Smith and Frankel quote Egyptian journalist Adel Darwish and "informed Iraqi opposition sources" on the early history of the Iraqi nuclear weapons effort, i.e., the period from 1974-1981.[8]

Origins, Modi Operandi, and Technical Accomplishments

Based on the above source material, as well as others as cited, in the following I summarize and comment on what is known about the origins, modi operandi, and technical accomplishments of the Iraqi nuclear program.

According to Darwish et al., the effort to develop weapons of mass destruction started in 1974 with the establishment of a three-man committee headed by Saddam Hussein, who was then vice-president of Iraq. The committee, with the advice of a Beirut-based consultancy called Arab Projects and Development, decided that efforts to develop nuclear, chemical, and biological weapons should be pursued

---

[7]See, e.g., David Albright and Mark Hibbs, "Iraq's bomb: Blueprints and artifacts," *The Bulletin of the Atomic Scientists*, Vol 48, No 1, January/February 1992, pp. 30-40, and "Iraq's quest for the holy grail: What can we learn?," Arms Control Today, Vol 22, No 6, July/August 1992.

[8]The material quoted by Smith and Frankel is discussed in more detail in: Adel Darwish and Gregory Alexander, *Unholy Babylon: The Secret History of Saddam's War*, Victor Gollanz Ltd, London, 1991.

in parallel. In the nuclear area, it was decided that the quickest route to the bomb was to use the cover of a civilian nuclear program and the quid pro quo of access to Iraqi oil to buy nuclear technology from countries in Western Europe and uranium from a variety of sources.

By 1976, agreements had been signed with France and Italy to supply a large research reactor fueled with highly-enriched uranium and equipment to separate plutonium from irradiated reactor fuel, respectively. At the same time, a major effort was initiated to recruit Arab scientists, engineers, and technicians from wherever they were working in countries throughout the world. Between 1974 and 1977, more than 4,000 such individuals arrived in Iraq to work on various high-tech military and civilian projects. A select group, most prominently the Iraqi physicist, Jaffar Dhia Jaffar, was employed in the nuclear program. In addition, as part of its nuclear agreements with France and Italy, about 200 Iraqi scientists and technicians were sent to France and 150 to Italy for training. Despite public and private warnings from Israel that Iraq intended to use the imported technology to make nuclear weapons, France and Italy refused to terminate their assistance. In June 1981, an Israeli air attack crippled the reactor, and started an international debate which continues to the present day about the use of military action as a non-proliferation strategy of "last resort."

> Comment: The concern that international safeguards are inadequate to prevent the misuse of "peaceful" nuclear activities to make nuclear explosives was first expressed in the Acheson-Lilienthal Report (1946), and continues to complicate life for nuclear non-proliferators. As the physicist Hannes Alfven has noted, "atoms for peace and atoms for war are Siamese twins." Even if nuclear technology, materials, and expertise declared to be for peaceful use are not subverted initially to make weapons, a civilian nuclear program provides a convenient cover for their acquisition and subsequent possible misuse for weapons. Even short of this, the cover of a peaceful program simplifies the task of acquiring what is needed for

a parallel, clandestine effort to develop nuclear weapons. According to Jaffar, he recommended that Iraq withdraw from the Nuclear Non-Proliferation Treaty – which it had signed in 1969 and ratified in 1972 – following the Israeli attack, but reconsidered after convincing himself and his superiors that it was possible for Iraq to comply with its obligations under the treaty with regard to declared facilities and materials with minimal risk of discovery of its clandestine weapons program.

To this end, Iraq made a major effort to conceal both the acquisition of needed equipment materials from abroad as well as the numerous dispersed facilities in Iraq, some of them large, involved in what was a major effort to both produce significant quantities of highly enriched uranium by various means, and to design and fabricate weapons using this material. addition, Iraq took every opportunity to demonstrate its commitment to peaceful nuclear us (playing an active role in various IAEA activities, while simultaneously carefully restricting access of IAEA inspectors and visitors at the Tuwaitha nuclear research center. The draco verification regime imposed upon Iraq following the Gulf war has made it much more difficult to implement its pre-war "carrot and stick" strategy for dealing with international inspect However, it has used, and continues to use, a variety of techniques including misdirection, threats and intimidation of IAEA/UNSCOM inspectors, destruction of relevant facilities, equipment and records, and numerous "full and complete" disclosures of its nuclear activities, to hide as much of its nuclear program as possible.[9]

> Comment: Besides the requisite equipment and materials, another essential ingredient for the success of a nuclear weapons program are scientists, engineers, and technicians with the needed skills. Iraq sought to increase its supply of such individuals by sending students

---

[9]For a detailed discussion, see Kay, op. cit.

to educational institutions abroad while concealing their intended mission.

According to Smith and Frankel:

> The focus of the Iraqi program shifted in the 1980s from recruitment in the Arab world to sending young Iraqis overseas to acquire technical training. Top graduates from Iraqi high schools and universities were promised exemption from conscription during the Iran-Iraq war if they would agree to study specific bomb-related subjects abroad. Many traveled to Britain, where the combination of advanced scientific knowledge and relatively lax visa regulations made it an irresistible magnet for a generation of Iraqi students.[10]

On a personal note, the author has been concerned with the issue of the proliferation implications of the education and training of foreign students in disciplines relevant to bomb-making since it was first raised in the U.S. during the Carter Administration.[11] In the face of the above evidence as well as similar concerns about the acquisition of expertise relevant to chemical and biological weapons and missiles, the U.S. and U.K. governments are considering new measures to deal with this problem.[12]

This is obviously a very sensitive matter: while it is legitimate to exclude "rogues from rogue states," identifying them as such is problematic, and restrictions on student access run counter to established notions of academic freedom and the benefits of raising the educational level of scientists and engineers from developing countries. Another hurdle is that the astute proliferator will not "put all his [student]

---

[10]Smith and Frankel, op. cit., p. A44; see also Kay, op. cit., p. 96.

[11]See John R. Lamarsh and Marvin M. Miller, "Weapons proliferation and foreign students," *The Bulletin of the Atomic Scientists*, March 1980, pp. 25-30.

[12]In the United Kingdom in July 1994, the government announced that it had reached agreement with the universities to accept official guidance about countries and technologies of concern which they will take into account when reaching decisions about accepting overseas researchers at post-graduate and post-doctoral levels in certain fields of scientific research. This, Parliament was told, is to inhibit access to technologies which could assist in the development of weapons of mass destruction. See, "Universities Act on Fear of Nuclear Proliferation," *The Independent*, London, July 22, 1994, p. 9.

eggs in one basket." That is, students will be sent to study various disciplines at different levels, e.g., undergraduate, graduate, and post-doctoral, at universities in more than one country. Detection then requires both pattern recognition and consultation between the targeted states, and may prove to be even more difficult to implement than "ordinary" export controls on the transfer of sensitive technology.

Technical Accomplishments: Was the Glass Half-Empty or Half-Full?

The initial reaction in the non-proliferation community to the evidence that Iraq had successfully concealed a large-scale nuclear weapons program was shock and consternation, followed by "finger-pointing" – mostly at U.S. intelligence services and the IAEA – and grudging admiration for what Iraq had accomplished based on the evidence gathered during the initial IAEA/UNSCOM inspections, i.e., observations of surviving facilities and equipment, some documentation, and statements by Iraqi officials such as Jaffar Dhia Jaffar. A good case in point was the initial assessments of the Iraqi effort to enrich uranium by electromagnetic separation.

In brief, Iraq had made a large investment in attempting to replicate the electromagnetic "calutron" (California University Cyclotron) technology used by the U.S. during World War II to produce highly-enriched uranium at Oak Ridge, Tennessee, for nuclear weapons. This technology had many drawbacks, i.e., it was capital, labor, and energy intensive, but it was producing significant amounts of enriched uranium in a time frame before the Oak Ridge gaseous diffusion plant was fully operational. After the war, the U.S. abandoned the calutrons in favor of gaseous diffusion as a means of producing enriched uranium on a large-scale, but electromagnetic separation is still the most versatile means for producing small quantities of isotopes for scientific research, as well as industrial and medical applications. For this reason, the technology is now widespread, and there is a large open literature devoted to innovations and new applications. Based on their World War II experience, U.S. scientists believed that no country would ever use these calutrons to produce highly-enriched uranium for nuclear weapons. Thus, nearly all of the information needed to build and operate calutrons, including the key U.S. patents, were declassified soon after the war.

Enter Jaffar Dhia Jaffar, the British-educated physicist who had a background in particle accelerators, and had worked at the European Center for Nuclear Research (CERN) in Geneva. The widespread assumption is that he decided that, given the availability of the U.S. World War II calutron documentation, the financial resources which could be devoted to the implementation of the process in Iraq, and the belief that no one would be looking for it, it made good sense for Iraq to try to use electromagnetic separation to produce highly-enriched uranium for nuclear weapons. Another important factor, I conjecture, was Jaffar's familiarity with the post-war innovations in this technology, and the consequent conviction that Iraq "could beat the U.S. at its own game." Imagine Saddam's reaction on hearing such news!

Research and development on electromagnetic separation started at the Tuwaitha research center in the early 1980s, and construction of a large production plant at Tarmiya began in 1986. The first large separators, designed to produce enriched uranium of intermediate assay (10-20% U-235) from natural uranium feed (0.7% U-235), were installed in February 1990. The plan was to install 70 such machines, whose output would be collected, processed and subsequently fed to 20 smaller separators which would further enrich it to weapons-grade (>90% U-235). None of this, of course, was known until after Desert Storm, although telltale indications of calutron enrichment were detected in samples from clothing worn by the foreign hostages who were released from detention at Tuwaitha in December 1990. Operations at Tarmiya were brought to a halt in January 1991 by two allied coalition bombing attacks; the Iraqis tried to hide the nature of the activity there by cleaning out the facility prior to the arrival of the first IAEA/UNSCOM inspection team in May 1991. However, an Iraqi defector had previously tipped off the U.S. government about the Iraqi calutron program, and the late John Googin, a veteran of the U.S. wartime calutron effort, confirmed the nature of the Tarmiya facility from photographs taken by the inspectors. Trucks carrying large calutron components removed from Tarmiya and other sites were observed and photographed by inspectors during the second mission; such components were later found buried in the desert at sites west and north of Baghdad.

Confronted with this evidence, the Iraqis changed tactics in their usual fashion, and provided information about their calutron program designed to impress the IAEA/UNSCOM inspectors, and through them, the larger non-proliferation community and the public. For example, the Iraqis stated that instead of using human operators to monitor and control the operation of individual calutrons as had been done during World War II, they would perform this task from a central location using computers. As reported in the semi-technical literature and the popular press[13], the significance of this with regard to increasing the productivity of the process was considerably exaggerated. Another change compared to U.S. wartime practice was to collect the uranium product after the ions had traveled through a circular arc of 255 degrees, instead of the 180-degree focusing used at Oak Ridge during the war. As with computer control, this idea is hardly new, and its application to large-scale separation of uranium is problematic. Focusing at 255 degrees – a technique pioneered at Oak Ridge during the 1960s for small-scale production of stable isotopes – gives a higher enrichment of the desired isotope, e.g., U-235, compared with operation at 180 degrees, but at the expense of a smaller amount of collected

---

[13]For example, in a special report on the Iraqi program which was published in the IEEE Spectrum in April 1992, it was stated that "Jaffar planned to bring the process into the computer age."

product. Moreover, there are serious problems involved in using this technique in the manner proposed by the Iraqis.

The above should not be taken as evidence that the innovations planned by Jaffer et al., including several not discussed here, would not have ultimately led to a more efficient process. However, the first task was to overcome the more mundane problems involved in getting the basic technology to work, and here, despite great efforts, the Iraqis had experienced major difficulties.[14]

Similar comments can be made with regard to the two other major elements of the Iraqi nuclear program, i.e., an effort, in parallel with that involving calutrons, to produce highly-enriched uranium using gas centrifuges, and the design, testing and fabrication of nuclear weapons, commonly called weaponization. The first workable weapons and centrifuges were made about 50 and 25 years ago, respectively. Since then, much has been done to improve the performance of both technologies. Moreover, as previously noted, the re-invention of basic bombs and centrifuges is simplified by the availability of both relevant information in the open literature and technologies such as precision machine tools, computers, and sophisticated diagnostic equipment in the international marketplace. In this light, it is surprising that more progress was not made.

Why? Perhaps because of such factors as the availability of almost unlimited resources and the desire to both impress the political leadership and avoid the consequences of failure, the people in charge of the Iraqi nuclear program bought much more equipment, built many more facilities, and studied many more production processes than required to make a bomb, while neglecting to do some basic homework. It was all very impressive, but as the experience in South Africa and other countries demonstrates, a more focused program can produce bombs with less time

---

[14]For a summary, see the discussion by David Albright in chapter II of David Albright, Frans Berkhout, and William Walker, *Plutonium and Highly Enriched Uranium 1995: World Inventory, Capabilities and Policies*, Oxford University Press, to be published.

and effort. To what extent this "lesson of Iraq" as viewed in Iraq will play a role in any future attempt to restart their nuclear effort is a matter of conjecture. "Our" main lesson should be to recognize the rising level of technology, wealth, and managerial skills in the developing world, and also not to underestimate the willingness of suppliers to sell sensitive nuclear and dual-use technology, with or without the knowledge of their governments, to buyers with cash in hand.

With regard to the new disclosures by the Iraqi authorities summarized in footnote 4, it is still too early to assess to what extent the seizure of the safeguarded research reactor fuel would have shortened the time to possession of a nuclear weapon. While the chemical and/or metallurgical steps necessary to convert research reactor fuel - both fresh and irradiated - to pure uranium metal for nuclear explosive use are extensively described in the open literature, and the Iraqis had carried out similar processing, they were unable to perform the needed operations during Desert Storm. In addition, we need a careful assessment of the new 198-page progress report on the Iraqi weaponization efforts to judge whether they would have been in any better position to incorporate the uranium metal into a nuclear explosive than indicated by the weaponization reports previously obtained. However, what is already clear is the folly of supplying bomb material to states for "peaceful use."

What if Saddam Hussein Had the Bomb Before Kuwait?

I summarize here some brainstorming by my MIT colleague Barry Posen about the possible consequences of a U.S. decision to go ahead, or not to go ahead, with its plans to evict Iraq from Kuwait by military action in the face of an explicit or implicit threat by Iraq to use nuclear weapons if such actions were taken.[15]

---

[15]Barry Posen, remarks at a U.S. - Israeli Seminar on Arms Control in the Middle East, February 18, 19 1993, Cambridge, MA (unpublished), and "U.S. Security Policy in a Nuclear-Armed World, or: What If Iraq Had Had Nuclear Weapons?" *Security Studies*, Vol. 6, No. 3 (Spring 1997), pp. 1-31. For other discussions of the prospects and problems involved in confronting nuclear-armed rogue

Consider first the costs and risks of not acting to retake Kuwait as a consequence of Iraqi possession of nuclear weapons. The first message this sends is the obvious one that nuclear weapons are the great equalizer that permits small powers to heavily, in fact, decisively influence the behavior of large powers. This will put a tremendous value on nuclear weapons in the world, and make countries want them. Second, nuclear weapons can deter conventional as well as nuclear attacks on your country. Third, nuclear weapons are good for more than deterrence, for more than preserving the status quo. If you don't act, the message you are sending is that if a state has nuclear weapons, and neighboring states don't have them nor do they have a large superpower presence on their territory, then if you have the conventional means to conquer a piece of their territory, you can do so with impunity.

This means that states that have anti-status quo objectives but no nuclear weapons will try to get them. But it also implies that no country with claims against it by a nuclear power would feel safe without its own nuclear weapons. So status quo powers who fear claims against them by a nuclear power will either try to get their own nukes or a superpower guarantee that works, i.e., one that involves the stationing of tens of thousands of superpower troops on their territory. In response, those with nuclear weapons and claims, seeing that their prospective victims are furiously trying to get either their own nuclear weapons or security guarantees, will start to think hard about preemption, conventional or nuclear. In sum, there will be more intense, regional nuclear and conventional rivalries, states that have nuclear weapons will not give them up, and the nuclear non-proliferation treaty will go up in smoke.

To deal with these potential consequences of not acting, we will have to give security guarantees, be prepared to take military action against rogue states with

---

states, see the articles by Robert D. Blackwill and Albert Carnesale, "Introduction: Understanding the Problem," and Philip Zelikow, "Offensive Military Options," in *New Nuclear Nations: Consequences for U.S. Policy*, Edited by Blackwill and Carnesale, Council of Foreign Relations Press, New York, 1993, pp. 3-19 and 162-194, respectively.

nuclear ambitions, and make our own nuclear defense and retaliatory capabilities more credible against such rogues. Obviously, this is not a pleasant prospect, but acting has its own costs and risks. We will have to make our nuclear deterrent more credible by, e.g., moving something into the region. Our coalition partners will get nervous, and only those who are most at risk from Iraq are likely to hang in. And we would have had to fight a limited war; this probably means no strategic bombing of Iraq or other actions which would put Saddam in a use-or-lose situation with regard to his nuclear weapons. Although the conduct of the war would be affected, the outcome with regard to the liberation of Kuwait would have been the same. However, the international community would not have been in a position to impose a draconian destruction and inspection regime on Iraq after the war.

Thus, even acting in this manner would still send the signal that nuclear weapons have some utility in your struggle with great powers. However, according to Posen there is an important distinction. In the decision not to act, to be deterred by nuclear weapons, there is an acknowledgment that these things have wholesale use for offense and defense. The decision to act and to act in a restrained way is an acknowledgment that you can protect your core values with nuclear weapons, but you can't conquer countries and hope.

Obviously, there will be differences of opinion and emphasis about these matters, and various aspects could usefully be fleshed out in more detail. For example, how does the analysis depend on the quantity and quality of the weapons that Iraq has, and how would we know this? And what if Saddam had announced or otherwise demonstrated that Iraq had nuclear weapons without invading Kuwait? However, such questions aside, it is clear that there are no free lunches in dealing with a nuclear-armed rogue state bent on throwing its weight around. The conclusion would seem to be that "an ounce of prevention is worth a pound of cure," i.e., everything should be done to prevent their acquisition of nuclear weapons in the first place. In the following, I discuss the prospects for this in the case of Iraq.

Are there nuclear weapons in Iraq's future?

The effort made by Iraq before the Gulf war to acquire nuclear weapons and the efforts since to conceal what was done has convinced most observers that Iraq is determined to get back into the nuclear weapons business as soon as possible, using the existing cadre of scientists and engineers and any relevant materials and equipment which remain hidden as a nucleus. However, under current conditions, it will be much more difficult for Iraq to restart and successfully complete a nuclear program compared to its original effort. In particular, the international community is now devoting greater resources to detecting and impeding nuclear weapons development in Iraq by various means. These include both technical and human-source intelligence collection by national governments and continued scrutiny by IAEA/UNSCOM personnel.

Re the latter, in October 1991, the UN Security Council passed Resolution 715 which extended the authority of IAEA/UNSCOM beyond the "destroy, remove, or render harmless" mandate of 687 to implement a plan for ongoing monitoring and verification (OMV) of Iraq's compliance with its obligations under Resolution 687 not to reacquire weapons of mass destruction and long-range ballistic missiles. As in 687, the lead in this task in the nuclear area is delegated to the IAEA, which is in the process of phasing in the OMV system while continuing to pursue its "search, destroy, and render harmless" mission.

The major issue, of course, is the effectiveness of such national means and international efforts in deterring Iraq. As might be expected, there is scant information about the former in the open literature. However, detailed descriptions of the work of UNSCOM and the IAEA in Iraq, including the latter's OMV system, are available;[16] I summarize some of the material relating to the OMV system in the appendix to this chapter. My own judgement is that as long as the international community keeps up the pressure on Iraq, especially in the form of strong support for the IAEA/UNSCOM mission in the face of Iraqi attempts to thwart it by various means, it will be difficult for them to develop nuclear weapons.

Let me be more specific. Production of significant quantities of highly-enriched uranium or plutonium would be the most difficult and potentially visible step in a renewed Iraqi nuclear program. Compared to this, it will be much harder to detect both theoretical studies and small-scale experimental research hidden in large industrial laboratories or at remote sites, perhaps underground. Such activities need not involve many people, and could significantly advance the state of its weapons art both with regard to weaponization and to weapons material production.

Thus, it is logical to assume that these activities are ongoing, but are being pursued in a manner which doesn't jeopardize the prospects for getting "a clean bill of health" from UNSCOM and the IAEA with regard to the fulfillment of its obligations under Resolution 687 and other relevant Security Council resolutions. Saddam's highest priority is to get the Security Council, despite the misgivings of the U.S., to lift the oil sanctions, hopefully followed in short order by the lifting of the constraint imposed by Resolution 707 (August 1991) which prohibits Iraq from engaging in nuclear activities of any kind except for use of isotopes for medical, agricultural and industrial purposes.

At that point, Iraq would have both the money and the possibility of getting back into the "peaceful" nuclear business in a more interesting manner. Of course,

---

[16]See, e.g., Tim Trevan, "The UN Special Commission's Activities in Iraq: 1994," in *Verification 1995: Arms Control, Peacekeeping and the Environment*, Oxford Press, 1995, Chapter 17, and Paul Stokes, "IAEA On-going Monitoring and Verification in Iraq," IAEA Action Team, Vienna, September 1994.

the IAEA/UNSCOM mandate would still be in place, including OMV activities which encompasses a mechanism to monitor exports to Iraq of dual-purpose items (See the appendix). The key issue is – for how long can/should the international community keep treating Iraq as a special case with regard to the imposition of a verification regime, which in the case of nuclear activities is much more severe than standard IAEA practice? The answer, I believe, depends to an uncertain extent, but perhaps significantly, on whether Saddam Hussein is still around and on whether a strong global norm against nuclear proliferation is being fostered.

At the moment, Saddam Hussein's fortunes seem to be at a low ebb. His support in his own country, and more generally in the Arab world, not to speak of the West, is dwindling – even King Hussein has stated publicly that Iraq would be better off without him. If one assumes that Iraq's quest for nuclear weapons derives wholly or in large measure from Saddam's personal conviction that the Arab state that attains such a capability – thus breaking the Israeli nuclear monopoly in the Middle East – would achieve hegemony in the Arab world and be treated with respect elsewhere, then his demise should be cause for celebration for nuclear non-proliferators, as well as many others. However, it can also be argued that Iraq has enduring security concerns that would be of central importance to any government of Iraq, and which provide an incentive for the development of weapons of mass destruction. Thus, according to Charles Tripp:[17]

> ... as became apparent during the war with Iran, the awareness of the relative lack of strategic depth in the country and the fear of the demographic and military weight of Iran, were powerful incentives to devise other means of defence. It seems almost certain that it was with this context in mind that the Iraqi government began to develop its programs for the production of weapons of mass destruction. The

---

[17]Charles Tripp, "The Future of Iraq and of Regional Security," in *Powder Keg in the Middle East*, eds. Geoffrey Kemp and Janice Gross Stein, Rowan & Littlefield, 1995, p. 149.

development of missile technology, and of chemical, biological and nuclear weapons were not perhaps primarily expressions of Iraqi ambition, but of the insecurity of the Iraqi leadership when contemplating its "frontier" location. There is good reason to believe that this is a factor which will shape Iraqi security concerns well into the future.

I believe that this emphasis on enduring concerns about the defense of borders, particularly with regard to Iran, is well-taken. The question is whether the development of weapons of mass destruction will be viewed by a post-Hussein Iraqi government as a logical response to such concerns, how this depends on the nature of this government and that in Iran, and whether states such as the U.S. will take a more relaxed view of the proliferation problem if rogues are replaced by regimes "that we can do business with." Or whether, with specific regard to the issue of nuclear proliferation, there is leadership by example in promoting such measures as a tougher IAEA safeguards regime incorporating elements of IAEA/UNSCOM practice, e.g., environmental monitoring, in Iraq, a more jaundiced attitude towards nuclear power in general and plutonium recycling in particular, and more progress towards reducing existing weapons stockpiles and their perceived utility for military or political ends.

With reference to the Middle East, recall that the large increase in the price of oil in 1973 fueled not only Iraq's nuclear ambitions, but also those of the Shah, whose grandiose nuclear power plans, including the building of 23 reactors by the mid-1990s and the training of large numbers of students abroad, was strongly supported by the U.S. government, despite evidence of a secret nuclear weapons research effort. Fortunately, this effort was not far along by the time he was deposed. Similarly, Iraqi troops crossed the Kuwaiti border before a major nuclear weapons program – hidden behind the fig leaf of peaceful nuclear activities and pro forma commitment to the Nuclear Non-Proliferation Treaty (NPT) – bore fruit.

Today, Iran is seeking to revive its nuclear power program with the aid of Russia, although electricity generation using indigenous natural gas – Iran has the world's second largest proven gas reserves - in a gas turbine/steam turbine combined cycle makes much more sense from an economic and environmental point of view.[18] Granted, one can argue, as Iran does, that Article IV of the NPT gives states party to the treaty an unalienable right to the benefits of peaceful nuclear technology. However, in Iran and many other developing countries this is equivalent to saying that a person has an unalienable right to shoot himself/herself in the foot. Unless, of course, one is interested in developing a nuclear weapons "option," in which case nuclear power has a decided advantage. Unfortunately, many governments, including that of the U.S., are loath to make this point. Thus we are forced to rely on an underfunded international safeguards regime, which is further constrained by limits on the intrusiveness of its inspection procedures, to find "the nuclear weapons trees in the peaceful nuclear forest." The "lesson" of Iraq is that this is a dangerous gamble; but who is listening?

---

[18]For a detailed assessment, see David Schwarzbach, *Iran's Nuclear Program: Energy or Weapons?*, National Resources Defense Council, Washington, D.C., September 1995.

Appendix

Ongoing Monitoring and Verification (OMV) in Iraq

Introduction

The following summarizes the OMV system as applied to the nuclear area in Iraq. A more complete description can be found in the references cited in footnote 16. The mandate for OMV with regard to all the weapons of mass destruction as well as ballistic missiles is UN Security Council Resolution 715 (October 1991). Iraq refused to accept this resolution until November 1993, arguing that the OMV system represents an unacceptable and indefinite infringement of Iraq's sovereignty, territorial integrity, and national security because of the extensive verification powers vested in IAEA/UNSCOM. It relented largely on the expectation that by so doing it would clear the way for the lifting of sanctions on Iraq, particularly those relating to oil sales. The IAEA plan for a nuclear OMV system in Iraq has been approved by the Security Council, and is now being implemented; similar OMV systems applied to chemical and biological weapons and missiles are being implemented by UNSCOM. However, the new disclosures about the nuclear (and biological) weapons programs mentioned in footnote 4 provide fresh ammunition for the U.S. government to argue that the lifting of sanctions is premature; thus, the situation with regard to future Iraqi compliance with the terms of Resolution 715 is unclear.

Basic Objective and Elements of the OMV System

The basic objective is to detect any activities relating to a nuclear weapons program before such weapons can be developed, and to deter Iraq from such actions through risk of detection. The basic elements of the system are:

- Extensive and detailed declarations by Iraq with regard to, inter alia, inventories of nuclear material, complete design information on any planned nuclear facilities, and information on all proposed imports and exports of nuclear and dual-use items;

- Technical monitoring of declared activities and searching for covert activities;

- Export and import monitoring.

The OMV system provides the IAEA with extensive rights to carry out the above, particularly with regard to monitoring and searching. These include: unrestricted freedom of movement, no-notice inspections, and continuous monitoring at facilities including installation of monitoring equipment. The system is being implemented with the assistance and cooperation of UNSCOM, e.g., in the sharing of intelligence information, data bases, and technical/administrative services.

The assistance of UN member states is essential for the success of OMV, particularly with regard to the identification of possible covert activities and the provision of monitoring equipment. In addition, there is a need for ongoing studies to assess how the effectiveness of OMV can be increased, e.g., by increasing its detection capabilities with regard to crucial elements of a nuclear weapons program such as clandestine centrifuge enrichment and high-explosive testing.

Thus, the OMV system will be an integration of IAEA, UNSCOM, and member state resources, which is both its strength and a potential Achilles' heel with regard to the need for sustained support from key member states.

Problems and Prospects

As previously noted, it is unrealistic to expect detection of small-scale weapons activities, e.g., theoretical studies and laboratory research, by technical means. Also, it is not clear to what extent it will be possible to monitor the present activities of Iraqis who previously have played key roles in the nuclear program. Overall, the success of OMV depends critically on the IAEA's fortitude and resources for conducting challenge inspections in the face of adversarial behavior on the part of Iraq.

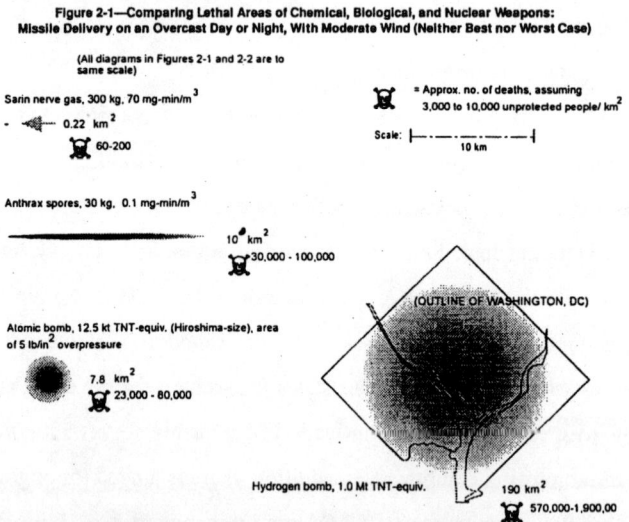

Figure 2-1—Comparing Lethal Areas of Chemical, Biological, and Nuclear Weapons: Missile Delivery on an Overcast Day or Night, With Moderate Wind (Neither Best nor Worst Case)

Figure shows the lethal areas of the agents delivered by a Scud-like missile with a maximum payload of 1,000 kg (note that the amount of biological weapon agent assumed would weigh considerably less than this; since the lethality per unit weight is great, the smaller amount considered here would still more than cover a large urban area). The estimates of lethal areas for chemical and biological weapons were prepared using a model that takes account of postulated release height, wind velocity, deposition velocity, height of temperature inversion layer, urban air currents, and residence time in air of the agent. The diagrams show approximate outer contours of areas with sufficient concentrations of agent that 50 percent to 100 percent of the unprotected people would receive fatal doses. Although some people within the defined area would survive, about the same number in the outer, less lethal areas, would die; therefore, the defined areas give approximations of the total number of unprotected people who could be expected to die in each scenario. With ideal (for lethality) population densities and weather, the chemical and biological agents could kill more people than shown here; under worse conditions, they might kill many fewer. The atomic weapons (fission and fusion) are assumed to be air burst for optimum blast and radiation effects, producing little lethal fallout. The lethal area is assumed to be that receiving 5 lb/in² of overpressure—enough to level wood or unreinforced brick houses.

SOURCE Office of Technology Assessment, 1993.

Afterword

Saddam Hussein remains in power and Iraq's quest for nuclear weapons competes with the Israeli nuclear arsenal as the world's worst-kept nuclear secret. However, over the last five years there has been a steady erosion of support among three members of the U.N. Security Council, Russia, China, and France, for the United Nations Special Commission (UNSCOM), specifically with regard to its search operations designed to uncover any evidence that Iraq retains Weapons of Mass Destruction (WMD) in violation of Security Council Resolution 687. This lack of support has been rationalized on several grounds, notably that while there were still some uncertainties with regard to the WMD capabilities Iraq had developed prior to the Gulf War, these were not significant, and the emphasis of inspections should shift to monitoring to insure that no new WMD capabilities are developed. There was also considerable disquiet - not confined to Russia, China, and France - with allegations that the U.S. had used UNSCOM to carry out intelligence operations aimed at destabilizing and overthrowing the Iraqi regime, a goal of U.S. foreign policy, which, however, is not mandated by Resolution 687.

The split in the Security Council between the positions of the U.S. and the U.K. and Russia, China, and France on inspections in Iraq was underlined by the air attacks on Iraq carried out by the U.S. and U.K. in December 1998 without requesting a specific mandate from the Security Council for such action. The rationale for the attacks was Iraq's unilateral suspension of all UNSCOM inspections at the end of October 1998. It charged that UNSCOM was being used by the U.S. to spy on Iraq, and demanded that the Security Council agree to carry out a comprehensive review of sanctions. In response to the attacks, Iraq refused permission for UNSCOM and IAEA personnel to carry out any further inspections pursuant to Resolution 687. This effectively ended UNSCOM's role, and its chairman, Richard Butler, resigned in June 1999.

After a year of arduous negotiations, the Security Council adopted Resolution 1284 on December 17, 1999, replacing UNSCOM with a new organization, the United Nations Monitoring, Verification and Inspection Commission (UNIVOC).

While 1284 refers back to 687, the emphasis of the new resolution is on monitoring and verification rather than trying to clear up the remaining uncertainties surrounding past efforts by Iraq to develop WMD. These are most significant with regard to biological and chemical weapons where there is compelling evidence that Iraq seeks to retain the capability to manufacture such weapons on short notice.

While there are also uncertainties in the nuclear area, e.g., the extent of external assistance to Iraq's indigenous efforts, the last report of the Director General of the International Atomic Energy Agency (IAEA) to the Security Council was cautiously optimistic with regard to constraining Iraq's nuclear ambitions provided that a system for ongoing monitoring and verification was in continuous operation:[19]

> The IAEA's extensive verification activities in Iraq, since May 1991, have yielded a technically coherent picture of Iraq's nuclear program. These verification activities have revealed no indication that Iraq possesses nuclear weapons or any meaningful amounts of weapon-useable nuclear material, or that Iraq has retained any practical capability (facilities or hardware) for the production of such material.
>
> However, there is an inevitable degree of uncertainty in any countrywide verification process that seeks to prove the absence of readily concealable or disguisable items or activities. It is this uncertainty which makes it essential for ongoing monitoring and verification (OMV) to be a continuous process. Nonetheless, the IAEA, despite its extensive verification measures, cannot provide absolute assurance of the absence of readily concealable items, such as components of centrifuge machines...nor guarantee detection of readily concealable or disguisable proscribed activities, such as computer-based weaponization studies...

---

[19]Seventh Consolidated Report of the Director General of the International Atomic Energy Agency, document S/1999/127, April 7, 1999, paragraphs 31 & 32.

A statement by the IAEA that it has found "no indication" of prohibited equipment, materials or activities in Iraq is not the same as a statement of their "non-existence." It is for this reason that the OMV plan takes into account the prudent assumption that Iraq has retained documentation of its clandestine nuclear program, specimens of important components and possibly amounts of non-enriched uranium. It is similarly assumed that Iraq retains the capability to exploit, for nuclear weapons purposes, any relevant materials or technology to which it may gain access in the future.

As of April 2000, the newly-named Executive Chairman of UNIVOC, Hans Blix, a former director general of the IAEA, has just submitted the organizational plan for UNIVOC to the Security Council for its approval. However, to date Iraq has not accepted the new organization, and it is unlikely to do so without considerable pressure from Russia and France, both of whom, along with China, abstained on the vote on Resolution 1284. Any such pressure is likely to be met by counterpressure from Iraq to implement 1284 in a manner which leads to an early declaration by UNIVOC and the IAEA that Iraq has cooperated fully in fulfilling the "key remaining disarmament tasks" (referred to in paragraph 33 of 1284) which would be required for Iraq to be in compliance with Resolution 687.

This would open the door to the lifting of sanctions on Iraq, which in turn would remove the main leverage on Iraq for accepting ongoing monitoring and verification. The OMV system might then either disappear entirely or devolve in the nuclear area to the standard safeguards procedures applied by the IAEA in non-nuclear states party to the Nuclear Non-proliferation Treaty. In theory, the Security Council could mandate the reimposition of sanctions or even military action if the OMV is either scuttled by Iraq or if it turns up evidence of new WMD activities. But such actions are unlikely unless Iraq threatens to use any WMD it acquires against other states.

Indeed, U.S. policy with regard to WMD proliferation in general and nuclear proliferation in particular seems to be evolving towards continued public disapproval but tacit acceptance of the acquisition of such capabilities, provided that there are no threats to use them against the U.S. or its allies. This has been defacto U.S. policy with regard to Israel for many years, and was also manifest in recent public statements by senior U.S. government officials including President Clinton about India's demonstrated nuclear capability. The result will be greater difficulty in maintaining both the global nuclear non-proliferation norm and a special focus on aborting the nuclear programs of "rogue" states such as Iraq, especially if the U.S. continues "to advocate water and drink wine" with respect to nuclear weapons.

Thus, the answer to the question of whether Iraq will acquire nuclear weapons, and if so, when, depends on several factors: who governs in Bagdad, the prospects for peace and democratic change in the region, and the leadership or lack of same of the U.S. in diminishing the perceived importance of nuclear weapons in international affairs. Given current trends, I am pessimistic that the proliferation of nuclear weapons to Iraq and other states can be prevented.

Chapter 5

Iraq's Approach to Proliferation and the Contrast to South Africa

Robert E. Kelley

Two case studies of nuclear weapons proliferation have occurred in the early 1990s – the cases of Iraq and South Africa.

Iraq's program was in the formative stages. It was discovered in a series of non-cooperative inspections. It was destroyed by military force. The Iraqi Program was extensive in scope, and remarkably unsuccessful in output despite huge sums of money and foreign procurement.

The South African program was disclosed after it was terminated and most evidence had been systematically destroyed. The South Africans succeeded in building six nuclear weapons in secret over a ten-year period. Their program was extremely modest in funding and yet very businesslike in execution.

This chapter explores the difference in approach by the two countries. Included are a review of the results found by the inspectors and an assessment of future prospects. The difference in management approach is another indicator of potential success for the determined proliferator.

The Nuclear Weapons Program of Iraq

What was the genesis of the Iraqi nuclear weapons program? It probably started with the planning of the Osiraq research reactor. This reactor represented the "simple" plutonium route to a nuclear explosive that was being pursued by several nations at the time. Iraq also has tried to characterize their whole civil nuclear program as a program to produce electricity. Some have found this incredible, in the world's second largest oil producer, a country where crude oil is burned directly to produce electricity. But there is a body of literature showing that Iraq had a program to build power reactors. The program was probably partly driven by Iraq's effort to educate many young nuclear engineers abroad during the 60s and 70s. When they came home, they did the obvious and tried to build a program consistent with their training. This continued even into the post Gulf War period when Iraq was rebuilding. Some of the captured documents the International Atomic Energy Agency (IAEA) found relate to power reactor plant siting studies even after the Gulf War.

Despite this civil program, Iraq embarked on a nuclear explosives feasibility study as early as the late 1970s. This program proceeded down multiple paths of uranium enrichment, plutonium production, fuel cycle facilities, and weaponization. Rough estimates suggest US\$3-4 billion may have been expended. The result was four grams of plutonium, a kilo or so of low enriched uranium, milligrams of highly-enriched uranium (HEU), and no clear plan for a bomb design. In addition, the indicators of the program so alarmed the West that destruction of Saddam's nuclear bomb was a major rallying point for the Allies in the Gulf War.

Given this poor record, why was the Iraqi program overestimated by so many in the post war period? The main reason is that the Iraqis are experts at inflating their accomplishments. They inflated their accomplishments in their top secret progress reports to their own management. And they could not resist bragging to IAEA inspectors about what they planned to do. But they weren't doing it.

The Progress Reports

In September of 1991 a gutsy IAEA team led by American David Kay inspected two Baghdad office buildings where they believed there would be classified documents related to the nuclear programs. The teams were enormously successful. They found hundreds of secret and top secret documents relating to materials production and weapons development. Were these documents genuine or counterfeits? The sheer volume of material suggests they were genuine. There were also many embarrassing revelations, names of personnel, post-war activities, and other odds and ends that argue strongly that this was a genuine find. If not, it would be the counterfeiting coup of the century. For this reason, the inspectors have generally evaluated all of the information from this cache as genuine and relevant.

There were two key classified progress reports that covered the nuclear weapons program captured during the "parking lot" incident in September 1991. These two reports are interesting for what they contain, and for the tremendous disparities between them.

The first of the reports is a collation of individual reports from a list of senior managers throughout the Iraqi program. These individual managers apparently answered a call for input that did not give clear guidance as to scope, or detail. Some managers responded with a terse page or two. Others waxed eloquently about accomplishments for many pages with tables, facts and dates.

All of the managers seemed to be interested in inflating their accomplishments. Those who wrote at length included a lot of "boilerplate" language about the great things they were going to do. An example is the report on weapons development – weaponization. In the introduction there is a great deal of discussion of the development of a fission bomb with a 20 kiloton yield. The narrative is chilling with descriptions of codes, implosion pressures, expected yield, hydrodynamic equations etc. Upon a first, even second reading, these facts seem to suggest that the Iraqis have made great strides in weapons development and are on the verge of building a bomb.

But a careful reading shows that the author is simply presenting a list of things that he has to do to design a bomb. He has read all of the available literature on the topic and is listing all of the important tasks that must be done.

This can be calibrated by facts in the text. For example, 20 kilotons is listed as the expected yield. The implosion pressure is an assumed value. All of the Iraqi criticality calculations are at an assumed compression of exactly twice the room temperature static density. There is no explanation or plan for how to achieve this density increase.

Any student can calculate criticality at double normal density. It is getting there that is the rub. The calculations for what have been called an "Iraqi design" are absolutely arbitrary and assumed. They are presented to the reader as if they were progress when, in fact, they are simply assumptions.

The progress report also lists many accomplishments for physical plant activities that could be monitored and verified. When one reads the accomplishments, and tours the facilities, you see that progress was inflated and made to look important. In fact, the inspectors could easily see what concrete had been poured, and what hadn't. The managers of the Iraqi program should have done the same. Progress was inflated.

The second progress report was radically different from the first. It was clear that a professional editor had been brought in to pull the inputs together and to produce a slick publication for consumption by upper management. The second report, covering the period immediately before the Kuwait invasion, was largely a fabrication.

The editor of this report pulled together many of the same facts as the first report from 1989-1990. In this case, the facts are smeared even more to hide what is happening. Goals are reported as accomplishments. Important-sounding scientific facts are listed to make it sound as if the workers are on the verge of a breakthrough. In fact they are just recycling readily available open literature goals, not accomplishments.

This is not just speculation. The inspectors were able to correlate many of the items in the second progress reports with visual observations. Equipment that was said to be moved from Tuwaltha to Al Atheer was found, just as the reports said. But it was unassembled, still in boxes, or damaged in transit. The reports that suggested Al Atheer was up and running were grossly exaggerated.

The Al Atheer Materials Science Center

Al Atheer has been described as if it were some 21st century science center. It was taking shape as a respectable laboratory, maybe one of the finest in the region. But over 50% of the laboratory floor space was still in the early stages of construction. Many of the buildings still had dirt floors or no roofs. Utilities were not even started. Construction of walls is just the initial stage. Internal finishing is the long pole in the tent. Key equipment was still boxed or not yet set up.

The Al Atheer was an exciting find. This center was going to have the capability to carry out many modern analytical and fabrication procedures in material science research. It would also have the capability to fabricate uranium, recycle enriched uranium scrap, press ceramic powders, coat molds with special coatings, and verify close machining tolerances with special inspection machines. And there were signs of a very modern set of facilities for testing high explosives, detonators, explosively driven metal plates, and nuclear weapons mock-up assemblies. This combination was obviously for a nuclear weapons program and was almost immediately recognized by the inspectors. Even without the document seizure in

September 1991, Al Atheer would have had to be destroyed for its very unique capabilities.

Why wasn't Al Atheer recognized and bombed during the war? The simple reason is that it was far from complete. Roads and infrastructure were complete as were many support buildings. But the key experimental facilities were mostly empty shells, in some cases with only dirt floors and no roofs. Several labs were complete and being used but in the most preliminary sort of way. Al Atheer was a priority construction project but it was only just coming together and was easy to overlook.

The captured documents provided a key piece of information – that Al Atheer was conceived and paid for by the nuclear weapons program. It was tainted with the clandestine program in the most complete sort of way. The decision to destroy the process buildings, even the incomplete ones, in 1992 has proven to have been a good one. One of the key concerns was allowing Iraq to have a fabrication site if hidden or purchased materials became available. The disintegration of the Soviet nuclear infrastructure was still over the horizon at this time. The destruction of Al Atheer at least means that Iraq does not have an easy route to utilizing illicit Soviet SNM if they can obtain it.

An important thing that Al Atheer was missing was any capability to synthesize or fabricate high explosive (HE) components. The proximity to the enormous Al QaQa ammunition plant cannot be coincidental. This is a site where many clues pointed to weapons program involvement. The Iraqis successfully stonewalled most attempts to link Al QaQa with the nuclear program despite obvious indications.

The destruction of Al Atheer included destruction of all the scientific equipment there. It seems unlikely that the Iraqis removed much equipment because some very significant and expensive items were there which could have been easily concealed. This is another reason to believe that this phase of their weaponization program was reset to zero.

The Gas Centrifuge Program

One area that the Iraqis did not exaggerate was their gas centrifuge program. They were not forthcoming about the program at first, but began to reveal it in some detail during the fourth inspection in July of 1991. They had bought a package deal from several German scientists who were willing to sell classified information, pure and simple. These Germans gave them material specifications, design dimensions, requisite equipment, key suppliers of turnkey equipment, and a general road map of how to proceed. They did not give them very much of the industrial art to put it all together and the Iraqis were trying to figure how to proceed.

The German technology was largely based on flow-formed managing steel rotors. This is a difficult manufacturing process. The Iraqis set up a flow forming machine at Al Furat and attempted to make rotors. The machine was an exact copy of what had been used in early URENCO programs. There is no sign that the Iraqis ever succeeded in making a single satisfactory managing steel rotor. Many out-of-specification rotors were found in a warehouse near Tuwaitha. If they did make any good ones, they would have had to weld in the endcaps with a welder that hadn't been unpacked. And the critical oxidation of the rotors would have had to be done in an oxidation furnace that was not yet operational.

An Iraqi program based on managing steel rotors was simply not yet off the ground. But they did manage to run two centrifuges using carbon fiber tubes produced on a filament winding machine. This machine was located far away in Germany. Twenty-two tubes were manufactured on this machine by an individual with inside knowledge of classified German programs. He shipped these tubes to Iraq for evaluation. Whether he was planning to supply a production run, or simply provide samples is unclear. It is likely that he was going to supply a winding machine and specifications. No raw materials seem to have reached Iraq for carbon fiber work.

A lot of managing steel related materials did reach Iraq. The steel for rotors and end caps arrived through clandestine procurement channels. The Iraqis used a tiny fraction of this material and destroyed the rest prior to inspections. IAEA learned of the materials and challenged Iraq. The steel, aluminum for centrifuge housings, and magnetic materials were disclosed. The Iraqis have a habit of declaring what they know is known!

The carbon tubes do not appear to have been on the most likely development path for Iraq. They were a convenient way for Iraq to do some rotational tests to satisfy management in a time when their indigenous steel tube project was a failure. Would they have switched to carbon at some point? Not unless their German advisors led them to do so. The Iraqis were risk adverse.

What is clear from all of this is that the Iraqis intended to build about 10,000 first generation centrifuges from managing steel end caps and rotors. Virtually 100% of the material was found by IAEA, unused. The turnkey equipment was found, unused. The centrifuge manufacturing facility at Al Furat was at the bricklaying stage. Some trial manufacturing work was going on in a shed at Al Furat. If Iraq got its act together, it could have had a centrifuge plant up and running within 5-10 years. This was definitely a limiting step in their quest for a bomb.

Another aspect of gas centrifuge development that gets overlooked is material production. Uranium hexafluoride gas (UF6) is a highly corrosive material produced using HF gas and elemental fluorine (F2). Both of these precursors are equally reactive and dangerous. They are not common in international trade and can lead to notice. Fluorine can be produced in special electrolysis cells, which have their own series of indicators. In fact, it would be very unusual to ship large quantities of F2.

It would be much more common to ship fluoride feed salts and build the cells near to the site of usage.

Iraq struggled with UF6 production. They used small scale batch furnaces to make a few grams at a time. Eventually they produced as much as a kilogram of UF6. This would have been more than adequate for their declared activities in gaseous diffusion and gas centrifuge research.

They described their UF4 and UF6 production activities in detail on more than one occasion. They were trying to avoid the use of HF by substituting Freon at the U02 to UF4 stage. This would have worked adequately for making UF6 later but would have introduced far too much carbon for metal reduction. This is another indication that the centrifuge program was separated from the direct weapons effort.

The progress reports discuss many elements of the metal and UF6 programs. There are reports of engineers trying to produce crucibles and furnaces from exotic fluorine resistant materials. Their success was limited.

Uranium Armor-penetrating Rounds

A red herring tossed out by the Iraqis was the uranium armor penetrator program. At first it looked like this was just a convenient cover story for uranium metallurgy but it shows up in one of the classified progress reports. Penetrators were probably a real program where the Iraqi AEC was trying to show its value to the war effort in the Gulf. They just never went anywhere but penetrators were billed as a major program to the IAEA.

Bullets made from uranium have enormous penetrating power through armor because of their hardness and density. They are a staple in the NATO arsenal. (Ironically, the Iraqis have made a great political point that uranium rounds expended by Allied forces are polluting southern Iraq and Kuwait.) Iraq declared a penetrator program as an excuse for their interest in uranium metallurgy. They claimed that the

500 or so kg of uranium metal they produced for this effort was their whole metallurgy interest. They also claimed in another declaration that the same 500 kg was for the nuclear program. These kinds of inconsistencies are not terribly embarrassing to them. This explains some of their progress reports to their own management. Facts are flexible.

One of the progress reports makes reference to the production of uranium penetrators. It is obviously a mirror and peripheral aspect of the program. The Iraqis actually had an out to explain all of the special uranium features of Al Atheer if they had been willing to expand on this tale. But instead, they stuck with the party line and maintained that Al Atheer was only for nuclear purposes. They could have justified the whole of Al Atheer by just extending their penetrator cover story a little, but they reacted defensively to the IAEA questions and lost their finest materials center. This is one of the disadvantages of having politicians coach scientists in the correct response!

The Electromagnetic Separation Program

The Iraqis surprised the world by resurrecting Electromagnetic Isotope Separation (EMIS) as a primary source of enriched uranium. The U.S. had declassified all aspects of this project because it was too inefficient and clunky to be a viable isotope separation process. Unless you were desperate like the U.S. in 1944 or Iraq in 1965. The Iraqis built major research and production facilities to exploit EMIS. They chose the process partially because it was all indigenous. They had to buy industrial equipment from abroad but it was innocuous by most standards and escaped detection. The program was also personality driven. The able Iraqi physicist, Jaffar Dia Jaffar, had training in related fields and felt he could pull off this coup.

Iraq's EMIS program sounded pretty frightening when it first got described to inspectors. The Iraqis were so proud of their accomplishments that they exaggerated them to the IAEA inspectors. They described the design goals as they had to their own management. It looked possible that the Iraqis would have been producing a critical mass or so of enriched uranium per year. There were some caveats though.

The process didn't work well at all. Efficiencies were only a few percent for the few separators that had been built. Classified records of actual runs showed problem after problem. The Tarmiya production plant was running at much lower efficiencies that the Tuwaitha research facility. The skill pool for operating the machines was very shallow. Iraq had intended to run Tarmiya as an integrated computer controlled plant. They found that the separators required individual attention, however, with a dedicated operating team for each machine. The 96 planned machines would have required 96 operating teams. They didn't have a fraction of the skilled manpower required for this task.

Jaffar even admitted to the inspectors early on that EMIS was failing and that gas centrifuges were the new favorite. The final proof is that the procurement records showed that the pipeline of materials for EMIS was empty at the time of the war. Iraq was reevaluating EMIS and was not wasting money on foreign procurement until problems were fixed or the process was abandoned. Iraq had also not engineered the second stage beta units that would take uranium from intermediate enrichment to the HEU levels for a bomb. This had not even been done in R&D. Clearly, EMIS was years away from contributing enough material for a nuclear explosive device.

There is speculation that Iraq could have used alpha stage EMIS to produce material that would be enriched to HEU by centrifuges. This is good speculation. But for a small country it is hard to imagine. The chemistry of the two processes is totally different and challenging in each case. Limited chemical engineering skills would have been stretched to the breaking point by these two simultaneous approaches.

Weaponization

Iraq was beginning to investigate the conversion of enriched uranium into an explosive at the onset of the Gulf War. They had been arguably planning the project for over ten years if you assume that Osiraq was a weapons plutonium producer. The progress reports clearly delineate the state of weapons research if they are genuine.

The arbitrary Iraqi assumption about device density being twice normal has already been mentioned. Another area of research was into a neutron initiator for lighting off the chain reaction when the bomb is compressed to super-critical.

Iraq conducted prohibited irradiations of bismuth to make polonium for an alpha-neutron source in the IRT reactor at Tuwaitha. The irradiation process and radio chemistry seemed to be well developed and well thought out. Many of the key Iraqi scientists were well trained in nuclear processes and chemistry. By their own declaration, and inspection team observation, they were becoming self-educated in shock physics and explosives processes.

Iraq was planning a series of experiments to determine the function and timing of their alpha neutron source. They were building a gas gun and a highly specialized explosive chamber for these tests. Simply put, the state of these construction projects indicated they had a long way to go.

The Petro Chemical-3) program built a massive instrumentation bunker for observing the final mock-up detonations of their nuclear device. The meter thick walls would protect people and instruments during these final tests on the way to a bomb. The site was barely used when it was critically damaged during the war. They had conducted a series of very small-scale tests to check out instrumentation. The tests were not remarkably sophisticated or successful. The instrumentation for these tests was never recovered. The Allied bomb that damaged the bunker burned up the contents. But the inspectors could see that whatever equipment that had remained, albeit destroyed, had been disconnected by cutting the power cords from the plugs! Remains of French oscilloscopes were found. The Iraqis could not recall these items. Irrespective of this diplomatic dance, the bunker was almost new and all intelligence indicated it was barely used.

Iraq was also building a very high quality test cell for contained explosive tests. The facility had wash down capability and had unusual separation from the control room to the test cell. This facility was going to be world class. It was destroyed by IAEA. The control building was surprisingly massive and required a huge quantity of explosive to destroy. The cell itself was far from being finished and could be destroyed simply by cutting up the steel reinforcing bar and molding shells. Iraq had very grandiose plans to simulate nuclear explosives in such a facility.

The Case of South Africa

The South African Nuclear weapons program was totally different in execution, purpose and outcome. The South African government developed a nuclear program over two decades to exploit naturally occurring minerals within their borders. They used their high technology to develop an isotope separation program that was entirely indigenous. This program may have originally been aimed at a civil program. But it is easy to imagine a series of meetings where the program was re prioritized to weapons purposes. As one of the South African weaponeers said, "we did it because we could."

South Africa really built a civil infrastructure and subverted part of it to weapons, unlike Iraq which had only one real goal - a bomb. The research center at Pelindaba was known for its research. The enrichment plants at Valindaba were obvious to the whole world and South Africa even leaked details of the process to diffuse speculation. The South African process was known as Helikon. It used UF6 gas in a hydrogen carrier to carry different isotopes at different radii around separating barriers. The scale of the plants was typically enormous for a UF6-based process and there was no attempt to keep it secret. Except for the ultimate enrichments and purpose.

By 1977 the South African AEC had designed a crude gun-assembled nuclear device and was considering testing it in a test shaft at the Kalahari site in Western South Africa. The Russians detected this activity and tipped off the U.S.. South Africa was a pariah but more closely connected with the U.S. than the USSR. South Africa was engaged in a war with Angola. Angola was supported by Cuban troops so it would be safe to say South Africa was at war with the Soviets, at least by proxy.

The U.S. demanded that South Africa desist from a nuclear test. In retrospect, it appears that the government directed the nuclear scientists to finish their work. But at the same time the government directed the quasi-government corporation South African Armaments Corporation (ARMSCOR) to take over the project. ARMSCOR built a nuclear weapons plant about 10 km from Pelindaba. When the nuclear scientists finished their first bomb in 1979, ARMSCOR took the design and bid them adieu. From then on, the project belonged to ARMSCOR and the Atomic Energy Corporation (AEC) was reduced to a supplier role.

ARMSCOR handled the project in a businesslike and unimaginative way. They set about to make the weapon deliverable and reliable. They established quality criteria and documentable engineering specifications. Problems were dealt within an engineering process that relied on deviations and specifications. The result was the gradual production of a stockpile of six weapons by 1990. Another was in production in 1990 when the change in government and attitude began to really shake South African society. Mr. de Klerk decreed secretly that the program should be stopped and dismantled.

Chapter 6

Iran and Nuclear Weapons:
Implications and Policy Responses

Shahram Chubin

The end of the Cold War replaced one set of worries with another. In at least some regions, the Cold War and bipolarity had constrained "the impetus to nuclear proliferation"[1] With its passing, in a more fluid world of fewer dependable security guarantees, the incentives for self reliance increased. In retrospect, the Cold War had a reassuring symmetry about it as well, which contrasts with the messier less tractable environment today, where "loose nukes," civil and ethnic wars and "rogue states" threaten mankind's well earned repose, its peace dividend.

This chapter argues that proliferation is not a general problem but an issue specific to certain countries. Iran is most likely seeking a nuclear weapon capability. Its current capability is rudimentary and it is unlikely to be able to move very quickly or very far under its own resources or even with external assistance. There are reasons to suppose that its move in this direction can be arrested. The implications of Iran's acquisition of nuclear weapons, admittedly worrisome, have nonetheless been exaggerated. In the process, policy has been conducive not to preventing its occurrence but rather to encouraging it, by threats and coercive measures. A policy that seeks to discourage reliance on such weapons should not demonize states seeking them, but look for ways to meet their concerns within the context of their

---

[1]George Rathjens, "Rethinking Nuclear Proliferation" *Washington Quarterly* Winter 1995(Vol. 18 No. 1) 183.

security environment. A policy comprising sanctions only, gives its target little incentive for compliance and little to fear. Isolating states tends to reduce the capacity for influencing them. Dialogue and engagement, however difficult, will tend to entangle these states and serve as a socializing process in case they do nonetheless proceed and succeed in developing nuclear weapons. In short, it could help change the direction of policy and in any case would act as a safety-net in case non-proliferation fails.

Although the security of most northern or western states has improved in recent years, this is not necessarily the case elsewhere. In the Middle East, regional dynamics were always the principal motor driving regional conflicts whether the Iran-Iraq or the Arab-Israel wars. These conflicts have persisted and overall security, in the Persian Gulf for example, has not materially improved since 1989. If nuclear proliferation is a question of security, it is important for Western policy-makers to get down on the ground and see what security looks like for those states that see themselves adversely, rather than positively, affected.

Such an act of empathetic understanding is difficult enough for the U.S. which sees proliferators as bloody-minded or criminal. It is made no easier by the short list of proliferators which includes some of the more unattractive and repugnant states, whose records cannot inspire confidence or occasion a spontaneous defense. However, if non-proliferation is to be a global norm rather than the product of U.S. dictation, it is necessary to attract support as widely as possible. This implies policies based on multilateral approaches and consensus.

Renewed concern about nuclear proliferation is largely a reflection of concern about the identity of aspirant proliferators. While targets of anti-proliferation policies rail on about discrimination and the "selective" non-proliferation policies of the U.S., the concerns of the U.S. and others revolve around how these states might view and seek to use and exploit such weapons. This reflects, in part, our inadequate and yet undigested understanding and assessment of the legacy of nuclear weapons in the Cold War. What was their role in preventing war, stabilizing Europe and reassuring allies? "Did nuclear weapons prevent war? What are the lessons of nuclear deterrence and different operational practices, or the use of nuclear threats? Which among the lessons would we want other states to emulate?"[2] Our attitudes about nuclear weapons are thus based not on recent history but on our fears. Much of the drive behind non-proliferation is thus based on assumptions about the responsibility and competence of potential proliferators and on uncertainty about the functions and utility of nuclear weapons and how they might be used.

Diminished reliance on nuclear weapons is not likely, soon if ever, to lead to total denuclearisation. But in a world where the two major nuclear powers are trying to reduce their stockpiles, their concern about horizontal proliferation necessarily increases. From their standpoint, emphasis on nuclear weapons by other states at this juncture, appears dissonant, anomalous and irrational. It may not look like that in specific settings. North Korea felt abandoned and vulnerable. Iran sees itself as subject to U.S. coercion, and potentially facing a rearmed Iraq. Although "threat perceptions" are notoriously susceptible to imagined or contrived scenarios, it would be difficult to deny the reality of the threat felt by these two states. They illustrate the essential point that specific states look to nuclear weapons for profound security reasons. They do not embark on this quest frivolously or without due cause. Nuclear weapons are likely to appeal to states threatened by larger more powerful states. Nuclear proliferation is likely to occur where external guarantees do not exist or are

---

[2]Janne Nolan, "Strategies for Nuclear Non-Proliferation and Against Proliferators" Paper presented to IISS Annual Conference, Vienna, September 6-8. 1995. 2 1.

in doubt: "Acquiring a nuclear capability is a statement of a lack of confidence in alternative security arrangements[3]

Iran's Motivations and Capabilities

Iran justifies its interest in nuclear technology by reference to its future energy needs and access to all aspects of scientific discovery. As a member in good standing of the Nuclear Non-Proliferation Treaty, it argues that it is entitled under its grand bargain, notably Article IV, to receive unimpeded access to the peaceful applications of nuclear technology. Apart from the legalisms and the access-to-technology argument, Iran points to the sunk cost of its nuclear power generating program, which in the form of two German-built reactors were largely completed before being partially destroyed in the war with Iraq. Iran now seeks to revive these in two stages with Russian assistance and to add to them in the future two smaller (300 megawatt versus the 1000 megawatt) reactors from China.

The details of the anticipated Iranian nuclear program need not detain us here. Its first power generating reactor at Bushehr will not be built for at least four years, and is itself problematic given the technical and financial problems involved.[4] More important are the motivations. The energy rationale is not plausible; the economics of nuclear power are not attractive to a country like Iran, especially if it is capital deficient. The 'sunk cost' argument is not persuasive either. The problems Russia will have in fitting its reactor on the German built foundation and the cost of recovering

---

[3]Lawrence Freedman, "Great Powers, Vital Interests and Nuclear Weapons" *Survival* Winter 1994/95 (Vol.36 No4.) 46.
[4]For a discussion of Iran's current nuclear infrastructure and plans see, David Schwarzbach," Iran's Nuclear Program: Energy or Weapons? *Nuclear Weapons Databook* (Washington D.C.:National Resources Defense Council September 7,1995; and Greg Gerardi and Maryam Aharinejad, "Report: An Assessment of Iran's Nuclear Facilities" *The Non Proliferation Review* Spring/Summer 1995 207-213; and U.S. , Congress, Office of Technology Transfer *Technologies Underlying Weapons of Mass Destruction*, OTA-BP-ISC-115 (Washington D.C.: U.S. Government Printing Office) December 1993) 182.

initial investment in the sites, make it a dubious economic argument for proceeding. The "right" to access to the latest technology is less easily dismissed, but the line between peaceful and weapons related technology in the nuclear realm is notoriously difficult to establish.

Western sources suspect that Iran is seeking a nuclear weapons option, using a "peaceful" program as a cover. These suspicions were based until 1995 on several indicators. Iran was actively engaged in a covert program of procuring materials useful for a weapons program. It was engaged in a weapons-oriented research program. It was cooperating in the nuclear field with states like China and Pakistan which had a background that was not reassuring to non-proliferators. Iran's interest in heavy water research reactors was also viewed with misgivings. Because of its limited indigenous infrastructure, the Iranian nuclear effort was seen as a problem which could be contained and postponed for a decade or so, as long as external sources of supply were dried up. Hence the U.S. effort to block Iranian access to fissile material and expertise in Kazakhstan and elsewhere.

This assessment changed virtually overnight with the publication of the terms of the Russian-Iranian agreement to revive the nuclear plants at Bushehr. The key parts of the agreement they were planning were 1) that at a later date a centrifuge plant might be added to the agreement and 2) that Russia would train some 2,030 Iranian technicians over a four to five-year period. The U.S. now accused Iran (in words reminiscent of Iraq) of being embarked on a "crash course" to develop nuclear weapons.[5] For the U.S. the issue was now out in the open: Iran was openly seeking technology that made no sense for its energy program (at least at its current level) and in emphasizing training was becoming acquainted with technology that it could then use as it wanted. With its power plant(s) in operation Iran could use the peaceful

---

[5]Lynn Davis, *Daily Bulletin*, USIS, Geneva Mission to UN, EUR-204/208, January 31, 1995, 1-2. See also *International Herald Tribune* March 18-19, 1995, 3.

cover to divert materials to a weapons program; improve the training of its technical cadre and accelerate its weapons related research. Major exchanges with Russia, including the presence of large numbers of Russian technicians (possibly up to 1,000) could increase the chances of nuclear smuggling as well.

In the U.S. view, the fact that no major identifiable installations currently exist in Iran, proves nothing. Similarly, current inspections can serve only as a deterrent or as a whistle-blower after the fact. What matters is intent or motivation. "The keys (to detection) in the future will more likely come from evidence of motivations and intentions or an unease about an overall pattern of activity rather than any specific observable deception."[6] The practical point is that it is harder to reverse or undo a program than to stop or at least delay it. Given the lead-times involved, the earlier they can be caught, the more chance of success.

Given evidence of interest in nuclear weapons, how quickly will Iran be able to attain a capability? At present it has no capability to enrich uranium or reprocess plutonium indigenously. To attain such a capability will take five to ten years. If, however, Iran were able to acquire fissile material – a critical bottleneck – and if it has the design capability, it could produce a weapon in less than five years.[7]

There are a number of factors favoring and constraining Iran in its quest for nuclear weapons which are worth briefly noting. Factors working to its benefit are the ambiguity and overlap between peaceful and weapons applications of nuclear

---

[6]David Kay, "The Lessons of Iraqi Deceptions" *The Washington Quarterly,* Winter 1995, (Vol. 18 No. 1) 102

[7]Iran has no bombs and will not be able to produce one on its own for at least seven years--five years for Russia to complete the reactor at Bushehr plus at least seven years to generate a bomb's worth of plutonium from the reactor's spent fuel and fabricate it into a warhead. Hence, according to CIA Director James Woolsey, Iran will have a weapons capability by early next century, see his testimony, U.S. Congress, Senate Select Committee on Intelligence, Hearing: *Global Threat Assessment,* January 10, 1995. Defense Secretary William Perry puts the time frame at between 7-15 years in Clyde Haberman, "US and Israel see Iranians Many Years' From A-Bomb," *The New York Times,* January 10, 1995 p.A-3. Perry's estimate differs from Israeli and American officials who argued that it would take Iran only five years, see Chris Hedges, "Iran May be Able to Build an Atomic Bomb in 5 Years, U.S. and Israeli Officials Fear," *The New York Times,* January 5, 1995, p.A-10.

technology and the possibility of a diversion of training and material from one to another. Iran has enough money and a scientific and technological base to support a program. Technical expertise and materials exist and are potentially available internationally for countries able to afford this route as short cut. Iran has had experience of clandestine purchases, dummy or front organizations and secret procurement networks in relation to conventional arms purchase s and should find this part relatively familiar. Dissembling and deception too are standard practice but Iran can benefit as well by learning from Iraq's mistakes in this area. Iran may also benefit from relations with China and Pakistan which may provide assistance. Iran's decentralized power structure with parallel agencies would make implementation of a covert program easier. Finally, through sheer persistence and ability to improvise, mixing domestic resources and foreign purchases, Iran may be able to attain some sort of weapons capability. The question is with what sort of confidence could it contemplate such a capability?[8]

What of the constraints? These fall into four categories, technical, organizational, financial and prudential. Iran's potential suppliers do not possess state of the art technology. Russia has technical problems in filling the Bushehr order in terms of fitting its 1000 megawatt reactors to the German built foundations intended for a 1200 megawatt reactor. China's prospective sales, which may have been canceled, depend on technology which has foreign components which it is not clear China can substitute or obtain permission to transfer. Another potential source of supply, clandestine purchases of fissile material or use of foreign expertise in weapons design, etc. is unpredictable. It may or may not work. But it can scarcely be counted upon to build a self-sustaining indigenous program. Such purchases or smuggling may work as a stopgap measure but will not substitute for a domestic program that can have a cumulative contribution toward a weapons program. They

---

[8]See Shahram Chubin, "Does Iran Want Nuclear Weapons?", *Survival*, Spring 1995 (Vol.37 No. 1) 1995, 86-104; and David Albright, "An Iranian Bomb?" *Bulletin of Atomic Scientists*, July/August 1995, 21-26.

cannot be the basis for a credible arsenal over the longer term. Organizational constraints include the apparent inability of Iran to integrate the various elements necessary to produce a relatively simple missile capability. After a decade, Iran is still reliant on North Korea as a source of technology for missiles, having been unable to substitute significantly for them by domestic manufacture. This would suggest a level of organizational (and possibly technical) deficiency which would bode ill for a nuclear program. Also from a political point of view, the ability to undertake a long term multi year program in secret which consumed resources and whose results might not be evident by the time its supporters were no longer in office, would appear implausible. Politically, Iran is not like Iraq; there is no equivalent Saddam Hussein figure sure of his tenure. Financial considerations would be another limiting factor. The opportunity costs of such a program are high and growing in light of other needs, including domestic reconstruction and the need for conventional weapons. This might make it sensitive to economies and subject to possible reversal. Finally, there are questions revolving around prudence and politics. The existence of an international norm against proliferation, the seriousness with which the Security Council and especially the U.S. treats the issue, the fate of Iraq and the current spotlight and resources devoted to detecting future proliferators, all of these would argue for extreme care in pursuing such a course and underscore the risks associated with doing so.

If not a deterrent, taken together all of these considerations would act to at least raise questions about the wisdom of Iran moving in this direction, the difficulties of so doing and the risks involved. None of them, however, is a guarantee that it is not doing so or that it will be unable to use foreign materials and expertise to circumvent the limitations of its own program.

Its arguments for nuclear power aside, if Iran is seeking a weapons capability, what are, or could be, its motivations? Iran would have general and specific reasons for acquiring nuclear weapons. It is a state dissatisfied with its status, wanting a wider role. It seeks recognition and acknowledgment; it wants equality and parity. It is a state with a sense of mission, to act as a "role model" for other (Islamic) states. It therefore has an incentive to demonstrate leadership qualities. Islamic Iran is also a state with a sense of grievance stemming from historical and recent experience. The Iran-Iraq war left it with a sense that the world was hostile to it and that it would have to rely on itself and not count on others for support. Self-reliance and "non-dependence" have since become catchwords in relation to security. Its sense of exclusion, (largely self-inflicted but also fed by U.S. policies of sanctions, isolation and exclusion from Persian Gulf arrangements) impel it to emphasize its own importance and insist that it cannot be ignored. insulted by the United States' designation of an old civilization as a "rogue state," beyond the pale, Iranians of all political stripes resent Washington's "arrogant" policies.

Considerations of prestige or status are not the principal reasons why states embark on the road to nuclear weapons. Even Britain and France had reasons beyond the "top table" and "grandeur" to seek or maintain an independent nuclear deterrent. In the case of Iran there are no urgent, overwhelming or existential threats to its existence. It is not comparable to Israel *vis-à-vis* the Arab states, or Pakistan *vis-à-vis* India or even India *vis-à-vis* China. Iran has no traditional foe with which it is in constant competition or conflict necessitating resort to nuclear arms.

Iran has other security problems. First, it is isolated with virtually no allies or dependable friends. Second, its access to conventional arms, which need rebuilding, is limited in part by the lack of dependable or suitable suppliers in part by its own shrinking financial resources. Third, over the past decade and a half Iran has been in a state of almost constant tension and hostility with the remaining superpower. The U.S. demonstrated next door in Iraq how wide the gap between the military capabilities of advanced and other states had become. From Tehran's perspective, the possibility of narrowing this gap in conventional weapons must appear well nigh hopeless, while the risks of an incensed U.S. "punishing" Iran may well be seen to be growing. (Iranian leaders may have convinced themselves also that that punishment is unrelated to their own actions, but simply a reflection of the U.S.' innate hostility toward independent Islam).

Nuclear Weapons and Security

What might be the specific security motivation for acquiring nuclear weapons (rather than the general incentives for seeking an option)? These, I believe, would be twofold: deterrence of any attacks on Iran by the United States and deterrence of a nuclear attack or threat by Iraq.

The U.S.' current military presence in the Persian Gulf, naval intervention in the region in the recent past including attacks on Iranian ships, oil rigs and civilian aircraft, all reinforce Iran's conviction that the U.S. is looking for an excuse to hit and cripple it. This conviction has grown with the United States' repeated attacks (1991, 1993) on Iraq, the formal designation of a Fifth Fleet for the Persian Gulf, and the imposition of a tougher trade embargo on Iran. Iran sees U.S. hostility as due principally to Iran's independent policies on the Middle East and elsewhere. Its leaders are determined to pursue these and to stand up to the U.S. implicit threats, to the extent of responding to military attacks if these should be forthcoming. U.S. hostility is not without its benefits for the regime, which can pose as truly independent and shift the blame for its economic mismanagement to external sources. The threat from the U.S. sensed by this regime in Iran is not necessarily "permanent" in the sense of being geopolitically or structurally determined or historically inevitable; it could change with a change of regime or even a radical shift within this regime. For the present though, security *vis-à-vis* the United States appears to be the main motive for Iran to acquire nuclear weapons.

Another key concern is Iraq. That state has shown a willingness to use weapons of mass destruction against Iran, eliciting only a perfunctory response from the international community. Iraq's nuclear program, which was accelerated in the 1980's, was sought by Iraq as a war-winning weapon against Iran.[9] The other elements in the program, chemical and biological weapons to be mounted on missiles, were doubtless intended for the same purpose. Continuing daily revelations about the degree to which Western intelligence sources underestimated Iraq's progress in all of these fields cannot be reassuring to Iran. Nor can the fact that after five years of UNSCOM inspections and monitoring, Iraq has managed through deceptions and evasions to preserve large parts of its programs from full disclosure. Iran can take little comfort from the fact that many analysts believe that Iraq may have kept the infrastructure, and certainly retains the human resources, to restart these programs very quickly, once sanctions are lifted. Iran cannot be confident that UNSCOM will continue long enough, or prove effective enough, to dispense with the need to develop its own deterrent.

Iran's incentive to look to its own resources for security in the light of future threats from Iraq, is underlined by the continued existence of disputes between the two countries. These include the unsettled border, support for each other's opposition groups, unresolved questions about many thousands of prisoners of war and claims and counterclaims about reparations and the return of assets. Iraq in the future may be belligerent and bent on vengeance rather than chastened. It may find access to arms or the ability to finance them difficult, and choose to develop weapons of mass destruction as alternatives. In the final analysis, Iran cannot count on Iraq for restraint or rely on others for its security. Iran's experience in the war with Iraq was underlined again by Desert Storm: whereas Iran was unable to threaten in kind retaliation against Iraq's chemical weapons, and therefore could not deter their use, the allies were in

---

[9] According to Robert Kelly, an UNSCOM Inspector in Iraq based on his interviews in Iraq, 1995.

such a position, and such weapons were not used against them.[10] The implication of this is clear and applies to nuclear weapons; nuclear weapons are the surest means of deterring the use or threat of use of nuclear weapons. Such a conclusion would be consistent with Iran's interest in developing nuclear weapons in recent years.

Another oft cited "target" for an Iranian nuclear capability is Israel. It is the case that Iran, like Iraq, has often made reference to Israel's nuclear capability as justification for others' interest in such weapons. This is referred to as a question of equality, of basic justice. It does not follow however that Iran sees Israel's nuclear weapons as a threat to its security or to its core interests, or that they constitute a prime motive for seeking equivalent weapons.

Iran has no border, and no bilateral dispute with, Israel. Iran has demonstrated no willingness or ability to pursue direct confrontation with Israel. I whether on its own or on behalf of Arab rejectionist forces Nor are there signs of a growing disposition to do so. There is every indication that apart from Hezbollah that quintessentially represents "oppressed Shi'ite" fighting for the liberation of their territory, Iran's involvement with rejectionist forces against Israel is largely hortatory and financial. Were Israel to withdraw from Lebanon following an agreement with Syria, Hezbollah's militia would probably be disbanded and amalgamated into a political party. Iran's potential for "direct" confrontation with Israel would thereupon end.

Iran has indeed taken a strong position on the question of Palestine depicting it as a Muslim issue, which its leadership can hardly evade. In using the issue to polish its credentials and acceptability in the Arab world, its target is as much the more "reactionary" Arab states as Israel. In so doing Iran has taken positions that are extreme, but have the merit of intelligibility to the "masses." Thus it does not

---

[10]Shahram Chubin, Iran's *National Security Policy: Capabilities. Intentions and Impact* (Washington D.C.:Carnegie Endowment for International Peace, 1994)

recognize Israel, its right to exist, or any United Nations' resolutions establishing it or ceding it Muslim territory. It opposes the Madrid "peace process" as capitalistic, compromising and equivalent to "treachery." It therefore supports in varying degrees and ways the different rejectionist groups, short of confronting Israel militarily. It has taken pains to signal a lack of any such intent. Leader Ayatollah Khamene'i recently distinguished between opposing the peace process and fighting: "We are not duty bound, according to Islamic commands, to go to distant frontiers to take part in fighting and Jihad. However, if we were close, it would be our duty to take part in the defence [against the aggressor]. In this case we cannot."[11]

For Iran, Israel is primarily a foreign policy not national security issue. It is a subject which Iranian leaders feel strongly about and which they have exploited. It is not, however, a question of national interest or a security question defined in military terms.

The Utility of Nuclear Weapons and Strategic Beliefs.

The nuclear era has been short and it would not be prudent to extrapolate over time from our experience to date. Furthermore that experience may not be applicable to other regions. Some analysts have suggested that some states are so insensitive to cost, irrational or other wise fixed on their own values, that they may be "undeterrentable."

A moderate version of this would argue that "Unfortunately, the United States knows comparatively little about what drives these regimes to act or, indeed, what deters them."[12] Yet surely the last fifty years have demonstrated certain verities even

---

[11]Ayatollah Khamene'i, speech in Babol, Voice of Islamic Republic of Iran Network 1, Tehran, October 17, 1995 in BBC ME/2438 MED/12, October 19, 1995. The comments were made in the context of replying to criticisms that Iran was "looking for enemies."

[12]Paul R.S. Gebhard . "Proliferation and Regional Security Strategies " *Washington Quarterly*, Winter 1995 (Vol. 18 No. 1) 174.

if these may not be iron laws. And surely, as Ken Waltz argues, the characteristics of nuclear weapons are so distinctive that they will have the same impact on all states. What are these results? Paraphrasing Waltz we can summarize them thus:

> Nuclear weapons concentrate the minds of those wielding them and against for whom they are intended. They tend to infuse moderation into every encounter, diminishing the chances of major confrontations. Uncertainty works in favor of deterrence in a nuclear world. Hence not many weapons are needed for deterrence to work. What is needed is a secure second-strike capability. This is not difficult to attain given the ability to move weapons around and protect them by dispersal or hardening, thus achieving a requisite degree of uncertainty for the state contemplating a first strike.

To date, nuclear weapons have not proven to be flexible instruments. They are not an equalizer – a shortcut to power or a substitute for conventional weapons. They are not suited to compelling or coercive uses (blackmail, intimidation, etc.). They are, in fact, quintessentially weapons favoring the status quo. Whatever the size of the inventory or means of delivery, nuclear weapons can do very little beyond defending core interests. It can do this by deterring threats from other nuclear weapons states and by deterring major conventional attack on its recognized vital interests (e.g., homeland). Beyond that, nuclear weapons have not been shown to have practical value.

Few would deny that this has been more-or-less the experience to date, but most would take issue with the proposition that this must invariably be the case elsewhere in the future. They see future proliferators as less likely to share the values of the Western states, as more prone to risk-taking and brinks-man-ship and therefore more disposed to try and stretch the utility of nuclear weapons to make them all-purpose weapons. Many analysts are concerned also about issues of command and control and organizational safety and the risks of accident and unauthorized use.[13]

Certain characteristics of Middle East politics do give cause for concern about proliferation. The existence of overlapping conflicts (Iran-Arab /Arab Israel/ Inter-Arab makes calculations harder. Regimes in the area are often subject to domestic pressures; there are "need driven" as well as "opportunity driven" regimes, to use Gassan Salameh's typology. Unrepresentative regimes that feel embattled may seek to use foreign adventures as a diversion. When isolated, the paranoia of such regimes can be aggravated increasing the chances of miscalculation, especially of the response of others to their own actions. A lack of empathy or understanding by outside powers may also lead to misunderstanding of regional politics. An overemphasis on stability and peace may tend to underestimate the value others put on justice or equality. Similarly the question of risks may be assessed differently if states put different value on human life or the worth of the individual versus that of the collectivity. Hence martyrdom may well be embraced as a blessing in a just cause more willingly by some cultures than others.

Against these considerations, there is the record of Middle East diplomacy, which is essentially pragmatic. States do not undertake risky ventures, especially when the costs are high. They do reign in extremism when their interests suffer. Regimes have proven to be sensitive to and prudent about, threats to their existence. Moreover it could be argued that such states while "ruthless are not reckless" and that nuclear weapons will surely concentrate their minds on their sense of survival.[14]

---

[13]See Scott Sagan and Kenneth Waltz, *The Spread of Nuclear Weapons: A Debate* N.Y.:Norton, 1995.
[14]Ken Waltz."Peace Stability and Nuclear Weapons" Unpublished Paper Presented at Conference on "Dealing With the Spread of Nuclear Weapons" Organized by the Dutch Atlantic Commission, The Hague, May 19, 1995.

Saddam Hussein may have misjudged the initial U.S. response but he did not choose to test it once activated, by the use of chemical weapons.

How does/would Iran look at nuclear weapons? Iran does not admit to the seeking of nuclear weapons, hence there is no debate about their utility or function. Iranian leaders have tended to disparage their utility. They depict them as immoral and not a source of power.[15] They make general statements that tend to focus on the inequality and discrimination involved in allowing one set of states this weapon while denying it to others. Implicit in this is a sense that these weapons are a possible source of status but not much more. As to their usability there is little public comment. We simply do not know enough about the program to be able to make helpful judgments about how nuclear weapons are viewed. For example we do not know the strategic beliefs of the leadership for we do not really know who is in charge of the program. Are the principal motors behind the weapons program civilians as in Israel; or the scientific-technical community as in India; or the military as in Pakistan or the leadership as in Iraq? Who controls the program? If it is the Revolutionary Guards, are they the interest group propelling its advance or simply its custodians? How are nuclear weapons viewed – as indispensable weapons for security or as last resort weapons as in Israel? Or as bargaining cards as in South Africa and possibly North Korea? With no clear or urgent threat is the weapon intended for prestige or for security? How entrenched or flexible is Iran's program? Would Iran seek to extend the uses of nuclear weapons to compensate for the inadequacies of its conventional forces? To counter attempts to exclude it from Persian Gulf security arrangements? What sort of doctrine will Iran eventually adopt with what targeting policy?

Iran's attitude toward nuclear weapons will, of course, affect how it will seek to exploit them. But it will be conditioned in turn by the characteristics of these

---

[15]See Chubin, *Iran's National Security Policy*, and "Does Iran Want Nuclear Weapons?"

weapons as well. These do not lend themselves very well to some the nightmare scenarios dreamed up by analysts. How Iran will behave with nuclear weapons is at least hinted at by the recent record of its behavior – militant in rhetoric, pragmatic in action. Iran has neither undertaken aggressions nor sought confrontations. Its support for terrorist groups oriented against other countries has been quite limited, Hezbollah being considered a "resistance" force fighting Israeli occupation of southern Lebanon. In light of the foregoing, what might one expect from a nuclear Iran?

Iran's Approach to Nuclear Weapons

In theory, Iran's acquisition of nuclear weapons would enable it to face the United States in the Persian Gulf with greater confidence. What would the acquisition of a modest nuclear capability by Iran do to the United States' role as balancing power in the region? With nuclear weapons Iran could expect that the United States would be more cautious in engaging it in combat. More specifically, the U.S. would become more inhibited about attacking Iran with a free hand whether gratuitously or as punishment or reprisal. Iran would thus achieve a measure of deterrence against major conventional strikes and any nuclear strikes against its territory, by being able to launch attacks on U.S. forces in theater or against the U.S.' regional allies.

What besides this type of deterrence could nuclear weapons achieve? In acquiring nuclear weapons, Iran would be challenging the United States' escalation dominance, imposing constraints on its ability unilaterally to dictate the amount and type of force to be used in a crisis. Would it also be weakening the United States' role as security manager of the region, by undermining the credibility of its security guarantees to the Gulf Cooperation Council states? As long as the United States maintained superior and dominant conventional forces in the region, its role as guarantor of the GCC states would remain intact. A nuclear Iran could credibly claim to rely on nuclear weapons only in a scenario involving its homeland and directly affecting its vital interests, defined narrowly. Any attempt to use nuclear weapons threats to confront the United States' presence or its guarantees, would be to enter into confrontation against a power superior on both nuclear and conventional fronts, a measure of risk that Iran has shown no sign of a willingness to undertake.

Could Iran through, nuclear intimidation, try to loosen the ties between the GCC states and the United States? It is difficult to see how. Nuclear weapons are not suited to coercion. In this case, the attempt to do so would be against states enjoying the backing of the foremost nuclear power whose commitment is attested to by its military presence in the region. Furthermore, an attempt at nuclear blackmail might not only drive these states closer together under the protection of the U.S., but provide the kind of excuse (or a pretext) that Iranians fear the U.S. seeks to launch attacks on it.

In brief, Iranian attempts to use nuclear weapons to confront the U.S., founder on the rock of American military superiority (at all levels) and the impracticality of seeking to extend the utility of nuclear weapons beyond homeland defense. Attempts to weaken the GCC/US link by nuclear threats risk prompting the reverse and sparking a confrontation. Attempts by Iran to undermine the United States' commitment and deterrent with what would be fledgling nuclear forces are remote. It would be assumed that while Iran would not be deterred by the United States' massive nuclear arsenal, the U.S. would be deterred by Iran's puny capabilities.[16]

The acquisition of nuclear weapons by Iran would not take place in a regional vacuum. The condition of Iraq and Israel would be an important factor. Iran's neighbors in the Persian Gulf would be directly concerned and feel threatened. On the analogy with Saddam's Iraq they might wonder whether Iran at some later date

---

[16]There is an analogous, equally improbable, scenario in the Korean case. "Our vast forces would not deter an attack on the South, yet the dinky force that the North may have would deter us?" Waltz, "Peace, Stability and Nuclear Weapons."

might not seek to use a nuclear force as a shield to sanctify its homeland from retaliation, while freeing its conventional forces for regional aggression? There is no record of Iran engaging in regional aggression and its conventional forces remain far from capable of this in the coming years. The concern remains nonetheless real, calling for a regional as well as global response.

Iran has a reputation for terrorism and there is concern that once acquired nuclear weapons might be used for terrorist purposes. This could involve the threat/use of nuclear weapons anonymously to extort certain results or the transfer of these weapons to terrorist groups, independent non-state actors. The threat/use of such weapons by a state without attribution would appear to be extremely risky for the state authorities. Just as (sea)mines are eventually traced, nuclear weapons are not so easily used and disavowed. The probability that responsibility will be allocated must play a role in deterring states from seeking to exploit nuclear weapons anonymously for blackmail. Similar considerations apply to the transfer to terrorist groups. In addition these weapons inherently are unsuitable for handling by terrorist groups, and out of all proportion to the aims of most of these groups. Nevertheless there are grounds for concern about the diffusion of nuclear weapons to non-state actors, though it seems unlikely that Iran would be in the lead of states active in such transfers, not least because it has as much to fear as to gain from it.

None of the foregoing is to suggest that the acquisition of nuclear weapons by Iran would contribute to regional security. It would certainly limit the United States' freedom of action, but not by all that much. It would not give Iran much room for maneuver or scope for coercion. It would increase Iran's confidence about its ultimate security and would strengthen its claim to be taken seriously in the region. Depending on how it responded to this increased confidence, it could make it easier or harder to accommodate and integrate into regional politics.

Iran's principal motive for nuclear weapons regionally is Iraq. There is no inherent reason why this should be so, after all, Iran with three times the manpower and greater strategic depth and frontage on the Persian Gulf should be able to assure its security *vis-à-vis* Iraq by conventional means. This it was able to do under the Shah and is preferable. The difficulty is that precisely because of the basic factors working in Iran's favor, Iraq has sought a "qualitative edge", and embarked on weapons of mass destruction as equalizers. While these are constrained at the moment, neither the quality of the restrictions nor their duration, are reliably assured. There remains the possibility of an eventual Iraqi " breakout," this time combining vengeance with technical knowledge. In such a scenario, Iran could not rely on Iraqi forbearance or international assistance. Its best deterrent would be a capability to respond "in kind" to any Iraqi use of weapons of mass destruction, nuclear or non-nuclear. Such reasoning is not reckless or unduly speculative. It combines Iran's own experience and the lessons it has learned from Iraq's two last wars.

An imbalance in nuclear weapons capability between two adversary states that are neighbors, neither of which can rely on significant external support, would be dangerous. It would be more dangerous if one, or both, states are territorially revisionist. A rerun of the Iran-Iraq war with either side in possession of nuclear weapons, would be frightening. However, much depends on the specifics. If both sides had had these weapons at the outset, would that war have started at all? If Iran alone had had these weapons, would Iraq have attacked? Would Iran have sought to spread its revolution using the nuclear umbrella as a shield? (see above). If Iraq alone had had nuclear weapons, would it have felt the need or impulse to attack Iran? If developed during the war, would it have used it to end the war, and warn Iran of the consequences of continuing its offensives? There is room for considerable speculation.

If Iran acquires nuclear weapons, its function against Iraq would be best served as a deterrent against possible use by equivalent weapons by that state. Iran has no territorial claims on Iraq and little interest in conquering it or annexing any of its parts. Iran's prime interest is in having friendly relations with a neighbor that is well disposed toward it. Since Iraq's aims are less certain, nuclear weapons could be a form of insurance policy for Iran. In the process, of course, they could also increase Iraq's own determination to retain or develop nuclear weapons, also for deterrence. At the least we can say that the potential threat of an Iran-Iraq nuclear confrontation is greater than that between Iran and the GCC states and roughly equal to the chances of reconciliation between the two states.

The nuclear scenario most discussed is also the most-distant one: Iran and Israel. From the Israeli view the discussion so far may appear "too rational," discounting too many uncertainties. From that perspective, a state that refuses to recognize it and supports the rejectionists against the peace process, looks like a serious danger. Furthermore, Israel feels acutely threatened by two trends in the region associated with Iran: the spread of fundamentalism and of nuclear weapons capabilities. Theoretically, Iran could become involved in a nuclear clash with Israel: a) directly, as a result of bilateral differences leading to conflict; and indirectly, whether as a result of support for; b) an opposition movement like Hamas or Hezbollah; or c) a fundamentalist or secular state (e.g., Syria) that is in conflict with Israel.

From the standpoint of Iran, none of these look very likely. Lacking borders, Iran has no tangible dispute with Israel. Its willingness to underwrite militarily the quarrels of others, however strongly its leaders might feel about the justice of the issues, is limited. Support for terrorist groups is unlikely to assume nuclear dimensions for reasons already outlined. Even assuming a "strategic partnership" whether with Syria or an equivalent fundamentalist state in the future, there is no reason to suppose that Iran would do more for that state than Syria did for Iran doing the Iran-Iraq war. Above all, none of these scenarios pass the test of being a vital interest. None of them would be worth jeopardizing Iran's security for, by confronting a state with a nuclear arsenal believed to be between 50-100 bombs. The balance of interest and commitment, as well as power, would clearly be and would be seen to be in Israel's favor.

Distinct from Iran's nuclear weapons acquisition, but related to it, is Iran's program to acquire long-range No-Dong missiles which can reach Israel.[17] These have aroused Israel's concern and should have been delivered to Iran by 1998. That concern, I believe, is less about any scenario that sees Iran using chemical, biological or nuclear warheads on these missiles, than it is about Israel's concern to maintain its freedom of action. Once Iran deploys these missiles, it will be able to threaten to retaliate against Israel if that state were to attempt to execute punitive or disarming strikes against Iran. For Israel, lacking land access and hence the ability to strike by conventional ground forces for retaliation against terrorist attacks, maintenance of an ability to threaten Iran directly by air, remains an important part of its overall conventional deterrent. It is this which Iran's long range missiles will call into question.

Israel understandably, is skeptical about change in her security environment. Iran proved willing to lose many lives in the prosecution of its war with Iraq Israel may contrast this with its own sensitivity to losses. Seeing Iran as capable of using deception as a strategic weapon, Israel is also reluctant to accept that what has held

---

[17]With a 1000kg warhead and 900-1000km range, they can easily be modified to an extended range of 1300kms range with a 1000 kg warhead. See Marvin Miller, "Weapons of Mass Destruction and Advanced Delivery Systems in the Middle East," Paper presented for Project on Future Security Arrangements in the Middle East, Sponsored by the American Association for the Advancement of Science to be published. 1995.

in the past need operate in the future. It cannot count on Iranian pragmatism or moderation.

The introduction of any nuclear weapons into the region would change the "rules of the game," with indeterminate results. Israel sees proliferation as an international not bilateral issue. It has reacted to the threat of the nuclearisation of the region in two ways. First, since 1992 it has sought to use it as an argument for conflict resolution, engaging the Arab states and parties in serious negotiations and attempting to build a domestic consensus in favor of a compromise peace. Second, it has issued warnings and threats principally directed against Iran.[18] Israel has acquired long-range F15 aircraft for possible strikes against Iran's installations. Israel has focused its intelligence resources on regional proliferation. It has also concentrated its diplomacy on seeking to dissuade supplier states (North Korea, Russia and China) from continuing their relationship with Iran, so far with no conspicuous results. Eventually, should Iran acquire nuclear weapons, there will be a need to establish a "strategic dialogue" in which "red lines" are clearly delineated. In the meantime, attempts to delay, stop and reverse Iran's weapons program should not be such as to encourage Iran in the belief that Israel is a potential adversary and strengthen Iran's case for acquiring nuclear weapons.

Non-proliferation Policy: From Symptoms to Causes

States embark on the road toward nuclear weapons to meet serious security problems. It is doubtful whether they can be dissuaded without addressing those concerns. Our attitudes toward proliferators are influenced by our relations with them and their regime type. These influence our policies toward them and our assessments of the implications for global and regional politics of their acquiring nuclear

---

[18]For examples see Chubin, *Iran's National Security Policies.* and "Does Iran Want Nuclear Weapons?"

weapons. in the case of Iran, as with other recent proliferators, apocalyptical scenarios have been unveiled about the uses to which nuclear weapons would be put. Exaggerating the impact of proliferation and the uses to which nuclear weapons could be put does little to dampen the incentives for proliferation. Latterly, U.S. policy has settled into a congenial mode of denunciation and diatribe affecting shock and moral dismay at the prospect of further proliferation.

Based on the premise that Iran's economic weakness makes it vulnerable, the U.S. seeks to extend and intensify its economic embargo on Iran. In theory sanctions "buy time." They impose costs on Iran for pursuing such policies, adding to its burdens and encouraging it to reassess its course. They delay the nuclear program, giving the regime a chance to change its mind and reverse itself or to stretch it out even further. Finally, by slowing the drive to nuclear weapons, they give time for other factors to work, for example for generalised discontent to make itself felt and to reverse the regime. Iran's economic difficulties have already slowed its nuclear ambitions and are likely to continue to do so. Given the opportunity costs of such a program, which will take time to produce results, it may become more controversial within the leadership itself. The regime may reverse itself or find itself replaced by more pragmatic figures less eager to exploit a conflicting relationship with the West for domestic purposes. Any and all of these may happen; and they might not. In case they do not, it might be wise to consider other policy options.

Policies that isolate proliferate states can only feed their sense of embattlement and paranoia.[19] Policies that focus on dental strategies, which may well be unsuccessful, divert attention away from motivations.[20] Ultimately, the best non-

---

[19]See Leon V Sigal, "Fighting Proliferation Without Waging War," Paper Presented to the Conference on "Fifty Years After Hiroshima," Organized by the Union of Scientists for Disarmament, Castiglioncello, Italy, September 28October 2, 1995.

[20]Rathjens, "Rethinking Nuclear Proliferation" 189.

proliferation policies are those related to conflict resolution.[21] Policies that emphasize sanctions and denial are unlikely to be effective alone; they need to be balanced by inducements and guarantees. States that are isolated are a rarely easily influenced.[22] They cannot be easily threatened either since they have little to lose or fear. If non-proliferation is to be reinforced as a global norm, it needs as wide support as possible. This implies the language of consensus, reciprocity and legitimacy rather than threat and menace.[23] Treating proliferators as outlaws misses the point. States do not s embark on such courses for amusement . If leading nuclear powers can set an example and reduce the salience of nuclear weapons, that would be a start. But it would not end the matter. If nuclear weapons states are unable to extend guarantees or offer inducements to would-be proliferators as substitutes, they should at least not aggravate the problem by threatening coercive measures against them, thereby underscoring the perceived need for such weapons among a certain category of state.

Ultimately to reduce the security incentives for nuclear weapons political relations will have to progress in the Persian Gulf region. In the first instance Iran and Iraq will need to settle their differences and begin to build on the common interests that each state shares with the other states. This may take time. It will only be reached by stages. The U.S. should do nothing to make such regional rapprochement more difficult. Attempts to keep Iran and Iraq at odds may be tactically beneficial but strategically unwise. An intensified Iran-Iraq nuclear rivalry would endanger more than those two states. Thus the U.S. should consider its regional policy in a wider perspective than merely reassuring the GCC states.

---

[21]Freedman, "Great Powers, Vital Interest and Nuclear Weapons" 48.

[22]John Simpson, "Nuclear non-proliferation in the post Cold War era," *International Affairs*, January 1994. (Vol. 70. No. 1) 38.

[23]Nolan, "Strategies for Nuclear Non-Proliferation," 20.

This chapter has argued that Iran may well be on a quest for nuclear weapons. It remains a long away from such a capability, which will take time to develop. In the interim, it may change its assessment of its situation or how to address it. It should be discouraged from its current course and its threat perceptions addressed. This would be easier to do if it was engaged rather than isolated. Threats against it may only work to convince many Iranians, not necessarily supporters of the regime, that U.S. bullying has to stop. If Iran were nevertheless to become a nuclear weapons state, the policy of engagement would not be without effect. To the extent such entanglement socializes that state into understanding the limits and liabilities involved in possessing nuclear weapons, and in instilling a sense of responsibility, it will have been rewarded. Even without such engagement however, it is difficult to believe that states undertaking such programs do not become aware of the enormous responsibilities and risks they run. For this reason I am not convinced that Iran with nuclear weapons will be substantially different in terms of propensity to run risks than it is now. It all probability it would be even more risk averse. Even so, it would be preferable if it could be convinced that it has other – better – ways of addressing its security concerns.

Chapter 7

Iran's Nuclear Program:
Is There a Negotiated Alternative?

Gary Sick

It is a truism in the anti-proliferation community that any country suspected of developing a nuclear weapons capability is, almost certainly, pursuing a nuclear weapons program. Despite denials and despite the ambiguity of many of the tell-tale signs, there really are no fundamental surprises in this field. The world may have been surprised in 1991 to learn how far Saddam Hussein had progressed toward having an operational nuclear weapon, but no one was surprised to learn that he had been trying. India, Pakistan, Israel, North Korea, and South Africa were all suspected of nuclear programs before those programs may have produced nuclear devices.

In the case of Iran, the latest addition to the list of suspected nuclear states, there is no reason to doubt that it has embarked on a development program whose objectives include the capability of producing a nuclear weapon at some point in the future. The pattern of known Iranian nuclear purchases, the stealth it displayed in pursuing some of its contacts, the weapons-related nature of some its attempted purchases, and the absence of a compelling rationale for an immensely expensive nuclear power program in a country with abundant conventional energy resources, all suggest that the international community is right to be suspicious of Iran's intentions.

Iran's interest in acquiring nuclear technology is not in doubt. Iran has a small research reactor that it purchased from the United States more than twenty years ago. It signed a contract with China in 1993 for two 330-megawatt nuclear power stations (rescinded in 1997), and with Russia for a VVER-440-213 (440-megawatt) nuclear power station with two pressurized water reactors. Iran has also expressed interest in three additional Russian reactors. Iran has purchased a mini-calutron and an electronic isotope separation unit from China. Iran also attempted to acquire more capable research reactors from Argentina and China, but the United States intervened to squelch both deals. Iran is attempting to persuade its exiled nuclear scientists to return home, and Iranian delegations have visited nuclear weapons production sites in Russia and the former Soviet Union.

These facts are well known and are not disputed. They do not, however, tell us very much about the nature of a prospective nuclear threat from Iran. Why is Iran pursuing this option? If Iran chooses to develop a nuclear weapon, what are the prospects that it will succeed? What can realistically be done to divert it from the nuclear weapons path? Those are the questions that this paper will address very briefly.

Why Is Iran Seeking a Nuclear Capability?

In historical context, Iran's effort to develop a nuclear infrastructure can be seen as a direct continuation of the more grandiose strategy of the Shah prior to the revolution. Beginning in the 1960s, the Shah developed a plan to build up to 20 nuclear power stations, each with more than 1,000 megawatt capacity. Although Iran's fossil fuel resources were considerably greater then than now, this was not regarded as quixotic. On the contrary Germany, France and the United States were in hot competition with each other for the business. The United States sold Iran a small research reactor, which is still in operation, and I happened to be present on

New Years Day 1979 when President Carter, himself a nuclear engineer, agreed to sell Iran two more large reactors during a visit to Tehran. Two German reactors at Bushehr were well on the way to completion in 1979 when the revolution and the Iraqi invasion intervened. France had also contracted to build two reactors at Darkhovin. Additionally, Iran bought a ten percent share of an enrichment facility being constructed in France by the Eurodif consortium, and loaned $1 billion to the French Atomic Energy Commission (CEA) toward the construction of a gaseous diffusion enrichment facility (later reclaimed). These arrangements would have allowed Iran access to enrichment technology and highly-enriched uranium.[1]

For anyone who watched Iran's military buildup in the 1970s under the Shah, the broad outlines of Iran's present strategy have a strong element of *dé jà vu*. Iran's interest in missile technology and its approach to acquiring such technology is also reminiscent of the Shah. The Islamic Republic negotiated first with China and then with North Korea and Russia to get access to ballistic missile technology. Reportedly, Iran helped to fund the costs of missile research and development in North Korea, presumably in return for access to the technology.

The Shah used exactly the same technique. During the 1970s, he provided large quantities of oil to Israel as part of a clandestine project to produce a surface-to-surface missile capable of carrying a nuclear warhead. The test firings were to be conducted in Iran. The United States had declined to sell a missile delivery system to either Israel or Iran, so the two countries secretly agreed to pursue the proto-

---

[1]For a thorough inventory and concise history of Iran's nuclear program, see Rodney W. Jones et al., Tracking Nuclear Proliferation, 1998 (Washington: Carnegie Endowment for International Peace, 1998), pp. 169-186. See also the interview with the head of Iran's nuclear program in Reza Abri, "The Situation of Atomic Energy in Iran," Daneshmand (Iranian Scientific, Technical & Cultural Monthly), September, 1996, No. 396, Vol. 34, pp. 10-17. For a thorough survey of the open literature, see Greg J. Gerardi and Maryam Aharinejad, "Report: An Assessment Of Iran's Nuclear Facilities," The Nonproliferation Review, Spring-Summer 1995, Volume 2 - Number 3. See also Mark D. Skootsky, "U.S. Nuclear Policy Toward Iran," Nonproliferation Analysis, Vol I No 1 Summer 1995, June 1, 1995.

nuclear option on their own, without informing their American ally.[2] The Islamic Revolutionary government has pursued an identical strategy, substituting China and North Korea for Israel.

During the Nuclear Non-Proliferation Treaty (NPT) debate in the United Nations in April and May 1995, Iranian delegates repeatedly called for the establishment of a nuclear weapons-free zone (NWFZ) in the Middle East. They noted with pride that Iran was the first country to call for such an arrangement in 1974 – a date that preceded the Islamic revolution by four years. Since then, Iranian representatives at the UN and elsewhere have been consistently outspoken in promoting an NWFZ that would include Israel. In private, senior Iranian officials have suggested that they would be willing to consider a more limited NWFZ in the Persian Gulf region before moving on to the delicate and difficult issue of Israel's nuclear program.[3]

There was widespread speculation at the time of the Shah that his very ambitious nuclear power program was a convenient cover for a weapons development program. In retrospect, those concerns appear to have been well

---

[2] The notes of the meetings in July 1977 between General Hassan Toufanian, the head of military procurement under the Shah, and Israeli Defense Minister Ezer Weizman concerning this plan were published in volume 19 of the "Documents from the Den of Spies" (documents taken from the U.S. embassy in Tehran in 1979). The documents were reported in the New York Times on April 1, 1986, p. 17. See also Samuel Segev, The Iranian Triangle, New York: The Free Press, 1988, p. 95. Iran in the end got nothing from its rather substantial investment with Israel. The final payment of $260 million worth of oil was made shortly before the Shah's regime collapsed, and the files were packed off to Israel on one of the last El Al flights out of Tehran. [Personal interview with General Toufanian, July 10, 1990.] Iran now claims that Israel owes it $2 billion for this program. See Uri Dan and Dennis Eisenberg, "Treachery in Teheran," The Jerusalem Post, July 13, 1995. According to majles member Hojjat ol-Eslam Hussein Sobhanian, the amount is $4 billion (see Reuters, July 16, 1995).

[3] This and other references in this paper are drawn from the author's extended discussions with seven Iranian officials directly engaged in Iran's nuclear program and/or who held senior policy positions. These discussions took place throughout 1997 and 1998 and were conducted on grounds of non-attribution.

grounded. The long-range ballistic missile that Iran was secretly developing with Israel would have had little military value without a nuclear warhead.

After the revolution, the new Islamic government renounced many of the Shah's policies, including the nuclear program. Reactor construction slowed to a crawl, and there were indications that the entire program might be scrapped. All work ceased when Iraq launched its invasion on September 22, 1980.

The Bushehr reactor site was a favorite target for Iraqi bombers, perhaps mimicking Israel's pre-emptive strike on the nuclear reactor site outside Baghdad in 1981. Unlike the Osiraq reactor, however, the Iranian site contained no radioactive materials and was still in the earliest stages of construction. According to Russian engineers who visited the site in early 1995, much of the sensitive material was carefully moth-balled and survived the ravages of both time and air strikes in good condition, although the plant's electrical equipment was beyond repair.[4]

Despite the war with Iraq, however, and despite Iraq's widespread use of chemical weapons against Iranian troop concentrations, Iran did not actively pursue a nuclear program. This decision, which was highly controversial within Iran, was sustained largely because of Ayatollah Khomeini's pronouncement that the use of indiscriminate weapons was contrary to Islam.[5]

According to one senior Iranian official, when Iran was being bombarded during the Iran-Iraq war and when weapons of mass destruction (WMD) were being threatened or used, Iran could easily have withdrawn from the NPT, had it been inclined to do so. In fact, he said, this was discussed at very high levels in Tehran at

---

[4]Interfax News Agency, March 22, 1995, citing a spokesman for Russia's Zarubezhatomenergostroy company, which builds nuclear power facilities abroad.

[5]Although Iranian pronouncements during the war repeatedly renounced the use of chemical and other weapons of mass destruction on grounds that the use of such weapons was inconsistent with Islam, the text of Khomeini's pronouncement was never made public. However, every senior Iranian official interviewed by the author referred to such a statement as a well-known fact and cited it as a major factor in Iran's weapons policy during the 1980-88 period of the war.

the time, and a decision was taken not to go for nuclear weapons and not to retaliate in kind. The reason for this was essentially religious, since WMD are indiscriminate and kill the innocent, which is forbidden by Islam. "The world may regard this as quaint," he commented, "but in an Islamic republic, it matters to us."[6]

During the eight years of the war, Iran discussed with Siemens (actually, Kraftwerke Union, a division of Siemens that had started construction of two units at Bushehr in 1974) the possibility of resuming work on the Bushehr nuclear power plant, in which Iran had invested a large amount of money. These discussions, however, were of little more than academic interest while the war was underway. They began again in earnest after the war ended in August 1988, but the Germans were reluctant to resume construction of the power plant in view of Iran's reputation as a radical state and the powerful opposition of the United States to any cooperation with Iran, particularly on nuclear issues. Iran explored the possibility of enlisting Argentina or Spain to assist with the project, but Siemens vetoed the idea.

As Ayatollah Khomeini became increasingly incapacitated and died in June 1989, there were some indications that his pronouncement would no longer govern Iranian policy. Ali Akbar Rafsanjani, who was Speaker of the Majles at the time, angrily denounced the international community for its silence about Iraqi use of chemical weapons. Iran, he said, should equip itself "in the offensive and defensive use of chemical, bacteriological and radiological weapons."[7] "Chemical and biological weapons are the poor man's atomic bombs and can easily be produced," he later added. "We should at least consider them for our defense. Although the use

---

[6] Interview, January 1997, on a non-attribution basis.
[7]Tehran Domestic Service, October 6, 1988, in FBIS-NES (October 7, 1988, p. 52).

of such weapons is inhuman, the war taught us that international laws are only scraps of paper."[8]

In the aftermath of Operation Desert Storm and Iraq's defeat in 1991, Iran was no doubt shocked, as was the rest of the world, to discover how far Saddam Hussein had progressed in developing an operational nuclear weapon. Iran had every reason to believe that it would have been the target for such a weapon only a few years earlier, and that it might well face that prospect again. Under those circumstances, Iran may have concluded that it had to be prepared to counter a renewed Iraqi nuclear program once international sanctions were lifted. That required, at a minimum, a nuclear infrastructure sufficient to permit Iran to keep pace with Iraq in a possible future nuclear arms race.

Iran may have had other rationales for its nuclear program. Having observed the ease with which the allied forces in 1991 defeated the Iraqi military – the same military that Iran had failed to defeat in eight years of bloody combat – Iran may have concluded that it needed a non-conventional deterrent to Western military intervention.[9] Iran has reportedly been identified as a potential target for U.S. strategic forces for many years.[10] Iran may also wish to have a counterweight to Israel's extensive nuclear arsenal, and it may believe that a nuclear program would bolster Iran's position as a regional power.[11]

---

[8] October 19, 1988, in FBIS-NES (October 19, 1988, pp. 55-56), cited in Peter Jones, "Iran's Threat Perceptions and Arms Control Policies," The Nonproliferation Review, Fall 1998, Vol 6 No 1, pp. 39-55.

[9] For an exposition of this rationale, see Zalmay Khalilzad, "The United States and the Persian Gulf: Preventing Regional Hegemony," Survival, Vol. 37, no. 2, Summer 1995, esp. pp. 104-6.

[10] Bruce G. Blair, Global Zero Alert For Nuclear Forces, Brookings Occasional Paper, The Brookings Institution, Washington, D.C., 1995, pp. 5-8. See esp. fn 10.

[11] For a detailed examination of the various political factors that may influence Iran's thinking on the nuclear issue, see Shahram Chubin, "Does Iran Want Nuclear Weapons?" Survival, Vol. 37, no. 1, Spring 1995, pp. 86-104.

The clearest indication of Iran's strategic concerns about nuclear weapons was provided by Seyyed Ataollah Mohajerani, the Vice-President for Legal and Parliamentary Affairs. In an interview with the daily newspaper Abrar on October 23, 1991, Mohajerani stated: "Israel should be totally deprived of its nuclear capacity. I mean what has been done to Iraq in respect of its nuclear capacity should be done exactly to Israel. In other words the atomic capacity of Muslims and Israel should be at par. If Israel should be allowed to have nuclear power, then Muslim states, too, should be allowed to have the same."[12]

Although this statement was widely interpreted as calling for the development of nuclear weapons by Iran or other Islamic states, his key point appeared to be a demand that regional non-proliferation efforts must include Israel. That theme was echoed by the Iranian delegates to the NPT conference, who called for a Middle East nuclear-free zone and for Israel to sign the Nuclear Non-Proliferation Treaty. Former president Rafsanjani frequently referred to the hypocrisy of the Western powers who call for nuclear controls but who acknowledge and condone Israel's nuclear stockpile. The same point was made vigorously by Iranian Foreign Minister Kamal Kharrazi in his maiden speech to the United Nations General Assembly in September 1997,[13] and has been a consistent feature of Iranian foreign policy.

As a non-nuclear state, Iran is the missing link in an almost unbroken arc of declared and undeclared nuclear (or near-nuclear) states starting with North Korea in the east and extending via China, India, Pakistan, and Iraq to Israel in the west. Each of these states has been willing to pay a high price – politically as well as economically – for its nuclear status. Iran now appears to have decided to take the

---

[12]As reported by the Islamic Republic News Agency (BBC/SWB October 24, 1991).
[13]"Statement by H.E. Dr. Kamal Kharrazi before the 52nd Session of United Nations General Assembly, New York, September 22, 1997," text distributed by the Islamic Republic of Iran Permanent Mission to the United Nations.

first steps along the path chosen by so many others in the Asian nuclear arc. What are the chances that Iran will become a nuclear weapons state?

Iran's Nuclear Prospects

Iran's nuclear program has attracted a great deal of international attention, much of it focused on estimates of how much time would be required for Iran to acquire a nuclear weapon. In early 1992, Robert Gates, then director of the CIA, estimated that Iran could have a nuclear weapon as early as the year 2000.[14] A year later his successor, James Woolsey, warned that Iran could have a nuclear weapon within eight to ten years.[15] Two years later, in January 1995, sources in Israel and the United States asserted that this date had been reduced to two to five years.[16] A few days later, after talks in Israel, U.S. Secretary of Defense William Perry and Israeli Prime Minister Yitzhak Rabin said they believed Iran could build a nuclear bomb within seven to fifteen years, though that time period could be shortened if Iran could buy plutonium or highly-enriched uranium from another country.[17] Two years later, however, high level sources in "the White House, the State Department, the Pentagon and the Central Intelligence Agency along with congressional and Israeli sources" reportedly had concluded that "Tehran seems to have shelved [its nuclear weapons] program two years ago after Mr. Yeltsin, under U.S. pressure, vetoed a Russian sale of weapons-related equipment."[18]

---

[14]Testimony before the House Armed Services Committee, 27 March 1992, cited in The Washington Post, March 28, 1992, p. 1.

[15]Testimony before the Senate Governmental Affairs Committee, Federal News Service, February 24, 1993.

[16]New York Times, January 6, 1995, p. 1.

[17]Joint press conference, January 9, 1995, as reported in Reuters.

[18]Joseph Fitchett, "Ousting Iranian, Russia Signaled U.S. on Arms: Yeltsin Cooperates in Curbing Tehran's Drive," International Herald Tribune, Tuesday, December 9, 1997, p. 1.

Based on these analyses, can we say with any measure of assurance that Iran will have a nuclear weapon by, say, the year 2010? No. In fact, the most important thing about the many official estimates and warnings is that they are intended to prevent what they are projecting. By drawing attention to Iran's initial efforts, they were intended to create a political climate that would make it more difficult for Iran to proceed. As political early warning signals, these statements are quite effective; as predictions, however, they are essentially worthless.

Whether or not Iran chooses to pursue the nuclear option to the weapons stage, and whether or not it is able to achieve its objectives, depends on a wealth of imponderables: the political evolution of the Islamic regime; the future price of oil; the political and military trajectory of Iraq once sanctions are removed; the willingness of outside powers to provide Iran a reprocessing capability; the state of U.S. relations with Iran and the other Persian Gulf states; even the outcome of the Arab-Israel peace process. Each of those factors, and probably many others, will affect the decision-making process in Tehran. Iran has started down the nuclear path. How far and how fast it moves down that path is no straight line projection.

The Khatami Phenomenon

The political system in Iran is in flux. The elation of the days immediately after the overthrow of the Shah subsided under the pressure of eight years of war with Iraq and the hard economic realities of the international marketplace. Well over half the population never knew life under the old regime. They were more concerned about jobs, schools, inflation and the daily business of survival than about the fine points of Islamic doctrine. Khomeini was once supposed to have remarked that "We did not have a revolution to determine the price of melons." Nearly two decades later, it was the price of melons and the quality of daily life – not revolutionary doctrine – that interested the man on the street in Tehran.

In the June 1993 Iranian presidential election, popular apathy and resentment was reflected in the fact that 42 percent of the voters stayed home, and of those who bothered to go to the polls 37 percent voted against the incumbent, President Rafsanjani. That trend was dramatically reversed in May 1997 when more than 29 million of the 33 million eligible Iranian voters went to the polls, and more than 20 million of them voted for Mohammad Khatami. It was the most overwhelming popular mandate since the post-revolutionary referendum in 1979 approved the Islamic Republic.

Khatami received especially strong support from women and young people, who were reacting to his campaign in favor of civil society, the rule of law, individual rights and freedom, and sovereignty derived from the will of the people. The conservative establishment, although humiliated by this outright vote of no confidence, soon recovered from the shock and began to fight back on several fronts against Khatami's reform program, indicting the popular mayor of Tehran, who had been a major architect of the Khatami landslide, and impeaching Khatami's minister of interior for being too lenient, among other things. Conservative elements maintained control of many of the military and security organs of the country, thus limiting Khatami's power to implement his program. In late 1998, a series of liberal writers and critics of the revolutionary regime were murdered by rogue elements in the intelligence ministry.

The stage was thus set for an internal struggle over the future direction of the revolution. This sharp division between the revolutionary old guard, which defined itself in terms of the slogans and aspirations of the 1979 overthrow of the monarchy, and a new generation with little memory of the revolution and an abiding interest in greater personal freedom, permeated every aspect of governance and decision-making.

Internal Disputes

Iran is not Iraq, where Saddam Hussein wields absolute power. Iraq is a one-party state with a dictator; Iran is a no-party state with a bickering collective leadership and no single locus of power. Shifting informal coalitions represent competing interests in a system that is not unlike the consensus-formation mechanism that has been used for centuries within Shi'i Islam. The process is messy and frequently fails to produce crisp decisions, especially when the national interest is unclear or where major political and economic interests are in conflict.

That is very much the case with the nuclear program. The shock of recognition about just how close Iran may have come to being the target of an Iraqi nuclear weapon may have been sufficient to produce a decision to resurrect a portion of the Shah's nuclear infrastructure and to begin laying the basis for a future weapons program on a contingency basis. It was not, however, clear that Iran had taken a firm decision to build a nuclear weapon or that the very substantial amount of hard currency required for a lengthy crash program would be allocated.

Iran was in debt, its oil revenues were decimated by the 1998 collapse in oil prices, and the demands of a young population for schools, jobs and housing could be ignored only at the peril of the populist revolutionary system itself. Would Iran be able to muster the political will and be prepared to make the necessary economic sacrifices in order to sustain a lengthy and costly weapons program? The answer was far from certain.

On one hand, Iran demonstrated that it was capable of developing a substantial ballistic missile program. During its missile war with Iraq in the mid-1980s, Iran declared its intention to produce its own ballistic missile system in order to avoid dependence on outside suppliers. After more than a decade of trying, on July 22, 1998, Iran successfully tested a prototype missile, the Shahab-3, with a range of about 800 miles. A second version, the Shahab-4, is expected to have a range of more than 1,200 miles.[19] Although the missiles are probably of Iranian design and are intended for domestic production, Iranian engineers had the benefit of Russian, Chinese and North Korean technology and components. This suggests, at a minimum, that Iran's ingenuity, technical capacity and perseverance in pursuit of a long-term military goal should not be underestimated.

On the other hand, there is no political opposition in Iran to a missile program. Having experienced the terror of missiles raining down from Iraq on Tehran and other cities during the eight-year war, and with no capacity to respond in equal measure, every Iranian appreciated the efficacy of a strategic missile defense. Yet, despite this consensus and access to foreign missile technology, Iran took more than a decade to produce its first test launch. Full-scale production and deployment was expected to require at least another four years, with a total elapsed time from inception to deployment of seventeen to twenty years.

At the end of the 1990s, Iran's access to the nuclear fuel cycle was scarcely more advanced than was its rudimentary missile production program in the mid-1980s. That suggests that, even if Iran should decide to proceed full-tilt toward the development of nuclear weapons, the formidable difficulties of mobilizing the financial, technical and human resources required for such a program will offer considerable warning time in which to explore diplomatic and other alternatives.

Again, Iran is not Iraq. By the time of the second gulf war, Iraq had been in the nuclear business for well over a decade and had acquired a cadre of thousands of nuclear technicians. Iran, however, is estimated to have fewer than 500 nuclear physicists, engineers and senior technicians. Iran has attempted to overcome this

---

[19]For initial reporting on the test launch, see the New York Times, July 23, 1998. For background on Iran's missile program, see the Senate testimony by Air Force Lt. Gen. Lester Lyles, director of the Ballistic Missile Defense Organization, cited in The Washington Times, March 27, 1998. The initial test of the Shahab-3 ended in an explosion only a few minutes after launch, but most observers believe this was an intentional self-destruct after a test of the launch system.

shortage by inviting Iranian scientists to return to Iran, by funding training facilities abroad, and possibly by seeking to hire foreign technicians.[20] But it cannot be done over night. David Kay, a former inspector in Iran for the International Atomic Energy Agency, told the BBC that "Iran, in many ways, is like Iraq at the early stages of the Iraqi programme . . . trying to acquire technical skills, training, technology and manufacturing capability on as broad a front as possible."[21] As a senior Iranian official told me, "Iran has no (nuclear) fuel cycle."[22]

In short, it is possible to say with some confidence that Iran has taken the initial steps of laying down a nuclear infrastructure that would permit it to proceed, at some point in the future, to build a nuclear weapon if it so decided. It is not clear that Iran has actually taken such a decision. On the contrary, the available evidence suggests that Iran is still in the earliest stages of a nuclear program, and there is time to consider policies that might divert Iran from the acquisition of nuclear weapons.

Preventing Proliferation

There are certain advantages in dealing with Iran that were not available, for example, in the case of North Korea. North Korea is one of the most insulated and mysterious countries in the world. It is very close to having a nuclear weapon and may already possess one or two. It took a remarkable feat of personal diplomacy by former president Carter just to establish contact with the Korean leadership. Iran is a very different place. It is more permeable, pluralistic and approachable. Mohammed Ayatollahi, Iran's ambassador to the IAEA, told an interviewer in 1992:

---

[20]Steve Coll, "Loan From Tehran Saved Third World Nuclear Research Center," The Washington Post, December 24, 1992.
[21]Agence France Presse, March 9, 1993.
[22]Interview, January 1997, on a non-attribution basis.

All the nuclear programs of Iran are peaceful and will remain peaceful. This is not propaganda. This is the policy the government has adopted . . . . A weapons program is not easy. It requires a complete (nuclear) fuel cycle and billions of dollars and you can't just buy it . . . . The (IAEA) knows exactly what we have. We reiterate that if there is any doubt in your mind, let us know. We are fully transparent.[23]

Even more simply and unequivocally, Iran's President Khatami in his "Address to the American People" in January 1998 stated: "We are not a nuclear power and do not intend to become one."[24]

Even if this – and many other similar statements by all levels of the Iranian government – is dismissed as self-serving and deceptive hyperbole, Iran is nevertheless a signatory of the Nuclear Non-Proliferation Treaty and a member in good standing of the International Atomic Energy Agency. Its known and suspected nuclear facilities have been regularly inspected by the IAEA, including occasional command inspections, with no evidence of a clandestine weapons program. Although that is not sufficient in itself to resolve doubts about Iran's nuclear intentions, it provides a necessary starting point for any analysis.

The Iranian Rationale

When asked privately to explain why Iran, as a state rich in fossil fuels, would choose to develop a nuclear power capacity, Iranian officials offer several explanations:[25]

[23]Steve Coll, "U.S. Halted Nuclear Bid By Iran; China, Argentina Agreed to Cancel Technology Transfers," The Washington Post, November 17, 1992.

[24]CNN transcript of interview of Christiane Amanpour with Iranian President Mohammad Khatami, January 7, 1998, http://www.cnn.com.

[25]The following is based on a series of interviews with senior Iranian officials during 1997 and 1998. All of the interviews were conducted on condition of non-attribution.

1. During the Shah's days, the country invested heavily in the nuclear power plants at Bushehr. The present Iranian government is determined to recoup some of that investment by completing the construction. They would have preferred to have Siemens complete the two plants, but since that was impossible for political reasons, they turned to the Russians. The price of nuclear fuel is also very attractive today, as Iran is well aware due to its ten percent stake and board membership in the French Eurodif consortium, also a remnant of the Shah's time.

2. Iran's oil reserves are finite,[26] and it is prudent for Iran to diversify its electrical energy sources – which also include hydroelectric, solar, wind and geothermal.[27] Iranian officials are quick to point out that neither the United States nor other western countries found it suspicious when the Shah initiated a nuclear energy program far greater than anything the Islamic Republic is planning.

3. Iran's gas reserves are immense, but its rapidly growing domestic demand for electricity has outstripped its ability to keep up. The demands for Iran's gas supplies are presently over-committed, including large quantities required for gas reinjection of its complex and aging oil fields. Moreover, the United States has threatened sanctions against companies investing in Iran's energy sector, including development of new natural gas fields for re-injection and electricity generation.

4. Nuclear power does not generate carbon dioxide and other gases associated with global warming. At present, Iran is one of the major contributors to global

---

[26]According to Iranian Deputy Energy Minister Hamid Chitchian, "With the rapid growth in energy consumption and regarding constant oil and gas reserves, it is predicted that there will be no oil for export by the year 2000." [Interview with the Islamic Republic News Agency (IRNA), cited in Reuters, July 3, 1995.] That is an extreme prognosis, and Iran will certainly take steps to bring domestic consumption under control before that happens, but it is a genuine policy concern.

[27]Reza Amrollahi, former head of the Atomic Energy Organization of Iran: "We have taken positive steps towards new [sources of] energy. We have supplied a village with solar power....In relation to wind power we have commissioned two units so far, one in Manjil and one in Rudbar....We get 1.1 megawatts from the wind....As for geothermal energy we are busy right now working in Ardabil and Western Azarbayjan Provinces and have achieved very good results. Voice of the Islamic Republic of Iran, May 18, 1995 (BBC/SWB May 22, 1995).

warming, largely because of the large quantities of gas flared as a by-product of oil production.

5. Iran is entitled to peaceful nuclear technology under the terms of Article 4 of the Nuclear Non-Proliferation Treaty, as a member in good standing and fully in compliance. To deny such technology – including the nuclear power plant at Bushehr – to a member state is hypocritical and casts doubt on the validity of the treaty itself.[28] This is particularly true when the United States has agreed to sell a comparable light water reactor to North Korea, a non-compliant state, as part of a non-proliferation package.

6. Iran's national pride is now intensely engaged in this matter. Iran sees access to peaceful nuclear technology as an emblem of a technologically advanced society. U.S. attempts to prevent Iran from acquiring such technology are seen as blatant political discrimination against an Islamic state, and U.S. opposition has strengthened determination to proceed with the Bushehr site.

Such arguments, though not lacking in merit, do not constitute persuasive grounds for a program that is likely to be inefficient, unduly costly, and strategically worrisome to much of the international community. Even Iranian officials in the nuclear hierarchy privately admit that the cost of electricity produced at the Bushehr plant would not be competitive with electricity generated from fossil fuels unless the price of oil exceeded $28 per barrel.[29]

More important than the official rationales are the hard realities of Iran's circumstances. Iran was invaded in 1980 by its neighbor, Iraq, which was engaged in developing weapons of mass destruction. These two states fought a brutal and

---

[28]Reza Amrollahi, the head of Iran's Atomic Energy Organization, commented that, "the peaceful use of nuclear power by countries that have signed the NPT should be facilitated. By this we mean that for instance Iran, which has signed the NPT, should not be harassed or bothered constantly and it should not have to face numerous problems and obstacles everyday." Interview, Vision of the Islamic Republic of Iran, February 28, 1995 (BBC/SWB March 2, 1995).

[29]At the end of 1998, with prices at historic lows, Iranian crude was selling for $10 per barrel or less.

bloody war for eight years. In addition, Iran has a nuclear power (Pakistan) to the east, another (Russia) to the north, and is within nuclear delivery range of Israel. Saudi Arabia has missiles capable of reaching every city in Iran. The United States, a hostile nuclear superpower, maintains a large military presence in the Persian Gulf, just off Iran's shores, as does the UK and, occasionally, France, among others. As a cold strategic calculation, Iran has grounds that would tempt many countries to pursue a nuclear program. That so little has been done to date, whatever the explanation, must be regarded as fortunate from a non-proliferation perspective. Iran's present position also offers unusually promising circumstances for implementation of a serious and sustained non-proliferation effort.

A New Opening to Iran?

Although Iranian President Mohammed Khatami's election agenda was purely domestic, his major achievement in his first eighteen months in office was to revolutionize Iran's foreign policy. Iran mended fences with its Arab neighbors in the Persian Gulf, invigorated its role in the United Nations, hosted a very successful Islamic summit, restored relations with the European community and promoted better relations with the new states of Central Asia. In January 1998, President Khatami used the occasion of a CNN interview with Christiane Amanpour to address the American people, setting in motion what appeared to be the beginning of a cautious rapprochement with the Great Satan.[30]

Khatami was both conciliatory and explicit. He went as far as any Iranian political figure could go in expressing regret about the 1979-81 hostage crisis, and he pledged that such "unconventional methods" would not and could not be employed in today's Iran. He directly address the "hot" issues of terrorism ("Any

---

[30]CNN interview, January 7, 1998, op. cit.

form of killing of innocent men and women who are not involved in confrontations is terrorism. It must be condemned, and we, in our turn, condemn every form of it in the world."); the peace process ("We have declared our opposition to the Middle East peace process, because we believe it will not succeed. At the same time, we have clearly said that we don't intend to impose our views on others or to stand in their way."); and weapons of mass destruction ("We are not a nuclear power and do not intend to become one").[31]

Secretary of State Madeleine Albright responded to this overture five months later, in a carefully drafted speech that avoided the harsh rhetoric that had characterized U.S. statements about Iran throughout the Clinton administration. She welcomed President Khatami's call for more exchanges and cultural contacts between the two societies and echoed his call to breach the wall of mistrust that had developed: "As the wall of mistrust comes down, we can develop with the Islamic Republic, when it is ready, a road map leading to normal relations."[32]

The Secretary of State, however, offered no significant changes in basic U.S. policy. Specifically, the sanctions on all economic interactions with Iran remained in place, as did U.S. vigorous opposition to any development of Iran's energy sector.[33] Iran, in turn, was caught up in a deepening struggle between the reformist camp of President Khatami and the traditionalists, who viewed any direct opening to the United States as a betrayal of the principles of the revolution and the "line" of Ayatollah Khomeini. The conservatives, who were angry and frustrated at Khatami's

---

[31]Ibid.

[32]Secretary of State Madeleine K. Albright Remarks at the 1998 Asia Society Dinner, Waldorf-Astoria Hotel, New York, June 17, 1998, as released by the Office of the Spokesman, June 18, 1998, U.S. Department of State.

[33]The primary sanctions imposed by the United States against Iran include Executive Order 12957 of March 15, 1995; Executive Order 12959 of May 6, 1995; and The Iran-Libya Sanctions Act of 1996 (ILSA). For an analysis of the origins and nature of the sanctions regime, see Gary Sick, "Rethinking Dual Containment," Survival: The IISS Quarterly, Vol 40 No 1 (Spring 1998), pp. 5-32.

call for more freedom of expression, began to resort to violence.[34] The United States and Iran each took the position that the first move was up to the other.[35]

There are a number of what one author calls "red button" issues that plague relations between Iran and the United States.[36] The question is where to begin to unravel these historical and policy grievances. The nuclear issue, unlikely as it might seem, is one potential starting point.

A Nuclear Non-Proliferation Strategy for Iran

The United States, and its friends and allies in the Middle East, are wary of Iran's nuclear potential. Iran, in turn, has found the financing of even one nuclear power station to be exorbitant, and there is ambivalence among many of Iran's top leadership both about the practical value of a nuclear energy program, and especially of a weapons program, primarily on Islamic grounds. There are no doubt others in the Iranian hierarchy who are less troubled by the Islamic implications; however, it would be an error to dismiss the importance of the religious element simply because it does not accord with Western strategic thought. It is one of the factors that should be incorporated in any non-proliferation strategy for dealing with Iran.

What are the components of such a strategy? The essentials are extremely simple: Iran renounces any nuclear ambitions, in a form that is explicit and verifiable;

---

[34]Mohammed Asgharzadeh, spokesman of the students who occupied the U.S. embassy, who had begun calling for reconciliation with the former hostages, was severely beaten in December 1998 by a gang of fundamentalists. A bus load of American visitors was attacked in Tehran in November 1998. And a series of murders of opposition writers and dissidents during the same time period was attributed to ultra-conservative elements in the intelligence services.

[35]Many other voices in the United States and Iran have offered alternative approaches. Former Secretary of State Cyrus Vance has called on both countries to begin by establishing diplomatic relations. See "US-Iran Relations: has the time come?" Speech Delivered by the Honorable Cyrus R. Vance, "Distinguished Speaker Series" of the American-Iranian Council, Inc. at The Asia Society, New York City, January 13, 1999.

[36]For an examination of these points of contention, see Geoffrey Kemp, America and Iran: Road Maps and Realism, The Nixon Center: Washington, DC, 1998, especially pp. 37-86.

in return, the United States withdraws its opposition and sanctions relating to the development of Iran's energy resources and undertakes a good faith effort to address Iran's legitimate security concerns. Such a process would not be simple, since it would force each side to confront the fears – real and imagined – of the other in a political context fraught with suspicion and mistrust. That process, however, would engage the two parties in a process of mutual learning and thereby potentially open the door to other issues. Its appeal as a starting point for a substantive dialogue is that each side potentially stands to gain something of vital interest in return for relinquishing something of much less moment. The elements of such a package would potentially include the following:

First, the United States and its allies and all prospective nuclear suppliers should insist that Iran formally renounce technologies that provide direct access to weapons-grade nuclear fuel, specifically enrichment (including centrifuge technology) and reprocessing. Iran has said that it has no interest in such technologies, but this should be reaffirmed in an official statement, subject to verification.

Second, the United States and other parties should maintain pressure on Russia, China, and other potential suppliers of nuclear technology and materials to Iran to prevent any transfer of enrichment and reprocessing technology. Any nuclear training of Iranians should be limited to what it takes to operate a reactor rather than providing broad access to nuclear technology. In the context of a general agreement on nuclear development, third parties should be prepared to reaffirm their commitments and cooperate in a suppliers regime. China has already demonstrated its willingness to limit nuclear cooperation with Iran, and such cooperation is very much in the national interests of Russia as well, since Moscow is within range of Iran's present and prospective delivery systems.

Third, suppliers should insist on clear-cut agreements about the disposal of spent fuel from the reactors. Iran has said that it would return the nuclear waste to the original suppliers, but safeguards should be imposed at every stage of the process to guarantee that the fuel is returned and that Iran exercises no control over it once it has been returned. Russia has already pledged that the spent fuel from the Bushehr nuclear power plant would be returned to Russia, where it will be reprocessed at its Mayak plant in the Urals region of Chelyabinsk.[37]

Fourth, if Iran insists on completing the Bushehr reactor, it should be sealed so that all movements of personnel and material into or out of the site can be monitored and so there is no interaction with the surrounding physical and social environment.

Fifth, there must be verification. Iran has said that it will permit frequent and intrusive inspections by the IAEA on demand and with little or no advance notice. That should be a condition of any continuing nuclear power assistance, which Iran will require for at least the next decade or more. An important step in that direction would be for Iran to adhere to the IAEA additional protocol, the so called 93+2 protocol, which permits more aggressive monitoring and inspections.

Finally, the international community should encourage Iran to adopt non-nuclear alternatives for its energy needs. Thus, if Iran is willing to provide both assurances and verification along the lines above, the United States should indicate its willingness to lift its opposition to development credits for "clean" energy, including commercial development of Iran's gas fields, access to high-speed turbines and combined cycle technology, and international credits for development of hydroelectric and other energy sources. It is to everyone's advantage to encourage, not oppose, development of new gas and alternative energy resources in Iran.[38]

---

[37]Russian First Deputy Atomic Energy Minister Lev Ryabev, August 14, 1995, as reported in Reuters.
[38]Executive Order 12957 prohibited all American companies from investing in the Iranian energy sector. Among other things, this nullified the proposed Conoco contract for development of two Iranian offshore gas fields. The French firm Total subsequently took the contract.

A negotiating package composed of these elements would be greeted with understanding and sympathy by most, if not all, U.S. friends and allies, including Russia. It is consistent with international law and with the compromise language of the Halifax summit.[39] Moreover, it is in the immediate national interests of potential nuclear suppliers. It is also consistent with Iran's own public and private statements about the objectives of their nuclear energy program.

A "Grand Bargain" With Iran?

Is this a reasonable starting point for a serious dialogue with Iran? Although it would be possible to initiate a dialogue beginning with "soft" issues (the environment for example) there is good reason to start with an issue of greater policy salience. The nuclear issue is a major impediment to improved relations, which impairs confidence on both sides. Its effects spill over into regional politics and have seriously affected relations between the United States and Russia.[40] It is a subject that Iran itself has been quick to raise in international forums, and Iran's official position is unequivocal and positive. The United States and others, however, are justified in being suspicious of Iran's intentions as a possible proliferator unless and until its nuclear energy program is subjected to verifiable assurances and to more systematic scrutiny than is presently the case.

Moreover, the West has some positive inducements (development of non-nuclear energy sources) that are immediately available and that are in the clear national interest not only of Iran but also of the United States and the international community more generally. Unlike the North Korean model, these inducements

---

[39]At the G-7 summit in Halifax in June 1995, the final communique called for all states to "avoid any collaboration with Iran which might contribute to the acquisition of a nuclear weapons capability."
[40]The United States has imposed a series of penalties on Russia for alleged dealings with Iran on nuclear and missile technology. See, for example, Robert S. Greenberger, "Russian Institutes Are Penalized By U.S. Due to Aid Given to Iran," Wall Street Journal, January 13, 1999, p. 1.

involve no cash outlay. On the contrary, Iran would finance development of its own gas fields and would potentially have access to credit financing from commercial sources as well as development financing from the World Bank and national sources.[41]

The U.S. administration can fulfill most of its prospective obligations in such a bargain by selective presidential waiver of existing executive orders and legislation. Thus, one of the major complaints voiced by Iran about the prospect of official dialogue with the United States – that such dialogue seems to promise nothing but stern lectures from the United States – could be overcome. By putting something on the table that is of genuine value to the other party, both sides would be better able to justify such contacts to their domestic skeptics and opponents.

Would such a "grand bargain" solve the many problems that plague U.S.-Iran relations? No. Such an agreement, in itself, would not resolve concerns about Iran's suspected chemical and biological development programs, nor would it directly address U.S. concerns about Iran's opposition to the Arab-Israel peace process and alleged support for international terrorism. It would also not address Iran's historical grievances about U.S. interference in Iran's domestic politics and would not resolve the outstanding issue of Iranian military assets, which remain under adjudication at the Hague Tribunal created as part of the settlement of the hostage crisis in 1981.

Such a dialogue would inevitably raise a series of questions going beyond the narrow limits of Iran's nuclear program. Iran would be expected to raise questions about the Israeli nuclear program, probably in the context of Iran's long standing

---

[41]Japan granted Iran credits for construction of a hydroelectric project in the south of Iran. Those credits have been held up for years under pressure from the U.S. government. Iran is a member in good standing of the World Bank, but all World Bank credits to Iran for development projects have been blocked by the United States.

proposal for an NWFZ in the Middle East.[42] As mentioned above, Iran has also raised the possibility of an NWFZ in the Persian Gulf region. Such issues would potentially raise a wide range of regional security concerns affecting Iran, its immediate and more distant neighbors, and the role of external powers. Further, Iran could be expected to focus on two elements of the Nuclear Non-Proliferation Treaty: security assurances for non-nuclear states and access to peaceful nuclear technology. Those are very thorny issues from a U.S. or Western perspective, but they are familiar issues that have been dealt within the negotiation of the NPT, *inter alia*, and should neither surprise nor dismay a skilled negotiating team.

Regardless of such considerations, there are real advantages of focusing discussion with Iran on a single, concrete issue with a clear quid pro quo, rather than insisting on a nebulous comprehensive review of all outstanding issues. Such a dialogue would provide a test of good faith on an issue of great national significance for both parties. That experience could establish a practical context for discussion of other troublesome problems. It is a rational starting point for breaking the impasse between the United States and Iran, where each side has insisted that the other must make the first move.

The absence of authoritative political contacts between Iran and the United States since January 1981 has been harmful to the larger interests of both states. That

---

[42]Robbie Sabel, Director for Disarmament at the Israeli Foreign Ministry, has expressed great concern about Iran's nuclear program, especially in conjunction with its missile development and cooperation with Russia. In his view, "Iran and Russia have to believe that the Western and other States see such proliferation as a very real threat to world security and are willing to take the necessary steps to prevent such proliferation. Such steps need to involve elements of both impedance and inducements...It is not yet too late." [See the comments by Robbie Sabel, Director for Disarmament at the Israeli Foreign Ministry, at the VIIth Carnegie International Non-Proliferation Conference, Washington DC, January 12, 1999. Text of remarks distributed by and available from the Middle East Project, SIPRI, directed by Peter Jones: <jones@sipri.se> and <ME-project@sipri.se>] However, neither he nor any other Israeli official has addressed directly the fact that one of the "inducements" in a negotiated package with Iran would involve discussion of Israel's WMD program. This is an issue that cannot be avoided if Iran is to be persuaded to adopt stringent restrictions on its nuclear activities.

stalemate has persisted because both sides have experienced a failure of political will and have indulged the strident voices of their respective domestic opponents of change. There is evidence that this inertia may be giving way to more constructive thinking in both Tehran and Washington. The nuclear issue may provide a productive starting point to begin unraveling the skein of hostility that has accumulated over two decades.

Chapter 8

Israel's Nuclear Posture:
Persistent Concerns, New Challenges

Yair Evron

This paper assesses the role that Israel's ambiguous nuclear posture has played in the country's strategy, its possible effects to date on the dynamics of the Israeli-Arab conflict, and, finally, its present and future role. The latter discussion is conducted against the background of current trends in the Middle East and the profound changes in the international arena. While the thrust of the discussion is historical-analytical and policy-oriented, it also refers in part to the theoretical debate about the causes and likelihood of proliferation.

Why States Build Nuclear Capabilities

States have developed nuclear-weapon capabilities or nuclear-weapon options for a variety of reasons. The most important motivation has been the search for security. Threat perceptions prompt leaders to opt for the ultimate weapon. This has been the case among the original five declared nuclear powers as well as among most of the new proliferators. Indeed, even where a state's security environment did not appear to demand resort to nuclear weapons, political and strategic leaders developed security rationales – in which they believed – justifying reliance on such weapons. Security considerations were the primary motivation for the five declared nuclear powers, which India and Pakistan joined with their tests in 1998, and the one undeclared – Israel, and the eleven states which have developed (and later abandoned) or are engaged in the development of a nuclear-weapon infrastructure: Canada, Sweden, Switzerland, Argentina, Brazil, South Africa, Iraq, Iran, Taiwan, South Korea and North Korea.[1] Clearly, in Argentina and Brazil these considerations appear strange and unreal,[2] and when these two countries decided to reverse their nuclear programs, their security was not adversely affected. In some other cases, it could have been argued that though security concerns were real, the country's defenses could have been best served by a non-nuclear strategy. This reasoning, indeed, convinced several of the potential proliferators among the eleven not to proceed with their effort. Others yielded to external pressures.

Although security was the primary motivation, international or regional prestige and political power served as a secondary reason. Indeed, in some cases this was an important aim and was only rationalized by security considerations. The notion that big power status, either internationally or regionally depends on an independent nuclear deterrent, certainly played a role in the British[3] and even more

---

[1] For good and useful books and edited collections published in the past few years on the causes for declared, undeclared and threshold states as well as for those who abandoned or reversed their capabilities see, inter alia, Regina Coen Karp, *Security with Nuclear Weapons? Different Perspectives on National Security* (Oxford: Oxford University Press, 1991); Regina Coen Karp (ed.), *Security without Nuclear Weapons? Different Perspectives on Non-Nuclear Security* (Oxford: Oxford University Press, 1992); Benjamin Frankel (ed.), *Opaque Nuclear Proliferation: Methodological and Policy Implications* (London: Frank Cass, 1991); Zachari Davis and Benjamin Frankel (eds.), *The Proliferation Puzzle: Why Weapons Spread (and What Results)* (London: Frank Cass, 1993); Michael Reiss, *Without the Bomb: The Politics of Nuclear Non-proliferation* (New York: Columbia University Press, 1988).

[2] On the Argentinian and Brazilian nuclear efforts see, inter alia, Virginia Gramba-Stonehouse, "Argentina and Brazil" in Regina Karp (ed.), *Security with Nuclear Weapons, ibid.*

[3] On the British nuclear program, see, inter alia, Richard Rosecrance, *Defence of the Realm* (New York: Columbia University Press, 1968); Lawrence Freedman, *Britain and Nuclear Weapons* (London: Macmillan, 1981); Stuart Croft and Phil Williams, "The United Kingdom", in Karp (ed.), *idem.*; Margaret Gowing, *Independence and Deterrence* (London: Macmillan, 1974).

the French decisions,[4] and was not absent from the Chinese[5] and Indian calculations.[6] It was also an important consideration in the Iraqi program[7] and in the Shah's decision in the late 1970s to initiate a nuclear R&D effort. In all these cases, however, security considerations were the primary ones, though mixed, as it were, in different degrees with political power and prestige calculations. Finally, in some of these cases domestic political and organizational considerations were also present. They were, however, only a secondary cause. The fourth motivation, which emerged only recently in the case of North Korea, is the search for international political legitimacy coupled with the attempt to create a bargaining card with which to extract economic and diplomatic aid.

Decisions to proliferate have three important features. First, although states decided to proliferate because of security considerations, cost/benefit security calculations could have led them in many cases to non-nuclear decisions. Second, the decision to develop a nuclear infrastructure was usually made by a small group of decision-makers dedicated to the nuclear option. Third, an ex post factum analysis could probably demonstrate, in most cases, that the security of new proliferators (and

---

[4]On the French decisions, see, inter alia, Klaus Schubert, "France" in Karp (ed.), *ibid.*
[5]On the Chinese nuclear decisions, see, inter alia, Avery Goldstein, "Understanding Nuclear Proliferation: Theoretical Explanation and China's National Experience" in Zachary Davis and Benjamin Frankel, *The Proliferation Puzzle*, op. cit.; Gerald Segal, "China" in Karp (ed.), op. cit.; Richard Drifte, "China" in Josef Goldblat, *Non-Proliferation: The Why and the Wherefore* (London: Taylor & Francis, for SIPRI, 1985).
[6]On the Indian case, see Girilal Jain, "India" in Goldblat (ed.), *ibid.*; Praful Bidwai and Achin Vanait, "India and Pakistan" in Karp (ed.), *ibid*; Devin T. Hagerty, "The Power of Suggestion: Opaque Proliferation, Existential Deterrence, and the South Asian Nuclear Arms Competition", in Zachary Davis and Benjamin Frankel (eds.), *ibid.* George Perkovich , *India's Nuclear Bomb* (Berkeley: University of California Press, 1999); Brahama Chellaney " After the Tests: India's Options" *Survival*, Vol. 40, No. 40.
[7]On the Iraqi program see *inter alia* Marvin Miller, *The Iraqi Nuclear Program*; Yair Evron, *Israel's Nuclear Dilemma* (London: Routledge, and Ithaca: Cornell University Press, 1994).

some of the old ones) would not have been adversely affected had they chosen not to develop their nuclear capabilities.

Israel's Ambiguous Nuclear Posture

Israel is clearly an example of a state that chose to develop a nuclear option exclusively for security reasons. A specific set of threat perceptions, shared by most of the political elite, served as the background for the nuclear decisions.[8]

However, though sharing the same assumptions about threats, many Israeli decision-makers would not have chosen the nuclear path had it not been for Ben-Gurion's decisions and leadership in that field. Moreover, several important strategic leaders opposed the nuclear decisions precisely on the basis of cost/benefit calculations.

It appears, therefore, that Israel would not have chosen the nuclear option, or would have done so at a different time or in a different manner, if some other decision-maker had led the country.

The ambiguity surrounding the Israeli nuclear posture was not a deliberate strategy but emerged gradually from disagreements inside Israel about the cost/benefit equation of an explicit nuclear posture. Even more important was the American pressure which began in late 1960 and persisted for a long time. An ambiguous posture seemed the appropriate response to these constraints and in addition, as time passed, also appeared to be less provocative toward the Arab states than an explicit one. Indeed, the ambiguous posture lessened Arab concerns, partially

---

[8]For various discussions of the Israeli nuclear decisions see inter alia Yair Evron, *Israel's Nuclear Dilemma, ibid.* Sholomo Aronson, *The Politics and Strategy of Nuclear Weapons in the Middle East* (Albany: State University of New York Press); Avner Cohen, *Security Studies*; Dan Raviv and Yossi Melman, *Every Spy a Prince*, (Boston: Houghton Mifflin, 1990); Uri Bar Josef, "The Hidden Debate: The Formation of Nuclear Doctrines in the Middle East", *The Journal of Strategic Studies*, Vol. 5 (1982), Avner Cohen, *Israel and the Bomb*, (New York: Columbia University Press, 1998).

reduced American opposition, and in general succeeded in making the nuclear effort seem less acute and menacing.[9]

Though Israeli decision makers have never explicitly referred to the country's capability, let alone its possible uses, there emerged over time a body of conjectural discussion about such uses. Following is a list of possible "uses" of the Israeli posture. In the absence of official Israeli reference to a doctrine for these "uses," they are partly speculative. After detailing them we shall consider to what extent the main categories of "uses" have already had an impact on the dynamics of the Arab-Israeli conflict, and to what degree they could still play an important function in the emerging new system of relationships in the Middle East.

"Uses"[10]

a.   Diplomatic pressure *vis-à-vis* the United States. Though never explicitly stated, it may be assumed that in the more remote past the nuclear issue was a tacit Israeli bargaining card in negotiations with the United States about the supply of conventional arms. This probably resulted from the American understanding of the security dilemma Israel continuously faces. However, since the early 1970s, and certainly since 1973, the special relationship between the United States and Israel has reached such a level of intensity that the supply of conventional arms of the most advanced types to Israel has been based on the fundamental interests and community of purpose that the two states share. The nuclear issue was partly raised in another context of negotiations between Israel and the United States, *vis-à-vis* the Israeli attempts to secure a defense alliance with the United States . This subject was partly

---

[9]For conceptualizations of the concepts of opacity and ambiguity of in the context of threshold nuclear postures in general and in the Israeli case in particular see *inter alia*; Evron, *ibid*. Yair Evron, "Israel and the Atom: The Uses and Misuses of Ambiguity," *Orbis*, Vol. 17 (1974); Avner Cohen and Benjamin Frankel, "Opaque Nuclear Proliferation" in Benjamin Frankel (ed.), op.cit.

[10]For a much more detailed analysis see Yair Evron, *Israel's Nuclear Dilemma. ibid.*

discussed in the Ben-Gurion/Kennedy correspondence of April-June 1963, as well as in other diplomatic interactions. Yet it was never stated in terms of a quid pro quo and both leaders refrained from explicitly considering such a deal.[11]

b.   Deterrence against conventional attacks. This broad "use" covers a whole range of scenarios, from limited attacks to major wars.

c.   Weapon of last resort (to be discussed below).

d.   Battlefield uses.

e.   Deterrence against the use of other non-conventional arms: chemical and biological agents.

f.   Compellent or conflict management instruments.

A brief historical-analytical review of the conflict since the early 1970s leads to the conclusion that the ambiguous (or undeclared) Israeli posture was largely irrelevant to the main developments in Arab-Israeli relations. An in-depth discussion is beyond the scope of this article. But a brief account is called for. Two main categories of "uses" will be discussed here: deterrence of conventional attacks and conflict management and resolution.

Deterrence of Conventional Attacks

Since Israel's nuclear image became more visible in the early 1970s, Arab countries have initiated one major attack against Israel – the 1973 War launched by Egypt and Syria. Its main objective was political – to convince the superpowers that

---

[11]Seymour Hersh, in *The Samson Option* (London and Boston: Faber and Faber, 1991) has even argued that during the 1973 War Israel directly threatened the U.S. that she would resort to the use or the threat of use of nuclear weapons if the U.S. did not begin the air lift of war materiel. This however, appears far-fetched and is not backed by evidence. On the contrary , according to the evidence of the Director General of the Israeli Prime Minister's Office at the time, Mordechai Gazit, the Israeli position transmitted to Washington on 9 October by Prime Minister Golda Meir's letter, had no reference whatsoever, even tacitly or indirectly to the nuclear dimension. For further details see Yair Evron, *Israel's Nuclear Dilemma, ibid.* On the Ben-Gurion- Kennedy dialogue see Avner Cohen, *Israel and the Bomb.*

the status quo was untenable, and consequently, unless the United States applied pressure on Israel to withdraw from Sinai and the Golan, there would be a high likelihood of another war leading to an international crisis.

The military objectives on both fronts were tailored to this goal and therefore limited.[12] In fact the assumption was that even a complete military failure would nevertheless shake the superpowers and bring about the desired political outcome. On the Egyptian front the objective of the first phase of the attack was to cross the Suez Canal and establish a corridor along the waterway under Egyptian control. In the second phase, the objective was to absorb the expected Israeli counter-offensive. If the two phases had been successfully accomplished, the Egyptians would have moved to the third and final phase: to extend the area under their control as far as the Sinai passes, thus placing a quarter to a third of the Sinai Peninsula under Egyptian control.[13] An analysis of pre-attack Egyptian casualty estimates shows the deep-seated Egyptian fear of Israeli conventional superiority. In fact, because of those estimates the Egyptian leaders had very grave doubts about the chances of success of even the first phase of the offensive. They were actually surprised by the relative ease with which they were able to cross the canal. Even after the Egyptian forces

---

[12]On Egyptian accounts of the political and strategic background, and on the unfolding and objectives of the 1973 War, see *inter alia*, Ismail Fahmy, *Negotiating for Peace in the Middle East* (London: Croom Helm, 1983); Mahmud Riad, *The Struggle for Peace in the Middle East* (London: Quartet, 1981); Anwar Sadat, *In Search of Identity* (New York: Harper and Row, 1978); Saad el Shazli, *The Crossing of the Suez* (San Francisco: American Mideast Research, 1980); Muhamad Hassenin Heikal, *The Road to Ramadan* (New York: Quadrangle Books, 1975). Hasan el-Badri, Teha el-Magdoub and Muhamad Diam el-Din Zhody, *The Ramadan War* (Dunn Loming VA: T.N. Dupuy Associates, 1978). On an Israeli account of the military campaign see Avraham Adan, *Al Shtei Gdot HaSuez* (On the Two Bans of the Suez) (In Hebrew) (Jerusalem: Adanim 1979). For a solid American account of the campaign see John Mearsheimer, *Conventional Deterrence* (Ithaca and London: Cornell University Press, 1983).

[13]Probably the best source on the Egyptian political and strategic objectives as well as its military planning of the war, is included in an article in the Israeli Defense journal *Maarachot*. This article made use of all the open available sources as well as of Egyptian classified military documents which fell into the hands of the IDF during the war. See Avi Shai, "Egypt toward the Yom Kippur War: The War's Objectives and the Attack Plan" (in Hebrew) *Maarachot*, 250, July 1976.

succeeded in withstanding the Israeli counter-attacks, they were not inclined to move to the third phase. They finally did so only after many internal doubts and under heavy Syrian pressure. Indeed, their fears were justified. The third phase turned out to be a catastrophe and enabled Israel to counterattack across the canal.

In summary, then, it was not Israel's assumed nuclear capability that forced the Egyptians to adopt a limited war strategy, but their estimates (which eventually proved correct) of the balance of conventional capabilities.[14] They assumed, however, and again they were right, that their political objective would be accomplished even in the face of defeat.

Conflict Management and Resolution

Another major event in the Arab-Israeli conflict was Anwar Sadat's decision to visit Jerusalem and proceed with peace negotiations. Here again the nuclear element was largely irrelevant or played only a secondary role.[15] The Egyptian goal since 1967 was to get back the Sinai Peninsula. This overrode any other aim. The Palestinian issue, pan-Arab solidarity and general "Arab" objectives, all paled compared to Sinai. Already in the period 1967-1970, long before the nuclear issue assumed any saliency, there were signs that Egypt, in consideration for the return of Sinai, would accept several political conditions though short of full peace with Israel. In any event, in view of Israeli political intransigence, Cairo did not believe that Israel would return the whole of Sinai under any conditions. Following the 1973 war, in which both sides became only too aware of the costs of continuing the conflict,

---

[14]The argument that it was Israel's nuclear image that forced the Egyptians to adopt a limited war strategy was advanced by Sholomo Aronson, "The Nuclear Dimension in the Arab-Israeli Conflict", *The Jerusalem Journal of International Relations*, Vol. 7, No.1-2 1984).

[15]For the argument that it was the nuclear issue that determined Sadat's move see in the first place, Sholomo Aronson, *ibid*. For a much more cautious variant of this general point, see George Quester "The Middle East: Imposed Solutions or Imposed Problems" in M. Leitenberg and G. Sheffer, (eds.), *Great Power Intervention in the Middle East* (New York: Pergamon, 1979).

and following Israel's undertaking to return the whole of Sinai, the ground was prepared for Sadat's visit to Jerusalem.

But several deeper processes in Egypt and throughout the Middle East created the necessary favorable context for that momentous move. First, the collapse of pan-Arab nationalism and the fragmentation of the Arab states' system. This profound ideological and political process of change, whose roots could be traced back to the 1967-73 period and to multiple developments inside different Arab states, changed the order of priorities in the Arab world and particularly in Egypt.[16] In the latter, it dovetailed with the rise of "Egypt first" sentiment and the specific Egyptian view of the world and of the Arab state system. Second, the 1967 defeat had triggered a painful reassessment in Arab political thought of the conflict and had produced a much more varied and complex attitude toward Israel. The new attitude allowed for greater flexibility. In addition, the deep revulsion within Egypt of the role played by the Soviet Union in the country, and the assessment that economically Egypt must open up to the West, all combined to contribute to the new Egyptian stance in the conflict and in foreign policy in general.

Jordan was never concerned about the nuclear issue and in any case sought already from 1967 to reach a peaceful accommodation with Israel.[17] Syria, on the other hand, though eager to get back the Golan Heights, refused to budge from its

---

[16]The classical description of the decline of Pan-Arabism is included in Fuad Ajami, "The Decline of Pan-Arabism", *Foreign Affairs* (Winter 1978-79). For works on the political and economic changes which took place in Egypt during the 1970s see *inter alia*, Alan Richards and John Waterbury, *A Political Economy of the Middle East* (Boulder, Colorado: Westview Press, 1990); Shimon Shamir, *Egypt under Sadat's Leadership* (in Hebrew) (Tel-Aviv: Dvir, 1978).

[17]Israeli-Jordanian relations have always been characterized by different mixes of conflict and cooperation. Both states have always were cognizant of the many shared political and strategic interests they have. These went back even before 1948, and certainly became more salient at different junctures since then. For some accounts see *inter alia*, Avi Shlaim, *Collusion across the Jordan* (Oxford: Oxford University Press, 1988); Aharon Kleiman, *Coexistence without Peace* (In Hebrew) (Tel-Aviv: Maariv, 1986); Dan Shuftan, *Jordanian Option* (In Hebrew) (Tel-Aviv: Hakibutz Hameuchad, 1986); Yair Evron, *The Middle East: Nations, Superpowers and Wars* (New York: Praeger, 1973).

refusal to sign a peace treaty with Israel similar to the one agreed to by Egypt. Even after the ambiguity surrounding Israeli nuclear capability diminished considerably following the Vanunu revelations, Syria persisted in its position. It was only the withdrawal of Soviet backing in the second half of the 1980s and the re-emergence of Iraq, Syria's most bitter enemy, as a main actor in the Arab states' system following the end of the war with Iran, that induced Syria to begin to revise its position. In other words, Israel's nuclear image may contribute to deterrence (though it is not needed in the conflict with Syria, which in conventional terms is inferior to Israel both militarily and strategically). But that image cannot compel Syria to sign a full peace with Israel unless many of its conditions are met. Indeed, the stubborn and inflexible posture Syria has adopted in its negotiations with Israel in 1995-1996 and again in 1999-2000, leads to the same conclusion.[18]

In sum, then, the gradual emergence of a new, peaceful relationship between Arab states and Israel was not dependent on Israel's nuclear image. It was, rather, and will continue to be, bound up with a complex process in which strategic, political (both inter-Arab and Arab-Israel) and international factors converge.

Current International Trends

The end of the Cold War and of competitive bipolarity, and the wide range of the superpowers' nuclear arms control agreements indicate the existence of a trend leading eventually to a diminishing international role for nuclear weapons. The

---

[18]On Syria's changing of regional orientations resulting from the re-emergence of Iraq as a leading Arab power during the Gulf crisis see *inter alia* Bruce Maddy Weitzman, *The Inter-Arab System and the Gulf War: Continuity and Change,* Occasional Paper Series No. 2 (The Carter Center of Emory University, 1992); On Syria's overall foreign policy see Patrick Seale, Assad: *A Political Biography* (Berkeley: University of California Press, 1988); Raymond Hinnebusch, "Revisionist Dreams, Realist Strategies: The Foreign Policy of Syria" in Bhagat Korany and Ali Dessuki (eds.), *The Foreign Policies of Arab States* (Boulder: Westview Press, 1984). On the Israeli-Syrian deterrence relationship see *inter alia* Yair Evron, *War and Intervention in Lebanon* (London and Baltimore: Croom Helm and Johns Hopkins University Press).

reversal in the nuclear policies of Brazil, Argentina, and especially South Africa and the U.S.-North Korea agreement, all reflects the same trend. Needless to say, considerable uncertainties persist.

Thus, for example, the "abolitionist" approach calling for the complete elimination of nuclear weapons has gained considerable legitimacy . On the other hand, both the United States and more so Russia, have refused to forgo nuclear weapons as an important element in their overall strategic and military postures. Of significant importance were also the Indian and Pakistani tests.[19]

At the theoretical level, several contending approaches are trying to assess future proliferation developments.[20] First, realists and neo-realists are divided among themselves as to future international trends and the potential stabilizing effect of proliferation. Some argue that proliferation is inevitable because of the "anarchical" nature of the international system. Furthermore, the end of bipolarity, which operated as a major stabilizing factor in the global international system, will give powerful impetus to proliferation.[21] Others, however, contend that proliferation could be prevented: Many states, relying on "realist" assessments, have in the past preferred non-nuclear strategies. In addition, preventive measures from the "realist" inventory

---

[19]For a comprehensive discussion of both trends toward diminishing role for nuclear weapons as well as the persistent uncertainties see Lewis Dunn, "The Proliferation Scene" in this volume. See James Leonard, in this volume. For a detailed discussion see also Yair Evron, *Israel's Nuclear Dilemma*, *op. cit.* On a reformulation of the Taboo against the use of nuclear weapons see Thomas Schelling, *The Role of Nuclear Weapons, 1993*. The "abolitionist" school is eminently represented in the *Report of the Canberra Commission on the Elimination of Nuclear Weapons* (August 1996).

[20]On a discussion of the various theoretical approaches to the question of proliferation see Janice Stein, "Proliferation, Non-Proliferation, and Anti-Proliferation..." in this volume.

[21]These points have been advanced primarily by Kenneth Waltz, *The Spread of Nuclear Weapons: May be Better*, Adelphi Papers No. 171 (London: IISS 1981) and *idem*, "The Emerging Structure of International Politics" (Unpublished manuscript) and in Kenneth Waltz and Scott D. Sagan, *The Spread of Nuclear Weapons: A debate*; John Mearsheimer, "Back to the Future: Instability in Europe after the Cold War", *International Security*, 15 (1990); Benjamin Frankel,"The Brooding Shadow: Systemic Incentives and Nuclear Weapons Proliferation", in Zachary Davis and Benjamin Frankel (eds.), *The Proliferation Puzzle, op. cit.*; John Weltman, "Nuclear Devolution and World Politics", *World Politics* Vol. 32, No. 2, 1980.

could be taken: alliances and guarantees coupled with punishments of proliferators.[22] Some realists and neo-realists argue that proliferation could stabilize the international and regional systems[23] while others speak of a destabilizing effect.[24]

Neoliberal-institutionalist theorists, "trade state" theorists,[25] and constructivist approaches argue that motivations to proliferate will not necessarily be powerful. International norms and institutions, the shift of the global emphasis to economic development and cooperation, the increase in international trade and the processes of democratization – all are seen to serve as powerful hedges against proliferation.

It appears to me that uncausal approaches cannot serve as exclusive predictors of future proliferation trends. Various realist and neo-realist approaches will probably be useful predictors of the majority of the variance of international strategic and political interactions, and liberal-institutional and trade-state approaches could probably serve as effective predictors for part of the variance. In most states both approaches should probably be considered and combined.

Most likely Western European states, as well as many East Asian and Latin American states, all of which are strongly committed to economic growth and many also to societal development and welfare, will tend to perceive that their international environment poses lower threats than was the case until the end of competitive bipolarity. Many of these countries are also protected by defense alliances with the United States. Thus, from a realist point of view, their security is altogether not threatened in the near or medium future.

---

[22]See for example, Zachary Davis, "The Nuclear Realist Regime", in Zachary Davis and Benjamin Frankel, *The Proliferation Puzzle, op. cit.* George Quester, "Knowing and Believing about Nuclear Proliferation", *Security Studies*, Vol. 1, No. 2, Winter 1991; Yair Evron, *Israel's Nuclear Dilemma*.
[23]See Waltz, *The Spread of Nuclear Weapons, ibid.* John Weltman, *ibid.* Pierre Gallois, *The Balance of Terror: Strategy for the Nuclear Age* (Boston: Houghton Mifflin 1961); Shai Feldman, *Israeli Nuclear Deterrence: A Strategy for the 1980s* (New York: Columbia University Press, 1982).
[24]See Quester *op. cit.*, Frankel *op.cit.*, Evron *op. cit.*, Sagan *op. cit.*
[25]For the best elaboration of the Trading State theory see Richard Rosecrance, *The Rise of the Trading State: Commerce and Conquest in the Modern World* (New York: Basic Books, 1986).

From a pure realist or neo-realist point of view, proliferation need not and does not necessarily stabilize international systems. On the contrary, there are valid "realist" reasons why proliferation might destabilize regional systems and possibly the whole international system. The main thing that realist approaches could effectively predict is that states which perceive themselves to face extreme danger and lack any external guarantee, might consider a nuclear option as a possible solution to their predicament. However, even then, they might prefer to rely on conventional deterrence and defense. The likelihood that states facing nuclear adversaries would opt for a nuclear option is certainly higher. However, even then they might prefer a defense alliance.

Finally, an international norm delegitimizing the use of nuclear weapons is likely to further discourage states from choosing the nuclear option. To be sure, states facing deadly threats which they cannot hope to deter by their own capabilities and lacking any external guarantee, might ultimately determine their nuclear posture not according to international norms but according to their assessments of costs/benefits resulting from their threat perceptions. However, in many international situations, in which the threats are not urgent and menacing and in which alternative strategies, including nonnuclear ones, are available, states' calculations might be influenced by the extent to which the use of nuclear weapons is internationally delegitimized. Steps toward more far-reaching nuclear arms reductions among the present nuclear powers might therefore discourage potential future proliferators from going nuclear.

However, since the future stability of the global international system depends ultimately on a measure of order which is underwritten by the United States, backed perhaps by some or all the other big powers, American nuclear disarmament might actually jolt the stability of the international system.

Current Situation in Middle East

The Middle East, and especially the Arab-Israeli region, is currently entering a transitory phase in which elements of the old and the new mix. The decline of radical pan-Arab nationalism, the commitment of many regimes to economic growth and some of them to societal welfare, the existent Arab-Israeli peace agreements and the prospects for additional agreements, the predominant position of the United States and its strong commitment to underwrite peace and stability in the area, all create the potential for a   continued trend toward a region with lower levels of violence than in the past.

As against this, forces of counter-stability are at work. To begin with, as long as Israel and Syria do not reach a peace settlement, there is a potential flash point from escalation along the Israeli-Lebanese border. Second Islamic radical militancy poses a challenge and a threat to several Arab regimes. Even if the militants fail in their efforts – s indeed appears now to be the case – they might have an influence on policy. In addition, other forces seeking democratic change in the Arab political systems might destabilize some of the current governments. The result could be a spillover into, and reversal of the Arab-Israeli peace system. Moreover, some of the traditional rules of the game of the Arab states and of the Middle East in general might persist even into the new era. These include competition for political influence among the main regional powers. Though such competition could, in principle, be resolved by political and diplomatic means, it might escalate into violence and again spill over into Arab-Israeli relations. Furthermore, Israel's greater integration politically and strategically into the Middle East gives rise to two cardinal issues. First, Arab states might consider Israel a competitor for political influence and this might lead to major problems. Second, a politically legitimized Israel in the Middle East might find itself allied with Arab states which are in conflict with other regional powers, leading again to possible crises in which Israel is involved. The role of military power and within it of nuclear weapons is of course relevant here.

Thus, peace and stability will have to depend on realistic measures designed to diminish mutual security concerns. These could be achieved by a combination of the further reduction of political grievances, as well as CSBM and stable deterrence.

Israeli Security Concerns

The following are the main security concerns that Israel still faces with varying degrees of probability:

a.   A total reversal of the peace process on all fronts. This might lead to major escalation and, ultimately, the formation of a grand war coalition directed against Israel.

b.   A breakdown of the Israeli-Syrian peace negotiations and the resulting possibility that under some new political configuration in the Middle East, Syria might resort in the future to the military option. An even worse scenario is the creation of an "eastern front" comprising Syria, Iraq, and possibly even Iran, which might resort to war on the Golan. The second scenario is certainly of a lower order of probability than the first, but neither can be entirely ruled out.

c.   The conclusion of an Israeli-Syrian peace agreement comprising as a Confidence and Security Building Measure (CSBM) the demilitarization of the Golan by the current regime, which is then replaced by a different one which disavows the peace. If the new regime should try to violate the demilitarization of the Golan, this would lead to a major war with Syria.

d.   The emergence of another regional power armed with nuclear weapons.

e.   A missile campaign launched by Iraq or Iran under some hypothetical political conditions. This campaign might involve also the use of chemical or biological agents.

It appears that all the scenarios of conventional attacks resulting from the above potential threats could be either deterred or – if deterrence failed – be defeated by Israel's conventional capability. The only scenario in which Israel – though not losing the battle might suffer very high costs which might verge on the unacceptable – is the emergence of a grand war coalition with a unified command mobilizing all the Arab capabilities against Israel. The probability for this is extremely low. However, Israeli decision-makers cannot completely discount it at present. Only a gradual process of political accommodation, coupled with the demonstration of complete Arab commitment to a stable peace, could gradually lower this concern.

Another concern has to do with a surprise Syrian attack on a demilitarized Golan which had been returned to Syria as part of a peace treaty. Here, Israel would have to develop conventional capabilities which could make it very costly for Syria to undertake such a venture. In any event, Israel would have to deploy in force on the Golan almost simultaneously with the advancing Syrian forces. This would require specific investments in military hardware. Still, none of these scenarios requires Israel's resort to deterring nuclear threats, let alone their actualization.

The possibility that a regional power such as Iraq or Iran might arm itself with nuclear weapons certainly poses the greatest threat to Israel. Although at present both countries are far from such a capability, the revelations about the past elaborate Iraqi program are a reminder that a similar program could also be conducted in secrecy in the future.

If Iraq or Iran (or another regional power) should succeed in developing a nuclear capability, the rules of the game in the Middle East would be transformed. All the regional powers would have cause for concern, and if international actions failed to bring about the denuclearization of the new proliferator, additional countries would also probably have to develop a nuclear-weapons capability.

The dangers involved in a Middle East under conditions of proliferation are very considerable. The – by now – historical model of the central balance of nuclear deterrence which produced a fairly high level of stability (although there was always the disturbing possibility of loss of control) cannot be replicated in the Middle East. Therefore, it is much likelier that in the Middle East, as compared with the superpowers model, deterrence would fail, giving rise to conventional confrontations and, finally, of escalation to the nuclear level.

In the absence of an effective regime, which would totally prevent proliferation in the Middle East, Israel must retain a strategic nuclear capability designed to deter another regional nuclear power. The situation would, however, be quite unstable.

Surface-to-Surface Missiles and the Non-conventional Threat

A more complex issue concerns the possible use of chemical and biological agents. Here the Gulf War is of some relevance. Though the exact situation is still unclear, UNSCOM accounts suggest that prior to the war, Iraq had a deployable biological weapon capability which could have been used against the coalition and against Saudi Arabia and Israel. Iraq refrained from using those weapons because this did not suit its purposes or because of American and/or Israeli deterrence. Apparently the American deterrence message was transmitted directly and in no ambiguous terms by U.S. Secretary of State James Baker to the Iraqi Foreign Minister, Tariq Aziz, at the Geneva Conference in January 1991. It is not clear, but should not be ruled out, that Iraq also weighed the implications of the ambiguous Israeli deterrent threats during that period.

Actual Use of Nuclear Weapons

Nuclear weapons differ from chemical and biological weapons in that, first, nuclear weapons cause instant enormous destruction, well beyond the damage that could be caused by the other two types of non-conventional arms (though biological weapons could potentially cause very considerable casualties); and, second, in that there are virtually no defenses against nuclear arms, whereas there are certain types of defense against the other two. These differences place nuclear weapons in a class of their own.

The special character of nuclear weapons has indeed led to the well-established notion – though far from being accepted by many experts – that they should never be used except as a deterrent against the use of nuclear weapons by the adversary or in the case of an existential threat to a country. On the global level this led to the emergence of the "nuclear taboo." This taboo is now even more entrenched and the global trend is toward making nuclear weapons less relevant to strategy. It is against this background that Israeli nuclear threats and Israel's possible use of nuclear weapons should be considered.

The use of chemical and especially biological weapons against Israel, though not an existential threat, could nevertheless inflict large civilian casualties and might lead the Israeli leadership to conclude that the cost to the country would be unacceptable. Israel might therefore decide to lower the threshold for the use of nuclear weapons.

Though, as mentioned before, the reliance on nuclear weapons still persists among the nuclear powers, nevertheless, the overall international trend is towards nuclear arms control and the decline saliency of the nuclear dimension. On that background an Israeli decision to use these weapons might result in enormous negative political fallout from the international community, particularly if others perceived the threat which prompted the decision as being less than existential. One possible outcome might be that constraints which had prevented some nuclear suppliers from delivering nuclear technology to Arab states would disappear, and such technology or even the actual weapons, might find their way to Arab arsenals.

On top of this, Arab states might be powerfully motivated to respond in kind, and this, in conjunction with the diminishing constraints on the suppliers and on Arab states themselves to produce nuclear weapons, could eventuate in a revenge nuclear strike against Israel. All these, however, might not deter an Israeli leadership in the face of a non-conventional attack.

In the past (before the Gulf War) the Israeli posture with regard to Syria's possible use of surface-to-surface missiles (SSMs) with conventional warheads was basically traditional. It involved measures of active and passive damage limitation coupled with an emphasis on a conventional attack designed to terminate the war within a few days and destroy the enemy's launching capability. The problem, however, would be much more difficult if SSMs with biological or chemical warheads were to be launched from Iraq or Iran or another peripheral country. Under such circumstances there would be greater emphasis on deterrence. This might escalate to the nuclear level.

All told, then, a consideration of the potential threats facing Israel leads to the conclusion that it has several reasons for maintaining a limited nuclear capability designed only for strategic deterrence. First, the remote possibility that under extreme (and quite unlikely) circumstances the whole political process currently unfolding between Arabs and Israelis is reversed and, in addition, the conventional balance deteriorates, so that Israel finds itself in a war, facing an existential threat. Second, if a regional power arms itself with nuclear weapons. Finally, although it seems, to me, possibly loaded with potential costs, a nuclear capability could serve as a deterrent against the threat of a large-scale biological attack (which could be far more lethal to the civilian population than a chemical attack).

In addition, albeit not as a strategic rationale, the knowledge of Israeli leaders that they have the capability to inflict unacceptable damage on all the other regional powers enables them to accept painful territorial concessions in the peace process.

Yet, even though security concerns justify, from the Israeli point of view, the existence of an independent nuclear capability, there are powerful reasons why it should be gradually controlled and limited. First, the continued existence of an Israeli capability provokes various regional states to choose the nuclear path as well. To be sure, the Israeli capability was only one cause for the development of the Iraqi option and is only a secondary one in the Iranian nuclear effort. Nevertheless, Israel's image as a nuclear power continues to serve as a justification for the latter and might eventually affect other regional powers. Even more important, it encourages political and commercial lobbies in the nuclear suppliers to pressure their governments to reduce the restrictions on the transfer of nuclear technology and hardware to hostile regional powers. Although at present there is no serious Egyptian lobby promoting the building of a nuclear option, this might emerge eventually if no CSBM is taken in this area. As long as Israel maintains an ambiguous posture, some of these reasons are somewhat blunted. Increasingly, though, that ambiguity has been eroding, and this requires that Israel undertake some limiting measures in the nuclear field.

Until 1998 the United States, at the head of an international coalition, had successfully restrained the Iraqi effort in all areas of armaments. Efforts to reimpose an UN arms control mechanism in Iraq have not (at the time of writing) yet succeeded; but, the U.S. continues its efforts to reintroduce such a control mechanism. Washington is also restraining the Iranian nuclear program. However, in the latter case, the position of some of the other big powers is more complex. They oppose the explicit Iranian military nuclear effort, but they are less supportive of the overall American strategy to constrain the Iranian military development. Moreover, Russia has transferred to Iran technology for the development and production of SSMs which could serve as delivery systems for nuclear warheads if the latter would eventually be produced. Russia's support for the Iranian nuclear effort has been apparently limited to the peaceful uses of nuclear energy, but there have also been unconfirmed reports concerning nuclear assistance which could potentially be used for military uses. The U.S. has been trying to limit the said Russian activity. The Israeli nuclear posture might therefore eventually complicate the general American anti-proliferation strategy in the Middle East.

Egyptian Concerns

The specific Egyptian concern has to do with the assumed purposes of the Israeli capability, and with the possibility that it will provoke other regional powers to choose the nuclear track.[26] In addition a pattern of concern has emerged about the *political* implications of Israel's nuclear posture.

Egyptian analysts, relying on some interpretations of the Vanunu revelations, argue that Israel's assumed capability extends beyond what should objectively be considered the minimum necessary for last-resort deterrence. Hence Cairo's concern as to the ultimate Israeli military objectives. One possible interpretation, according to Egyptian analysts, is that Israel has opted to develop tactical nuclear weapons for battlefield use. Since Israel is perceived as superior in conventional capabilities, and since the most appropriate terrain for the use of such weapons appears to be Sinai, Egypt fears that an Israeli government with expansionist intentions might try to recapture the Sinai peninsula.

Another Egyptian concern could be implicit in a broad "realist" systemic interpretation. It is that Israel, equipped with a very broad range of nuclear weapons, has gained strategic superiority in the Middle East. Again, one might surmise that a small Israeli capability, whose mission is only to deter and defend in last-resort situations, though still unacceptable to Egypt, might nevertheless be tolerable.

---

[26]See the contributions of Moustafa Saif and Abdul Halim in this volume.

Cairo is also worried that an uncontrolled and extensive Israeli nuclear arsenal is so provocative that other Middle Eastern countries would unavoidably have to follow the Israeli example and develop their own nuclear capabilities. This would place Egypt in a precarious position. In a multipolar nuclear Middle East, Egypt, too, must choose the nuclear option for both strategic and political reasons. However, since Egypt has several other priorities for investing its scarce resources, such an option is not welcomed. Moreover, to date Egypt has done well strategically and politically without the nuclear option. Investing in it would seem a painful and unnecessary diversion of resources.

Egyptian concern about the Israeli capability is possibly also part of a larger feeling of growing uneasiness about Israel's overall political power.[27] Precisely the success of the peace process, something Egypt has been interested in since 1979, created a paradoxical new situation. The relatively powerful (in regional terms) Israeli economy, coupled with Israel's greater diplomatic maneuverability in Middle Eastern politics due to its more legitimized position in the region, are perceived by Cairo as creating the potential for Israeli regional leadership. A nuclear-weapons capability would, in this view, only augment this political power. Thus, another paradoxical situation is emerging. While, as I argued earlier, in fact the image of a nuclear Israel did not alter the *political* situation in the region, and the peace process was basically due to other factors, at present, Egypt sees the nuclear capability as playing a political role, albeit in a very different way: by enhancing Israel's political power in the competition for influence. The Egyptian position should therefore be interpreted not as part of an adversarial strategy *vis-à-vis* Israel but precisely as part of a strategy designed to create a new political and strategic pattern of a peaceful Middle East, but one which is still marked by political competition and fluidity.

---

[27]See, for example, references by Amru Moussa, Egypt's Foreign Minister.

Israeli Preferred Options

In view of the various factors mentioned before – the persistent potential threats; the international trends; the emerging new system of peace and stability in the region; Egyptian concerns and the need to apply various CSBM and arms control measures in the region in order to strengthen strategic stability – Israel should try to accommodate its policies to the new situation. Such new approaches could be encouraged by various regional and superpower policies.

First, additional political steps would undoubtedly strengthen readiness to adopt unilateral arms control measures. Thus, the conclusion of peace between Israel and Syria, and following that with other Arab states, would reduce the potential for reversals in the peace system. In addition, deepening "normalization" would also indicate that the forces in the Arab world which oppose peace are weakening.

Second, cutbacks in the conventional capabilities of the Arab standing armies could lessen Israeli fear of a surprise attack in case of political crisis and reversal of the peace process. Currently, under conditions of full mobilization, Israel's conventional forces could withstand a concerted conventional attack by an Arab coalition though casualties would be heavy. However, the profound asymmetries in the size of the standing armies could present a serious problem for Israel in a surprise attack. Hence the Israeli demand to link conventional and non-conventional arms control negotiations.

Third, the establishment of a regional security system (which in another place I termed a "common security regime"[28]) with the participation of Israel would strengthen   political and strategic relationships among the parties and make defections less likely. It could also help deter destabilizing attempts by anti-status quo regional powers outside the alliance. Needless to say, there are major problems

---

[28]See Yair Evron, " Towards the Emergence of a Common Security System in the Middle East" in Lenore Martin (ed.) *New Frontiers in Middle East Security* (New York: St. Martin's Press, 1998).

involved both in the creation of an alliance and in its operation. To begin with, given the background of ongoing persistent hostilities and suspicions, much time would pass before Arab states and Israel could join in a coordinated security system. As against this, it could be argued that, albeit tacitly, Israel already cooperates with certain Arab states in security areas.[29] So the move to open cooperation would not constitute an insurmountable difficulty. However, problems arising from open formal cooperation will remain. Then again, meaningful Arab inter-state cooperation in the realm of security has always been marked by uncertainty and fluidity. The Arab state system has always allowed for rapid changes of alliances and a complex power-balancing "game."[30] In addition, were such an alliance to be formed, it might invite precisely what it would desire to deter, namely, the emergence of a counterbalancing regional coalition of anti-status quo powers. Nevertheless, the idea should be pursued and – if acceptable to some Arab parties – could be adopted.

Fourth, an American-Israeli defense treaty would be beneficial. This depends in the first place on the United States. In the past, whenever Israel sought such a treaty, Washington hesitated about entering a formal commitment. At present and in the near future there are two opposing arguments as to the likelihood of a positive American response. On the one hand, the present domestic mood in the United States opposes the undertaking of additional formal security commitments. On the other hand, the U.S. would probably be ready to consider such a treaty positively within the context of an Israeli-Syrian peace treaty and were Israel to insist on it. It should, of course, be added that there are deep hesitations in Israel concerning a formal defense treaty with the United States. Indeed, it is more likely at present that

---

[29]See, for example, the references to the Israeli-Jordanian relationship in fn. 17.

[30]On power balancing in the inter-Arab state system see Stephen Walt, *The Origins of Alliances* (Ithaca: Cornell University Press, 1987); Yair Evron, "Gulf Crisis and War", *Security Studies*, Winter 1994; Yair Evron and Ya'acob Barsimantov, "Coalitions in the Arab World", *The Jerusalem Journal of International Relations*.

Israel would try to gain a different type of an American strategic commitment. However, the subject of a defense alliance will most probably remain alive.

By now, indeed, American-Israeli relations have become so close that were Israel to find itself in a dire military situation, the United States would probably provide military support. But a formal defense treaty would further augment and deepen the American commitment. Moreover, it would considerably enhance Israel's deterrence against several types of military attacks.

It should be added that in real terms American military support need not take the form of ground troops, a contingency which could cause domestic concern inside the United States. Large-scale air support is more likely, as well as the delivery of needed materiel.

A formal defense treaty could also be effective in changing the cost calculus of states distant from Israel which might consider launching long-range strikes with SSMs armed with conventional or non-conventional warheads.

CSBM in the Nuclear Area

As part of the various elements detailed above, which are designed to increase regional security, Israel should consider measures which could decrease Arab and specially Egyptian concerns about its nuclear capability.

First, freezing fissile materials production. President Bush's proposal of 1991, followed by the Clinton proposal for a "cut-off" and the various initiatives to push the freezing initiated in the UN within the context of the Fissile Material Cut-Off Treaty (FMTC), will probably be reintroduced in the near future to international diplomacy. This should receive serious consideration by Israel. However, several problems arise. First, a freeze could affect not only the production of future weapons capabilities, but could, for technical reasons, gradually and over time, affect present capabilities. Another problem has to do with the kinds of *quid pro quo* which Arab states will have to provide. A much more stringent inspection and verification system of nuclear activities in the Arab states and Iran would be necessary. But beyond that Israel might find it necessary to insist on other measures affecting other non-conventional arms in Arab hands. It is also debatable whether all the Arab states would accept the freeze (though to an extent they are formally bound not to produce fissile materials already by the NPT) as it maintains the Israeli capability in the future. Nor can we foresee their reactions to other arms control measures connected with the freeze. However, this is an area which could, in principle, provide scope for various CSBM and arms control measures.

Another CSBM – one which might match the deterrence dimension of the assumed Israeli capability – refers to the missions of that capability. As argued before, the main rationales for an Israeli capability are deterrence of "last resort" or existential threat contingencies and to deter another regional nuclear capability. Deterrence of the use of other non-conventional capabilities might be added with the mentioned complexities and difficulties.

Further clarifying these missions may be an important positive step to allay the concern of Egypt and some other Arab states about Israeli nuclear capability. One way to go about this is through Israeli-American understandings about those missions. These could be transmitted to Egypt and other concerned Arab states. That the U.S. would act as the channel for these communications would add to their credibility.

Another possible CSBM could be to combine two sets of declarations and undertakings: a regional multiparty nonaggression pact coupled with a declaration of "no first use" of WMD. Declarations as such have of course only a limited effect, yet they do have some efficacy. Furthermore, the possibility that the United States would play a role in underwriting such pledges should be weighed and considered, since this might enhance their effectiveness.

The combined declarations would first emphasize that no state would try to violate the status quo; second, since "no first use" depends on adherence to the non-aggression pact, that the Israeli capability is designed only for defense of the status quo and for deterrence against existential threats; and, third, that the Israeli capability would not be used as an instrument for political coercion.

As mentioned, Egypt's position is probably due in part to its perception that the Israeli capability might become an important attribute of overall political power. Earlier in the article we noted that a quest for political power and prestige has always been one of the considerations motivating some of the nuclear powers or the late proliferators to acquire a nuclear weapon capability or option. However, the causal relationship between nuclear weapons capability and political power and influence is complex and unclear. Several examples suggest that nuclear weapons do not really confer political prestige and power on their holders. The nuclear capabilities of Britain and France have not truly enhanced their overall political power. Germany and Japan, on the other hand, though without nuclear weapons, wield great political power. Then again, Russia, with its enormous nuclear capability, is currently in a miserable political situation.

This should not be construed to mean that nuclear weapons have absolutely no correlation with some dimensions of political power. It does however, mean that other variables, primarily economic and technological power, are more important politically. Nuclear capability might become more important in political terms, for example, when an alliance depends on one nuclear power to deter a powerful nuclear adversary. Beyond that, it appears that conventional military power is probably more correlated to overall political influence. This is so because conventional capabilities are so much easier to deploy, threaten with, and use in the service of a range of political objectives.

Therefore, it would serve the interests of both Israel and Egypt if it were made as clear as possible that the Israeli capability cannot under any circumstances be perceived as having any political relevance. Indeed, by maintaining an ambiguous posture Israel has in fact already sent a clear message that its capability is devoid of political significance. This posture should be further reemphasized. The Israeli capability has only one mission: deterrence of existential threats!

One of the Egyptian demands is for transparency of the Israeli capability, to be followed later on by gradual reductions of whatever stocks there are. It appears, however, that transparency might prove counterproductive in different ways. While it is true that the ambiguity surrounding the Israeli posture has eroded considerably, it still serves several important purposes. First, an explicit Israeli capability coupled with greater transparency could strain and complicate Israeli-American relations. The U.S. is committed to non-proliferation by practice as well as by law. An explicit Israeli capability might force the U.S. to act against Israel or, short of this, to undermine its overall anti-proliferation policy. And Israel itself is interested in the persistence of that policy, which it considers an important hedge against further proliferation in the Middle East by some of its bitterest adversaries, such as Iraq and Iran. Second, disclosure would be an irreversible act. Following it, it is difficult to imagine that any Israeli government would be willing to forgo whatever capability the country might have. Once things become explicit, attitudes and interests tend to coalesce around them, bringing into existence a powerful lobby which would most probably preempt any move toward nuclear arms control. Indeed, an explicit posture might increase the pressures on Arab governments to invest greater resources in nuclear development. It might also reduce the inhibitions of nuclear suppliers against transferring sensitive technology and knowhow to Middle Eastern states including those opposed to the status quo. Finally, a breakdown in the political process after disclosure would create a stalemate and would again increase pressures on Arab governments to invest in the nuclear path, thus in turn inhibiting Israeli readiness to limit and reduce its own capabilities. It appears, therefore, that we can adduce a whole series of arguments why disclosure, transparency and an explicit Israeli posture might strain Israeli-American relations and, more important from the Arab point of view, also create difficult dilemmas for them, finally perhaps making nuclear arms control even more difficult to achieve.

Finally, Israel's concerns about present and future security threats makes her extremely suspicious of any discussion of the nuclear issue. This, in combination with the Egyptian insistence on precisely this issue led to the breakdown in the ACRS negotiations. This led Israeli decision makers to the "slippery slope" theory, *vis-à-vis* any discussion of the nuclear issue in whatever context would lead inevitably and invariably to the domino effect whereby Israel will have eventually to accept all the Egyptian demands. It is possible however, to develop negotiating forums within which some dimensions of the slow and very long process towards nuclear arms control could be discussed between Israelis and Egyptians.

Deterrence and Reassurance

The Middle East is presently in a transitory phase. Continuation of the peace process and better relations between Israel and Egypt could create the framework within which the main regional powers at the heart of the Middle East might gradually move from mutual suspicions and concerns induced by the continuous specter of the security dilemma, to a system in which "common" security characterizes interstate relations. As mentioned before, this would involve major changes in the "rules of the game" between Arab states and Israel as well as among the Arab states themselves. During the transitory stage, which might extend over many years, the emphasis should be put on different packages of cooperation, CSBM and stable deterrence. The role of deterrence will begin to diminish only when the region moves into a more distant phase of "common" security. It should be added in this context that areas of even "cooperative" security (which goes beyond "common" security) might emerge even before then. It is likely, for example, that if the Israeli-Palestinian peace process proceeds, Jordan-Israel and the Palestinian entity could create an area of cooperative security. Deterrence, however, might continue to characterize Israeli relations with other regional powers. The question then should be how to allow deterrence to be attuned to different strategies of reassurance. This relates also to nuclear deterrence.

Several mechanisms could be envisaged to fit deterrence and reassurance. First, Endorsement by all regional actors of strategies designed to defend the *status quo* which would be formed following the completion of the peace process.

Second, trade-off transactions of measures on different levels of inter-state relations. For example, Israeli political measures through territorial concessions, in exchange for security measures designed to enhance Israel's strategic situation.

Third, the non-use of WMD threats for the achievement of political purposes.

Fourth, a high level of American involvement in the emerging structure of peace, designed to compensate parties in case other parties defected from the agreements.

Fifth, creating frameworks for non-provocative deterrence. This could be done, for example, through de-emphasizing capabilities which could be best used in surprise attacks.

Sixth, gradual and steady movement toward different types of common security through a whole range of CSBM.

The fit between deterrence and reassurance is by no means an easy one. It depends to an extent on a change in the overall political-strategic relations in the Middle East. But even before that, some of the ideas mentioned here could help to develop "defensive deterrence" rather than "offensive deterrence" with the former being more conducive to the evolvement of reassurance strategies.

Summation

Since the beginning of the peace process with President Sadat's visit to Jerusalem in November of 1977, Israeli security has undergone a major change for the better. The probability of another war initiated by a leading Arab state or a coalition has diminished considerably. However, different types of security threats persist with the most serious being the possible proliferation of nuclear weapons in the Middle East. In view of that, Israel is likely to maintain her ambiguous nuclear posture for quite a long time. At the same time, because of a combination of political and strategic reasons, efforts should be made to modify and limit some dimensions of the Israeli nuclear posture. These comprise unilateral Israeli measures as well as formal and informal measures agreed upon between Israel and the U.S. as well as between Israel and Egypt (and other Arab states). While an ambiguous nuclear posture will remain one of the elements of the overall Israeli strategic posture, its role should be limited only to deterrence against the most extreme existential threats, and – with the peace process continuing – should allow scope for the gradual development of a package of reassurance strategies.

Chapter 9

Israel's Nuclear Opacity:
a Political Genealogy[1]

Avner Cohen

The Israeli bomb has been referred as both "the world's worst-kept-secret" and "the bomb-that-never-is." These two phrases together capture the sense of political and epistemological oddity associated with this issue: its presence lies in its absence, its familiarity resides in its unacknowledged status. The Israeli bomb is invisible but known, absent but ever-present.[2]

Israel was the sixth nation in the world, and the first one in the Middle East, to acquire nuclear weapons capability. Its nuclear program started in earnest about four decades ago when it built its main infrastructure in Dimona. Around 1966-67 Israel passed the significant nuclear threshold and on the eve of the Six-Day War it already had rudimentary nuclear capability.[3] By 1970, Israel's nuclear status became presumed worldwide.[4]

Yet Israel's nuclear behavior has been distinctly different from that of the first

---

[1]This paper was written originally in the summer of 1995 and subsequently it became the basis for the introductory chapter in my book, *Israel and the Bomb* (New York: Columbia University Press, 1998). Certain updating and adjustments were made in April 2000 to fit it to this volume.

[2]The editors of *The Economist* manifested this semi paradox in their choice of language. First referring to it as "The Bomb that Never Is," (*The Economist*, October 19, 1991), the next week they called it "The World's Worst-Kept Secret," (*The Economist*, October 26, 1991).

[3]Even Israeli reliable sources have recently acknowledged this. See, Yuval Ne'eman, "Israel in the Nuclear Weapons Age," *Nativ*, September 1995, 38. More about this in later chapters.

[4]Hedrick Smith, "U.S. Assumes the Israelis Have A-Bomb or Its Parts." *New York Times*, July 18, 1970.

five members of the nuclear club. To this day, Israel has not declared itself a member of the nuclear club. Three decades have passed since Prime Minister Levi Eshkol pledged that Israel would not be the first nation in the Middle East to introduce nuclear weapons and none of the subsequent seven Israeli prime ministers – Golda Meir, Yitzhak Rabin, Menachem Begin, Yitzhak Shamir, Shimon Peres, Benjamin Netanyahu and Ehud Barak – have changed an iota in this formula. To this day, the Israeli bomb has remained invisible, veiled and unacknowledged. While Israel's nuclear status has since the early 1970s no longer been ambiguous, its posture and policy have remained fundamentally *opaque*.

Nuclear opacity is a distinct Israeli contribution to the nuclear age. It is Israel's way of "being nuclear." By "nuclear opacity" I refer to a situation where a state's nuclear capability has not been acknowledged but it is firmly recognized in a way that makes a difference in other nation's perceptions, strategies, and actions.[5] Around 1970 Israel had moved into this category.

Since then, opacity became Israel's mode to navigate its way through the maze of paradoxes and dilemmas associated with the advent of nuclear weapons. During the 1970s and 1980s "nuclear opacity" became the fundamental modus operandi of all second-generation nuclear proliferators. In 1974 India crossed the nuclear threshold by conducting a "peaceful nuclear explosion" without calling itself a nuclear weapon state. Less than a decade later, two other states – Pakistan and South Africa – followed the Israeli model, initiating clandestine programs and building weapons, apparently without testing. While apartheid-ruled South Africa eventually rolled back its program in anticipation of the coming of an African National Congress (ANC) led government, Israel, India, and Pakistan became known as the "threshold" states in arms control vernacular, nations that kept their bombs

---

[5]Avner Cohen and Benjamin Frankel, "opaque Nuclear Proliferation," in Benjamin Frankel (ed) *Opaque Nuclear Proliferation* (London: Frank Cass, 1991), 14-44.

undeclared and invisible. India and Pakistan shattered the non-testing norm in May 1998. Israel has remained, at least for now, the sole practitioner of nuclear opacity.

Over the last three decades, Israel's posture of nuclear opacity has become a sturdy element of its national security strategy. Since the 1970s opacity (in Hebrew, *amimut*) became canonized and formalized as Israel's official nuclear doctrine. It is considered by Israelis now as one of their nation's most successful policies, a national strategy that fits perfectly the unique complexity and particularities of Israel's security predicament. Israeli policy-makers – past and present, left and right alike – have learned to view it as both politically indispensable and strategically natural.

While it is true that nuclear opacity looks now to Israelis natural even indispensable, it was not the product of well-thought strategy. The doctrine was formulated to rationalize an existing reality. Opacity grew piecemeal, progressed through distinct stages, and in response to contingent particular political needs. Although the Israeli declaratory posture gives the impression of continuity and uniformity, the particular contours of the Israeli policy were shaped as a result of dynamic and dialectical interactions and unforeseen among many players on different levels.

Like much else in the history of Zionism, opacity is a product of a series of improvisations. It evolved and matured in historical stages that followed one another. Historically, I discern four such stages from the late 1950s until 1970: secrecy, denial, ambiguity and finally, opacity. The sources of opacity are multiple. Generically, I distinguish among four types of sources: domestic, international (first France and later, most importantly, the United States), regional and conceptual-technical.

This paper is an effort to outline briefly the genealogy of Israel's policy of nuclear opacity. It focuses primarily on the period from the mid and late 1950s until around 1970, during which the Israeli nuclear program became a full technological, strategic and political reality.

The Domestic Sources

The domestic sources of opacity involve attitudes of individuals, deliberations and debates among elite groups inside and outside the government, and broader societal-cultural attitudes regarding nuclear weapons. Prior to the disclosure of the Dimona reactor' in December 1960, during the phase of complete secrecy, the attitudes of David Ben-Gurion – Israel's first prime minister and the father founder of the nuclear project – played a crucial role in shaping the contours of Israel's nuclear policy. Though Ben-Gurion had no sense of the idea of nuclear opacity, let alone the terminology, his instinctive attitudes on this matter proved fateful for future opacity. His dual role as minister of defense and prime minister allowed him to make all the big decisions on his own. Until the deal with France was finalized in late 1957 there were hardly any political-domestic consultations. When the big decisions concerning Dimona and related issues were made in 1957-58 Ben-Gurion shared with his senior colleagues only the minimum necessary; it was only discussed on a "need to know" basis.

Secrecy, concealment and vagueness were Ben-Gurion's traits in dealing with this subject, at home and abroad, for the entire period that he was Israel's prime minister. Michael Bar Zohar, one of Ben-Gurion's biographers, elaborated on his tendency to avoid discussing long-term policy objectives, unless it was absolutely necessary and unavoidable.[6] Shimon Peres focused on this general point with regard to the nuclear issue when he commented on Ben-Gurion's reluctance to "nail down" Dimona's long-term objectives.[7] In another occasion Peres recalled that in the days

---

[6]Michael Bar Zohar, *Ben Gurion*, (Tel Aviv: Zamora Bitan, 1987), Vol., III, 1400 (in Hebrew).
[7]Shimon Peres, "About Shalheveth," in *Shalheveth Freier: 1920-1994* (Tel Aviv: Israel Atomic Energy Commission, 1995), 12-13 (in Hebrew).

of the project "we never talked about nuclear weapons, not even in internal discussions, we always talked about an 'option.'" Even with his close political colleagues who knew something about the project, Ben-Gurion was vague about the security motivation of the Dimona project, making ambiguous references to the need to develop a national nuclear energy infrastructure in a manner that would create a "nuclear option" for both civilian and military applications available for future decision-makers.

Apparently, Ben-Gurion himself was not clear in his own mind in those days how far Israel should go with its nuclear pursuits, and what posture he should pursue. So he improvised one step at a time. To discuss long-term goals prematurely could compromise the security of the entire young project, at home and abroad. This reluctance at the very highest level to "nail down" long-term objectives was among the early tenets of opacity. To this day, this taboo has persisted.

Another important tenet of opacity involves the strategy Ben-Gurion chose to present the project to the United States in December 1960. Ben-Gurion chose the path of denial: he denied that Dimona was about security; he presented Dimona as exclusively civilian-peaceful infrastructure. Why did Ben-Gurion choose to be less-than-honest from the very start with the United States? It may be that part of the answer resides in Ben-Gurion's domestic situation. The American exposure came in a most unfortunate time for Ben Gurion: at the height of the Lavon Affair.[8] Though the two issues were substantially unrelated, they were politically related. In

---

[8]The Lavon Affair is commonly regarded as Israel's biggest political scandal. It originated in 1960 when Pinhas Lavon, then the Secretary General of the Union Federation (Histadrut), demanded that Prime Minister David Ben Gurion exonerate him of the charge that he had been responsible for the so-called intelligence "mishap" in Egypt, in 1954, when Lavon was Minister of Defense. Ben Gurion refused and the affair led to a major crisis in Israel's ruling party, MAPAI. The controversy over the [7]"Lavon Affair" continued until the mid-1960s, weakening both MAPAI and Ben Gurion's leadership. The American disclosure of the Dimona reactor, as well as the domestic debate about the Dimona project, were overshadowed and entangled with the controversy over the "Lavon Affair." See, Shabtai Teveth, Ben Gurion's Spy: The Story of the Political Scandal that Shaped Modern Israel (New York: Columbia University Press, 1996.

December 1960 Ben-Gurion was a weakened national leader, exhausted by the Lavon Affair and by the bitter generational struggle over leadership that it produced. The Dimona project was an item in this political struggle. His weakness at home was probably a factor that shaped his choice of strategy in response to the American demand for explanation about Dimona. Constrained by earlier assurances he had given to Charles de Gaulle and by his struggle at home, Ben-Gurion was determined to avoid a path of confrontation with the United States over Dimona. He could not control the outcome of such confrontation, and he recognized that it could be disastrous both for the Dimona project and his own leadership. Denial involved no immediate public confrontation with the United States.

Ben-Gurion's strategy of denial, however, had profound consequences on Israel's nuclear discourse. It created a climate that made public nuclear debate difficult, if not impossible. To criticize Ben-Gurion on the Dimona project would imply that his statement to the Knesset was not truthful; this could be damaging to Israel and would be looked upon as an unpatriotic act. Virtually all Zionist parties, left and right alike, felt inhibited to voice reservations in public. For one thing, due to secrecy and the technological complexity of the issue, few were competent and informed to debate the issue. For another thing, even those who understood Ben-Gurion's interest in a nuclear option were instinctively reluctant to debate the issue in public. Notwithstanding reservations about how the project had been decided and executed, Zionist parties were committed to the imperative of *Kdushar Ha-bitachon* – the sanctity of security. For those few who did insist on debating the issue in public, the procedures of the Military Censor made it difficult for them to state their case properly. All in all, the taboo was more self-imposed than imposed by law. This taboo, too, is among the most powerful societal sources of opacity, and has endured the present time.

Around 1962, more than four years after the Dimona project had been initiated, the hidden nuclear dilemma resurfaced politically in two ways. First, the Knesset was no longer ready to be bypassed and ignored. Parliamentarian leaders demanded that Ben-Gurion share information with them on a strictly secret basis. Ben-Gurion agreed and a seven-member sub-committee, made of the leaders of the major parties, was secretly formed to oversee the nuclear project. It became the most distinguished and prestigious Knesset sub-committee. By sharing sensitive information (mostly financial and technological) with this committee on a strictly secret basis (members were not even allowed to take notes in those briefings), Ben-Gurion assured that public debate would not take place. Being sworn to secrecy, these Knesset members became, for all practical purposes, the project's gatekeepers, they almost never questioned the principles, they never discussed the issue in public, and they made the issue off-limits to domestic politics. This fundamental pattern, too, was a domestic source of opacity.

The second action Ben-Gurion took in 1962 was opening the nuclear dilemma to a selected group of Israeli defense leaders, past and present. The issue at stake was whether Israel should make fundamental changes in its military doctrine and force structure: whether Israel should invest its limited sources on non-conventional capabilities (nuclear, missiles) or continue to modernize its conventional forces. The timing of those high-level discussions was triggered in part by Egypt's missile project and by the necessity to make basic decisions since Dimona was moving towards completion. By that time there already had been a quiet but fierce doctrinal debate between those who supported investment in modernizing the conventional forces (armor, tactical air force) and those who were advocating revolutionary shift to non-conventional technologies, missiles and nuclear. In 1962, Ben-Gurion decided to conduct a seminar-like debate between the two schools before a decision was made. Peres and Dayan represented the pro-nuclear view, advocating what Peres called in those days "the doctrine of self-reliance" and the view that for the long-run

Israel would not be able to compete in a conventional arms race with the Arabs. Ultimately, nuclear weapons would force the Arabs to abandon hopes of settling the conflict by military means. Allon and Galili represented the other view, disagreeing with Dayan's pessimism and warned of the danger in applying the nuclear deterrence calculus to the Israeli context.

Ben-Gurion was reportedly reluctant to make a final doctrinal choice. He left the big issue open, while making small decisions. For the time being Israel would not invest its limited funds in order to shift towards nuclear doctrine. Instead, it would continue to invest most of its funds on strong tactical air force and tanks. Still, Ben-Gurion initiated a missile project and continued with the plans to finish the nuclear infrastructure but not as a crash program. It turned out that the way Ben-Gurion handled the dilemma in 1962-63 had a lasting effect, much beyond the particulars of the time. This way of resolving the dilemma by default and postponement, while in the meantime maintaining the conventional balance and treating the nuclear option as insurance, became the mark of Israel's pattern of proliferation. Israel had been reluctant to accept the nuclear reality through the front door. Inevitably, it created a situation in which the nuclear issue sneaked in quietly through the back door. This was another early source of Israeli opacity.

The seeds of opacity that had been planted during the Ben-Gurion era deepened during the Eshkol era. The nuclear issue remained greatly isolated and insulated from the rest of the domestic politics agenda. Eshkol, like his predecessor, made nuclear decisions in consultations with a handful of ministers and aides. Until his resignation in 1965, Peres was still the man in charge of the project under the prime minister. Later, Zvi Dinstein replaced him, while Galili, Allon, Eban and Rabin became among Eshkol's closest advisors. Eshkol rarely brought the nuclear issue to the cabinet, except to approve his plans for its reorganization in 1966.

During the bitter rift between Ben-Gurion and Eshkol, which led in 1965 to a split within the ruling MAPAI party, the special apolitical status of the nuclear issue was put to a test. Ironically, it was Ben-Gurion's new party, RAFI, which had now an interest in using Dimona as its own achievement and to charge Eshkol with dangerous concessions to the United States. While Ben-Gurion and Peres hinted in that direction, they refrained from using the issue politically in an explicit way. Here, too, Ben-Gurion's nuclear legacy lasted; the taboo prevailed and the nuclear issue kept its non-partisan status. This pattern, too, became an important tenet of Israeli opacity.

Prior to the Six Day War, as Israel was approaching the realization of its nuclear option, Eshkol ordered that a nuclear policy consistent with his political commitment to the United States be formulated. New advisory bodies were secretly formed to deal with those new challenges; they were small, highly secretive, and a-political. Eshkol shifted Ben-Gurion's denial policy into a policy of ambiguity. In line with his commitment to President Johnson not to introduce nuclear weapons into the Middle East, Eshkol deepened his commitment to a strong posture of conventional deterrence through arms purchases from the United States. Eshkol thought of the nuclear option not as an instrument for deterring the Arabs, but rather as a last resort option and a security hedge vis-a-vis the United States. The pledge not to introduce nuclear weapons became the mark of Eshkol's ambiguous nuclear policy. This was another step in the journey towards opacity.

After the 1967 war and in the wake of the advent of the NPT in 1968, Israel drifted towards a bomb-in-the basement posture. It was the post-1967 geopolitical environment, compounded with bureaucratic momentum, which fueled the drift from ambiguity to opacity. The war created a new national agenda in which the nuclear issue had an even lesser role to play. As domestic politics became less relevant to the nation's nuclear policy, bureaucratic politics became more of a factor. It was appointed guardians, not politicians, who made the real decisions. On the matter of the NPT, for example, the issue was hardly discussed in the cabinet. By 1970, a solid tradition had been established which held that the political arena was not the appropriate forum to decide the nation's nuclear policy. This pattern, too, was an important tenet of opacity.

The International Sources

The second generic source that shaped Israel's nuclear posture was interaction with outside powers. In the period prior to 1970, two international powers were especially important to that effort. France was the country that introduced Israel not only to nuclear technology but also the delicate art of opaque nuclear politics. The United States was the superpower that was in search of its own global non-proliferation policy at the time that Israel was making its first steps in this area. In retrospect, the United States shaped Israeli opacity more than any other state. In return, the United States was Israel's unknowing partner in the making of opacity.

France

France of the Fourth Republic was Israel's first and foremost guide to the nuclear age. In Paris, in the mid-late 1950s, Shimon Peres and his associates learned first-hand how a democratic nation can go nuclear without making an explicit national decision to do so. France was the nation that (unknowingly) "introduced" opacity to Israel as a political mode of "going nuclear." Under the Fourth Republic, important nuclear activities were made piecemeal by sympathetic politicians and administrators acting on their own, while the official government could maintain, and rightly so, that no final political decision on nuclear weapons had been made. However, the period of French nuclear opacity was short-lived. It ended in April 1958 (two months before the Fourth Republic ceased) when France openly decided to conduct a nuclear test in the Sahara in early 1960. Still, the French pattern seems to shape the early Israeli nuclear behavior, even in determining the nuclear understandings and agreements with France itself.

The political sensitivities and constraints both in France and Israel forced Ben-Gurion and his nuclear lieutenants not only to maintain strict secrecy about their nuclear activities in France, but also to be non-explicit, tentative, ambiguous, even deceptive about their long-term intentions, ideas and plans. Israel, unlike France, had a strong and autocratic leader who decided single-handedly to initiate a national nuclear project, however, like the French case (but for different reasons), he was reluctant to make an explicit nuclear decision. On the domestic scene the French way of doing nuclear business fitted Ben-Gurion's ever-present desire to keep vague about the program's objectives. As in the French case, the Israeli project's leaders fragmented their activities into smaller sub-projects, all officially explained in terms of exploratory and preliminary preparations for a future national energy program – not a final decision about anything. As to military applications, reference was vague, tentative and always in terms of an "option." This kind of discourse was influenced by the French domestic discourse. In retrospect, Israel excelled in applying the French pattern beyond the limits of the original.

But even more important was the manifestation of opaque discourse on the external scene in France itself. Peres and Ernst David Bergmann, the chairman of the Israeli Atomic Energy Commission (and the head of research at the Ministry of Defense), identified France as Israel's most likely source of nuclear assistance, fashioning an alliance with France's nuclear enthusiasts at a time that French political leadership was still undecided and divided about France's own nuclear future. Both sides of the deal, French and Israeli, shared similar nuclear dreams of an independent deterrent that they could hardly speak about freely and explicitly. Those French nuclear enthusiasts greatly helped Peres in 1956-57 to put together the Dimona deal in a way so that its significance was kept concealed. According to French sources, on both content and format, the Dimona agreements manifested the art of doing business opaquely. By separating the political, technical and commercial aspects of the deal, its architects made it look innocuous – its real significance was compartmentalized and concealed. In the political document Peres signed, Israel committed itself to use the reactor for peaceful purposes. Apparently, no reference to the reprocessing plant and other sensitive issues appeared anywhere in the state-to-state agreements.

It was during Ben-Gurion's last three years in office that he learned the externally imposed limits on Israel's freedom of action in the nuclear field. He had to protect the Dimona project on two fronts: first, quietly with President de Gaulle of France and second, more publicly with American Presidents Eisenhower and Kennedy.

The United States

If France was the nation from which Israel had learned how a democracy can go nuclear opaquely, the United States was the superpower whose response to Israel's nuclear program greatly shaped the way Israel stumbled into opacity. The historical record indicates that Israel's unique political way of acquiring nuclear capability, and the mode of nuclear proliferation it developed, was closely related to the evolution of American non-proliferation policy in the 1960s.

The United States was not in a position to stop the Israeli nuclear program, but the American security/nuclear dialogue significantly determined the political mode under which Israel went nuclear. Israel went nuclear opaquely, not overtly, in a way that carefully considered American policies and deliberately avoided defying American non-proliferation policy. During the 1960s, while four American administrations came and went, the United States and Israel groped for answers that would satisfy strategic needs, national goals and political requirements. The search continued for nearly a decade. Three pairs of American-Israeli leaders made the critical and distinct stages in that search: Kennedy-Ben-Gurion, Johnson-Eshkol and Nixon-Meir. In a kind of Hegelian-like dialectical path, the search progressed through three distinct political stages, for each pair of interlocutors: confrontation, ambiguity and reconciliation. Israel's nuclear opacity was the ultimate answer to this decade-long search.

In turn, the Israeli nuclear case was an important factor in the shaping and evolution of American non-proliferation policy throughout the 1960s. In a sense, Israel was the first case of nuclear weapons proliferation with which the United States had to contend, beyond Russia, Britain, France and China, at a time when the United States had not yet developed a coherent non-proliferation policy. Israel was a case of a friendly and small state surrounded by bigger enemies and (unlike Germany) outside the sphere of superpower containment. Moreover, unlike the cases of the Soviet Union, the UK, and France (and later China or India), Israel did not aspire to the status of the great powers. And, most significantly, Israel enjoyed strong domestic support in America. The challenge of how to apply the long-held American opposition to the spread of nuclear weapons to the complexity of the Israeli case had lasting effect that went far beyond the Israeli case. The Israeli case was an important learning experience for those three American administrations in their search for a coherent non-proliferation policy.

The Israeli nuclear case evolved in the 1960s as the Kennedy and Johnson administrations grappled to form American non-proliferation policy aiming at creating a non-proliferation order based on international treaty. Israel was a key state for the evolution of American ideas about non-proliferation. Israel's nuclear posture evolved in the 1960s in interaction with the evolution of the U.S. non-proliferation policies. Viewed in this way, opacity came into being as a joint American-Israeli effort to respond to their respective dilemmas, as the co-evolution of Israel's proliferation policy and American non-proliferation policy. The complexity of the Israeli case was an important impetus for the United States in seeking the NPT. By the same token, the specter of such a treaty was an important factor in moderating Israeli nuclear ambitions.

On at least eight occasions during the 1960s, the United States came to the point of a confrontation or near-confrontation with the Israeli government over Israel's nuclear program. The first time was in December 1960, when the Eisenhower administration revealed publicly the existence of Israel's plans to build a nuclear reactor in Dimona and demanded Israeli explanations and reassurances about the reactor's peaceful purpose. Ben-Gurion responded by providing public and private assurances that the Dimona reactor was for "peaceful purposes." But no agreement about American visits to Dimona was struck. That confrontation was short-lived because it started in the last few weeks of the departing Eisenhower administration. The challenge was left to the incoming Kennedy administration.

After it took office in January 1961, the Kennedy administration dealt with the political sensitivity and technical reality of the Israeli nuclear program as a long-term policy issue. If the United States wanted to draw the line on nuclear proliferation, as Kennedy believed it should, the Israeli program had to be curbed. Kennedy found himself in a dilemma. He had a deep personal commitment to the cause of nuclear non-proliferation, but he also had a strong commitment to the security and well-being of Israel. This was a time when the United States had not yet developed a coherent global nonproliferation policy. The Kennedy administration found itself searching for a nonproliferation policy *vis-à-vis* Israel while other allies of the United States – the UK and France – were developing their own nuclear arsenals.

President Kennedy twice tried to intervene in Israel's nuclear affairs, but confrontation was averted in each case through delicate quiet diplomacy at the highest level. In early 1961, shortly after he took office, Kennedy was determined to obtain verifiable assurances, by way of American visits on site, of the peaceful nature of the Dimona project. Ben-Gurion agreed and invited two prominent American scientists to visit Dimona. The visit revealed no indications of a weapons program. It was also a precedent. In the wake of the scientists' positive report the two leaders met in New York on May 30, 1961. No better example of that high-level compromise exists than the discussion of nuclear issues at that meeting. The two leaders wanted to avoid a confrontation, and each had a sense of his own political limits, at home and abroad. Kennedy did not raise questions which went beyond Ben-Gurion's tentative assurances on the peaceful purpose of the Dimona reactor. Ben-Gurion respected Kennedy's political needs and did not question American non-proliferation policy as it applied to Israel. Both nations thereby planted the seeds of opacity.[9]

The meeting in New York presaged the future by setting, unintentionally, the parameters by which both nations would conduct their dealings on the nuclear issue. The verbal understandings reached at that meeting allowed the nuclear issue to be left off the bilateral agenda for almost two years. The issue of Dimona, however, resurfaced in the spring of 1963, as the Dimona reactor was about to become operational. Kennedy was focusing on the problem of global proliferation in connection with the anticipated negotiation of a test ban treaty, what became the Partial Test Ban Treaty (PTBT) of July 1963. Ben-Gurion's pressure on the United States for American security assurances to Israel was his response to Kennedy's pressure on the nuclear issue. Delaying his response to Ben-Gurion's request for U.S. security guarantees, Kennedy wrote of his concern about the introduction of advanced weaponry (nuclear arms and ballistic missiles) into the Middle East. This dramatic correspondence between the two leaders continued until Ben-Gurion's

[9]Avner Cohen, *Israel and the Bomb* (New York: Columbia University Press, 1998), 99-113; Cf., Avner Cohen, "Most Favored Nation," *The Bulletin of the Atomic Scientists*, January-February 1995 (Vol. 51, No 1), 44-53.

resignation on 16 June 1963, the day on which Kennedy's tough letter was to be delivered to him. The letter was never delivered to Ben-Gurion because on that very day he resigned from office.[10]

However, Kennedy did not cease his pressure on Israel. Prime Minister Levi Eshkol took office in late June 1963 during the most severe American-Israeli confrontation over the nuclear issue. Days after he took office, he received one of the toughest messages an Israeli prime minister had ever received from an American president, a slightly modified version of Kennedy's letter to Ben-Gurion. Kennedy demanded of Eshkol a verified implementation of the arrangements Ben-Gurion had agreed to in principle, which would confirm the peaceful purpose of Dimona. The key to these arrangements was Kennedy's demands for "semi-annual" visits by American scientists to Dimona. After weeks of a near-crisis situation, on 19 August 1963, Eshkol proposed a formula, allowing American visits in Dimona, which appeared to satisfy Kennedy's demands. Eshkol's formula, however, left somewhat vague the issue of timing and exact nature of the American visits to Dimona. Once again, a showdown was averted, as Eshkol was able to offer a compromise that seemed to meet Kennedy's demands.[11]

Although the nuclear understandings reached in August 1963 were vague, they proved lasting and decisive. Lyndon Johnson, who succeeded Kennedy in November 1963, had to implement the Kennedy-Eshkol understanding. Johnson was not as personally committed as his predecessor to the cause of nuclear non-proliferation. The Johnson administration pressed Eshkol to allow it to reassure Nasser on Dimona during Eshkol's first visit in Washington in 1964. In the coming years it made at least two high-level attempts to place Dimona under International Atomic Energy Agency (IAEA) safeguards – in the Harriman-Komer visit to Israel

---

[10]Ibid, 115-36.
[11]Ibid, 153-74.

in 1965 and in connection to the negotiations over the sale of Skyhawks in 1966 – but it backed off in face of Israeli resistance. Eshkol was not ready to go beyond his ambiguous pledge that Israel would not be the first country to introduce nuclear weapons into the Middle East and the Johnson administration had no recourse but to accept it. The era of confrontation was replaced with the era of ambiguity.

The seventh time that Israel and the United States had a confrontation over the nuclear issue was during 1968, Johnson's last year in office and the year in which the NPT was signed. The Johnson administration exerted pressure on Israel to sign the NPT. At first Israel seemed to acquiesce in the American request, but by summer 1968 it became clear that Jerusalem was determined not to sign the treaty. The issue came to a point of confrontation in late 1968 as Israel negotiated for the first sale of Phantoms. The American pressure was mounting, but on the eve of the presidential election in November 1968 Johnson decided to put an end to the pressure. Israel received the Phantoms and did not sign the NPT.

In July 1969 the United States conducted the last visit to the Dimona site. Later that year, Prime Minister Golda Meir reached a new kind of tacit understanding with President Richard Nixon which ended the American visits in Dimona. According to this understanding, Israel refrained from making public reference to its nuclear capability – no declaration, no testing – while the United States looked the other way at the Israeli nuclear case. With this understanding, nuclear opacity emerged in its full-blown form. This was the transition from ambiguity to reconciliation.

As a whole, the American-Israeli security/nuclear dialogue throughout the 1960s evolved gradually around three fundamental axes: (a) supply of American conventional weapons to Israel; (b) American assurances on Israeli security; (c) inhibitions on Israel's nuclear program. A few times they came to the verge of collision but always a public showdown was avoided because ultimately neither party was interested in that. These confrontational and near-confrontational episodes created a binational learning curve. It was a process of trial and error, largely tacit, through which both the United States and Israel learned how to cope with the Israeli nuclear case.

The Arab "Contribution" to Opacity

The third generic source of influence on the Israeli nuclear posture was the Arab world, in particular Egypt (which in the 1960s was called the United Arab Republic, [UAR]). Just as Israel was committed to attain a technological edge *vis-à-vis* the Arabs, it was also committed not to provoke the Arabs to take a nuclear path of their own. It was obvious that if Israel provoked the Arabs to initiate their own nuclear project, it might be even more dangerous for Israel than a situation in which neither side has a nuclear program. That is, the Israeli nuclear project, under adverse circumstances, could undermine its own cause: instead of creating stable deterrence that could eventually lead to peace, it could actually make Israel less secure and more vulnerable. Ben-Gurion's nuclear critics in Israel warned that his nuclear obsession could bring about his ultimate nightmare: a pan-Arabic nuclear project headed by Egypt's Gamal Abdel Nasser. Secrecy, denial and ambiguity were essential to keep the Arabs at bay.

In the late 1950s, prior to the exposure of Dimona, a key aspect of the total secrecy policy was to keep the Arabs uninformed as long as possible. It was recognized that the French assistance could be jeopardized due to Arab pressure. One of the major reasons for adopting the denial path was to lessen Egyptian suspicions. In his meeting with President Kennedy in May 1961 Ben-Gurion agreed that the reassuring report of the American scientists' visit in Dimona would be passed on to Nasser. Since the first visit to Dimona in 1961, the United States consistently insisted on the need to reassure Nasser that Dimona was believed to be peaceful, as

Israeli leaders declared. Without such reassurances the Americans were concerned about the possibility that if Egypt believed that Dimona was about to produce nuclear weapons this could trigger an Egyptian military attack on the Dimona site.

This concern was a constant feature of the American-Israeli dialogue in that period. In the early-mid 1960s there was a common view in Washington (White House, State Department, CIA) that an Israeli bomb could inevitably lead to regional hostilities. The United States was concerned that, apart from the possibility of Egyptian preemption, Israeli nuclearization could lead to the Soviet Union becoming directly involved in nuclear escalation in the region, either by providing Egypt with actual nuclear weapons or by backing it with explicit Soviet nuclear cover. Nasser, himself, declared that he could not tolerate the development of nuclear weapons in Israel, and both the United States and Israel were concerned about the possibility of Egyptian military action against Dimona.

These predictions did not materialize. It appears that Israel's low-key declaratory policy, along with the American reassurances, had a calming effect on the behavior of the Arab world. As long as Israel kept a policy of low profile, Arab governments and leaders tended to marginalize the Israeli nuclear issue. By and large, the Israeli nuclear program did not become in the 1960s a major political issue in the Arab world. The issue usually came out publicly only in response to news reports overseas. Egypt, the country that had been expected to lead the Arab reaction to Dimona, had a surprisingly mild attitude on this issue. When Nasser came out with a series of tough declarations on Dimona, the Eshkol government responded by publicly stating that Israel would not be the first to introduce nuclear weapons to the region.

Still, there are indications that the Israeli nuclear issue played some role in the series of inadvertent miscalculations that led to the 1967 Six Days War. While it was not the hidden cause of the war, nuclear-related events and considerations, on both the Egyptian and Israelis sides, played a significant role in the evolution of the crisis that preceded the war. In particular, Egyptian reconnaissance flights over Dimona during the May 1967 crisis – at the time the issue was kept secret – changed dramatically the mood among Israeli policy-makers in a dramatic way; it reinforced the intelligence indications that the nuclear complex at Dimona was a top priority target in Egyptian war plans. On the Israeli side, in the days prior to the war Israel moved its rudimentary nuclear capability into a state of operational alert. The Egyptian defeat created circumstances that eased the Israeli drift from ambiguity to opacity. However, the Arab pattern of "taking advantage" of Israel's nuclear opacity in order to maintain a low profile on the nuclear issue continued.[12]

In retrospect, and somewhat ironically, there was a certain pattern of interaction between the Israeli nuclear policy and the Arab attitudes on the nuclear issue. As long as the Israelis kept the nuclear issue low profile, so did the Arabs. As in the Israeli case, the Arab nuclear pattern seemed a product of evolving historical contingencies, combined with societal-cultural attitudes. In a peculiar way, then, the Arabs were also a partner, junior perhaps, in the making of opacity.

The Conceptual-Definitional Source of Opacity

Finally, an important aspect of the makeup of Israel's nuclear opacity involved a cluster of conceptual-epistemic-technical issues concerning the definition of nuclear weapons: What does constitute a state crossing the nuclear weapons status? Where is the nuclear weapons threshold? What is the meaning of Israel's "non-introduction" pledge?

---

[12]Ibid, 159-76. Cf., Avner Cohen, "Cairo, Dimona and the June 1967 War," *Middle East Journal*, Vol. 50., No. 2, (1996), 190-210; see also Avner Cohen, "Nuclear Arms in Crisis Under Secrecy: Israel and the 1967 and 1973 Wars," in *Planning the Unthinkable: Military Doctrine for the Use of Weapons of Mass-Destruction*, Eds. Peter R. Lavoy, Scott D. Sagan and James J. Wirtz, (Ithaca: Cornell University Press, forthcoming).

In the case of all five declared nuclear states – the United States, the Soviet Union, Britain, France and China – crossing the nuclear threshold was symbolized by a distinct act: a full-yield nuclear test. For years a nuclear test was taken as a necessary step in the nuclear proliferation ladder both for technical and political reasons. Technically, testing of weapons system – any weapons system – was considered the last stage in the development process. The development process cannot be completed without a series of field tests of the entire system. Testing, in this technical sense, is a measure of operational reliability.[13] As early as the Soviet Union exploded their first atomic bomb in August 1949 it became evident that traces of a full-yield nuclear explosion cannot be concealed. Politically, a first full-yield nuclear test is the act that signifies the transition from the phase of secrecy to the public phase; the test is an act of "political introduction." The test provided a clear-cut and visible criterion for recognizing when and how the nuclear threshold had been crossed.

Viewing the nuclear threshold in this way, nuclear proliferation was perceived as an either/or process: as long as country did not conduct a test it was still given the benefit of the doubt concerning its nuclear status. In the absence of solid information, it is difficult to determine how far a nation has advanced in its nuclear development. Furthermore, even if solid intelligence information exists, there could be powerful political and operational inhibitions against exposing it.

Israel made its nuclear pursuit piecemeal and by taking advantage of this conceptualization of the proliferation ladder. It went nuclear while avowing privately and publicly not to be the first to introduce nuclear weapons. If "introduction" means

---

[13]It was known early on, of course, that a state could manufacture a yield producing first-generation fission bomb even without testing it, as the United States did with its Hiroshima bomb. Testing is required for more sophisticated weapons, small-enhanced radiation weapon or H-bomb. See, "Nuclear Tests and Nuclear Weapons," in Benjamin Frankel (editor*), Opaque Nuclear Proliferation* (London: Cass, 1991), 175-190.

conducting a full-yield nuclear test, Israel avoided – even defied – the political act of "introducing" nuclear weapons. As noted previously, Prime Minister Eshkol resisted pressure from the project's leaders to conduct a nuclear test, keeping his word to Johnson that Israel would not introduce nuclear weapons. Israel crossed the nuclear threshold in a way that made it most difficult to track and to identify. In fact, it went nuclear so opaquely that it appears that its own leaders did not even internalize and digest the strategic and political meaning of the transition. This lack of synchronization came to its peak on the eve of the Six Days War.

A brief analytic detour may illuminate the conceptual-definitional issue involved here. The NPT requires non-nuclear weapon signatories "not to manufacture . . . nuclear weapons or other nuclear explosive devices" (Article II). The NPT itself contains no definition as to what constitutes a "nuclear weapon" apart from a broad reference to all "nuclear explosive devices" (which includes "peaceful nuclear explosion"). As part of the NPT negotiation record suggests, the phrase "nuclear explosive devices" should be understood as the capacity to "release large quantities of energy in a very short period of time from sources of relatively small volume and light weight."[14] The critical operational element in the NPT is the obligation not to *manufacture* a nuclear explosive device. On this matter, too, the NPT itself does not explicate the meaning of this phrase, but its negotiating record (the so called "Foster criteria") suggests a broad interpretation that includes *all* activities that entail the intention to make nuclear weapons.[15]

Based on the available records, during the Eshkol-Johnson period, Israel

---

[14]Cited in George Bunn and Roland M. Timerbaev, *Nuclear Verification Under the NPT*, PPNN Study, No. 5, 1994, 7.

[15]The problem is that, except for the reference to manufacture or acquisition of nuclear explosives, nowhere in the NPT is there an explicit effort to draw the line between legitimate and illegitimate nuclear research activities. The Foster criteria, the authors stress, put the prohibition on manufacture in terms of activities much earlier than just "the final assembly of an explosive device," as Sweden suggested. Nevertheless, it did not list what those activities are but rather defined them by their purpose. Bunn and Timerbaev, ibid.

never explicitly pledged not to manufacture or develop nuclear weapons. All it did pledge was not to introduce such weapons. These are conceptually and politically very different pledges. If the NPT framers intended to overcome the lack of definition of "nuclear weapon" by imposing a general prohibition on all activities connected with "manufacturing" of such weapons, the Israeli pledge was inherently vague as to what exactly "introduce" amounted to. Due to this vagueness, Israel took upon himself in effect no specific limitations on its activities in the area of nuclear weapons, apart from the obvious one not to cross the nuclear threshold, that is, not to test a nuclear device. This allowed Israel to maintain maximum fog on its nuclear activities (short of a nuclear test). From an Israeli perspective, the virtue of the formula resided in its great degree of vagueness

One can say, of course, that the American visits in Dimona were supposed to verify that Israel did not separate plutonium from its reactor fuel, and they seemed to do that. However, the fact remains that elements within the United States intelligence community had suspicions about the credibility of these visits. Since the early to mid 1960, the United States intelligence community believed that Israel had been actively working on nuclear weapons, and that the information obtained from the American visits at Dimona might be misleading. One gets the strong impression that the highest political level of the Johnson administration, as well as the chiefs of the intelligence community, had little appetite to probe the Israeli nuclear issue. Given the extreme sensitivity of the matter, and Israel's absolute opposition to IAEA safeguards in Dimona, the United States had little choice but to accept the "non-introduction" pledge and to make the best of it.

It appears that in the pre-1967 period the United States understood the Israeli pledge as technologically vague but politically clear. It was taken as a political commitment, made at the highest level in Israel, not to cross the nuclear threshold. When Prime Minister Eshkol stated publicly in the Knesset in July 1966 that Israel did not have nuclear weapons and would not introduce them he seemed to equate the absence of weapons with the "non-introduction" pledge. Everything depends, of course, on the exact definition of "nuclear weapons" and the "non-introduction" pledge; such definitions, however, were apparently not discussed in those days between the United States and Israel. Under the circumstances it was better off to leave the operational content of the pledge vague rather than to confront it. The fact that the United States lacked solid evidence as to how close Israel had gotten got to the bomb made it easier for both sides.

The definitional issue about Israel's nuclear status became subtler after the 1967 war. By that time Israel had an interest in "upgrading" the perception of its nuclear program but without breaking its earlier pledge. Professor Amos de-Shalit, a man known to be closely involved in the Israeli nuclear program, acknowledged in a rare interview days after the 1967 war that Israel had the technical knowledge to produce an atomic bomb, and could do so if the government so chose, but that thus far the cabinet opposed such a move.[16] During the battle over the NPT in October 1968 Prime Minister Eshkol and Foreign Minister Eban stated, in almost identical language, that Israel "has now acquired the technical know-how" to produce nuclear weapons, even though, both emphasized, "it was a long way from this to producing nuclear weapons."[17]

While these statements sought to "upgrade" the notion that Israel was technologically advanced in the nuclear-weapons area, they also aimed to maintain the fog about what Israel was exactly doing in the nuclear field. They amounted to a public acknowledgment that Israel had advanced in the nuclear field and should be regarded as having a weapons "potential," "capability," or "option"; at the same time

---

[16]*Ha'aretz,* July 21, 1967.

[17]"Eshkol: Israel Knows the Secret of the Production of Atomic bomb," *Ha'aretz*, October 4, 1968; "Eshkol and Eban Comments on Nuclear Knowledge Without Prior Discussion," *Ha'aretz*, October 8, 1968; "Israeli Nuclear Deterrent Urged by Jerusalem Paper," *New York Times*, October 5, 1968.

they were meant to be consistent with the Israeli pledge not to "introduce" nuclear weapons. The ambiguities that had been avoided for some time became a matter of contention between the United States and Israel in late 1968 during negotiations for the sale of the U.S.-made F-4 aircraft. Indeed, until the 1968 Warnke-Rabin nuclear discussions in November 1968, I found no evidence indicating that the United States officially probed Israel to clarify what it exactly meant by the "non-introduction" pledge.

In those discussions Paul Warnke pressed Ambassador Yitzhak Rabin about the exact status of the Israeli nuclear program. Rabin evaded those efforts first by reiterating the "non-introduction" pledge, and subsequently, in a response to Warnke's pressure to explicate what "non-introduction" really means, he proposed to equate "non-introduction" with a policy of non-testing and non-declaration. Rabin remained silent about whether Israeli actually manufactured nuclear weapons, but insisted on the point that without a test and declaration a state cannot be considered to have introduced nuclear weapons. All weapons systems, he insisted, conventional and unconventional alike, must be tested prior to operational deployment. Without a test it is impossible to introduce any weapon-system from the developers to the users; this is even more so about nuclear weapons. Rabin insisted that for a state to have nuclear weapons means to test and to declare them.[18] He noted that Israel's commitment not to introduce nuclear weapons amounts to a commitment not to make any political use of its nuclear capability. As long as Israel had not conducted a nuclear test, by definition and by practice, it could not be said to have introduced nuclear weapons.[19]

During the early period of the Nixon administration similar questions were

---

[18]Avner Cohen, *Israel and the Bomb*, 311-19. Warnke's own version of that exchange appears in his, "Nuclear Israel," a review of Seymour M. Hersh, *The Samson Option*, in *The Bulletin of Atomic Scientists*, March 1992, pp. 41-42.

[19]Interview with General (Res) Mordechai Hod, Tel Aviv, May 28, 1996.

raised again about the Israeli "non-introduction" pledge. Ambassador Rabin reiterated his explication of the non-introduction formula.[20] The issue was left pending for the Meir-Nixon meeting in late September 1969. The United States no longer asked Israel for clarifications about its nuclear project; as of 1970 there were no more American visits in Dimona. By that time another nuance was added to the scholasticism about the meaning of the "non-introduction" pledge. In conversations between Israelis and Americans on this topic "non-introduction" was often believed to mean that the bomb was there, lacking only one screw (or the equivalent) to make it operational. Only when this "screw" was "screwed in" would a weapon have been "introduced."[21] In any case, the nuclear issue was dropped from the bilateral agenda.

By 1970 it became public that "for at least two years the U.S. Government has been conducting its Middle Eastern policy on the assumption that Israel either possesses an atomic bomb or has component parts available for quick assembly."[22] While there was some disagreement over the issue of the "last screw" – whether Israel should be judged to have atomic weapons before the last screw or piece of the mechanism is hooked up – it was undisputed that Israel was for all practical purposes a nuclear weapons state. Israel had crossed the nuclear threshold. .

The road to nuclear opacity had been traveled.

---

[20]Yitzhak Rabin, *Pinkas Sherut* (Tel Aviv: Ma'ariv, 1979), Vol.2., 251-2 (translation AC).

[21]A letter from former a former senior intelligence official to the author, November 9, 1996. In his letter, the author adds another twist to this matter: "Among Americans it was often said that the Sixth Fleet had long since "introduced nuclear weapons into the Middle East area" therefore if the Israelis built and deployed nuclear weapons, they would, in light of the above, not be technically or legalistically the first but rather the second to introduce etc. American thinking along this line was based on past experience with the Israelis where the placement of a comma or lack of an article definite or indefinite, would often be used to evade the intention of an agreement by providing a legalistic or semantic loophole."

[22]Hedrick Smith, "U.S. Assumes the Israelis Have A-Bomb or its Parts," *New York Times*, July 18, 1970.

Chapter 10

Israel's Position on Arms Control and the Nuclear Non-proliferation Regime

Emily Landau

Introduction

In the past decade, the notion of arms control has assumed a much more prominent role on Israel's security agenda. Before the 1990s, the concept of arms control was relatively foreign to the security debate in Israel – while certain arms control measures had been employed in various aspects of the Arab-Israeli conflict, the term had not been conceptualized or even recognized as having particular relevance to Israel's security concerns. As far as the global non-proliferation regime was concerned, Israel made no real effort to take part in these initiatives. This situation began to change in the late 1980s, with increased reports on the development of weapons of mass destruction (WMD) and their delivery systems in the Middle East. The arms control proposal put forth by Egyptian President Mubarak in April 1990, the 1991 Gulf War, and the arms control proposal introduced by U.S. President Bush in May 1991 in the direct wake of that war, also served to significantly elevate the awareness of all states in the Middle East to the dangers that the presence of weapons of mass destruction posed to the region. This in turn led to a growing acceptance of the need to deal with them.

Due to the increased interest in arms control, it was not surprising that with the launching of the Madrid peace process in 1991, arms control and regional security became the designated topic of one of the five working groups that made up the multilateral track of the Middle East peace process. Israel was involved in these talks during the years 1992-95; they created for the first time a regional framework for conducting an ongoing discussion of arms control issues. Attention was directed to developing an understanding of the relevance of such measures for dealing with the security concerns of states in the Middle East. In the past decade, for the first time Israel also took clear steps in the direction of strengthening the global non-proliferation regime. Signing the Chemical Weapons Convention (CWC) in 1993, and the Comprehensive Test Ban Treaty (CTBT) in 1996 are steps that underscore the significance that Israel attaches to efforts to reduce the global non-conventional weapons threat, and to strengthen the international norm of non-proliferation.

Efforts to take part in arms control initiatives in the non-conventional realm – whether in the regional or global contexts – have consistently placed Israel in a delicate position due to its steadfast policy of ambiguity in the nuclear realm. This policy – whereby Israel neither confirms nor denies any information regarding its assumed nuclear option – is the outgrowth of an understanding reached with the US, and has bolstered Israel's deterrence over the years. Strategic deterrence has been a constant of Israel's security policy, upheld by successive governments. It was endorsed by Prime Minister Ehud Barak as recently as early October 1999. Barak said that "even in peace time, Israel will continue to keep a strategic deterrent potential – for as long a range as necessary, in terms of geography and time."[1] The reason for this is that Israel will continue to face strategic threats from the peripheral states, even after agreements are reached with the Palestinians and Syria. Barak made it clear that he will not agree to concessions regarding Israel's nuclear potential, and will not respond to pressure in this area. The Barak government's position is to continue to uphold the policy of previous governments, whereby Israel will agree to a nuclear weapons free zone (NWFZ) in the Middle East only in the distant future,

---

[1]*Ha'aretz*, 5 October 1999.

after achieving comprehensive peace and conventional and missile arms control. The U.S. continues to support this Israeli stand. According to media reports, the most recent expression of this support came in the form of a letter from U.S. president Bill Clinton to former prime minister Binyamin Netanyahu in which he promised that the U.S. would guard Israel's strategic deterrent, and ensure that Middle East arms control initiatives would not hurt it in the future.[2]

In fact, Israel's position on promoting the non-proliferation of WMD is impacted by a complex web of conflicting strands: Israel accepts the importance of WMD non-proliferation, and the idea of creating a WMD free zone in the Middle East, but faces a real dilemma in terms of having to deal simultaneously with demands in this regard put forth by states with which it has established peaceful relations, and those (not participating in the Middle East peace process) that make the same demands on Israel, but they continue to pose a real threat to Israel's security. Thus, Israel cannot ignore the existence and possible further proliferation of Arab states' WMD capabilities, but is faced with pressing demands from Arab states to deal with its assumed nuclear arsenal by joining international treaties virtually immediately. A related dilemma is that Israel's long-standing policy of ambiguity in the nuclear realm serves its deterrence needs, but is perceived by Arab states as undermining global and regional arms control efforts. The question is whether and how under these circumstances nuclear and other WMD non-proliferation can nevertheless be advanced in the Middle East context.

The proposition that will be advanced below – that the proper framework for dealing with arms control in the Middle East is the regional one – is perhaps not a novel one, but an attempt will be made to base this idea on an assessment of what has

---

[2]Aluf Ben, "Clinton Gave His Word to Netanyahu: Israel's Nuclear Capability Will be Kept" *Ha'aretz*, 14 March 2000.

been achieved so far, the problems that have been encountered, and what is likely to be achievable in the future.

I will begin by providing the background to global efforts to control proliferation of WMD with an emphasis on the nuclear realm. I will then briefly review the major non-proliferation initiatives, highlighting the current dilemmas Israel faces with regard to these efforts. The second part of this article will deal with the regional arms control effort carried out in the framework of the Arms Control and Regional Security Working Group (ACRS), and the possibility for renewing this effort in a manner that would address the concerns of the various parties in the Middle East.

The Global Arena

The global nuclear non-proliferation regime was initially formulated and put into force during the Cold War years. In the context of the bipolar Cold War dynamics, the U.S. and the Soviet Union were investing their energies primarily in the direction of dealing with the bilateral nuclear balance between them, and in preventing the dangers of misescalation and surprise attack. The dangers of unintended use of nuclear weapons by either side were viewed to be so devastating that both recognized their common interest in working toward minimizing this threat. In order to further stabilize the global balance, it was also perceived that additional nuclear proliferation must be prevented. This was the context in which the Nuclear Non-proliferation Treaty (NPT) was formulated in the late 1960s.

In the Cold War period, global dynamics were largely influenced by the dynamics between the two superpowers – the US and the Soviet Union were the major world actors and global politics were framed in light of their strategic interests. Thus, it was not surprising that the NPT treaty was formulated in such a way as to preserve the global balance of power. Nuclear Weapons States (NWS) would remain nuclear (with only a commitment to "pursue negotiations in good faith" on nuclear disarmament, as set out in Article VI of the treaty), and non-nuclear states would also remain non-nuclear. This discriminatory state of affairs became a basic truism of the non-proliferation regime.

With the end of the Cold War, there has been growing pressure on the NWS to meet their commitment to pursue nuclear arms control and disarmament. The Comprehensive Test Ban Treaty (CTBT) and the Fissile Material Cut-off Treaty negotiations (FMCT) have been presented as a means of strengthening the NPT, especially as far as the commitment of the nuclear states to deal with their arsenals. It also constitutes an effort to include Pakistan, India, and Israel in this regime.

But, the question remains whether the overall approach to non-proliferation as developed in the Cold War years is still relevant to the post Cold War world; and whether the NPT regime (even a bolstered one that attempts to tie NWS to their obligations as set forth in the treaty) is still the most relevant framework for dealing with the dangers of global proliferation of nuclear weapons. For the US itself, the post-Cold War world has created a new strategic reality in which the perceived threat of WMD proliferation has become much elevated due to the disappearance of its major Cold War threat: the Soviet Union. In its emerging threat perception, the U.S. believes that it faces non-conventional threats from different states (most notably, Iran, Iraq, and North Korea). This in itself calls into question some of the existing arms control agreements, as has been demonstrated by the debate over the need for national missile defense systems, which may call for certain amendments to the 1972 Anti-ballistic Missile (ABM) bilateral treaty signed between the U.S. and the USSR. The U.S. also recognizes the new significance of regional dynamics in dealing with the threat of proliferation of weapons of mass destruction, and has invested much energy in regional arrangements, such as was the case with ACRS. Nevertheless, in its thinking on global arms control, the US has continued to rely heavily on the international regime as developed in the Cold War years.

As far as Israel is concerned, there are problems with the global approach. Israel faces certain pressures and dilemmas regarding the global regime that can only be dealt with through a sober analysis of regional realities.

Israel and the Global Nuclear Non-proliferation Regime
Nuclear Non-Proliferation Treaty (NPT)

At the NPT Review and Extension Conference in 1995, it was agreed to extend the NPT indefinitely. The conference also adopted a set of principles and objectives, a template against which to measure future implementation of the treaty. The conference empowered PrepComs or review conferences to evaluate implementation on an annual basis. Regarding the Middle East, toward the end of the Conference, an Egyptian draft resolution – supported by most Arab states – was introduced calling on Israel, by name, to accede without delay to the NPT and to place all of its nuclear activities under International Atomic Energy Agency (IAEA) full scope safeguards. An amended Resolution, which did not specifically call on Israel by name, but rather called for all Middle Eastern states to adhere to the NPT and the implementation of comprehensive IAEA safeguards, was in fact adopted by the Conference, although the status of this Resolution was not agreed upon by all sides.

At the May 1998 PrepCom meeting, there was discussion of whether the Resolution is in fact linked to the decisions that were taken at the 1995 Review Conference (Egyptian position) or whether it should be treated as an isolated document (the US view). The May 1999 PrepCom (as formulated in the draft Chairman's working paper) recommended that the provisions of the Resolution on the Middle East adopted by the 1995 Review Conference be reaffirmed at the next

Review Conference to be held in 2000, and that deep concern be expressed that Israel continues to be the only state in the region which has not yet acceded to the Treaty and refuses to place all its nuclear facilities under the full-scope IAEA safeguards without further delay and without conditions. A consensus was not reached on this Chairman's working paper; however, as might have been expected, the Resolution was reaffirmed at the most recent Review Conference that took place in April-May 2000: "The Conference reaffirms the importance of the Resolution on the Middle East adopted by the 1995 Review and Extension Conference and recognizes that the resolution remains valid until the goals and objectives are achieved."[3]

In anticipation of this conference, Israel faced pressure from Arab states – most prominently Egypt – to sign the NPT, as had been the case in the months preceding the NPT Review and Extension Conference of April-May 1995. At the outset of the conference, there were reports of an U.S.-Egyptian understanding that the U.S. would accept Egypt's initiative for specifically naming Israel as the only Middle Eastern state that has not adhered to the NPT, on condition that clear mention would be made of the three additional states who have not yet signed: India, Pakistan and Cuba. This understanding was in fact reflected in the final document; however, Egypt's attempts to also include a decision to appoint a special UN representative to follow up on means for getting Israel to join, failed. As Israel in fact remains the only country in the Middle East that has not signed the NPT, it is not troubled by this statement, especially as no operative steps were taken against it. Taking a decision to sign the NPT would obviously mean an end to Israel's policy of ambiguity in the nuclear realm, and this is clearly not something that the Ehud Barak government intends to do.

---

[3] 2000 Review Conference of the Parties to the Treaty on the Non-Proliferation of Nuclear Weapons, Final Document, 22 May 2000.

The Comprehensive Test-Ban Treaty (CTBT) :

At the 1995 NPT Review and Extension Conference it was also decided to adopt a program of action calling for a CTBT, a Fissile Material Cut-off Treaty and a statement to pursue systemic and progressive efforts to reduce nuclear weapons globally in order to reach the goal of eliminating these weapons.

The goal of the CTBT is to ban all nuclear weapons test explosions and all peaceful nuclear explosions. The treaty will enter into force after ratification by 44 members of the Conference on Disarmament (CD) that have nuclear reactors or nuclear research reactors. As of October 1999, only 26 of the 44 states which are listed under Article XIV as states that must sign and ratify the CTBT before it can enter into force have ratified the treaty – the U.S., Russia and Israel have not yet ratified. Israel's position regarding the treaty is that it can contribute to the elimination of global nuclear weapons, and thus strengthen the norm of non-proliferation, without this endangering Israel's national security. For this reason Israel signed the treaty in 1996 and agreed to participate in international seismic monitoring. Toward the end of 1999, as part of this agreement, Israel conducted a series of explosions near the Dead Sea in order to calibrate the Israeli seismic system.

Israel's remaining concerns regarding ratification of the CTBT were stated in 1999 by Gideon Frank, Director General of the Israeli Atomic Energy Commission. He cited concerns regarding the level and readiness of the verification regime achieved by the PrepCom, its effectiveness and immunity to abuse. Israel regards it as a precondition to ratification that the operational manual regarding On-Site Inspection be completed. He also noted concerns regarding Israel's sovereign equality status as reflected in actions taken by the PrepCom and other policy making organs of the CTBT, without making this a precondition to ratification. The final factor that Israel will take into consideration, again without posing it as a precondition, are developments in the Middle East, including adherence to the CTBT by regional states.

The Fissile Material Cut-off Treaty (FMCT):

In March 1995, the CD members agreed to establish an ad hoc committee with the mandate to negotiate a treaty banning the production of fissile material – known as the Cut-off Treaty. As noted, the Cut-off Treaty was designed to bring India, Pakistan and Israel into the global non-proliferation regime. All parties to this future treaty would have to put their relevant nuclear sites under international inspection. The provisions of the treaty that have been discussed thus far seem to relate to future production of these materials, without placing current stockpiles under any international supervision. The negotiations on the Cut-off Treaty stalled due to the opposition of some states, and were revived only following the nuclear tests carried out by India and Pakistan in May 1998, and the massive pressure placed on these two countries to remove their opposition to going forward with negotiations.

According to reports in the media, in August 1998 Israel remained the only country that had not given its approval to setting up a committee to begin formulating the treaty. As decisions in Geneva are taken by consensus, Israel's opposition could have blocked the initiation of negotiations. The U.S. pressed Israel to remove its effective veto, and Israel finally agreed. Israel clarified, however, that it does not view this as obliging it to be a party to the future treaty.[4]

The FMCT could provide unprecedented international oversight over nuclear states' nuclear sites, and demonstrate their commitment to Article VI of the NPT. Israel most likely fears that by accepting this future treaty, it could establish a dangerous precedent that could be seen as a step down the "slippery slope." An additional concern for Israel is the Egyptian position whereby the Cut-off Treaty

---

[4]See *Jerusalem Post*, 7 August 1998, 12 August 1998; *Ha'aretz*, 11 August 1998.

should relate not only to future production, but should place existing stockpiles of plutonium under inspection.

What Can Be Learned?

Two elements seem to emerge clearly from the above account of the global non-proliferation regime as far as Israel's participation is concerned. First, despite its consistent policy of ambiguity in the nuclear realm, in the past decade Israel has nevertheless taken steps in the direction of strengthening the global regime. It has signed the CTBT, and taken part in the seismic monitoring associated with it. Israel also removed its 1998 opposition to the initiation of negotiations on the pending Cut-off Treaty, although it views this treaty as highly problematic in terms of its potential ramifications. It is also noteworthy in this context that at the signing of the Chemical Weapons Convention (CWC) in January 1993, then foreign minister Shimon Peres made specific mention of nuclear weapons as one category of WMD to be dealt with in a regional context.[5] Thus, while Israel will not take steps viewed as endangering its national security, it has nevertheless shown unprecedented commitment to the global arms control effort.

But, the second, and perhaps more significant element is that Israel's efforts to take part in the global non-proliferation regime have demonstrated that the global dynamics of non-proliferation are inseparable from regional security concerns. The Resolution on the Middle East adopted at the 1995 NPT Review Conference on Egypt's initiative, Egyptian insistence that the FMCT relate to existing stockpiles, and also the tie created by some Arab states between their signature on the Chemical Weapons Convention and Israel joining the NPT (that has been reinforced by

---

[5]In his address, Peres said, "In the spirit of global pursuit of general and complete disarmament...Israel suggests to all countries of the region to construct a mutually verifiable zone, free of surface-to-surface missiles and of chemical, biological and nuclear weapons." *Reuters News Service*, 13 January 1993.

Egyptian president Mubarak as recently as September 1999[6]), all underscore the inescapable linkage of the global non-proliferation regime to the regional balance of power. Egyptian president Mubarak has also recently drawn a link between Egypt's ratification of the CTBT and Israel's willingness to do so.[7]

In fact, it should be noted that Israel's increased willingness to take part in international arms control efforts came only after the initiation of the Madrid peace process, and initial progress was achieved in the multilateral region-wide Arms Control and Regional Security (ACRS) working group. The fact that the establishment of a regional framework for dealing with issues related to arms control predated initial steps in the direction of strengthening the global regime reflects the preeminence of the regional context. Taking into account, the impact of specific regional concerns, especially Israel's particular situation within the Middle East, makes it imperative to go beyond global treaties when searching for new means of dealing with the threat of WMD proliferation in this region.

When considering Israel's participation in the global regime, beyond the difficulties mentioned above, it must also be kept in mind that there are real problems inherent in the international treaties themselves. The fact that in the Middle East Iran and Iraq are both party to the NPT, and at least in the case of Iraq (but most likely Iran as well), it is clear that the commitment to this treaty has not been upheld. This is perhaps only the starkest example of the difficulties in ensuring compliance when a state has made a decision to acquire nuclear weapons capabilities. While the norm of nuclear non-proliferation has been established, this does not guarantee that party states will adhere to it when highly motivated to do otherwise. Moreover, additional weapons of mass destruction exist in the region that must be dealt with as well.

---

[6]Cairo MENA in English, 1423 GMT, 15 September 1999 (*FBIS-NES*-1999-0915).
[7]*The Egyptian State Information Service*, 10 February 2000.

Israel and the Middle East Arms Control and Regional Security Talks

The Arms Control and Regional Security (ACRS) Working Group was active between the years 1992 and 1995, as one of the five working groups that made up the multilateral track of the Madrid peace process.[8] In his address to the first meeting of the multilateral track, held in Moscow in January 1992, then US Secretary of State James Baker set forth the basic objective of the multilaterals as addressing those issues that are common to the region and do not necessarily respect national or geographic boundaries. Specifically regarding the ACRS, he referred to the Gulf War as a vivid reminder of the destructive nature of new patterns of arms acquisition and production – undermining the very security they were intended to promote. He set forth the agenda of these talks as: "In the first instance . . . offering the regional parties our thinking about potential approaches to arms control . . . From this base, the group might move forward to considering a set of modest confidence-building or transparency measures covering notifications of selected military-related activities and crisis-prevention communications. The purpose would be to lessen the prospects for incidents and miscalculation that could lead to heightened competition or even conflict."[9] Progress was in fact made in the area of Confidence and Security Building

---

[8]For a representative sample of articles written on ACRS, see: Shai Feldman, "Progress Toward Middle East Arms Control" in Shlomo Gazit (ed.) *The Middle East Military Balance, 1993-94* (Tel Aviv: Jaffee Center for Strategic Studies, 1994); Gerald Steinberg, "Middle East Arms Control and Regional Security" *Survival*, 36:1, Spring 1994, 126-141; Bruce Jentleson, *The Middle East Arms Control and Regional Security (ACRS) Talks: Progress, Problems, and Prospects*, IGCC Policy Paper no. 26, September 1996; Emily Landau, "The Arms Control and Regional Security Working Group: 1994-96" in Mark A. Heller (ed.) *The Middle East Military Balance, 1996* (NY: Columbia Univ. Press, 1998); Peter Jones, "Arms Control in the Middle East: Some Reflections on ACRS" *Security Dialogue*, 28:1, 1997, 57-70; and Bruce Jentleson and Dalia Dassa Kaye, "Security Status: Explaining Regional Security Cooperation and Its Limits in the Middle East" *Security Studies*, 8:1, Autumn 1998, 204-238. On arms control in the Middle East see: Steven L. Spiegel and David J. Pervin (eds.) *Practical Peacemaking in the Middle East, Volume I: Arms Control and Regional Security* (NY: Garland Pub, 1995), and Shai Feldman, *Nuclear Weapons and Arms Control in the Middle East* (Cambridge, MA: MIT Press, 1997).

[9]Remarks by Secretary of State James A. Baker, III Before the Organizational Meeting for Multilateral Negotiations on the Middle East, House of Unions, 28 January 1992, US Department of State, office of the Assistant Secretary/Spokesman (Moscow, Russia).

Measures (CSBMs)[10], but the talks were put on hold indefinitely toward the end of 1995 due to an inability to reconcile basic differences between Israel and Egypt over the nuclear issue. Egypt wanted the nuclear issue to be placed on the agenda of ACRS, and Israel said that it could only begin discussing this issue after comprehensive peace had been achieved between Israel and the Arab states, including Iran and Iraq.

Return to Regional Politics

The end of global bi-polarity has ushered in a return to regionalism in international relations. The regional context has taken on new meaning for states in terms of their threat perceptions – states have been both enabled and challenged to define their security concerns in a regional setting. With regional players taking a more prominent role in international affairs, it will become more and more apparent that global arms control efforts themselves will have to take regional states seriously and devise a means of addressing specific regional concerns within the overall arms control regime. In the Middle East as well, the control of weapons of mass destruction will have to be dealt with from a regional perspective.

Taken strictly in terms of the agreements reached, progress in the ACRS working group was limited, and the talks were put on hold before even the initially agreed-upon CSBMs were able to have an effect. In these terms, it might seem that efforts on the regional level are no more of a potential means for moving forward on arms control than the attempt to include Israel in the global non-proliferation regime. Here, as is the case regarding global arms control initiatives, the nuclear issue has become an insurmountable stumbling block to progress. However, a closer look at the structure of the working group, as well as the dialogue that took place in the

---

[10]See in particular Jentleson, *The Middle East Arms Control and Regional Security (ACRS) Talks*, 1996.

framework of ACRS, reveals that it was set up in a manner that was geared toward achieving results, making it at least potentially more significant than might seem at first glance.

The ACRS working group created a unique framework for learning about, and creating shared understandings of arms control – learning about the experience of other states and regions with arms control, and developing new and possibly innovative ideas related to arms control that could serve as a basis for moving forward in the Middle East. There was an appreciation of the need to come to a true understanding of the security concerns of all parties involved as a first step in this direction. This was evident in James Baker's initial remarks on the establishment of ACRS, when he pointed out that an arms control working group would tackle destructive patterns of arms acquisitions, "but in a way that recognizes the vital security interests at stake for all the parties of the region."[11] Beginning these talks with definitions of threat perceptions and participating states' security interests reflected an understanding that the arms control process must address the strategic realities of the region; that there is much to be discussed that goes far beyond the mere addition of one's signature to an existing international treaty for the control of WMD proliferation. The regional context is important not only for dealing with existing security interests and concerns, but for creating a shared interest in achieving arms control agreements that meet and address those concerns. Building a common interest in upholding arms control agreements is the best means of ensuring future compliance with these agreements.

All this is not to say that devising an agreed-upon means of addressing the nuclear capability that Israel is assumed to possess is not a real problem that will need to be confronted by the regional parties. What it does mean is that the place to look for a means of beginning to deal with this issue is the regional dialogue process.

---

[11]Remarks by Secretary of State James A. Baker, III, 28 January 1992.

It should also be made clear that for this process to succeed (however success is defined), there must be recognition of the fact that it is a process – that it will most likely be long-term and that allowance must be made for this. This simple fact is often ignored, which creates unrealistic expectations for rapid progress. The process will be long-term not only (and not even primarily) due to the fact that Israel has made it very clear that it will not proceed in the direction of establishing a Weapons of Mass Destruction Free Zone (WMDFZ) before comprehensive peace is achieved with all the Arab states including Iran and Iraq, but because success demands that a security dialogue culture be created. States must establish the normative basis for conducting a regional security dialogue in the Middle East, which entails common norms, identities, and dialogue procedures.

As noted, this is not to say that global efforts are not important or relevant to the Middle East. Global dynamics remain important from Israel's point of view in order to control both indigenous development of nuclear weapons as well as transfers of technology and weapons parts to non-nuclear states. The norm of global non-proliferation in the nuclear realm is recognized as an important one. However, it must be understood that the major arms control effort must be carried out in the regional context.

Moving Forward

In a statement to the 43rd IAEA General Conference (late September 1999), Gideon Frank reaffirmed Israel's commitment to establishing "in due course and in the proper context, the Middle East as a zone free of WMD and missiles." It seems that in order to proceed in the regional context, Israel should really take this commitment seriously and actually consider taking the decision to place the issue of a WMDFZ on the agenda of the Middle East multilateral arms control talks – to agree to begin discussion of this issue.

Such a step would perhaps facilitate the resumption of ACRS. It would also ensure that all weapons of mass destruction as well as conventional weapons and missiles are dealt within a context that is geared toward creating a stable and secure regional security system. In this framework, CSBMs would be regarded as an integral stage in the arms control process; movement in the CSBM process itself could be instrumental in creating the necessary institutional dialogue framework for states in the Middle East in order to deal with the more difficult arms control issues. Once the issue is being discussed in a regional forum, if regional and global dynamics are proceeding at a different pace, it will have to be recognized that certain concessions regarding the global regime will have to await progress in the regional context. As far as implementation is concerned, due to regional strategic threats from states not involved in the peace process or the regional security dialogue, Israel cannot realistically alter its basic position whereby the precondition to actually creating a WMDFZ in the Middle East is in fact the conclusion of comprehensive peace in the Middle East.

Chapter 11

The Impact of the Egyptian-Israeli Debate on Nuclear Weapons on the Middle East Peace Process

Gerald M. Steinberg

Since 1990, arms control has been an increasingly important issue in the Middle East. The combination of the increased Weapons of Mass Destruction (WMD) threat from Iraq and Iran, the Middle East peace process, the efforts made in the multilateral working group on Arms Control and Regional Security (ACRS), and the exceptionality of the region with respect to the expansion of the global non-proliferation regime, all contributed to this increased emphasis on arms control.

The issues involved, such as the implementation of Confidence and Security Building Measures (CSBMs) and the status of the various WMD programs of the states in the region, were discussed in a number of overlapping venues. In addition to ACRS, debate and conflict took place in the annual meetings of the First Committee of the United Nations, the annual meetings of the Board of Governors of the International Atomic Energy Agency (IAEA), the Conference on Disarmament (Geneva), the 1995 Nuclear Non-Proliferation Treaty (NPT) Review and Extension Conference (NPTREC), the Prepcoms prior to the 2000 NPT Review Conference as well as the conference itself, the meetings of the Arab League, Middle East summits, and bilateral discussions between many of the states.

As will be seen in this chapter, these discussions and debates had a major impact on the political relations between the states in the region, between the states and the U.S., and the overall Middle East peace process. The Egyptian campaign focusing on the Israeli nuclear weapons capability became the major issue in bilateral relations between Jerusalem and Cairo, and the atmosphere of conflict that resulted over this issue had a negative impact on the negotiations between Israel and the Palestinians. This conflict also created an impasse in the ACRS discussions, and led to tensions in relations between Egypt and the United States.

ACRS

The 1991 Madrid Middle East peace conference established a number of multilateral working groups, including a group on Arms Control and Regional Security (ACRS). The multilateral framework was designed to tackle regional issues that extended beyond the bilateral negotiations, and to establish a basis for discussion and mutual recognition between Israel and the wider Arab world, extending from North Africa to Saudi Arabia and the Gulf States.

The ACRS working group was the most ambitious, and manifested the growing emphasis of arms control and non-proliferation initiatives in the region. Prior to the beginning of the ACRS process, the belated discovery of the scope of the Iraqi nuclear weapons program, the establishment of UNSCOM to search for, monitor, and destroy Saddam Hussein's efforts to maintain weapons of mass destruction and missiles to deliver them, and President Bush's 1991 Middle East Arms Control Initiative had already increased the focus on these issues. In 1990, Egypt presented a framework to create a Middle East Zone Free of Weapons of Mass Destruction (known as the Mubarak Initiative). Although the regional conception for ACRS was similar to the Bush Initiative, ACRS emphasized the direct negotiation of Confidence Building Measures (CBMs) and step-by step development of regional security, rather than focusing on long-term objectives, as in the Bush proposal.[1]

---

[1]The sessions of the ACRS are closed and information is limited. For a discussion of the primary issues, see Alan Platt, editor, *Arms Control and Confidence Building in the Middle East*, (Washington DC, United States Institute of Peace Press, 1992); Steven Speigel and David Pervin, eds. *Practical*

However, a number of key states, including Syria, Iraq and Iran were not involved in the multilateral process, and this constituted a major limitation on the negotiation of regional security arrangements.

At an early stage in the ACRS meetings, Egypt began to press Israel to agree to include its nuclear policy on the agenda. The Egyptian representatives stated that progress in the regional peace process was linked to the end of Israel nuclear monopoly.[2] Israel rejected the Egyptian demands to discuss the nuclear issue in detail, arguing that the development of regional security must be based first on progress in implementing regional peace agreements, as well as a broad network of CSBMs.[3] Until these conditions were reached, the Israeli policy based on the maintenance of the ambiguous nuclear deterrent would remain, and thus, the type of detailed negotiations demanded by Egypt that would lead to a change in this policy was unacceptable. As a result, by early 1995, the ACRS process was blocked over this issue, long before other issues led to the impasse in the Palestinian-Israeli negotiations in 1996. Because of this conflict, ACRS continued to be blocked following the election of Ehud Barak in 1999 and the resumption of the bilateral negotiations that led to renewed activity in the other four multilateral working

Peacemaking in The Middle East, Vol. I: Arms Control and Regional Security (NY: Garland Publishing, 1995); Joel Peters, *Pathways to Peace: The Multilateral Arab-Israeli Talks* (London, Royal Institute of International Affairs, 1996); and Bruce W. Jentleson, "The Middle East Arms Control and Regional Security Working Group (ACRS)," in *Building a Middle East Community: The Future of the Middle East Multilateral Peace Process*, A. Makovsky, ed., Washington, DC, Washington Institute for Near East Policy,(forthcoming).

[2]Mohamed Nabil Fahmy, "Egypt's disarmament initiative," *The Bulletin of the Atomic Scientists* (November 1990), pp.9-10. In 1978, President Sadat had sought to include agreement on the Israeli nuclear capability in the context of the Camp David Agreements that led to the Egyptian-Israeli Peace Treaty, but this rejected by the Israelis, and the issue was dropped for many years. See William Quandt, *Camp David: Peacemaking and Politics* (Washington, DC: Brookings, 1986), p.222, and Ariel E. Levite and Emily B. Landau, *In the Eyes of the Arabs: Israel's Nuclear Image* (Hebrew), (Tel Aviv: Tel Aviv University Press, 1994)

[3]Some of the other Arab participants also sought to include discussion of the Israeli nuclear policy in the context of CBMs, but with less fervor than in the case of Egypt. See Jentleson, "The Middle East Arms Control and Regional Security Working Group (ACRS)"

groups. For this entire period, the Egyptian and Israeli positions did not change noticeably.

The meetings and other activities in the ACRS working group, as well as similar exchanges between Egypt and Israel in the annual meetings of the International Atomic Energy Agency (IAEA) and the United Nations General Assembly were closely intertwined with the preparations for the upcoming NPTREC. This sparring provided a prelude to the intense debate that took place prior during the meetings in New York.

Arms Control and the Peace Process

In 1993 and 1994, the Middle East peace process had made substantial progress, with a number of agreements and treaties. However, Egypt was not a party to any of these agreements (having made its peace with Israel in 1979), and Egyptian-Israeli relations were dominated by the nuclear issue.

In late August 1994, Egyptian Foreign Minister Amre Mousa paid his first official visit to Israel.[4] This was a highly charged and conflictual visit, beginning with Mousa's initial refusal to visit the Yad Vashem Holocaust Memorial, which is an important part of official visits for all diplomats and official guests. From the beginning, Mousa clearly stated that this visit was focused solely on Egypt's demand that Israel sign the NPT. A number of Israeli analysts commented on Mousa's insensitivity in efforts to avoid Yad Vashem and confrontation with the Holocaust, and the links between this and the Egyptian pressures to "strip Israel of its weapon of last resort."[5] The issue dominated the press conference held by Peres and Mousa, in which the Egyptian foreign minister sought to gain support from the Israeli public.

---

[4]Mousa had come to Israel before for short periods in the context of the negotiations between Israel and the Palestinians.

[5]Avi Beker,"Israel's Long Corridor: Ambiguity and Nuclear Non-Proliferation," *Institute of the World Jewish Congress, Policy Forum* No. 7, (1995), p.6.

When Mousa argued that the Israeli capability posed a danger to Egypt, Peres noted that although the United States "has a very large arsenal, . . . it has a policy of peace . . . . I know that our Arab neighbors generally, and clearly Egypt, know that Israel doesn't have any belligerent intentions..."[6]

Mousa's meetings in Jerusalem marked the beginning of a new and more intense phase of the conflict. This period included frequent bilateral or multilateral meetings, as well as a series of summits (two way, four way, and various other combinations) in Cairo, Washington, New York, Europe, and Jerusalem, focusing primarily on the Egyptian-Israeli conflict with respect to the NPT.

In December 1994, Israeli President Weizman paid an official visit to Egypt. Although the office of the Israeli President is largely symbolic, and he plays no policy-making role, Weizman's visit had important political significance in the context of Israeli-Egyptian relations, and, in particular, the growing conflict over the nuclear issue. Egyptian government officials and the press (both government and opposition) used Weizman's visit to emphasize the demands for Israel on the NPT.

The intensification of the Egyptian campaign led to internal debates within the Israeli government regarding possible responses. Rabin consistently rejected proposals to change the Israeli position,[7] and the Israeli foreign ministry and military intelligence officials prepared documents analyzing the long-term implications of the Egyptian policy, as well as the options for exerting counter-pressure. Summaries, including the prospects for "punishing Egypt" and the possibility of war in the next

---

[6]Joint Press Conference, Israeli Foreign Minister Shimon Peres, Egyptian Foreign Minister Amre Mousa (questions and answers in English) Israel Information Service, Israel Ministry of Foreign Affairs, Jerusalem, 31 August, 1994

[7]The White House, Office of the Press Secretary, 26 July, 1994, President Clinton, Prime Minister Rabin of Israel, and King Hussein of Jordan (transcript); Zeev Schiff,"The Reinforced Nuclear Wall," *Haaretz*, 27 January 1995, p.C-1

decade were leaked and published in the Israeli press.[8] However, the Israeli response was limited and indirect, since the Mubarak government was honoring the security aspects of the 1979 Treaty, and was preferable to likely alternatives (such as a fundamentalist Islamic regime) in Egypt. Some Israeli officials saw the Egyptian campaign as domestically driven. Mubarak was perceived as under internal threat, and the hostility to Israel (known as the "Cold Peace") and pressures on the NPT issue were partly interpreted in this context.[9]

Nevertheless, the rhetoric of the conflict escalated, and following the leak of the Israeli Foreign Ministry's assessments regarding the possibility of war, the Egyptians responded in kind. In January 1995, *Ruz-El-Yusuf*, one of Egypt's leading weeklies, carried a lead article on the prospects of war with Israel. Retired General Farik Sa'ad Eldin Shazli, who led the Egyptian military in the 1973 War, and is a major member of the opposition, was quoted extensively. He declared that "The combined weaponry possessed by the Arab states today exceeds that of Israel, if all of these weapons were directed against Israel the Arab states would defeat Israel." Amin Elhawidi, former Egyptian Minister of War and Head of General Intelligence and another opposition figure, stated "I expect war with a certainty because the agreements which have been signed and are being signed today lead to war." This exchange did not contribute to the Middle East peace process or normalization of relations.

During this period, meetings between Egyptian and others Arab leaders also focused on the issue of Israel and the NPT. On December 28 and 29, 1994, Mubarak met with Saudi Arabia's King Fahd and Syrian President Hafez el-Assad in Alexandria. In their communique, the leaders called for Israeli withdrawal from the

---

[8]Eytan Rabin and Aluf Benn,"Intelligence Report: Egyptian Arms Buildup Worrying," *Haaretz,* 17 January 1995, p.1; Guy Bechor, "Foreign Ministry Will Hold Discussions on Relations between Israel and Egypt; Senior Official: "This is a Cold Peace" *Haaretz,* 25 November 1994, p.A5
[9]Gerges, pp.71-72.

Golan Heights and return to the pre-1967 borders, while they endorsed the Mubarak Initiative and the "immediate" negotiation of a Middle East nuclear weapons-free zone (MENWFZ).[10]

Israeli Foreign Minister Peres was closely identified with the peace process, and he expressed concern that the growing political conflict with Egypt over the nuclear issue would weaken support in Israel for concessions and security risks.[11] If Egypt, which was the first state to sign a peace treaty, exhibited such hostility, aligned itself with Syria, and placed primary emphasis on "stripping Israel of its deterrent," Peres noted that many Israelis would question the wisdom of continuing the process.[12] As a result of this assessment, Peres actively sought an accommodation with Egypt that would remove the issue from the agenda.[13] He noted that the solution "does not include Israel signing the treaty," but rather was based on less far-reaching (and undisclosed) policy changes that would satisfy the Egyptians and defuse the conflict. In his annual address before the U.N. General Assembly, Peres explicitly presented Israel's vision of "A Middle East which will be nuclear-free,

---

[10]*Nuclear Proliferation News*, No. 18, (17 February 1995); "Egyptian, Syrian, and Saudi Leaders Conclude Summit in Alexandria," *Yediot Ahronot*, 30 December, 1994, p.2

[11]Etel Solingen, "The Political Economy of Nuclear Restraint," *International Security*, 19 2, (Fall 1994), pp.126-169 argues that domestic political and ideological differences between Israel's major parties has led to conflicts over nuclear policy. While some individuals, such as Shimon Peres and some of his proteges, are reportedly more "willing to embrace a regime," as Solingen claims, the evidence for the broader claim regarding parties and ideologies is not supported by the evidence. While Peres made some isolated statements indicating greater enthusiasm for the concept of a Middle East Nuclear Weapons Free Zone following implementation of comprehensive peace agreements, including Iran. However, this was far from the Egyptian demands for immediate Israeli accession to the NPT. More importantly, with the possible exception of Peres, between 1977, when Likud first formed a government, and 1995, there was no discernible difference between the nuclear policies of Labor (particular during the government of the late Prime Minister Yitzchak Rabin) and Likud-led governments. Many of the key policy makers in the Ministry of Defense (such as Director General David Ivri) and the Israel Atomic Energy Commission served under both governments.

[12]30 December, 1994 (Israel Line Computer News service, Israel Information Service, Israel Foreign Ministry).

[13]Reuter News Reports, "Peres says nuclear row with Egypt near solution," 2 February 1995; Reuter News Reports, "Israel won't join Nuclear Treaty – Peres," 11 January 1995; cited in *Nuclear Proliferation News,* No. 18 (17 February 1995).

missile-free, hunger-free, discrimination-free, tyranny-free.[14] His remarks at the Nobel Prize award ceremony a few months later contained similar language.[15] In the next month, a series of meetings between Israeli and Egyptian officials focused on various compromise proposals to defuse the conflict.[16]

However, Egypt continued to insist on a specific Israeli commitment to sign the NPT, and Israel refused.[17] The growing conflict between Israel and Egypt began to impede the broader Middle East peace process, particularly with respect to public support for security risks and territorial withdrawal in Israel.[18]

The stage and the leaders shifted to Washington, where the conflict continued, along with efforts of the U.S. government to mediate. The Mubarak government interpreted U.S. policies, such as the Bush Initiative and interest in the fissile material production cut-off, as being supportive of the Egyptian position, and American officials spoke of an Israeli "gesture" to satisfy Egypt.[19] However, as the conflict over the nuclear issue began to affect the peace process adversely, the United States started to pressure Egypt to alter its position on NPT extension, and the focus shifted from conflict between Israel and Egypt to an Egyptian-American confrontation.

---

[14]Address by H.E. Shimon Peres, Minister of Foreign Affairs, to the 49th session of the United Nations General Assembly, 29 September, 1994 (Israel Information Service, Israel Ministry of Foreign Affairs, Jerusalem).

[15]Remarks by the Minister of Foreign Affairs upon Acceptance of the Nobel Peace Prize, Oslo, 10 December, 1994 (Israel Information Service, MFA, Jerusalem).

[16]David Makovsky, "Peres plans meet with Mubarak over NPT crisis, *Jerusalem Post*, 20 February 1995, p.1; Nitzan Horowitz, "Egypt and Israel will resume contacts on the NPT, After U.N. discussion," *Haaretz*, April 7, 1995, p.A3

[17]Statement from Cairo Summit, Israel Government Press Office, Israel Information Service, Jerusalem, 3 February 1995.

[18]David Makovsky, "Ministry to air problems with Egypt," *Jerusalem Post*, 25 November 1994, p. A-3; Alon Pinkus, "Egypt using NPT dispute to slow normalization," *Jerusalem Post*, 22 February 1995, p.2; "US: Egypt's 'no' on NPT damaging ties, *Jerusalem Post*, 17 February 1995, p.1

[19]APS Diplomat, "Perry pressing Israel on nuclear treaty" 27 January 1995 cited in *Nuclear Proliferation News* No. 18 (17 February 1995); Aluf Benn, "The U.S. Expects an Israeli Gesture to Insure Egyptian Support for the NPT," *Haaretz* 7 December, 1994, p.A-4

The NPTREC

On April 1995, 175 NPT signatories met to consider the extension of this agreement beyond the initial 25 years specified in the text.[20] The U.S. government and the Clinton Administration had made the indefinite and unconditional extension of this treaty a central objective of foreign policy, and dedicated extensive resources towards seeking this outcome. Four months before the opening of the conference, the numerous conflicts and disputes that were raised in the PrepCom meetings that had taken place led to discussion of various other options, including short-term extensions, suspension of the conference, splits among the signatories, or even the collapse of the NPT regime.[21]

In addition, the Egyptian demand to link indefinite extension to a change in the Israeli nuclear policy threatened to block agreement. Egyptian government representatives defined their objectives in different language at various times, but the ostensible goal was to force Israel to accept the NPT, place all its nuclear facilities under safeguards within a fixed period of time, and end the long-standing Israeli policy of nuclear ambiguity.[22] Egypt actively sought the support of the Arab League and the non-aligned movement (NAM), and at one point, Mubarak indicated that "Egypt would withdraw from the NPT unless the issue of Israeli non-membership is

---

[20]The research for this paper was supported by a grant from the Ihel Foundation, and Yona Cymerman and Lea Rappaport provided research assistance.

Article X.2 of the NPT Treaty, which entered into force in 1970, specifies that "Twenty-five years after the entry into force of the Treaty, a conference shall be convened to decide whether the Treaty shall continue in force indefinitely, or shall be extended for an additional fixed or fixed periods. This decision shall be taken by a majority of the Parties to the Treaty."

[21]Judy Aita and Jacquelyn S. Porth, "Last-Minute Egyptian Move Sets Back NPT Conference Deadline," United States Information Agency, NEA 306, Washington, DC, May 10 1995

[22]See for example, Abdallah Hammudah and Sawsan Abu Husayn, "Interview with Foreign Minister Amr Musa," *Al-Sharq Al-awsat* (London), 24 August 1995, p.7 in FBIS-NES-95-167 29 August 1995, p.9

addressed specifically in the NPT Extension Conference.[23] (There was a great deal of confusion in the Egyptian policy, particularly in statements made by Mubarak. The Egyptian leader stated that "the day Israel signs, I will sign" and that "Egypt will not renew its signature" if Israel refuses to sign. Other sources discussed the possibility that "Egypt is contemplating withdrawing from the Treaty or 'suspending' its membership," and Mousa stated that "All options are open."[24])

In the period preceding the opening of the NPT Extension Conference, Egyptian officials had good reason to expect some support for the United States in the effort to force a change in Israeli policy. Some American analysts called for pressure on Israel to "shut down its Dimona reactor[25]," and policy-makers and analysts were concerned that the appearance of a "double standard in US policy on the NPT and Israel" would complicate NPT extension.[26] Simpson noted concerns that "lack of any movement towards a ZFWMD would result in a refusal by Arab governments to accept a long extension of the NPT."[27] Mitchell Reiss, an American academic specializing in arms control issues, warned that the Israeli nuclear program

[23]*Nuclear Proliferation News* No. 18, (17 February, 1995), citing Agence France-Presse International News, 15 January, Agence France-Presse International News, 16 January; Reuter News Reports, 24 January 1995

[24]Under the terms of the NPT, Egypt had two options. it could vote against extension, but still be bound by the majority, or it could withdraw in accordance with the provisions of the treaty. *Davar*, 31 January 1995, p.3; Fawaz A. Gerges, "Egyptian-Israeli Relations Turn Sour," *Foreign Affairs*, (May/June 1995) 74, pp. 69-78; "Egypt ties NPT policy to Israeli Moves," Reuter News Service, 10 February; "Egypt Refuses to Budge on Nuclear Non-proliferation Stand," Agence France-Presse International News, 12 February; "Arabs won't sign NPT without Israel," Reuter News Reports, 16 February; "Egypt Makes Israeli Adherence Condition of NPT Extension," Agence France-Presse International News, 16 February; cited in *Nuclear Proliferation News* No. 19, 7 March 1995, p.13.

[25]Mitchell Reiss, "The Last Nuclear Summit?," *The Washington Quarterly*, 17:3, (Summer 1994), p.11.

[26]Answer by Richard Falk, in Symposium: The Middle East: What Is Our Long-Term Vision," Bruce Riedel, William Quandt, Richard Falk, *Middle East Policy*, 3:3, (December 1994), p.12; Eugene Bird,"Israel Nuclear Program Blocks U.S.-Backed Non-Proliferation Initiative," cited by Paul Power, "Middle East Nuclear Issues in Global Perspective," *Middle East Policy*, 4:2, (September 1995), p.202.

[27]Simpson and Howlett, p.59

would be a central issue, and"without American pressure on Israel to close Dimona, "the concerns of Arab parties may dominate the Review Conference."[28] In addition, some argued that the conference provided an opportunity to "cap the nuclear capabilities" of the three threshold states. [29]

However, by early 1995, it had become clear that Israel was not going to accept the Egyptian demand that it agree to sign the NPT or proposals to close Dimona. Israel rejected the assertion that Dimona was "nearing the end of its operating life,"[30] noting that the small reactor in not technically comparable to much larger and power reactors, designed earlier than Dimona. (The Israeli government has declared that the reactor meets the highest safety standards.) Also, it was apparent that pressures in this direction in the context of the peace process would reduce political support in Israel for concessions and security risks.

As a result, the United States began to pressure Egypt to accept the proposed Israeli gestures and endorse NPT extension. Under-Secretary of State Lynn Davis stated that "we are impressing upon Egypt our desire to have them support an indefinite extension" while noting that the United States did not realistically expect Israel to sign the NPT or to "take steps inconsistent with how they see their security today."[31] Robert Pelletreau, Assistant Secretary of State for Near Eastern affairs, went to Egypt in late January, and reportedly warned Egypt that some members of Congress had raised the possibility of reviewing American aid to Egypt ($2.2 billion per year) in light of the Egyptian threats to obstruct NPT extension.[32] However,

---

[28]Reiss, p. 11

[29]McGeorge Bundy, William J. Crowe Jr., Sidney D. Drell, *Reducing Nuclear Danger* (New York: Council on Foreign Relations Press, 1993),p.68-9; Roger Molander and Peter Wilson, "On Dealing with the Prospect of Nuclear Chaos," *Washington Quarterly,* 17:3, (Summer 1994), pp.36-37.

[30]Reiss, p.11

[31]*Nuclear Proliferation News* No. 18 (17 February 1995).

[32]Akiva Eldar, "To Strike Egypt in the Pocketbook" *Haaretz*, 30 November 1994, p. A-1; Akiva Eldar, Aluf Benn and news agencies, "Mubarak warned on possible US aid cut, if Egypt obstructs NPT Extension," *Haaretz*, 4 April 1995, p.1; Gerges, p.73

Osamah El Baz, special advisor to President Mubarak, dismissed the prospects of a cut in U.S. aid. The Egyptians were aware that both Israel and the U.S. were loathe to do anything that might weaken the Mubarak regime and lead to increased support for radical Islamic groups seeking to overthrow the Egyptian government.

On February 12 1995, the leaders of Israel, Egypt, Jordan and the Palestinians met in Washington for talks on a number of issues linked to the peace process, particularly on the bilateral Israel-Palestinian track. However, the Blair House summit was dominated by the Egyptian campaign. In the opening session, Mousa delivered a vitriolic attack on Israeli policy, demanding to know when Israel would sign the NPT, and tabled a document that included allegations of environmental dangers to Egypt resulting from the Israeli reactor complex. Peres again responded, declaring that "Since Camp David, there has been no change in our position and the distance between Dimona and Egypt has also not changed."[33] In an interview with the London-based paper *El Hayat,* Mubarak was quoted as saying that "Egypt will sign the NPT when Israel does," and claimed support from Syria and a number of Persian Gulf states. The summit concluded just as the other such efforts had, without an agreement, and the issue remained unresolved. The crisis in the relations between Israel and Egypt intensified, and became personalized, with Rabin referring to "a bad wind blowing from the Egyptian foreign ministry." [34]

The full-scale American campaign to obtain consensus in the NPT Extension Conference continued, and in early March, Secretary of State Christopher visited the

---

[33] Akiva Eldar, "Israel and the Palestinians Agreed that to End Closure only if Steps are Taken Against Terror" *Haaretz,* 13 February, 1995, p.1.

[34] *Nuclear Proliferation News* No. 19 (7 March 1995), p.13. Rabin's statement reflects the view of some but not all Israeli analysts and officials, that Mousa and Fahmy were the primary forces in this anti-Israel campaign, while Mubarak acted to limit this tension, in response to American requests and a recognition of the importance to Egyptian interests and regional stability of fostering better relations with Israel. As a member of the Egyptian delegation in the UN in the 1980s, Mousa developed a reputation for deep antipathy towards Israelis, and Fahmy's father resigned as Foreign Minister in protest to President Sadat's peace initiative in 1977.

region. Following the meeting with Christopher, Mubarak softened his position, declaring that he did not expect Israel to "demolish or remove everything now," but that it was reasonable to expect an announcement of "a timetable or something on any concrete steps."[35] A few days later, Mubarak announced that Egypt would not withdraw from the NPT, even if Israel refused to change its policy. Mubarak indicated that while protesting the Israeli position, Egypt would support extension.[36]

However, shortly thereafter, Egypt hosted a special meeting of delegates to the Arab League with the goal of gaining the support of the 22 members in linking NPT extension to Israeli accession. On February 6, a preliminary meeting of the foreign ministers of the eight "Damascus Declaration" states – Egypt, Syria, Bahrain, Kuwait, Oman, Saudi Arabia and United Arab Emirates – officially endorsed the Egyptian hard line. In their final statement, they repeated the demanded that "Israel sign this treaty and put its nuclear installations under the system of guarantees of the International Atomic Energy Agency."[37]

This led the U.S. government to undertake what was described as "a concerted diplomatic counter-offensive" focusing on the GCC and other moderate Arab states threatened by Iraq and Iran. According to reports, American representatives stressed the link between the policies of these states and the continued alliance with the U.S., as well as the relation between NPT extension, the security of these states, and the stability of the region. (This was similar to the successful American strategy on the Chemical Weapons Convention (CWC) in 1993, when the Egyptian government sought to forge an Arab block that would remain outside the Treaty, and to link the positions of Arab states on the CWC to the Israeli position on the NPT. Despite the Egyptian effort, many other Arab states have signed the CWC.)

---

[35]*Nuclear Proliferation News* No. 20 (21 March 1995).
[36]Ibid.
[37]Reuter News Reports, 6 February 1995, "Arabs Take Stand Against Israeli Nuclear Privilege," cited in *Nuclear Proliferation News* No. 19 (7 March 1995), p.8.

The leaders of the Gulf and North African states reportedly agreed that the primary sources of regional instability and insecurity came from the nuclear, chemical, and biological weapons programs of Iran and Iraq, and that the indefinite extension and strengthening of the NPT regime was in their own national interest.[38]

On March 23, Egypt hosted a special full meeting of the Arab League ministers, which was designed to create a unified position for the NPT Extension Conference. This would have served as a nucleus to gain wider support of the members of the NAM. Vice President Gore arrived in Cairo at the same time and strongly reiterated the U.S. policies in direct and blunt talks with President Mubarak and the representatives of the other Arab states attending the Arab League meeting. As a result of the American pressure, and the interests of some of these states to distance themselves from the Egyptian attempt to establish hegemony, the meeting did not endorse the Egyptian effort, and the Secretary of the Arab League declared that "some Arab countries are leaning toward signing without an Israeli commitment to do so."[39]

Thus, the Egyptian effort to forge a unified Arab position prior to the NPT Conference failed, as did Cairo's attempt to speak for and represent the Arab world. Egypt still had the support of Syria, and worked closely with the Syrian delegation in the Extension Conference, but without firm backing from the Gulf States and North Africa, the Egyptian position was much weaker than had been sought. This also weakened Egypt's capability to forge alliances or gain the support of other states in the NAM in the attempt to link NPT extension to a change in the Israeli policy.

The extensive discussions between the U.S. and Egypt continued until the opening of the NPT Extension Conference. From April 5 to 9, Mubarak was in

---

[38] Although Jordan formally tended to follow the Egyptian position, the 1994 Jordanian-Israeli Peace Treaty calls for a Middle East free from WMD, "both conventional and non-conventional," without specific reference to nuclear weapons or the NPT and IAEA.

[39] *Nuclear Proliferation News* No. 19 (7 March 1995), p.13.

Washington, and, once again, the Egyptian policy on the NPT and Israel was a major focus of official discussions and media appearances. The U.S. government, including President Clinton, continued to seek an Egyptian agreement to end the efforts to block indefinite extension or link its policies to explicit condemnation of Israel. In his meetings with Clinton, Mubarak again pledged that Egypt would not disrupt the conference, and "would not be lobbying other governments against extension of the NPT."[40] In contrast, Mousa, who accompanied Mubarak, declared that Egypt has not modified-and will not modify-its demands, which, he stated, were Israeli agreement, prior to the NPT conference, to discuss a nuclear-free Middle East in "the next meeting" of the multilateral arms control and regional security (ACRS) negotiations, and a commitment to joining the NPT within two years of signing peace treaties with Syria and Lebanon.[41] The apparent contradiction between Mubarak and Mousa raised questions regarding Mubarak's authority and divisions in the Egyptian leadership, or perhaps a division of labor between the leaders.

Throughout this period, Peres continued his efforts to work out a formula with Egypt before the NPT Extension Conference opening. According to press reports, in late February, in yet another meeting (this time in Paris), Peres presented a more specific version of the Israeli policy, pledging to "begin negotiation of a MENWFZ two years after bilateral peace agreements are signed with all states, including Iran." (The same source reported that Foreign Ministry proposals to agree to discussions of the proposed MEWMDFZ in the ACRS talks were rejected by Rabin.)[42]

---

[40]Press Briefing By Ambassador Robert Pelletreau, Assistant Secretary Of State For Near Eastern Affairs And David Satterfield, Assistant Director For Near Eastern And South Asian Affairs, The White House, Office of The Press Secretary, April 5, 1995
[41]Hillel Kuttler, "Moussa: Israel's Fears of NPT Baseless," *Jerusalem Post,* April 5, 1995, p.7
[42]Aluf Benn, "Israel will agree to Nuclear Free Zone to Begin Two Years after Signing of Regional Peace Agreement," *Haaretz,* February 21, 1995, p. 1.

Although Peres presented this as another gesture to end the impasse, it was apparently not understood as such, and the conflict, as well as efforts to resolve it, continued. On March 21, Yosi Beilin, a member of the Israeli cabinet and Peres protege, went to Cairo again, and spoke about the goal of a nuclear-weapon free Middle East – after the achievement of a lasting peace, and that both objectives could be negotiated "in parallel." (This was a major departure, since Israeli official policy has and continues to be that detailed negotiations can only begin after peace in the region has been fully achieved.) Beilin also noted that the concrete language and commitment to join a MEWMDFZ, included in the Israeli ACRS paper on the goals of the process, marked a major change in policy. Beilin claimed that "It was the first comprehensive Israeli paper about this issue and I believe that the common denominator between Egypt's view about it and the Israeli one is not a very small one. I think the idea of an agreement on a nuclear-free zone, which is an idea of President Mubarak, is something mutual."[43] A few days later, Peres presented a further elaboration of the Israeli position on the MENWFZ, emphasizing the development of a system of mutual inspection and comparing this with the discredited NPT/IAEA verification system.[44] However, while the Israelis might have felt that the gap was closing, no such evaluation came from Cairo.

Endgame

Despite Mubarak's pledges to Clinton and declarations in Washington, the Egyptian-Israeli confrontation continued through the NPT Extension conference, which opened in New York on April 19 1995. By this time, it was apparent that Egypt could not block indefinite extension, but hoped to reach a compromise with

---

[43]*Nuclear Proliferation News* No. 21 (4 April 1995).
[44]Ibid.

the U.S., which sought to gain an agreement by consensus.[45] In his opening statement, Mousa declared that "the treaty as it stands today and in view of the absence of accession to it by a neighbor with well known nuclear capabilities, is incapable of safeguarding the national security of Egypt. Consequently, Egypt finds itself today in a position where she cannot support the indefinite extension of the Treaty." He even raised the option of "suspending the Conference for a reasonable period of time." Other Arab states, particularly Syria, supported the Egyptian position.[46] In his opening statement, the Syrian foreign minister attacked the Israeli policy, and declared that "Syria cannot agree to the extension of the NPT unless Israel accedes to the Treaty and subjects its nuclear installation to international inspection." He repeated the Egyptian call for suspension of the conference "to correct the loopholes in the Treaty." (As a non-signatory, Israel did not participate formally in the conference, and maintained low-level representation based on its permanent United Nations delegation.)

The conference began with eight days of General Debate, in which 116 speeches were made. After the General Debate, the three Main Committees (Disarmament, Safeguards, Peaceful Uses) as well as other committees, held meetings, and there were numerous informal consultations. On May 5, Canada presented a proposal for a consensus decision to extend the Treaty indefinitely. (The United States and other supporters of extension sought to avoid a divisive vote and split decision, that might weakened the role of the NPT.) Although this proposal would have gained a majority (its was cosponsored by over 100 states), the Canadian text may not have gained consensus approval. (A group of NAM states proposed

---

[45]Paul Power, "Middle East Nuclear Issues in Global Perspective," *Middle East Policy 4* (September 1995), p.203.
[46]Statement by Farouk Al-Shara, Minister of Foreign Affairs of the Syrian Arabic Republic, to the Conference of the State Parties to the Treaty on the Non-Proliferation of Nuclear Weapons (NPT), April 19, 1996, New York

rolling extensions for 25 years.[47]) South Africa then introduced a draft of principles linked to indefinite extension.[48] The language was largely based on U.S. draft proposals, and, because of the South African government's prestige, also gained the support of the non-aligned movement. This had the effect of severely weakening the Egyptian leverage and potential for gaining the support of the NAM in linking some action specific mention of Israel.

The South African draft led to the negotiation of a declaration adopted by acclamation (explicitly endorsed by 111 of the participating 178 nations) that extended the NPT indefinitely.[49] In addition, the conference adopted documents on Strengthening the Review Process, and on Principles and Objectives for Nuclear Non-proliferation and Disarmament. They addressed general issues, but had specific importance with respect to Israel and the Middle East. These resolutions emphasized the goal of universality and provisions for a strengthened review process, consisting of annual 10-day Preparatory Committee meeting in each of the three years preceding a five-yearly Review Conference. Among the stated objectives of this process are the consideration of "principles, objectives and ways in order to promote the full implementation of the Treaty, as well as its universality," thereby insuring that the Israeli exceptionality will continue to receive attention. In addition, the resolutions specified the goal of reaching agreement on a Comprehensive Test Ban Treaty (CTBT), and a fissile material production cut-off agreement.[50] Israel was active in negotiations for the CTBT, and backed this treaty. However, cut-off proposals are

---

[47]Rauf and Johnson, pp.28-42

[48]Tom Zamora Collina, "South Africa Bridges the Gap," *Bulletin of the Atomic Scientists* (July/August 1995), p.30.

[49]Continued dissension and dissatisfaction by some states, including the Arab states, blocked adoption of a formal Final Declaration and assessment of the status of the NPT and its operations. This also occurred in the 1980 and 1990 NPT Review Conferences (See Epstein, p. 29).

[50]"Indefinite Extension of the Non-Proliferation Treaty: Risks and Reckonings," *Report of the 1995 NPT Review and Extension Conference,* New York, 17 April to 12 May 1995, *Acronym* No. 7 (September 1995).

problematic for Israel, as they are viewed as "back-doors" to the NPT and external inspection on the activities at the Dimona facility. As noted, the Israeli government has not taken an official position on the cut-off, but Rabin once termed these proposals "unworkable."[51]

At the same time, these resolutions were also seen as providing support for the Israeli position, particularly with respect to the direct negotiation of a regional nuclear-weapon-free zone among the countries in the region. Section five of the Set of Principles, calls for the "establishment of internationally recognized nuclear-weapon-free zones, on the basis of arrangements freely arrived at among the States of the region." Section six mentions the Middle East specifically in this context, and noting that the "specific characteristics of each region" should be considered.

Although officials of United States government reported that Mubarak promised Clinton that Egypt would not disrupt the extension process by seeking to isolate Israel, the American and other delegations expected that to obtain complete consensus, some form of compromise with the Egyptian demands would be necessary. The U.S. delegation had been working with delegates from some moderate Arab states on such a compromise resolution. There was also some hope that the Egyptians would view the language in the other resolutions and reports, cited above, as an acceptable achievement. However, the efforts to devise a compromise failed and the Egyptian delegation demanded that Israel be explicitly singled out. On 9 May, just one day before the scheduled adoption of the three main conference extension documents and three days before the end of the conference, Egypt and 13 other members of the Arab League, (Algeria, Bahrain, Egypt, Iraq, Jordan, Kuwait, Libyan Arab Jamahiriya, Mauritania, Morocco, Qatar, Saudi Arabia, Sudan, Tunisia

---

[51]David Makovsky, "PM: Egyptian Model of Full Withdrawal Difficult To Change" *Jerusalem Post*, 24 September 1995, p.1.

and Yemen), tabled a draft resolution focusing explicitly on Israel. The text called for Israel's immediate acceptance of the NPT and IAEA safeguards, and sought to link the consensus on the South African package to endorsement of this draft. Egypt insisted that its resolution be adopted prior to the formal decision on the NPT extension, thereby complicating and delaying the overall conference activities and threatening to block consensus.[52]

The U.S. government recognized that approval of such a document would have a negative impact on Israeli policy in the peace process, without changing Israeli policy with respect to the NPT or other arms limitation measures. This move, just before the scheduled end of the conference, was a direct violation of the pledges Mubarak had made to Clinton, and according to reports, the U.S. President called Mubarak from Moscow "and warned him against playing such a dangerous game."[53] Members of the U.S. delegation met intensively with the Arab delegations, and during a caucus of the Arab states, many of the co-sponsors declared that they would not vote for this resolution, leaving Egypt and Syria isolated.

At this stage, various other proposals were discussed, including one that would have linked Israel with other non-NPT signatories in the region (Oman and United Arab Emirates), but the representatives of these states objected, reportedly because they did not want to be included with Israel.[54] After another round of intense consultations, and phone calls from Washington to the national capitals, the representatives most of the Arab cosponsors indicated that their representatives were prepared to support the consensus for NPT extension, regardless of the response to the Middle East resolution.

---

[52]*Nuclear Proliferation News,* No. 18 (17 February 1995); Power, p.204; Epstein, p.28.
[53]Shmuel Segev, "Egypt Moving Toward Anti-US Anti-Israel Policy" *Jerusalem Post* 17 May, 1995, p.5. There are also reports that Vice President Gore's foreign policy aide, Leonard Furth, called Osamah El-Baz, (Gore was the formal head of the American delegation to the NPT Extension Conference) and both reports may be correct.
[54]Power, p. 204; Segev, p.5

Based on these discussions, the U.S. delegation prepared an alternative Middle East resolution, which, in marked contrast to the Egyptian proposal, included a specific endorsement of the peace process and linked the MEWMDFZ to this process. Israel was not mentioned by name (although the report produced by Committee III and attached to the final document named all non-NPT states). The objectives of this decision were not stated explicitly, but was apparently designed to provide Egypt with something to show for its efforts, avoid embarrassment for Mubarak, and a deep rift in relations between Cairo and Washington, while also not pushing Israel into a corner.

At this point, a sponsor (or sponsors) had to be found, and the three NPT depository states (the United States, Britain, and Russia) agreed to play this role. Although some analysts later called this "an inspired political maneuver" by Egypt and the Arab states[55], the role of the depository states was the result of a proposal from a member of the American delegation, and the political implications were apparently not recognized at the time. (Israel, as an non-NPT signatory, is not bound by any of the resolutions, although U.S. officials contacted Israeli policy makers in Israel, and sought their response to some of the events and resolutions.)

The conclusion of the NPT Extension Conference marked an important point in the conflict over Israel's NPT status and the ambiguous nuclear deterrent. The conference ended with a unanimous decision to extend the NPT indefinitely, without a change in Israeli policy or status. However, the provisions in the formal decisions and in the Middle East Resolution left the opportunity for continuing the conflict in future review conferences and other meetings. Indeed, immediately after the end of the conference, the Egyptian government indicated that the issue was far from resolved, and that the conflict would continue. In a meeting of the plenary of the

---

[55]Indefinite Extension of the Non-Proliferation Treaty: Risks and Reckonings, *Acronym* No. 7 (September 1995) p.60

permanent Conference on Disarmament in June, Egypt's Ambassador Mounir Zahran urged implementation of the Middle East resolution, and called for "concrete actions" in its implementation with respect to Israel.[56] The process and conflict between Israel and Egypt disrupted and set-back the Arab-Israeli peace process and would continue to do so.

Shortly after the assassination of Rabin in November 1995, Shimon Peres, who became the prime minister, met with Mubarak and Mousa in Egypt. Peres sought to strengthen support for the peace process in Israel by demonstrating improved relations with Egypt. In the wake of this meeting, Peres is reported to have stated that he had received a pledge from Mubarak for a year's "cease fire" on the nuclear issue, and resumption of cooperation in the ACRS process.[57] However, there was no official confirmation from either government. Shortly thereafter, Mousa and other Egyptian officials resumed their campaign, and continued to block efforts to resume the ACRS with discussions on non-nuclear weapons limitations and CSBMs. In addition, public pressure on Israel continued. In November, after an earthquake in the Red Sea, Mousa said that "Egypt was following up" reports that this might be related to Israeli nuclear tests, and this theme has been repeated frequently by Egyptian officials.[58]

[56]*Nuclear Proliferation News* No. 27 (15 June 1995). An Egyptian view of the Conference was presented by Mahmoud Karem, Director of Department of Disarmament Affairs, Egyptian Ministry of Foreign Affairs, in "The 1995 NPT Review and Extension Conference: A Third World Perspective," a paper submitted to the Institut Francais des Relations International (IFRI), June 1995

[57]Guy Bechor, "The Nuclear Scarecrow is less Threatening," *Haaretz*, 3 January 1996, p.b-2; *PPNN Newsbrief*, (Fourth Quarter 1995), p.2, citing the *New York Times*, 17 December 1995 and 23 December 1995

[58]Salamah Ahmad Salamah, "Closeup: Nuclear Tests in al-Aqaba?," *Al Ahram*, 28 November 1995, p. 10; in FBIS-NES-95-233, (5 December 1995), p.10. In contrast, the Egyptian Minister of Science announced that the seismic evidence showed that the movement was the result of an earthquake.

The Next Round: NPT 2000

In the three preparatory conferences "PrepComs" prior to the 2000 Review Conference, and in the conference itself during April 2000, the debate and much of the conflict was repeated. However, the events of 1995 created a pattern, and the subsequent conflict more or less repeated this pattern. Prior to the conference, Israel was pressed again to make concessions to Egypt to avoid confrontation, and while some important CBMs were taken, such as signing the Comprehensive Test Ban Treaty, and conducting a cooperative regional calibration test in coordination with the CTBTO in 1998, Israeli policy on the NPT did not change in any way.

In the 2000 conference, which also took place during a critical phase of the peace process, the interaction lacked the drama and some of the tension of the previous round, and the outcome more or less reinforced the precedents set earlier. Egypt again pressed its campaign to isolate Israel on the nuclear issue, and the U.S. took the lead in negotiating with the Egyptians. In a series of meetings that again took place in the weeks prior to the NPT conference, the U.S. government reached agreement with Egypt on acceptable language regarding Israel and the Middle East, but this time, this agreement held. (The Clinton Administration was careful to avoid a repetition of the confusion in the last days of the 1995 conference, that led to the co-sponsorship of the ME resolution, and departed from the guidelines that had been agreed before the conference.) Once again, Israel, as an non-NPT state that had no wish to be put on the docket and forced to defend its policies in a hostile environment, maintained a low profile.

The final document went a bit further than the 1995 text, naming Israel specifically in the Middle East resolution, rather than merely calling on states, without name, in the region to adhere to the NPT. Egypt could claim a victory, while for Israel, this could be seen technical change, since in the intervening years, the Gulf States joined the NPT regime, leaving Israel, whether named explicitly or not, as the only non-signatory in the Middle East. For its part, the U.S. could claim to have prevented further erosion in Israel's position. For the first time, the lack of Iraqi compliance (or rather, the inability to certify Iraqi compliance) with the NPT obligations was included in the final text, introducing a new element into the Middle East resolution.

In other words, the conflict has clearly become ritualized and repetitive, with little impact on the policies of either Egypt or Israel. In upcoming PrepComs (the first of which is due to take place in 2002), it will start again, reaching a climax in 2005. There is no evidence to suggest that Israel is likely to alter its policies in the intervening period, but developments in Iran and Iraq could have a significant impact on the status of the NPT in the region. In terms of bilateral relations between Egypt and Israel, every sign points to a continuation of the conflict.

Assessment

For both Washington and Jerusalem, the outcome of the 1995 NPT extension conference, and, to a certain degree, the next conference in 2000, were major diplomatic achievements. The United States succeeded in obtaining indefinite extension without causing divisions or dissension among the signatories (although not quite the consensus or unanimous support the administration had initially sought) and without a negative impact on other foreign policy objectives, most notably the Arab-Israeli peace process. Israel was able to maintain its nuclear deterrent posture while avoiding conflict with the U.S. (indeed, the close coordination had the effect of enhancing bilateral ties and increasing the understanding of each other's interests and objectives).

The conflict also forced the Israeli government to provide a rationale for the policy of nuclear ambiguity, and the underlying logic of this option was articulated in public domestic and international frameworks. This was a major change from past policy, in which Israeli leaders generally avoided any public discussion of nuclear and deterrent policy, and sought refuge behind standard phrases that provided no explanation or justification. Rabin, Peres, and other Israeli leaders clearly articulated the links between the maintenance of the nuclear capability and the continued threats to national survival, linked to the military, geographic and demographic asymmetries in the region. Perhaps the clearest example of this new formulation, developed in the course of the conflict with Egypt, was presented by Ehud Barak shortly after he became Foreign Minister in January 1996. In the absence of proven and reliable regional peace agreements, Barak declared, "Israel's nuclear policy, as it is perceived in the eyes of the Arabs, has not changed, will not change and cannot change, because it is a fundamental stand on a matter of survival which impacts all the generations to come."[59] Israel's increasingly active role in international organizations and forums dealing with arms control and non-proliferation, such as the Conference on Disarmament and the OSCE, enabled the government to consolidate and strengthen the domestic political commitment to these policies. Despite the exceptionality of its policies, Israel avoided the political and diplomatic isolation that sought by Egypt.

The Indian and Pakistani nuclear tests in May 1998 and their transformation from the status of threshold states and NPT-holdouts to nuclear weapons states also

---

[59] Aluf Benn, "Barak: Nuclear Policy has not and will not change" *Haaretz* 31 December, 1995, p.10a

changed Israel's status. Israel was now the only remaining non-NPT state that had not tested or become an overt nuclear power. In addition, and in contrast to the cases of India and Pakistan, the Israeli government's decision to sign the Comprehensive Test Ban Treaty marked an important confidence building measure, indicating Israel's readiness to contribute to global arms control regimes when this was compatible with its national security. All of this helped to reduce Israel's political vulnerability in the face of the Egyptian campaign.

In addition, the U.S. government accepted the Israeli position that nuclear arms control and the status of the Israeli deterrent was inextricably linked to the Middle East peace process, and discussions of the former are dependent on substantial progress in the latter. This link can be seen in the language adopted by the NPT Extension and Review conferences of 1995 and 2000, in the resolutions on the Middle East and in formal statements issued by the U.S. State Department.[60] The United States and Israel also established a formal forum for bilateral consultations on non-proliferation and arms control issues in order to increase coordination and prevent misunderstanding and conflict.

Going further, in October 1998, following the Wye Plantation Summit in which the Netanyahu government agreed to specific conditions and a timetable for further redeployments in the context of negotiations with the Palestinians, the U.S. and Israel signed a new strategic Memorandum of Agreement. In this agreement, the U.S. pledged to "enhance Israel's defensive and deterrent capabilities" against threats of ballistic missiles, as well as to upgrade the strategic and military cooperation with

---

[60]United States Information Agency Near East/South Asia English Washington File, Tuesday, June 25, 1996, Transcript: State Department Briefing, Tuesday, June 25, 1996, Briefing from Acting State Department Spokesman Glyn Davies

Israel.[61] In the 2000 NPT Review conference, this agreement was important in strengthening coordination between Israel and the U.S. on these issues.

The policies adopted by the U.S. government also reflect a shift from exclusive emphasis on the universal nature of the NPT regime to a regional approach to arms control. For many years, the United States had consistently placed primary or exclusive emphasis on the NPT and IAEA framework. The policies adopted by the United States in the context of the NPT extension process demonstrate acceptance of the Israeli position that its nuclear policies are linked to the regional security environment, which is beyond the scope of global regimes such as the NPT. The first steps in this process of change in the American approach to non-proliferation can be seen following the Gulf War, and the realization that the effectiveness of the application of the NPT on a global basis was flawed in regions such as the Middle East.[62] These changes were expressed in the 1991 Bush Initiative, but then, the regional framework was still closely coupled to the NPT and IAEA. After 1995, this link became much looser.

From the Egyptian perspective, the results were mixed, at best. The Mubarak government did not succeed in its stated objective of forcing Israel to accede to the NPT or pledge future acceptance, and to place all nuclear facilities under safeguards. As in the case of the CWC, Egypt was unable to gain sustained support from the Arab states or recognition as the leader of the Arab world, even on this issue. In various meetings of the Arab League prior to the Extension Conference, as well as during the conference itself, representatives of these states distanced themselves from

---

[61]No author, "Israel and U.S. sign strategic agreement," *Ha'aretz*, November 1, 1998; "U.S. Signs Accord to Protect Israel From Mass-Destruction Arms," *New York Times*, November 2, 1998; Danna Harman, "US, Israel upgrade strategic relations," *Jerusalem Post*, November 1, 1998

[62]Gerald M. Steinberg, "Non-Proliferation: Time for Regional Approaches?," *Orbis* 38:3 (Summer 1994) pp. 409-424

the Egyptian position. For the most part, in their interactions with Israel, the other Arab states did not follow the Egyptian lead with respect to placing exclusive emphasis on the nuclear issue.

In addition, as a result of the continued and single-minded campaign, the Egyptian government is seen by many, both in the region and outside, as carrying some responsibility for the difficulties in the peace process. The hostility from Egypt and the conflict generated over this issue had a negative impact on Israeli public opinion and reduced support for risk taking. Critics of the Labor Government's policies argued the high level of hostility from Egypt and attempts to isolate Israel were negative precedents for proceeding with withdrawal from the Golan Heights in order to reach a peace agreement with Syria.

This does not mean that the outcome of this campaign was a total defeat for Egyptian diplomacy. The Middle East Resolution in the NPTREC and the frequent review conferences provide mechanisms for maintaining pressure on Israel, for seeking to isolate Jerusalem, and for giving the Egyptian government a cause around which to build domestic legitimacy and claim inter-Arab leadership.[63] Despite the outcome, Egypt is able to claim a pivotal diplomatic role in the region, and gain the attention of the United States. Domestically, the role that Egypt played in confronting both Israel and the United States on this issue was very popular, thereby strengthening the legitimacy of the regime.[64]

---

[63]Prepared Statement by Ambassador Mounir Zahran (Egypt) Before this Second Session of the Preparatory Committee for the 2000 Review Conference of the Parties of the Treaty on the Non-proliferation of Nuclear Weapons Geneva April 28, 1998

[64]For a discussion of the role of Egyptian domestic factors in this process, see Gerges, pp.69-78, and Guy Bechor, "The Egyptian Campaign on the NPT Increased the Popularity of Mubarak and Mousa on Cairo's Streets," *Haaretz*, 19 April, 1995, p.2

In this sense, the NPT conflict should be seen as only one issue, albeit the most visible, in a series of Egyptian efforts to assert dominance and slow the acceptance of Israel in the region. The Egyptian government has also urged the Arab states to suspend regional economic cooperation with Israel in the context of the Casablanca and Amman Economic Summits and the Barcelona conference, (sponsored by the European Union). Cairo has blocked progress in all of the multilateral working groups, accused Israel of planting mines in the Sinai (this accusation was later retracted), and strongly protested Israeli-Turkish military cooperation agreements[65]. From the Israeli perspective, the multiplicity of conflicts, and the stated Egyptian objective or "reducing Israel to its 'natural' size'[66]," indicate that Cairo's campaign on the NPT was not fundamentally motivated by threat perceptions, but rather is a means of slowing the process of normalization between Israel and other Arab states, in the effort to enhance Egypt's own power in the region.[67] For Egypt, the NPT Extension and ACRS processes and the bilateral discussions with Israel were not seen as the basis for stability that would serve the interests of all states in the region, but rather an arena of political conflict in a broader zero-sum game.

In addition to the global and regional factors that shaped Egyptian policy (Iraq and Saddam Hussein, the end of the Cold War, a decline in Egyptian influence in the Middle East and Arab world due to the wider Middle East peace process, and the domestic political support for efforts to weaken Israeli military capabilities and ending the nuclear monopoly), expectations of support, particularly from the U.S.

---

[65]Arieh O'Sullivan, "Turkey Denies Letting IAF Train There," *Jerusalem Post,* April 8, 1996
[66]Amre Mousa, cited in *Davar Rishon*, April, 11 1996; cited by Zeev Schiff, "Six Difficult Nuclear Questions," *Haaretz*, 24 February 1995, p.C-2
[67]Segev, p.5

government, appear to have influenced the Egyptian perceptions. The available evidence indicates that until late 1994 or early 1995, the U.S. did not convey the message, that it would not press Israel for concessions or compromise, to Cairo.[68] By this time, the Egyptian campaign was in full gear, and both domestic and regional political commitments had been made. In an area where policies change slowly, even if the Egyptian leaders had decided that the anti-Israel campaign was too costly in terms of bilateral relations with Israel, the regional peace process, and relations with the U.S., (and there is no indication that the major actors in Cairo reached these conclusions), it would have been difficult to suddenly abandon its policies in the few months that remained before the Extension Conference.

This analysis suggests that in dealing with Egypt, U.S. government officials should be extremely wary of creating expectations in the future regarding pressure on Israel. As the evidence presented above indicates, the long-standing policy of nuclear ambiguity is deeply ingrained in Israeli security doctrine, and is widely supported by the national security bureaucracy, the political leadership, and the press. In the absence of fundamental political changes in the region, going far beyond the small steps towards conflict resolution taken to far, this is not likely to change.

Similarly, the Egyptian policy and emphasis on this issue are likely to continue. Despite some initial efforts and agreements to resume the multilateral talks, including the ACRS process, following the election of Barak in 1999, and the Sharm el Sheik agreement shortly afterwards, in practice, the obstacles remained

---

[68]Egyptian policy makers viewed many of the statements and publications of American officials and analysts regarding NPT universality and expressions of concern and critiques of the Israeli policy of nuclear ambiguity as indications of support for the Egyptian position. The 1991 Bush Middle East Arms Control Initiative was seen as explicit endorsement of the 1990 Mubarak Initiative. See Yahya M. Sadowski, *Scuds or Butter: The Political Economy of Arms Control in the Middle East*, (Washington DC: Brookings, 1993) p.41; and Moshe Zak, "The Bush Plan: Between Shamir and Mubarak" *Ma'ariv*, May 31 1991, p.B-2

unchanged. ACRS remains frozen for the foreseeable future, and Egypt and Israel maintain opposing positions in the U.N., IAEA, CD and other international forums. The NPT conferences reinforced the positions of the major actors, and the pattern of Egyptian demands, Israeli resistance, and U.S. efforts to contain the tensions and limit damage to the political relationships in the region will be repeated . After 10 years in which this issue has been the focus of the Egyptian government's policy with respect to Israel, and in the absence of any evidence to the contrary, it appears that the conflict is likely to continue.

Chapter 12

Israel Today: Strategic Options

Ze'ev Schiff

This will not be a discussion of the history of Israel's nuclear history. It is a very long and complex story, deserving a separate survey. My point of departure will be the peace process between Israel, the Arab countries, and the Palestinians. My intention is to take stock of the changes which followed the peace process. It is against this background that Israel is examining its policy.

Five tough questions now face Israel. The answers will reveal the strategic alternatives available to Israel and, to a great extent, its policy and conduct in the foreseeable future. Let me begin with the questions:

1.   Has a drastic change already occurred, one that calls for an immediate Israeli revision of its security policy? A policy which attaches an important role to the nuclear factor?

2.   Do these changes justify compliance with the call on Israel to sign the Non-Proliferation Treaty (NPT) at a set future date? And furthermore, has the time come to undertake the proposed cutoff of production of fissile materials?

3.   Has the time come for Israel to change its ambiguous nuclear policy? Namely, that Israel should display its nuclear inventory to the world?

4.   Would Israel and the region be in greater danger if a number of Middle East countries become nuclear?

5.   Should Israel make some reassuring moves, even if it is not prepared to join the NPT?

Undeniably, the Middle East has undergone a great transformation. It began when peace was signed with Egypt. Most Arab countries opposed it and turned against Egypt. The changes that followed did not happen in a vacuum. They happened against the backdrop of the collapsed Soviet Union (opening dangerous arsenals of fissile materials as well as releasing nuclear weapons production experts anxious to make a living) and the consolidation of the United States as the only great world power.

The peace process which started in the wake of the Gulf War, and the defeat of Iraq, led to the Madrid conference and to the mutual recognition of Israel and the mainstream of the Palestinian national movement. Then peace between Israel and Jordan followed. These changes allowed Israel to sit, for the first time, on multilateral international arms control committees including a number of Arab countries. Although important countries like Syria and Iraq are not participating, and although there are substantial differences with the Arab participants, a new dialogue has evolved and a different view of the problems related to regional security has emerged.

Alongside this positive development, Israel cannot turn a blind eye to persistent reports reaching various intelligence services that Iran is working to obtain nuclear weapons and that Iraq has also developed biological weapons. Up to this day Iraq refuses to reveal to the UN special control commission the identity of the countries and firms from which it has procured materials for the manufacture of weapons of mass destruction. Incidentally, three other countries refuse to divulge information on the subject. They are North Korea, China, and Egypt. Egypt claims that such disclosure would put its national security at risk.

The new threats take various forms. One of these threats stems from the rise of radical Islam. In reviewing the changes, careful attention should be given to the fact that the Middle East is the only region where, in the past five years, two countries were eliminated. The one, Kuwait, emerged by the skin of its teeth seven months later. The other, South Yemen, was ignored by the international community and ceased to exist after being occupied by the North. It follows that there have been some significant changes in the Middle East, but no substantial transformation so far. The peace process is only beginning, and many pitfalls still lie ahead. The dramatic turning point will occur when Syria signs a peace treaty with Israel and two important countries, Iraq and Iran, with their nuclear ambitions, join the peace process.

Which means, in answer to the first question, that for the moment not enough has happened to reassure Israel that the strategic threat to its survival has been eliminated. For the time being, Israel sees no satisfactory justification to review its basic security policy regarding these threats, even if they seem less menacing right now.

All the same, unavoidable changes in Israel's approach to security can be expected to take place as the peace process progresses. This process will oblige Israel - which geographically speaking is very small - to give up large territories. Its small strategic depth will shrink even further. A study of Israeli policy should clearly bear in mind that even the most moderate Israeli government could not give up territories, dismantle settlements and evict a large population from its homes and settlements in the territories. What the Arabs are demanding is sure to tear the nation apart. To meet Syrian, Palestinian and Jordanian demands, Israel would also have to give up a great deal of water, and absorb large numbers of Palestinian refugees. On top of all that, Israel would have to give up its strategic deterrent capability. To make these demands on Israel is to display enormous naivete, unless they are intended to bring about the destruction of the Jewish state. Israeli public opinion will not have it, and rightly so.

It should be pointed out that Israel must take great care to maintain the tangible stability and effectiveness of its strategic deterrent. According to the polls, this is a widely accepted fact in Israel. Let me quote Jean Pierre Chevenement, the former French minister of defense who resigned in protest against the Gulf War. He supported Israel's having what he described as minimal nuclear deterrence at a certain level. So long as Israel is threatened, it would not be realistic to expect it to give up its estimated nuclear weapons, he said.

This explains why Israel will not agree to commit itself here and now, as vigorously demanded by the Arabs, to precisely say when it would sign the NPT. That answers the second question. Israel has rejected these pressures on the eve of the NPT conference. It is quite clear that Israel will strongly reject international control of vital Israeli security matters. Jerusalem will not tolerate international bodies running its affairs.

Not a single Egyptian objective in this struggle has been achieved. Egypt has also failed to induce Washington to pressure Israel on the NPT issue. But Egyptian failure does not necessarily please Israel. Naturally, Israel must protect its vital interests, but it does not wish to humiliate Egypt. That has not been the object, as the Israelis have repeatedly explained to the Egyptians. From Israel's standpoint, the international conference on the extension of the NPT ended without any apparent changes: there were five recognized nuclear powers and another three de facto countries – Israel, India and Pakistan. Israel wishes this situation to remain unchanged for the time being.

Can Israel at this point be reasonably expected to cut off the production of fissile material? Israel's prompt reply is negative, but it is my impression that the last word on this has not been said. One thing is clear: Israel will insist that such a settlement be concluded within the framework of the Middle East peace agreements. The agreement should be based on mutual supervision, including Israeli and Arab teams, and not just visits of international inspection teams.

The third question addresses the proposal that Israel take the initiative and review its nuclear policy. To this day, Israel has neither confirmed nor vigorously denied possession of nuclear weapons. To my mind, such a change would be a serious mistake. It would plunge Israel into a serious and superfluous confrontation with the American Congress which is committed to take action against countries in possession of nuclear weapons. American aid to Israel will be in jeopardy. But there is another reason for rejecting that proposal. It is rather doubtful that in ceasing to be inexplicit, Israel would be doing Egypt – the driving force behind the demand for change – any great favor. The immediate outcome of an official Israeli statement will be the rise of radical demands in the Arab world that Egyptian and other Arab countries develop their own nuclear weapons. By unfolding its nuclear situation Israel will provoke the Arabs unnecessarily. It would be pointless and ill-timed to revise a policy which has been regarded as highly successful.

The answer to the fourth question may well be the most problematic and not just for Israel. Could Israel not be faced with a more dangerous nuclear situation than it is in today? The danger is that the Middle East could, all of a sudden, be transformed into a multi-polar nuclear area. That is certainly a greater danger. Such nuclearization does not necessarily depend on Israel. The Iranian nuclear project is not necessarily motivated by fear of Israel. The Iranians have decided to go nuclear after the findings in Iraq. But what may be of the utmost importance is that there is no guarantee that the nuclearization of additional countries would come to light after an early warning. What we have here is an invisible "red line," unlike the clearly visible geographical borderlines. The crossing of the nuclear borderline can be sudden and undetected by even the best intelligence services. Once the lessons of

Iraq and its nuclear weapons have been learned, no effort will be spared to avoid exposure.

Israel is facing two grave dangers which need to be addressed as its strategic objectives. First and foremost is the danger posed by the combination of nuclear weapons with unbridled Islamic radicalism. It could threaten Israel's very existence and cannot be ignored. The second danger would be posed in a state of war when a negative coalition is between the ring of countries bordering on Israel and the ring of countries outside, such as Iraq and Iran.

The second danger can be reduced by peace with Syria – the only way to fix a buffer between Israel and the countries of the outside ring. That would greatly reduce the threat from Iran and Iraq.

If such a settlement is accompanied by progress on the Palestinian course, the levels of hostility towards Israel will drop considerably. Without it the danger of nuclear weapons in the hands of a country guided by Islamic radicalism is greater. Multipolarized nuclearization will plunge the Middle East into a very serious situation. In that type of Middle East, Israel would be exposed to still greater dangers.

There will be people in Israel who will argue that if such a danger does exist, a danger that does not necessarily depend on Israel, its nuclear policy must not be changed. Others will argue to the contrary that because of this danger urgent steps should be taken to exclude weapons of mass destruction from the area. At present, Israel favors the first approach. It opposes a substantial and hasty change. A multipolar nuclearization of the Middle East is a situation Israel would obviously be unable to handle by itself. Israel would also require unequivocal American deterrence in that new situation.

We are left with the question of the reassuring steps Israel should take. Especially because Israel is refusing to join the NPT, it should be as flexible as possible in its measures to reassure its neighbors. These measures should form a part of Israeli policy. Concerning the NPT, it is worth remembering Israel's declaration that no later than two years after regional peace is achieved, including peace with each member of the Arab League and with Iran, Israel would agree to discuss nuclear demilitarization and the exclusion of other weapons of mass destruction from the Middle East. For the first time Israel has named a time, open and conditional though it may be. An important principle of this policy is that regional peace must be reached first. Once that is achieved, negotiations on the regional demilitarization of nuclear and other weapons will follow.

In fact, Israel has already taken a few steps. It is prepared to join the treaty banning the production and possession of chemical weapons (CWC), a treaty which involves extremely intrusive inspections. Most Arabs did not join it. Israel has signed but not yet ratified the Missile Technology Control Regime (MTCR) which is not joined by Egypt either. Israel has declared that it would be willing to join a treaty banning nuclear tests – Comprehensive Test Ban Treaty (CTBT). Israel has also joined the UN register for the sale and procurement of arms whereas most Arab countries have abstained.

The road ahead is long. Nobody can expect Israel to disarm and give up its deterrent capability just because declarations of readiness for peace can be heard from across the lines. Israel cannot disregard the many asymmetries enjoyed by the Arabs. Their vast territories provide strategic depth, they have large populations and a wealth of natural resources. All these are fixed asymmetries while Israel's technological and scientific edge could be temporary and cease to exist. The road is long indeed. Progress along that road will be with measured steps and the order of things should not be reversed. First peace must be achieved and later, as concurrently as possible, the disarmament of threats must be established. As far as I can see there is no chance that Israel would agree to reverse the order by disarming itself and giving up its capability to defend itself before peace is firmly established.

Chapter 13

Egypt's Position towards the Israeli Nuclear Arsenal

Ahmed Abdel Halim

The Middle East of the Future

Before tackling the main issue, we should try to envision the region we live in within a general framework of security and peace. Peace in the Middle East is a desirable and possible objective. We understand peace not only as a series of politico-security and economic arrangements, but also as a state of mind, a human condition and a framework for thinking. It rests ultimately on the conviction of its necessity. To our minds, peace involves not just state-to-state relations, but should also include society-to-society interactions based on mutual benefits, growing interdependence and a balance of interests.

The Middle East we want for our children is a region which values human dignity, democratic practices, economic development, social welfare and regional integration, and which excludes military superiority. We envision a region in which ideas, human beings and goods can flow freely and without restrictions. Borders between states will continue to exist but they will be more demarcation lines for jurisdiction purposes than battlefield lines. Lines of polarization between states will dissipate, and although cleavages will not be totally resolved, they will be overcome.

On the domestic scene, democratic regimes based on political pluralism will be the dominant form of government. Political tolerance and acceptance of others will be crucial values. Religious trends and movements will increasingly embrace democratic ideas similar to those of European Christian parties. Human rights will be monitored and protected. Political parties of similar persuasions in different states are likely to interact with each other, and similarly syndicates and professional associations. Economically, free market economics will allow the flow of factors of production across frontiers. Regionally, the Middle East will have its political, economic and security structures.

On the military-security side, the Middle East will be free from all weapons of mass destruction: chemical, biological, and nuclear. Defense policies will be based on conventional weapons and all states will adopt defensive military doctrines. Military industries will be converted, or at least most of them, into civilian industries and some forms of military cooperation will be instituted.

Regionally, it is difficult to envision the achievement of any significant decrease in the level of armament in the absence of peace and stability in the region. The nature of any arms arrangements must reflect the willingness of the countries involved to live in peace with each other, moving from a state of war to one of peace. These conditions will transform former adversaries into, first, neighbors and then partners. Consequently, in the Middle East of the future, there should not be a place for policies that aim at achieving stability and security through military superiority, especially in the nuclear field, but only through economic, social and political interaction.

Regional security and arms limitation agreements in the region would be based upon the quantitative and qualitative symmetry in the military capabilities of the region's states including domestic military industrial capabilities. Security would be achieved through agreed upon political arrangements, the coupling of arms control or disarmament arrangements with effective verification regimes, and the application of these principles to all states of the region without exception in a balanced and non-discriminatory manner. The objective of arms limitation arrangements would be the achievement of "increased levels" of national security for all parties at the "lowest levels" of armaments, and not the achievement of security for one party at the expense of others.

Thus, for the Middle East to be stable it requires an integrative process on three levels: a political settlement, economic development, and defense arrangements which involve a stabilizing role for the United Nations, the United States and Europe. The maintenance of peace requires a certain degree of understanding and economic development and opens the door for the further enhancement of both.

We also note that peace is not a fairy tale full of happy events, but rather a complex and painful process. It has its agonies and frustrations, and in its early phases it can be a destabilizing element. In a situation of protracted social conflict that has lasted for almost a century, change will not be easy and requires time and perseverance. It follows that the conclusion of a peace treaty or agreement will unleash forces of both stabilization and destabilization. In this context, a transitional period during which the foundations for the shift to peace are laid down seems of crucial importance. Of great significance here is the further investigation of the peace process mechanisms and the requisites for a breakthrough.

Just as we need mechanisms for the initial phase of the peace process, we also need corrective mechanisms to maintain the peace once it has been established. Studies in this field should be a crucial part of our endeavors in this conference and others. In other words, for the peace process to endure we must invest in its continuity. In conclusion, we should see the Middle East, now and in the future, as a peaceful region in which all parties live in peace and security within their international boundaries. We should also see the Middle East as a region of cooperation and coordination among its peoples in all spheres of interest. But most importantly, we should see the Middle East as an area free of all types of weapons of mass destruction and their means of delivery, and this should be the final goal that we all seek to realize.

Clear and present danger

The striking military asymmetry in the Middle East, especially in the nuclear field, constitutes a clear and present danger, both now and in the future. Such an asymmetry in Israel's favor has always been emphasized by the Israelis as a condition conducive to peace in the region. However, this is viewed by the Arabs as a dictated peace and cannot be accepted for the long term. Thus, a discussion of a significant decrease in all levels of armaments and a negotiation about regional security and arms control arrangements in the region is a prerequisite for peace and stability in the Middle East.

Regional security and arms control agreements in the region should be based upon: 1) the importance of quantitative and qualitative symmetry in the military capabilities of the region's states including domestic military industrial capabilities; 2) achieving security through agreed-upon political arrangements excluding military superiority; 3) arms control or disarmament arrangements should be coupled with effective verification regimes, and these principles should apply to all states of the region without exception in a balanced and non-discriminatory manner. The objective would be the achievement of increased levels of national security for all parties at the lowest level of cost and armaments, and not the achievement of security for one party at the expense of others. This objective could be achieved through taking effective steps to make the Middle East a zone free from nuclear weapons and other weapons of mass destruction, preventing an arms race among the region's states, and achieving greater military transparency in the different weapon systems.

The most important factor in this regard is the necessity of reaching a reasonable and acceptable regional balance of power that takes into consideration the threat perceptions of each state while not creating a situation in which one state's perceived security needs creates a perception of threat among other states. The balance is crucial for stability. Once this principle is accepted, it is necessary to determine the size of each state's armed forces, as well as the quantity and quality of their equipment, their operational plans, and their strategic needs according to the security considerations of each country individually, taking into account the concerns of other states in the region. Quite clearly a state that has not only conventional superiority but a monopoly on nuclear and space capabilities has an excess of military power that gives it the potential for offensive action, which can be seen as a threat to other states.

Peace should be maintained by using the tools of peace, including economic cooperation and social exchanges, and not the tools of war. Peace cannot be secured through the use or threat of military force, even if that threat is only implicit. A key concern in Egypt's military thinking and planning is the extraordinary imbalance caused by Israel's military program in the nuclear and space fields. As Israel has refused to join the Nuclear Non-Proliferation Treaty (NPT), its nuclear capabilities face no international restrictions. The argument, or pretense, that Israel's nuclear weapons cannot be used for strategic or military purposes are not tenable and ignore the danger that these weapons pose. Similarly, the arguments that the Arabs should not be concerned about Israel's nuclear capability now that there is peace, or that these weapons constitute a guarantee of continued peace, ignore the fact that a peace based on international pressure is not a real and secure peace.

Regional states cannot permanently accept such an Israeli threat and will seek to eliminate it by finding a compatible and equivalent means if, and when, regional and international conditions change. This would multiply the clear and present danger in the Middle East. The only alternative, and the only real basis for true peace, is for all parties to accept the Egyptian initiative for the creation of a region free of nuclear weapons and other weapons of mass destruction. The adoption of a program for a region free of nuclear weapons is a crucial step in arms control, and towards peace and stability in the region.

Perceptions

Before going any further, we should examine some of the perceptions that constitute a major obstacle facing arms control, peace and stability in the Middle East. The protracted nature of the Arab-Israeli conflict has resulted in mutual mistrust, thus creating a situation conducive to misperception. Such misperceptions will continue to exist at the policymaking elite and mass levels for quite some time, but will likely be downplayed with the enhancement of constructive behavior. However, several factors might hinder such a process. For example, differences between parties as to what constitutes security, differences over the distribution of peace dividends, and differences over what constitutes a model type of interaction between both sides. Distrust and suspicion might lead to questioning the whole notion of peace. This could be the case in view of the instability of the region and the side effects of other conflicts in the area.

Mutual mistrust and suspicion will probably be further exacerbated by the tendency of policy makers, elites and masses to fit incoming information to their existing theories and images. They will probably adhere to their established views and resent alternative ones, thus fixing each side's exaggerated negative images of the other.

Changing perceptions in a protracted social conflict is a long term process. It is easier to assimilate a new image of the opponent if information establishing and sustaining such an image is transmitted and considered bit by bit than if it comes all at once. Thus, socialization is a cornerstone in this regard. However, in order for socialization to materialize, a change in behavior is a prerequisite. Israeli behavior is a fundamental obstacle. Actual concrete changes in Israeli behavior would reinforce a change of image. For example, Israel should follow better measures in treating the Palestinians in the occupied territories and, most importantly, Israel should accept declaring the Middle Fast as a zone free from nuclear weapons and other weapons of mass destruction.

While the afore-mentioned obstacles may constitute formidable obstacles to peace, they can be overcome. The Middle East could be a region characterized by peace, a peace which would insure the survival, security, welfare and prosperity of all its members.

What to do

For half a century, the Arab-Israeli conflict has had a clear and substantial impact on the mobilization and allocation of all parties' resources. With the phase of conflict coming to an end, marked by peace agreements and the difficulty of using military power for the foreseeable future, it is becoming increasingly necessary for regional states to think about the reallocation of their resources in a way that will bring the full benefit of peace and enhance regional cooperation, which will in turn strengthen peace. Given international trends, a state that is not economically strong and has not joined a viable economic bloc will not be able to play a prominent role in the world, even if it has extensive military power. That is, a country's status is increasingly related to what it has to offer economically rather than militarily. The key task is to convert from mobilization directed towards military and strategic goals to mobilization for economic and social aims, while not ignoring perceived security requirements.

In the case of Egypt, the main factors influencing its perceived security requirements include:

1.   The continued existence within the region of states with non-conventional capabilities, combined with the possession of superior conventional capabilities, of which the use or even threat of use to achieve foreign policy objectives constitute a direct threat to Egypt.

2.   The need for a balance of power in a region where one state has complete military superiority which allows it to threaten its neighbors at the time of its choosing and for reasons of its own.

3.   The ability to secure and defend all economic and social development goals. Such goals require the existence of a defensive umbrella able to protect such efforts. That there is little point in pursuing the objectives of economic and social development if these goals are vulnerable to external threats is a recognized international principle.

4.   The necessity of the elimination of nuclear weapons and all other weapons of mass destruction, and their means of delivery, is a legitimate objective that should be pursued by all parties in the Middle East.

5.   The continued existence of a dependable Egyptian armed force as a guarantor of regional security and stability is crucial. Of course, Israel sees its superior military might as such a guarantor. But two things should be recognized: first, there is a need for a military balance, for reasons already noted; and second, Israel's military forces cannot be used to stabilize the region, and indeed are seen by its neighbors as one of the causes of instability.

For these factors, and others, the issue under consideration is of a very complex nature, as it involves issues belonging to the political, economic and security spheres. We deal here with the appropriate responses to the existence of nuclear threat in the region, from the perspective of a single country (Egypt), in an area of conflict (the Arab Israeli Conflict).

The present situation in the Middle East remains complicated and volatile despite the current peace negotiations. The proliferation of unconventional weapons endangers not just the region, but world peace as well. The intensive race to accumulate more sophisticated and destructive weapons, and the development of methods for their use, affect different facets of regional and international stability and constitute a major obstacle to the peace process in the region. This situation would prevail until a ban is imposed on the diffusion of technology of nuclear weapons, and until the region is declared as a Nuclear Weapons Free Zone (NWFZ).

Concerning the Israeli nuclear issue, there is a radical contradiction between the Egyptian and the Israeli positions. Israel insists on keeping its nuclear arsenal intact and contends that it should be institutionalized in any peace agreements in the region, while Egypt wishes to abolish all nuclear weapons from the Middle East, and establish a region free from all sorts of weapons of mass destruction. Egypt argues that without solving the nuclear issue, it is highly probable that the non-nuclear states in the area will seek to develop the nuclear option in order to minimize any future threat against them emanating from Israel.

On the other hand, acceptance of the Egyptian point of view could result in two basic facts:

1.   The elimination of all weapons of mass destruction in the region would enhance confidence and trust among the parties and could lead to the realization of common interests and the increase of economic interaction among them, making all parties keen to preserve the peace established.

2.   If Israel accepts, it will still continue to have the infrastructure, experts, technology and know-how necessary for the reproduction of new nuclear weapons if circumstances necessitate that. This will continue to be an advantage that Israel would have.

These two facts could be reinforced by the notion of maximum transparency and verification and inspection regimes that would assure the compliance of all parties to any agreement that would be reached concerning this matter. This could be also supported by Israel's showing of good faith, through its joining – sometime in the future – the Non-Proliferation Treaty, and signing safeguard agreements with the International Atomic Energy Agency (IAEA). It would also be supported by tightening export controls and requesting supplier states to limit their export of nuclear material that is intended for peaceful purposes only to countries that have signed the NPT.

Conclusion

The secrecy surrounding a country's WMD capability leads to varied degrees of misperception by the countries directly affected by the presence of the threat. This becomes a vicious circle leading to the production of more weapons and increases in their effectiveness. The cost is extremely high and shows the serious imbalance between military expenditure and development. If such a situation continues, the economic burden will increase, and allocations for military production will rise.

It goes without saying that the cost of production of nuclear weapons is increasing every year. An agreement on the elimination of such weapons might ease the burden imposed on state's budget and hence its tax payers. In the final analysis, we must emphasize that a concentration on the elimination of one type of mass destruction weapons leaving aside other types cannot be the right answer to the worries and concerns of parties in the region. We believe firmly that there should be a linkage between chemical and nuclear weapons, if we are really thinking of putting controls on the diffusion of technology associated with the production of mass destruction weapons, and in particular on the nuclear capabilities in the Middle East.

❈

Appendix

Egypt's stand towards Weapons of Mass Destruction.

The idea of the elimination of weapons of mass destruction (WMD) from the Middle East is not new but needs further elaboration. This idea has been brought into focus by the accumulation of such lethal weapons in the Middle East, thereby creating a destabilizing environment that endangers international peace and security. The broad parameters of this proposal lie in regional arrangements which are the key to realizing this objective.

It is important, therefore, to concentrate time and effort on such a regional approach. As the NPT recognized in Article VIII, "Nothing in this treaty affects the right of any group of states to conclude regional treaties in order to assure the total absence of nuclear weapons in their respective territories." In this context it is appropriate to recall that as far back as 1948, the UN Commission of Conventional Armaments advised the Security Council that it considered weapons of mass destruction to include "atomic explosive weapons, radioactive material weapons, lethal chemical and biological weapons, and any weapons developed in the future which have characteristics comparable in destructive effect to those of the atomic bomb or the other weapons mentioned above." This is a somewhat generic definition, old in nature, but could be used as a point of departure to deal with basic concepts.

The concept of the establishment of a Nuclear Weapon Free Zone (NWFZ) in the Middle East was first brought to the attention of the United Nations General Assembly in 1974, when Iran dispatched an Explanatory Memorandum on July 5, 1974. The period from July until October 1974 witnessed considerable consultations between Egypt and Iran, after which Egypt decided to support and join the Iranian initiative as a cosponsor following a slight change to the title of the item in order to read "Establishment of a Nuclear Weapon Free Zone." The addition of the word "weapon" was done in order to account for, and legitimize the quest by, both countries to prevent the dangers of the proliferation of nuclear weapons while securing nuclear energy for peaceful purposes.

Finally, in October 1974, both Egypt and Iran presented a joint draft resolution to the First Committee of the General Assembly. In introducing the item, Egypt argued that:

1. The states in the region of the Middle East should not, as a point of departure, produce, acquire or process nuclear weapons;

2. Nuclear weapon states should not introduce or use any nuclear weapons against any other state in the region of the Middle East;

3. There should be immediate establishment of an effective system of safeguard for both nuclear and non-nuclear states in the region; and

4. If Israel obtained nuclear weapons, Egypt would not be able to stand idly by in view of such a serious development that would drag the region into a costly arms race and endanger international peace and security.

Israel stated, on the other hand, that it would not be the first to introduce nuclear weapons into the Middle East, which proved to be untrue.

Again, on April 8, 1990, Egyptian President Hosni Mubarak presented an initiative to establish a zone free from weapons of mass destruction in the Middle East. The rationale of the proposal was to spare a region fraught with tension from the scourge of investing precious resources in any type of weapons of mass destruction. The three components of that initiative are compelling:

1. That all weapons of mass destruction without exception in the Middle East be prohibited, including nuclear, chemical or biological;

2.   That all states of the region without exception make an equal and reciprocal commitment in this regard; and

3.   Verification measures and modalities be established to ascertain full compliance by all states in the region with the full scope of that prohibition without exception.

This initiative enjoys several paramount characteristics. It is intra-regional, takes account of the present complex configuration, cautions against the specter of future stockpiles of lethal weapon systems of mass destruction, and has acquired a well-established international status.

Nevertheless, Israel did not abandon its initial position of continuing to possess its nuclear arsenal, and refusing to join, or promise to join, the NPT at any time in the future. On the other hand, Arab fear of an Israeli nuclear weapon is augmented by periodic revelations concerning Israel's nuclear capabilities. In addition, Israel's refusal to join the NPT and place all its nuclear activities under IAEA safeguards deepens Arab anxiety. Unofficially, Israel argues that the Arabs have learned, over the years, to coexist with a latent but undisclosed Israeli nuclear posture and continue, officially, to deny the validity of any reports, or allegations, concerning its nuclear position.

Naturally, the denuclearalization process is not easy and cannot be implemented overnight, but Egypt asks Israel to commit itself within a certain period, or at least to take a few measures to show its goodwill. Stopping further production of nuclear weapons, issuing an inventory of its nuclear arsenal and making moves toward the signing of the NPT, are some of the possible measures that could be taken. Any positive steps taken on the part of Israel would be reciprocated by Egypt.

Chapter 14

The Arab-Israeli Nuclear Debate: Reality or Myth?

M. Zuhair Diab

The Issue Under Debate

Before the conference on extending the Treaty on the Non-proliferation of Nuclear Weapons (NPT) was held in New York in May 1995, the Arab League had prepared a position paper on the common Arab conception of this extension. A committee of Arab experts also presented a plan for establishing a Middle East weapons of mass destruction-free zone.[1] Undoubtedly, it is a step in the right direction when the Arab states think seriously about problems of arms control, particularly as the peace process to settle the Arab-Israeli conflict is under way. The main Arab demand, according to the position paper, was that the Arab states should not agree to the indefinite extension of the NPT unless Israel joined it. Moreover, Israel should accept international inspection of its nuclear facilities by the International Atomic Energy Agency (IAEA) and stop producing fissionable materials for military purposes. In the event, there was disarray in Arab voting, which was not unusual, and certain states like Egypt and Syria abstained as the NPT was indefinitely extended by a substantial majority.

The episode renewed the debate over Israel's nuclear capability and its relevance to the settlement of the Arab-Israeli conflict, whether by political or military means. The Arab stand, with some variations in emphasis, maintains that

---

[1]*Al-Hayat* (Beirut), March 17, 1995, pp.1 and 4.

Israel's nuclear capability poses a serious threat to the security and stability of the region and is fueling an arms race. The question whether nuclear weapons, by themselves, are a source of instability or have been instrumental in preventing a general war is still open. Furthermore, the problem of proliferation, as it was perceived in the 1960s, has so far proven to not be very acute and nuclear weapons have not been used regionally. However, the contention that they exacerbate the arms race among states involved in a conflict is valid with some reservations, depending on the major assumption underpinning the argument. If we believe that weapons, and arms races, are symptomatic of conflict, then disarmament or curbing the arms race ultimately depends on resolving the conflicts between the states involved. The advocates of arms control, however, argue that certain weapons systems, including nuclear ones, present a problem which is different in magnitude from conventional weapons. Hence, they call for immediate steps to prevent nuclear proliferation and to ban chemical and biological weapons. Here, a link is established between these weapons since states that are not capable, for a variety of reasons, of acquiring nuclear weapons may resort to manufacturing chemical and/or biological ones as a deterrent to their nuclear opponents. In this sense, the Arab argument is valid, since Israel's nuclear capability has partly motivated certain Arab states, like Egypt, Syria and Iraq (until the Gulf War of 1991) to acquire chemical weapons. Nevertheless, it should be borne in mind that chemical weapons also have battlefield uses that are independent of their deterrent role, although their use could be viewed as an escalating step towards the threat or use of nuclear weapons.[2]

Regardless of the argument over the dangers attendant to nuclear proliferation, in my view it is an international problem and it has to be tackled on that level if the nuclear powers are sincere about controlling it. To be selective, namely,

---

[2]Gordon M. Burck and Charles C. Flowerree, *International Handbook on Chemical Weapons Proliferation* (New York: Greenwood Press, 1991), pp.189-190.

to exempt some states, such as Israel, from adhering to the Non-proliferation regime while putting pressure on other states not to develop a nuclear capability, even a peaceful one, or to develop chemical arsenals, is discriminatory and counter-productive. The justifications that certain leaders are irrational or that they support terrorism, and that there is more propensity for regional states to resort to nuclear weapons than is the case with the great nuclear powers, are not objectively defensible. Rather, they reflect an element of ethnocentrism and bias towards certain states which happen to have common interests with the West. However, I do not wish to make an issue of Israel's nuclear capability, as Egypt, and to a lesser extent Syria, tried to do during the period before the approval of the NPT's indefinite extension, because it is futile and could negatively affect the peace process if Israel is pressured on this question at this crucial time. The appropriate time for adopting arms control measures, including nuclear non-proliferation, will be following the settlement of the substantive issues in the Arab-Israeli conflict, particularly Israel's occupation of Arab territories. The fact that the multilateral talks among the regional states, excluding Syria, Lebanon, Iraq, Iran, Sudan, Yemen, and Libya, are still going in circles supports this point. Furthermore, because of the linkages between the two strategic environments (the Arab-Israeli and the Gulf), the problem has become more complicated as Israel has perceived an Iranian threat, whether real or contrived.

The focus of this essay is to throw some light on the arguments concerning the role of Israel's nuclear potential, or weapons, in the context of the Arab-Israeli conflict. The relevant questions are whether this capability has affected the course of the conflict? And if it has done so, what is its impact on the strategic calculations of the parties to the conflict? A third question is whether it has prevented a settlement?

Israeli Motivations

The standing Israeli position is that it will not be the first state to introduce nuclear weapons into the Middle East.[3] It has opted for an undeclared deterrent, or a bomb in the basement, seeing in it more political advantages internationally. The argument that it is intended to discourage other states in the region from developing their nuclear capabilities is untenable, as Iran is now suspected of harboring such intentions and as Iraq tried to do before the Gulf War. The debate over the strategic utility of this vagueness is still going on, although it has, to a certain degree, abated in intensity since the revelations of the Israeli former technician Mordechai Vanunu in 1986. Whatever the Israeli perspective, the Arabs have assumed, even taken for granted, that Israel was developing a nuclear capability since the 1960s, when the existence of the Dimona reactor was publicized.

Two main motives have been presented to justify Israel's efforts to opt for a nuclear military program since the 1950s. First, the Arab side would gain a numerical advantage over time and since its presumed intention was to destroy the state of Israel, Israel had to possess the ultimate weapon. The aim is to dissuade the Arabs from planning for this objective by signaling to them that if such a venture had a chance to succeed, Israel would then retaliate with a devastating nuclear strike. The second motive is that owing to the traumatic Holocaust experience, Israel cannot place its trust in any international guarantees, even those issued by the United States.[4] Although it could be argued that Israeli fears are exaggerated, the unofficial, and sometimes official, Arab political discourse following the 1948-49 War and up to 1967, contributed to a certain extent to the development of these threat perceptions.

---

[3]Leonard S. Spector with Jacqeline R. Smith, *Nuclear Ambitions The Spread of Nuclear Weapons, 1989-1990* (Boulder, Co.: Westview Press, 1990), p.158.
[4]Yair Evron, *Israel's Nuclear Dilemma* (London: Routledge, 1994), pp. 1-14; and Avner Yaniv, *Deterrence Without the Bomb: The Politics of Israeli Strategy* (Lexington, Mass.: Lexington Books, 1987), pp.12-19.

It goes beyond the scope of this essay to demonstrate the discrepancy between the official and popular Arab attitudes, but suffice it to mention that the signing of the Armistice Agreements between Israel and four Arab states, Egypt, Syria, Jordan and Lebanon, in 1949 constituted a de facto recognition of Israel as an existing state, though they remained at war, legally speaking. Moreover, in 1950, the Arab League Council adopted a resolution setting forth the conditions of peace with Israel. Thus, Israel's perception that the ultimate Arab intention was to destroy it, combined with the expectations of Arab numerical superiority is actually a misperception and has not been substantiated in reality despite Arab rhetoric. One should bear in mind that no Arab accepts the historical and religious claims of the Zionist movement in Palestine. This attitude is basically responsible for the rhetoric. However, accepting the reality and legal existence of Israel is a different matter.

As for the question of numerical superiority, it has not materialized in any of the Arab-Israeli wars so far.[5] There is also a difference between adding up the populations of the Arab states and the actual combat-effective units which they can field in wars, bearing in mind that not all Arab states involve themselves in the war efforts against Israel. This is due to the socioeconomic structures of Arab societies, which are basically peasant ones, which make it difficult for them to have the required trained manpower to operate the machinery of modern warfare. The Israeli counter-argument is that in time the major Arab states, namely Egypt, Syria and Iraq, will develop economically and technologically so that they could be able to mobilize superior forces and even close the technology gap. Hence, Israel must have its

---

[5]For the forces actually engaged in combat and their fighting effectiveness see: Chaim Herzog, *The Arab-Israeli Wars: War and Peace in the Middle East from the War of Independence to Lebanon* (London: Arms and Armour Press, 1982); Nadav Safran, *From War to War: The Arab-Israeli Confrontation, 1948-1967* (New York: Pegasus, 1969); Richard A. Gabriel, Ed., *Antagonists in the Middle East: A Combat Assessment* (Westport, Con.: Greenwood Press, 1983); and Anthony H. Cordesman, *The Arab-Israeli Military Balance and the Art of Operations* (Lanhan, MD.: University Press of America, 1987), passim.

nuclear capability until such conditions of peace prevail in the region for some time to allow for the testing of Arab intentions. Whatever the merits of the Israeli argument, it loses its strength if the Arab parties directly involved in the conflict have entered into contractual peace with Israel.

With regard to trusting international guarantees, the West, particularly the United States, has demonstrated, time and again, its resolve to protect the existence of Israel as a political entity and to enhance its military posture to the point of saturation. Every American president since Harry S. Truman has made this resolve abundantly clear and left the Arabs no room to doubt it.[6] Furthermore, Israel's qualitative edge has been proven in all of its military engagements with the Arabs. One may argue that there are no formal treaties of mutual defense or guarantees between Israel and a European power or the United States. Yet actions speak for themselves. The Israeli-French cooperation in the nuclear and missile fields in the late 1950s and until 1967,[7] and the American-Israeli strategic cooperation since 1981 are ample proof of the commitment to Israel's national existence.[8] The network of military relationships created by this agreement whether in the form of cooperating on research and development of advanced weapons, holding joint training exercises, or prepositioning military materiel, is ample proof of this commitment, at least to the Arabs.

In citing these facts and arguments, it is not my purpose to refute Israeli reasoning or to challenge how Israel perceives its national security requirements. It has decided, whether rightly or wrongly, to have a guaranteed "national insurance policy," which can be cashed in the event of unforeseeable contingencies. However,

---

[6]George Lenczowski, *American Presidents and the Middle East* (Durham: Duke University Press, 1990). passim.
[7]Leonard S. Spector, op.cit., pp.151-151.
[8]Avraham Tmir, *A Soldier in Search of Peace: A Inside Look at Israel's Strategy* (London: Weidenfeld and Nichlson, 1988), pp.213-222.

the Israelis should be aware that these facts have not escaped Arab strategic thinking, regardless of Israel's nuclear capability. Whether Israel's estimated nuclear arsenal is 50 or 200 warheads, depending on the source,[9] they are redundant in the context of the conflict with its Arab adversaries.

Arab Perceptions

Egypt has taken the lead in outlining Arab threat perceptions arising from Israel's nuclear capability. Dr. Osama al-Baz, Political Advisor to President Hosni Mubarak, said that the future problem between Egypt and Israel would be "the Israeli nuclear program, because it is a military program and not an economic one. This will lead to the destabilization of regional balance and security."[10] General (Ret.) Ahmed Abdul Halim has explained this threat perception.[11] Briefly, his basic assumption is that Egypt regards the main security problem in the Middle East to be the imbalances in power relationships and in military capabilities, particularly in the nuclear field, among the regional states, which affect their relations on the regional level and with external powers. Israel's superiority is signified by its continued monopoly of nuclear capability, in addition to its maintenance of its technological edge in the conventional field with American help. He also dismisses Israel's fears of Iran's and certain Arab state's efforts to acquire nuclear capabilities as not based in reality or on rational reasoning. For General Halim, there is a difference between the point when Israel possessed about ten to fifteen warheads, which were explained as weapons of "last resort" to be used in case Israel was defeated conventionally or the existence of the state was threatened, and the current situation where its arsenal is estimated to be between 200 to 300 warheads. In the latter case, this capability becomes a tool of

---

[9]Leonard S. Spector, op.cit., p.160.
[10]*Al-Hayat*, June 21, 1995, p.17.
[11]Ibid., April 11, 1995, p.17.

foreign policy which by necessity will be used by Israel to dominate the region and to force the Arab parties to yield to all of its demands, whether legitimate or not. However, he makes a contradictory remark by saying that Israel cannot completely dominate the Middle East region as a result of certain geographic, demographic, geopolitical, geostrategic and many other restrictions. To maintain that the power relationships in the region are in favor of Israel, whether diplomatically or militarily, is to state the obvious. But to make nuclear capability a chief component in the equation is not clear-cut, since it depends on the political objective of both Israel and its Arab opponents, and the military means that are employed to achieve them.

The Relevance of Nuclear Capability

To define the role of nuclear weapons in the Arab-Israeli power equation, we first need to define the strategic context in which they could be utilized for deterrence or compellence. A caveat should be added here, however, which is that Israel's nuclear deterrent up to now does not fall within the framework of traditional theories on nuclear deterrence for two main reasons. First, Israel is the only putative nuclear power in the Arab-Israeli equation. Second, both sides belong to a subinternational system, unlike the two superpowers, where neither Arab and nor Israeli freedom of action is absolute if they decide to threaten the use of nuclear weapons or to actually use them. If in the future an Arab state acquires a nuclear capability, then it is possible to contemplate the operation of strategic rules defining options and limitations that are different in nature from the current situation.

Deterrence

Putting aside Israel's previously mentioned motivations and exaggerated fears, it should be emphasized that the Arab side has acquiesced to the reality of peacefully coexisting with Israel since the 1967 war, and could be interpreted as having had the intention of living with Israel since 1950, as argued earlier. The 1967 war ended any lingering hope of destroying Israel as a political entity.[12] Two principal factors were responsible for this dramatic change of perception. First, the Arabs discovered that the technological gap between them and Israel was so wide on every level, especially the conventional military one, that such an objective was unrealistic. The second factor was that the international community, in particular the United States and the former Soviet Union, would not have tolerated it. The 1967 war actually transformed the nature of the conflict as the Arab states confirmed that their demands for a settlement were limited to the liberation of the territories occupied in 1967 and the recovery of the national rights of the Palestinians according to the UN resolutions. Although the Resolutions of the Khartoum Summit of 1967 rejected peace with Israel, its recognition and negotiating with it, they implicitly acknowledged its existence.[13] Indeed, Egypt and Jordan accepted Resolution 242 of 1967 at the time, and Syria followed suit in 1973 when it accepted Resolution 338. The Arab position was made clearer after the October War of 1973 in the Algiers and Rabat Summits of 1973 and 1974, respectively.[14] Moreover, the Fez Summit of 1982 openly accepted the notion of two states in the land of Palestine.[15] The fact that Egypt signed a peace treaty with Israel in 1979, and as a result of the Madrid Conference of 1991, Jordan signed a Treaty in 1994 following the Palestinian-Israeli Declaration of Principles of 1993, testified to the credibility of Arab intentions. Furthermore, the negotiations between Syria and Israel since that Conference provide a clear indication that Syria has accepted the notion of coexisting with Israel. The central issues between the Arab parties and Israel have narrowed down to the conditions of a

---

[12]M. Z. Diab. "A Proposed Security Regime for an Arab-Israeli Settlement."
[13]*The Israeli-Palestinian Conflict: A Documentary Record*, ed. Yehuda Lukacs (Cambridge University Press, 1992), pp.454-455.
[14]Ibid., pp.463-465.
[15]Ibid., pp.478-479.

comprehensive settlement, namely, the territorial dimension and Palestinian national rights.

If the knowledge of Israel's nuclear capability in 1967 was a factor in the Arabs' acknowledgment of the impossibility of destroying Israel, it was not evident in their behavior. Moreover, that knowledge did not prevent Syria from calling for military action to stop Israel from diverting the waters of the Jordan River and to support the Palestinian infiltrators in the few years preceding the 1967 war. Although Syria's moves were rejected by Egypt and other Arab states, they did not do so because of Israel's putative nuclear capability.[16] Even during the crisis period, Egypt's behavior was of a more deterrent nature, namely, trying to dissuade Israel from attacking Syria rather than trying to destroy it, bearing in mind that at the time there was no Israeli threat of using nuclear weapons to deter Egypt.

By 1973, more information came to light about Israel's nuclear capability, but that did not prevent Egypt and Syria from planning and executing the October War. This was evident in the fact that Syria did not plan to go beyond the 1967 line and Egypt did not even plan to go beyond a few kilometers from the east bank of the Suez Canal.[17] Therefore, even if the argument that Israel's nuclear capability played a role in convincing the Arabs to give up their goal of destroying Israel is accepted, it had no impact on Arab strategic thinking in planning a limited liability war.

Looking at the role of nuclear weapons from the Israeli side, it was claimed that Israel developed them following the 1967 War in order to preserve the status

---

[16]Nadav Safran, op.cit., pp.46-47.

[17]Muhammad Zuhair Diab and Amid Khouli, *Al Muna'ataf al Kabir* (Damascus: Yishreen Establishment for Press and Publication, 1979), pp.28-40; and President Hafez al Assad's speech on October 6, 1973, ibid., pp.245-248 (Arabic).

quo.[18] Again, this argument was proven incorrect by the fact of the October War and the way Israel perceived the different kinds of threats it could be exposed to. It has been always stressed by the Israeli military establishment that what they need is a credible conventional deterrent that can be translated into military action in case deterrence fails.[19] Countering the Palestinian guerrilla activities with retaliation against their bases in neighboring countries requires conventional forces and not a nuclear threat. Repulsing limited incursions by an Arab army also requires conventional forces and cannot be done by tactical nuclear weapons. The War of Attrition between Egypt and Israel from late 1968 till early 1970, and the conflict between Israel and Syria in the year preceding the October War and during the months before the Disengagement Agreement of 1974, all demonstrated this military reality. As further evidence, one can add the Israeli invasions of Lebanon in 1978 and 1982. Furthermore, any suggestion of contemplating the use of tactical nuclear weapons in the areas adjacent to Israel's borders is based on complete lack of knowledge of the geography and meteorological conditions in the region. The short distances and the proximity of population centers on both sides of the borders mean that the radiation could be carried in any direction and affect any side. One exception might be if they were used in the Sinai Desert, but even there the winds could carry the radiation to Israel. If their use is meant to be inside the territory of Arab states, then we are moving in practical terms to strategic use even though the effects of such a nuclear strike would be meant to be tactical. Clearly, the calculations of, and restraints attached to, such use are on a different level.

Although Syria has joined the common Arab position in demanding Israel's signing of the NPT and regarding the American refusal to exercise pressure in this

---

[18]Fuad Jabber, *Israel and Nuclear Weapons: Present Option and Future Strategies* (London: The International Institute for Strategic Studies, 1971), p.133.
[19]Yair Evron, op.cit., p.12.

direction as another case of applying double standards,[20] its perception of the role of nuclear capability is more relaxed and sophisticated. In its declaratory policy, it views Israel's nuclear capability as a manifestation of an aggressive policy that poses a potential threat to the security and stability of the region. However, operationally it does not give the nuclear question priority over reaching a peaceful settlement of the pressing issues of the conflict, namely, the occupied territories and Palestinian national rights. It is interesting to note that up until the late 1980s, there were few official pronouncements or any public debate on Israel's nuclear policy or the demand for it to join the NPT.[21] When the peace process has been put in motion with the accompanying multilateral talks that cover, inter alia, arms control, Syria has adopted a public stand that considers Israel's refusal to sign the NPT and its obstruction of the establishment of a free-zone of all weapons of mass destruction in the Middle East as tantamount to a unilateral disarmament.[22] It is reasonable to assume that this stand has been put forward as a bargaining position in case Syria comes under pressure over its chemical weapons and missile capabilities, whether it joins the multilateral talks in the future or not. Regarding the appropriate time for the implementation of arms control in general, the Syrian stand is that it has to be within the objective condition of peace, and if arms limitation is to be adopted before, then it should be discussed on the basis of its "comprehensiveness and justness."[23]

An interesting observation on the role of nuclear weapons in the context of the Arab-Israeli conflict and whether they affected Syria's pursuit of strategic parity

---

[20]Interview with Vice-President Abdul Halim Khaddam with Mideast Mirror (London), March 20, 1995, p.13.

[21]Shai Feldman, *Israel Nuclear Deterrence: A Strategy for the 1980s* (New York: Cambridge University Press, 1982), pp. 12 and 68.

[22]Interview with the Syrian Foreign Minister Farouk al-Sharal cited in Peter Herby, *The Chemical Weapons Convention and Arms Control in the Middle East* (Oslo: International Peace Research Institute, 1992), p. 53.

[23]Al-Assad's speech on March 8, 1992, al-Thawra (Damascus), March 9, 1992, pp. 1-5.

with Israel was made by President Hafez al-Asad in 1987. In his view, the interaction among the world's peoples creates strong mutual concerns which restrict the use of such weapons and he cited the example of the United States' involvement in Vietnam and how it was defeated without being able to resort to nuclear weapons. He also referred to the Lebanese conflict between 1982 and 1985 which saw the participation of the United States and Israel, yet both were defeated and could not use the atomic bomb. The reason for this lay in the fact that both these conflicts involved ordinary people, which made it difficult for both states to make use of their nuclear capabilities. He went on to say: "There are conditions for the use of the atomic bomb. In my opinion, these conditions are more difficult for Israel than for the United States. They are difficult in terms of technology and geographic location." And after citing the effects of the Chernobyl incident, he said: "...If Israel attacks Damascus with a nuclear bomb, Israel itself will be affected and it will not be safe from the dangers." He concluded by maintaining that rights would not change whether or not there was an atomic bomb.[24]

By 1990, President Asad was able to declare his technical answer to Israel's nuclear capability. In a public speech he referred to the closing of the technological gap between the Arabs and Israel and said that the wars of today would not be like those of the past; namely, they would not be short and inexpensive. He continued by saying: "Israel is still technologically superior and can inflict on the Arabs human disaster in case of war. However, the Arabs can also inflict on Israel the same disasters with what they have. Israel knows that and knows that its technological superiority cannot prevent the exchange of disasters . . . Bearing in mind the

---

[24]*Al-Zabas* (Kuwait), January 24, 1987.

demographic depth possessed by the Arabs which the Israelis lack, this exchange of disasters will be much heavier on them."[25]

In effect, in this speech, President Asad announced the existence of limited mutual deterrence on the strategic level. The Syrian answer to Israel's nuclear threat has been to build a massive missile force equipped with both conventional and chemical warheads. The existence of such deterrence was recognized by the late Israeli Prime Minister Yitzhak Rabin in 1994, when he said: "Syria has surface-to-surface missiles in a quality and quantity that make what we suffered during the Gulf War like child's play."[26] Israeli sources estimate that Syria has at present around one thousand missiles of the Scud-B/C types, as well as a reported assembly line.[27]

It could be argued that this Syrian capability cannot neutralize Israel's nuclear one in absolute terms owing to the difference in kind and the resulting magnitude of damage. Nonetheless, deterrence works in relative terms according to the political objectives sought in a conflict. Syria's objectives are not to destroy the state of Israel or to start a war with it; Damascus is quite aware of the awesome retaliatory strike Israel would launch if it did try to start a war. What Syria is signaling is that in case Israel resorts to a nuclear threat to obtain political concessions or tries to expand a future war to civilian and strategic targets in Syria, the latter has the capability to inflict unbearable damage according to Israel's cost/benefit calculus; namely, immense human losses that would not justify the objectives sought by Israel. Hence, it could be safely asserted that Israel's nuclear capability has no bearing on the military equation between Syria and Israel under the current parameters of the conflict, since Syria has already accepted the coexistence of a Jewish State on part

[25]Hizb al-Baath Arabi al-Ishtraki, al Qyadh al-Qawmya, Circular No. 474 (Damascus, June 11, 1990), pp.14-15.
[26]*Al-Hayat*, June 23, 1994, pp. 3 and 4.
[27]*Jerusalem Post*, March 16, 1995, as quoted in *al-Hayat*, March 17, 1995, p.5.

of the land of Palestine.[28] Such a situation is in fact a rebuttal to the Egyptian argument cited above. Paradoxically, the strategic stalemate that exists between Israel and Syria has prevented the reaching of a quick settlement between them due to the fact that neither side is in a position to dictate its terms to the other. Israel recognizes that launching a war against Syria will be prohibitive in terms of cost. For its part, Syria's efforts to continue building an offensive conventional capability to wage a limited war to liberate the Golan Heights have been retarded for the time being because of the Russian refusal to maintain its military support at the same level as the Soviets had previously. Evidence that this is still the Syrian operational military thinking has been provided lately by the Chief of General Staff Lieutenant General Hikmat alShihabi. He stated that the military option to recover the Golan Heights would be exercised in case the diplomatic option failed to achieve this objective.[29] He later added that if Israel chose to start a war, Syria would be in a position to inflict enormous damage.[30] Clearly, Shihabi was implying the use of missiles, albeit with conventional warheads, if Israel were to extend the theater of war to civilian and strategic targets.

Three inferences can be drawn from these statements: First, on the strategic level, the Syrian leadership feels confident because it has succeeded in building a deterrent force consisting of missiles and chemical warheads which, to a certain degree, would neutralize the impact of Israel's nuclear deterrent on a Syrian decision to launch a limited-liability war once the necessary level of conventional forces is attained and the regional conditions are appropriate if diplomacy fails. Second, on the tactical level, Syria belittles the possibility of Israel's use of tactical nuclear weapons to contain an armored thrust deep into the Golan Heights; and if such a possibility

---

[28]M. Zuhair Diab, "Have Syria and Israel Opted for Peace?" op.cit.
[29]*Al-Hayat*, July 31, 1996, p.4.
[30]*Al-Arab* (London), August 8, 1996, p.2.

arose, then Syria could retaliate with chemical weapons. It stands to reason that mutual deterrence, namely nuclear vs. chemical, is more credible on the tactical level than on the strategic one. This is because the tactical level involves inflicting damage on a smaller scale; i.e., destroying and immobilizing military forces, as opposed to needing to destroy value-targets such as cities, dams and industrial complexes. In other words, on the tactical level both tactical nuclear and chemical weapons are relatively equal insofar as the desired effect is concerned. This equality is harder to achieve on the strategic level because of the nature of the targets involved, which gives an edge to nuclear weapons over chemical. However, since deterrence is in the eye of the beholder, one should take into account the value placed on human life by the Israelis and the density of their population and industrial centers. Thus, several salvos of missiles with sufficient payloads of chemical and incendiary warheads are quite enough to cause unbearable damage to Israeli value-targets which would dissuade its leadership from resorting to the use of nuclear weapons except in the extreme case where the existence of the state is threatened. Third, despite the new Syrian declaratory position on Israel's nuclear capability regarding it as a threat to its national security and regional stability, it has had no operational impact on Syrian military policy in terms of imposing constraints on the exercise of a military option for a limited war if it is needed in the future. The declaratory position is actually for bargaining purposes in the context of both the Convention on Chemical Weapons of 1993, which Syria has refused to sign, and American pressure over acquiring medium-range missiles. In sum, the Syrian position remains essentially the same as before the peace process in the sense that Israel's nuclear capability does not have priority over recovering the Golan Heights either diplomatically or by military means.

Compellence

Drawing on Schelling's differentiation between deterrence and compellence, where in the latter case a state initiates an action to force the adversary to respond, Israel has so far not used its nuclear monopoly for compelling purposes.[31] Whether this is by choice or out of fear of the unpredictable consequences and international pressure is irrelevant. The best chance for Israel to exercise such an option was probably in the 1970s through the mid-1980s while Syria was still in the process of building up its missile and chemical capability.

It is unclear why the Egyptians are so worried about this scenario, given their having concluded a peace treaty with Israel in 1979 that satisfied both sides' demands, as well as their enthusiasm about the Madrid process, and the multilateral talks about arms control in particular. However, it would be more useful in the context of the Arab-Israeli conflict to stretch the meaning of compellence by posing the question whether Israel's nuclear capability has played any role in forcing the Arab parties to conclude peace agreements with Israel by exercising tacit compellence? Up to now Egypt, Jordan and the Palestine Liberation Organization (PLO) have concluded such agreements and in none of these cases can one detect any impact, whether tacit or explicit, of Israel's nuclear capability, either in the Arab decision to choose this course or in dictating the terms of the agreements. Although in all the Arab-Israeli wars the Arab side was defeated militarily, Israel has not been able to impose a strategic surrender on its opponents, either because of international intervention and/or the Arabs' advantage in territory and manpower leading them to opt for a prolonged war of attrition, in which Israel cannot afford to engage. In other words, the Arab side has always retained the power of denial if they decide to exercise it. Hence, the decisions by Egypt, Jordan and the PLO to opt for peace were

---

[31]Thomas C. Schelling, *Arms and Influence* (New Haven: Yale University Press, 1971), pp.69-78.

motivated by considerations completely divorced from Israel's military power, either conventional or nuclear.

In the case of Egypt, it was quite clear that the late President Sadat intended the October War to be the last war that Egypt would enter with Israel. This was evident from his statements both before and after the war.[32] Moreover, the siege of the Third Egyptian Army at the hands of the Israelis in the final stages of the war broke Egyptian morale, amounting to a psychological strategic surrender.[33] As for the conditions of a settlement, Sadat asked only what Israel would accept: the return to the international borders during the British Mandate period over Palestine and not the 1967 borders which would have included the Gaza Strip. Sadat also disengaged Egypt from the Palestinian problem by offering the Camp David Agreement on self-rule. When the PLO refused to accept it at the time, Sadat decided to go ahead with the Peace Treaty of 1979. Furthermore, Egypt normalized relations with Israel before the full withdrawal from the Sinai Desert had been completed. Obviously, for Israel there were tremendous strategic advantages in that deal, since it obtained the defection of Egypt, the largest Arab country, from the Arab-Israeli military equation. In addition, Israel realized that the Sinai would be more valuable as a demilitarized, natural geographic early warning system than as the site of costly Israeli garrisons, particularly when Egypt also accepted the presence of American early warning posts. It is very hard to detect any influence exercised by Israel's nuclear capability either in Sadat's decision to go to Jerusalem and break with the Arab ranks, or in the conditions of the Treaty which he accepted quite freely and willingly. We should also bear in mind that Sadat's domestic base allowed him to disengage from the

---

[32]Anwar al-Sadat, *Al-Bahth an Al-Zat: Qssat Hayati* (Cairo: Al-Maktab Al-Misri Al-Hadith for Printing and Publication, 1976) (Arabic).

[33]Chaim Herzog, *The War of Atonement* (Jerusalem: Steimatzkils Agency Ltd., 1975), pp. 246-250.

Palestinian question quite easily, even when the PLO refused to go along with the Camp David Agreement.

With the end of the Cold War, the second Gulf War and the demise of the Soviet Union, both the international and regional strategic landscapes have changed. The acceptance of President George Bush's peace initiative of 1991 by Syria, Jordan, Lebanon and the PLO was a foregone conclusion. It was actually an attempt by the United States to balance its interests in the region and was simultaneously viewed by the Arabs as a useful means of containing Israel's hegemony, having lost the military power of Iraq and the protection of the international strategic balance. Nonetheless, the Arab side still retained the power of denial if they chose to pursue it. Moreover, the Likud government at the time was not very anxious to enter negotiations and it required some American pressure to engage it. Clearly, the change to the Labour government in 1992 helped the peace process to produce results. In regard to the Arab side, Syria tried to get the other parties to coordinate their demand that Israel withdraw to the 1967 borders and then each party would be free to negotiate its own specific agreement.[34] However, it was clear from the start that the PLO did not intend to stick to this coordination and conducted secret talks with Israel to reach the Declaration of Principles Agreement of 1993, which was of an interim nature. Jordan, on the other hand, was waiting for this opportunity to domestically justify its disengagement from the Palestinian problem. Both of them claimed that the status of regional and international power relationships did not give them any bargaining power to resist. Instead, both Jordan and the PLO ended up financially bankrupt and politically isolated in the Arab world. In other words, their own lack of judgment and miscalculation led to their weakened postures, in addition to their desire not to coordinate with Syria and Lebanon. It would be a figment of the imagination to claim

---

[34]Statement by Foreign Ministers of Syria, Jordan, Lebanon, and the Head of the Political Department in the PLO, July 25, 1995, in *al-Ba'ath* (Damascus), July 26, 1992, pp. 1 and 10.

that Israel compelled both the PLO and Jordan to accept the conditions of their separate peace agreements through any form of nuclear blackmail.

In contrast, after eight years of negotiations between Syria and Israel, it is obvious that neither side has been able to impose its terms. One reason for this has already been mentioned; namely, limited mutual strategic deterrence. More importantly, however, Syria did not miscalculate during the Gulf crisis and war. Thus, neither is it financially bankrupt nor is it politically at odds with the most powerful Gulf state, Saudi Arabia. For Syria, its relationship with Saudi Arabia is its most vital Arab alliance and it regards the behavior of other Arab states as simply irrelevant. Again, one cannot see any evidence of Syria's fear of Israel's nuclear capability which could make it submit to Israel's conditions or to be in a hurry to conclude an agreement that does not meet its demands of withdrawal to the 1967 line. Any scenario that envisages Israel's resort to nuclear compellence to force Syria to sign an unfavorable agreement, if hypothetically tolerated internationally, will be akin to a bluff that could be very easily called by Syria. Such a threat would simply lack any credibility regionally and internationally, bearing in mind the awesome political consequences of the misuse of a nuclear capability which is supposed to be solely for the defense of national security.

Conclusion

It is one thing to maintain that nuclear proliferation is destabilizing regionally and that it negatively affects the national security of non-nuclear states, and quite another to ascribe to Israel's nuclear capability the Arab failure to reach a settlement with Israel on their own terms. As has been demonstrated, Israel's nuclear capability has not played a crucial role either in the Arabs' acceptance of the reality of Israel and the need to co-exist peacefully with it, or in their decisions to enter into peace agreements with Israel. If Israel's need for the capability has been made redundant from the Arab point of view, psychologically the Israelis have not fully adjusted to the condition of peace with the Arabs. Hence, the Arabs have to set their priorities in the proper order. The pressing question now is the Palestinian problem and ending Israel's occupation of the Arab territories under its control. On both issues Israel's nuclear weapons are irrelevant. On the contrary, it is counterproductive to put pressure on Israel regarding its nuclear capability while the Arab side is still struggling to convince the Israelis of the need to respond to Palestinian national aspirations. The assassination of Rabin was proof of the complications that Israeli society is facing in adjusting to a settlement, although, unfortunately, the Israelis created the problem for themselves by encouraging the building of settlements in the territories. The continued rotation of Labor and Likud governments is symptomatic of the Israelis' indecision about whether their ultimate security is better served by expansion or responding to the Arabs' demands.

The noise made by Egypt smacks of selfishness and is short-sighted, since it has recovered its territory and the Palestinian problem does not directly impinge on its national security as in the case of Jordan, Syria and Lebanon. The Egyptians claim that they are doing this for the sake of Arab security and not only for their own national interests. Regrettably, the net result of their actions is not only negative, but may also prove harmful to common Arab security when the Palestinian problem is still being tackled and Israel's occupation has not been fully terminated. The Egyptians also claim that stressing the question of Israel's nuclear capability does not arise out of any problem related to Egypt's foreign or domestic policies. It is not unreasonable to conceive of two main motives behind Egypt's behavior. First, to demonstrate on the Arab level that although they were the first to sign a peace treaty with Israel, they are still at odds with it on this question because they care about Arab security. Incidentally, this stand helps the regime domestically as well by adopting such a propagandistic campaign. Their separate peace dealt the most severe blow to

Arab bargaining power *vis-à-vis* Israel as it destabilized the Arab-Israeli military equation and it took over a decade for Syria to make it up with a great deal of expense and effort. The second motive is that Egypt realizes that it is losing the arms race in the region to Israel, Iran and Syria (and potentially Iraq after the removal of the present regime). Egypt has always pretended to be the leading Arab state in the region but it lost this position long ago and cannot recover it due to its economic constraints and overpopulation problem. Under such conditions, Egypt is hardly in a position to keep up in the arms race which is essential to its military posture. Finally, the proper time for an arms control regime including weapons of mass destruction, particularly nuclear ones, is when a condition of comprehensive peace prevails in the region, a peace that encompasses Iran as well.

Chapter 15

International Law and the Dynamics of
Middle East Nuclear Proliferation

Abdulhay Sayed[1]

A complete account of the dynamics of Middle East nuclear proliferation requires consideration of, among other factors, the nature of the pressure exerted by the related legal framework on the various regional actors, as well as the way with which these actors perceive and deal with such pressure. As long as the existing law on nuclear weapons has the pretense of ordering international relations on the basis of the principle of non-proliferation as a step towards nuclear disarmament, and actors in the Middle East strive, in varying degrees, to assert their independent decision in relation to nuclear weapons, the dynamics of this interaction may be rich in lessons about present trends and prospects for change.

International law on nuclear weapons as it is applicable to the Middle East includes a general prohibition on the use of nuclear weapons, with a marked uncertainty when such use is invoked in an extreme circumstance of self-defense where the survival of the State is at issue. The law also contains a general prohibition on the possession of nuclear weapons by any non-nuclear-weapon State as defined by the Nuclear Non-Proliferation Treaty (NPT), though the law remains uncertain as to the universal application of such a prohibition especially to non-signatory States[2].

---

[1]Abdulhay Sayed is a Syrian lawyer. I am indebted to Steve Tulliu, Hani Sayed and Prof. Keith Krause for their valuable comments and criticisms.
[2]It is interesting to note how, in practice, the normative energy of the NPT is used to overshadow non-party States. In the Security Council resolution adopted in response to the recent nuclear

The same can also be said with respect to the comprehensive test ban contained in the Comprehensive Test Ban Treaty (CTBT), assuming that the treaty is in force. The calls, within the UN or in the Israeli-Jordanian peace treaty, for the establishment of a nuclear-weapon and other weapons of mass destruction-free zone in the Middle East remained in the realm of wishful thinking. They constitute what lawyers would characterize as pronouncements de *lege feranda* (or desired law as opposed to what law is). They provide a substantive direction, worthy to look at more closely. They are, so to speak, carried away by the law's normative impulse. Anyhow, experience has shown that the Security Council resolution 687 which regulates among other items the procedure for the chemical, biological, nuclear and missile disarmament of Iraq, is backed by an unusually heavy military pressure to support its normative energy.

Generally, the relevant law on nuclear weapons in the Middle East is at best elusive. Indeed, the practice of the regional actors mirrored, in their practices, the perplexing character of the law.

I

Israel, a state widely believed to have developed an arsenal of nuclear weapons[3], is not a party to the NPT, despite the repeated international pressures on it to join as a non-nuclear-weapon State. It rather adopts a posture of ambiguity

---

detonations of India and Pakistan - who are not parties to the NPT - the Council expressed "its firm conviction that the international regime on the non-proliferation of nuclear weapons should be maintained and consolidated and that in accordance with the Treaty on the Non-Proliferation of Nuclear Weapons India or Pakistan cannot have the status of a nuclear-weapon State." See S/RES/1172 (1998) of 6 June 1998. The Indian response was quick to affirm that those tests "had not violated any legal obligation entered into by India." See a summary of the Indian statement to the First Committee of the UN General Assembly in (First Committee, 10, Press Release GA/DIS/3110 5th Meeting (AM 14 October 1998)

[3] For an account on the Israeli nuclear arsenal see for example Frank Barnaby, *The Invisible Bomb: The Nuclear Arms Race in the Middle East*, (London: I.B. Tauris & Co. Ltd., 1989); see also the UN *Study on Israeli Nuclear Armament*, (UN Doc. A/37/434, 1982).

regarding its nuclear capability,[4] which allows it to muster the necessary strategic deterrent vis-à-vis the "existentially threatening" Arab neighbors, while contributing in the deflation of any excessive international pressure to join the NPT. The Israeli official discourse has often repeated the argument reminiscent of realism, that the current system of safeguards under the NPT is not viable, and thus cannot be relied upon in insuring that all other Middle Eastern countries parties to the NPT would not covertly develop their own program despite International Atomic Energy Agency (IAEA) control[5]. The argument is now reinforced by the example of the reported Iraqi nuclear program which was undergoing before the second Gulf war, and which is now being brought to halt thanks to the work of the Security Council's special commission for the disarmament of Iraq (UNSCOM). The fear of cheating is eminent in the Israeli choice not to join the NPT. Israel did not hesitate to strike the nascent Iraqi reactor Osiraq, in order to prevent any likely shift in the balance of power. The default from signing the NPT, reveals however an understanding that should Israel join, the treaty will greatly affect its deterrent nuclear ambiguity posture. Indeed by not joining, Israel would be able to conserve such a posture and resist any lawyerly attempt to broaden the scope of the principle of non-proliferation as carried by the universally prone NPT, to include non-signatory threshold states.

Despite such a realist understanding, other Israeli practices lead to believe that they may be inspired by liberal institutionalist theories. The Israeli attack on the Iraqi reactor Osiraq was legally justified, by Israeli officials, as a legitimate measure of "self defense" according to article 51 of the UN Charter[6]. Of course such an

---

[4]Among the many accounts on the Israeli posture of nuclear ambiguity see the recent work of: Shai Feldman, *Nuclear Weapons and Arms Control in the Middle East*, (Cambridge: The MIT Press, 1997), 95 ff. In support of such an ambiguous posture Shimon Peres is reported to have said in a conference in 1995, in Geneva that: "[s]ome people would like us to clarify where we stand. But if a fog is part of a deterrent, let's keep the fog." See Shai Feldman, *Nuclear Weapons and Arms Control in the Middle East*, 245.

[5]Shai Feldman, *Nuclear Weapons and Arms Control in the Middle East*, 246.

[6]See the Israeli statement before the Security Council concerning its actions regarding the Osiraq reactor, June 12, 1981: "In destroying Osiraq, Israel performed an elementary act of self-preservation, both morally and legally. In so doing, Israel was exercising its inherent right of self-defense as

interpretation widely stretched the right of self-defense to include unlikely cases. In fact, this argument failed to prove the eminence of a prior Iraqi "armed attack," to justify self defense. Indeed, this Israeli behavior and stance called for the Security Council's condemnation[7]. Yet, Israel could not afford to state a purely realistic argument and sought instead to appeal for a certain legal legitimacy.

Israel has also signed the CTBT, and intends to be an active participant in the Organization the treaty establishes. From the Israeli perspective, the verification regime established by the treaty is more reliable than that of the IAEA. The Israeli signing of the CTBT also demonstrates, according to Israeli officials, a substantial degree of commitment to the global promises of nuclear non-proliferation[8]. But more importantly, the CTBT does not in itself jeopardize the Israeli posture of nuclear ambiguity, although some of the intrusive verification provisions in the treaty such as those related to on-site inspections[9] may well force Israel to disclose damaging information about its nuclear program[10]. Indeed, Israel had to make sure that other provisions in the treaty might be invoked to denounce "abusive"[11] demands for on-site inspections.

As to the Advisory Opinion of the International Court of Justice on the legality of the threat or use of nuclear weapons, Israel remained silent. It simply did not allude to it during the General Assembly First Committee's deliberations when

---

understood in general international law and as preserved in Article 51 of the United Nations Charter." UN Doc. S/PV. 2280 (1981); see also the Israeli statement before the Council on June 19, 1981 (UN. Doc. S/PV. 2288 (1981).

[7]Resolution S/RES/487 (1981) of June 19, 1981 strongly condemned "the military attack by Israel in clear violation of the Charter of the United Nations and the norms of international conduct."

[8]See the Israeli statement before the First Committee of the General Assembly at the date of the signing of the treaty: (UN Doc. A/C.1/51/PV.7 of October 18, 1996, at p. 10)

[9]Article IV. D. of the CTBT.

[10]See Shai Feldman, *Nuclear Weapons and Arms Control in the Middle East*, 256.

[11]Article IV. D. 36 of the CTBT: "The requesting State Party shall refrain from unfounded or abusive inspection requests." See also Article IV. D. 67 on "Frivolous or Abusive On Site Inspection Requests."

the Opinion was issued,[12] and abstained from voting on a related resolution,[13] which merely noted the Court's call to pursue nuclear disarmament negotiation in good faith[14].

Regardless of such Israeli indifference, the thrust of the opinion comforts in many ways the Israeli policy of deterrence through nuclear ambiguity. Indeed, it appeared clear from the Court's pronouncement that while there is no legal license to use nuclear weapons in an extreme case of self-defense in which the very survival of the state is at stake, there is equally no prohibition on such use. A condition where the very survival of the State is at stake, though of indeterminate nature (does survival refer to the continuation of the governing political regime or to the physical annihilation of the population; who determines the aggressor and the victim; who determines that the very survival of a state is threatened), has been a source of unresolved hesitation. The underlying question that hovers above the Court has been: could a State faced with a total disregard of the principle of proportionality which ought to guide action in armed conflicts, and thus suffering an eminent threat of annihilation, be guided by the same proportionality principle, to retaliate proportionally to such unlimited attacks? The Court was unable to resolve the question on the basis of law, as the law, appeared driving itself by its own mechanism towards its own negation[15]. The Court's non-pronouncement on the issue simply highlighted this negation. With the law's negation, prohibition or permission become both irrelevant. From the Israeli perspective, the law's negation would signify a license "in times of gloom"[16]. Indeed, the Court's positing of the situation where the survival of

---

[12]See the Israeli statement before the First Committee of the General Assembly at the date of the issuing of the Opinion: (UN Doc. A/C.1/51/PV.7 of October 18, 1996)

[13]See the minutes of the First Committee's meeting (A/C.1/PV. 22, at p. 7)

[14]See the UN General Assembly resolution: A/RES/51/45 M of December 10, 1996

[15]See Abdulhay Sayed, *Quand le droit est face à son néant*, 143 ff.

[16]See Shalheveth Freir, "A Nuclear Weapon Free Zone and its Ambiance," paper presented as part of UNIDIR's project on "Confidence-Building in the Middle East", July 13, 1993, p. 2.

a State is at stake represents an alternative articulation of the "Samson option,"[17] for which an Israeli nuclear arsenal was sought to be built in the first place. As weapons of last resort, the Israeli nuclear weapons would certainly not be spared in the event of Israel facing what it unilaterally determines to be an attack threatening its very survival. It is however less clear what the impact of the Advisory Opinion would be on any Israeli threat or use of nuclear weapons to prevent or respond to threats that do not amount to annihilation. Past experience indicates that, given Israel's sensitive threat perceptions, allusion to actual use of nuclear weapons as part of deterrence, has indeed been made with serious resolve[18]. While stating the law, the Advisory Opinion would have little if any impact in altering Israel's position in the future. The Court's determination that the use of nuclear weapons is "generally" contrary to international law applicable in armed conflict lives the door open for a wide range of exceptions, which would not fit with the word "generally". Such exceptions, barely recognizable today for the shortage of precedents (the bombings of Hiroshima and Nagasaki though remain as stark reminders), may well be invoked by Israeli officials to justify any use of nuclear weapons unilaterally deemed of military necessity. On the whole, while Israel remained inattentive to the findings of the Court, this did not mean that

---

[17]This expression has formed part of the title of a book about the Israeli nuclear capability by: Seymour Hersh, *The Samson Option, Israel's Nuclear Arsenal and American Foreign Policy*, (New York: Random House, 1991).

[18]Shai Feldman depicts in the Israeli official discourse an evolutionary "diminished nuclear ambiguity." See Shai Feldman, *Nuclear Weapons and Arms Control in the Middle East*, 101. Also, experience suggests that the Israelis have already threatened to use nuclear weapons in specific periods of tensions has also occurred. Indeed in response to Saddam Hussein's statement on April 2, 1990 that if Iraq were attacked Iraq is capable of burning half of Israel, the Israeli defense minister declared: "[w]e have the means for a devastating response, many times greater than Saddam Hussein's threat". Of course, such a statement seems to have been resonating in Iraqi ears throughout the second Gulf war, Ibid., p. 102. There had also been reports circulating about Israel thinking to use nuclear weapons during the 1973 October war. See the recent article of Mohammed Abdelsalam, "Nuclear Threats and the October 6th War", in Arabic, *Al-Siassah Al-Dawliah*, 34:134, (October, 1998), 83-86. The author reviews accounts on the possible Israeli nuclear alters during the war. The author concludes: "Thus nuclear weapons were not remote from the October 6, 1973 war, in a manner that warrants ignoring them, nor were they close to a degree that simply renders them as just another weapon system that could be used like any of the destructive conventional weapons."

Israel would be indifferent. The Court's opinion has somewhat diluted the normative energy of law by the uncertainty, vagueness or hesitation in its findings. While such inconclusive findings are incapable of affecting State behavior, they may still be manipulated to justify political choices.

The regional and international pressures, which called upon regional States to form a regional nuclear-weapon-free zone (NWFZ), while carrying little normative energy, have somewhat forced Israel to moderate its stance on the future of nuclear weapons in the Middle East. Israel officially subscribes to the idea of the establishment of a NWFZ. Since 1980, Israel approves the related resolution in the UN General Assembly[19]. Israel has displayed its willingness to work towards a Middle East free of weapons of mass destruction as soon as possible, in the peace treaty it signed with Jordan in 1994. However, Israel reiterates its reservations as to the dependence of such a zone on the existing IAEA verification mechanism. Rather it sees a regionally-based, intrusive verification mechanism, negotiated and embedded in a formal treaty, a better alternative to pursue[20]. The Israeli stance on the establishment of a nuclear-weapons-free zone in the Middle East combines trust with the law's potential at the regional level, a distrust of the law's achievement at the global level and a mistrust because of the law's limits. Israel resisted however to even discuss the matter of a nuclear-weapon free zone within the regional multilateral negotiating group on arms control, requiring first that all Arab countries as well as Iran conclude a genuine peace with it[21].

---

[19]UN General Assembly A/RES/35/147 of December 12, 1980.

[20]For a review of the Israeli position see: Shai Feldman, *Nuclear Weapons and Arms Control in the Middle East*, 249 ff.; see also the Israeli statement before the First Committee of the General Assembly (UN Doc. A/C.1/51/PV.7 of October 18, 1996), 8 ff.; and the most recent Israeli statement before the First Committee of the General Assembly (First Committee, 9, Press Release GA/DIS/3115 10 Meeting (AM), 20 October 1998).

[21]The *Al-Hayat* newspaper reported that the Israeli Chairman of the nuclear energy committee, which is affiliated with the Office of the Prime Minister, declared that "the Arab states must apply democracy for years before Israel gives up its nuclear capability." *Al-Hayat*, May 24, 1997, p. 7.

Many have questioned, however, the Israeli seriousness in pursuing a track that would ultimately lead it to give up a deterrent capability which constituted for decades a guarantee of statehood, in times where the national trauma still afresh[22]. Political hawks and the military elite in Israel would indeed both conclude that Israel cannot show any sign of weakness in the middle of the hostile Arab environment. Israel needs to remain at all times superior in capabilities so that Arabs would never consider its elimination[23]. Some have argued that the Israeli position on the establishment of the NWFZ in the Middle East, or on the CTBT is part of those rhetorical moves which are designed to defuse the political pressures associated with the existing legal instruments, knowing that problems in the region would still surface in a way so as to render any controlling endeavor nearly impossible.

On the whole, it becomes now clear that the interaction between the existing law on nuclear weapons and the Israeli understanding of such law seems to have produced a hardly classifiable hybrid Israeli position.

II

The Arab and Iranian practices can hardly be grouped under a single rubrique. Arab states and Iran generally pursue different and sometimes contradictory policies at the regional and international level. However, their reception of and dealing with the law's call to apply in the area of nuclear weapons in the Middle East may be similar at the official level, though regime understandings and practices may differ and sometimes collide. An important unifying factor can be found in the striking

---

[22]See on this argument Shai Feldman, *Nuclear Weapons and Arms Control in the Middle East*, 250; see also Avner Cohen, " The Nuclear Issue in the Middle East", in a New World Order", *Contemporary Security Policy*, 16:1, (1995), 58.

[23]Many have indeed encouraged Israel to adopt an overt nuclear posture as threats are likely to increase as a result of the peace process: See for example: Lous René Beres, "The Peace Process and Israel's Nuclear Strategy", *Strategic Review*, (1995), 38; Walter Schilling, "Israel's Nuclear Strategy in Transition", *Aussenpolitik, German Foreign Affairs Review*, 46:4, (1995), 319-326, 323.

similarity of popular reaction to what came to be known as the "Arab street(s)," or in an underlying Arab or Islamic fever that shapes and moves the opinion of the Arab and Islamic masses. The degree of the regime search for legitimacy as well as that of its internal stability both converge to shape the regime's understanding and practices regarding the law on nuclear weapons.

The preceding findings are particularly relevant in the case of the Arab and Iranian handling of the demands of the NPT. All Arab countries as well as Iran are now State parties to the NPT and their installations are fully and regularly verified. Some countries such as Egypt or Algeria have been hesitant to join the NPT[24]. Others, such as Syria and Iran have adhered to the NPT since its inception[25]. Indeed, adherence to the NPT has affected the Arab states' behavior in the direction of non-proliferation. The cost of defection from the treaty or covertly running contrary to its provision is understood to be of high price. Indeed, with ratification, many Arab countries have made the strategic decision not to pursue nuclear weapon programs in compliance with the global non-proliferation promise. Some may have been motivated by the consideration that such development is too costly, or too difficult. But this did not prevent popular and regime sentiments of injustice, because of the aggressive Israeli policies against fellow Arabs and Muslims and frustration with the Western tolerance of the Israeli nuclear-weapons program, to develop in the direction of demanding the pursuit of nuclear-weapon programs in order to balance the Israeli

---

[24] Egypt ratified the NPT on February 26, 1981 and concluded a safeguard agreement with the IAEA on June 30, 1982, IAEA Annual Report 1997, Algeria ratified the NPT on January 12 1995 and concluded a safeguards agreement with the IAEA on January 7, 1997, IAEA Annual Report 1997.
[25] Syria ratified the NPT on September 24, 1969 and concluded a safeguards agreement with the IAEA on May 18, 1992, IAEA Annual Report 1997, Iran ratified the NPT on February 2, 1970 and concluded a safeguards agreement with the IAEA on May 15, 1974, IAEA Annual Report 1997.

capability despite the NPT commitment[26]. The quest for regime prestige[27] and the perception by the governing elites of other external threats has also added to the incentive to proliferate covertly. Thus, Iraq[28], Iran[29], Libya[30] and Algeria[31] have been

---

[26]Columnists in the Arab press increasingly appear supportive of the idea that Arab governments need to proliferate because of the Israeli intransigence regarding its nuclear capability. One article argues that: "[I]srael, whether it joins the NPT or not, it shall retain the nuclear weapons to realize what it wants to realize. It must be clear to all regional countries that the balance is in favor of Israel, unless the Arab countries acquire this weapon, and especially Egypt, for if such weapons remains with Israel alone, this will render it the most powerful and influential country in the region, and will at the same time weaken the influence of Egypt and reduce its role in the region." See Jaffar Hassan Hadi, "Israel and the Nuclear Bomb: The Nuclear Weapon Pressures the Arabs and Damages Peace", in Arabic, *Al-Hayat*, 25 March 1995; see also Mohammed Abdelsalam, "Working Paper", in the Seminar on the Future of the Israeli Nuclear Monopoly, in Arabic, *Al-Mustaqbal Al-Arabi*, 19:208, (1996), 50-87. Mohammed Abdelsalam, who reported the above excerpts, also concluded that: "there exists a reigning climate in the region during 1994 and 1995, whose characteristics are now crystallized with the peace process, that pushes towards the necessity that the countries in the region ought to develop their nuclear capabilities, considering the importance of such capabilities notwithstanding their substances (whether civil or military), for to continue halting such development, and to voluntarily give up the nuclear option for regional and international considerations, or as evidence of good faith, is not a wise policy at the international level, or an acceptable one at the internal level." (p. 82) See also Abdeltawab Abdulhay, "The Arab Nuclear Bomb", in Arabic, *Al-Alam Al-Yaoum*, July 30, 1995; Nadia Mahmoud Moustafa, "The Nuclear Option in Egyptian Policy," in Arabic, *Al-Siassa Al-Dawlia*, 25:97, (July, 1989), 24-58.

[27]See Mohammed Abdelsalam, "Working Paper", in the Seminar on the Future of the Israeli Nuclear Monopoly, in Arabic, *Al-Mustaqbal Al-Arabi*, 19:208, (1996), 50-87. The author specifically concludes that "considerations of prestige may greatly influence the drive in the direction of nuclear proliferation in the period after the settlement of the Arab-Israeli conflict", at p. 71.

[28]It is reported that Iraq was secretly pursuing a multi-billion-dollar nuclear weapons program, code named "Petrochemical 3," with thousands of workers in numerous facilities. The IAEA investigations following the second Gulf war revealed details of the Iraqi effort to design an implosion-type nuclear explosive device and to test its non-nuclear components, including Iraq's plans to produce large quantities of lithium-6, a material used usually for the production of "boosted" atomic bombs and hydrogen bombs. For further details see Rodney W. Jones et al (ed.), *Tracking Nuclear Proliferation: A Guide in Maps and Charts*, 1998 (Washington, D.C.: Carnegie Endowment for International Peace, 1998), 187 ff.

[29]Iran is reportedly seeking to accelerate nuclear weapons development by direct purchase of fissile material from sources in the former Soviet Union. Russia is reportedly supplying Iran with a gas centrifuge uranium enrichment facility, which though under IAEA safeguards could enable Iran to build and operate a similar plant clandestinely to produce weapons-grade uranium. Iran has also sought the assistance of China but cooperation is now stumbling. For further details see Rodney W. Jones et al (ed.), *Tracking Nuclear Proliferation*, 169 ff.; see also Mohammed Abdelsalam, "Working Paper", 82 ff., who alludes to reports about the importance of a secret nuclear program under the supervision of the military establishment in Iran which parallels an ambitious 2.2 billion $US civilian nuclear program for the establishment of 10 nuclear reactors, in the course of two decades, for the

among the countries subject to reports on possible development of nuclear-weapons programs. Syria has recently been subject to reports suggesting that nuclear cooperation with Russia may well signify a quest for a nuclear-weapons option[32]. In addition, the Egyptian president Mubarak is reported to have said that Egypt would acquire nuclear weapons to counter Israel's arsenal if deemed necessary[33]. Each of those countries may be moved by a combination of reasons peculiar to their particular situations. Popular demands[34], regime perception of the surrounding internal and

---

production of electricity. The paper concedes however that no credible evidence is substantiating such reports. See also Ahmed Ibrahim Mahmoud. "The Iranian Nuclear Program: Development, Motives and the Strategic Significance," in Arabic, *Al-Siassah Al-Dawliah*, 34:131, (January, 1998), 311-319. The author considers among other things the various motives that are pushing Iran to develop a nuclear capability.

[30]Intelligence reports indicate that Libya continued its attempts to purchase sensitive nuclear technology. Libya is reportedly trying to recruit nuclear scientists to assist in developing nuclear weapons. For further details see Rodney W. Jones et al (ed.), *Tracking Nuclear Proliferation*, 215 ff. In addition the Libyan President Qadhafi periodically issues contradictory statements that give little insights on Libya's nuclear intentions. He declared "even if we obtain such a (nuclear) bomb or produce it, we would not be able to drop it on Palestine, because if we bomb Palestine it would be as if we had bombed Syria, Lebanon, Egypt and Jordan. Namely, all Arabs will be lost. No one is thinking of using an Atomic bomb on Palestine. It is impossible to use weapons of mass destruction in this area. The entire world remembers Hiroshima and Nagasaki." cited by Shai Feldman, *Nuclear Weapons and Arms Control in the Middle East*, 135. But Qadhafi has also said: "Arabs must be able to develop a nuclear bomb to balance the Israeli nuclear arsenal", *Al-Hayat*, May 18, 1995.

[31]Reports indicate that as part of a Chinese-Algerian nuclear cooperation agreement, China would provide know-how to enable Algeria to operate hot cells in a facility under construction since 1992 at a site adjacent to a 15-MWt heavy water research reactor in the Es salam location. These hot cells would give Algeria the capability to separate plutonium from irradiated fuel, although there are no signs that Algeria is now pursuing any secret development effort, especially after its recent ratification of the NPT. For further details see: Rodney W. Jones et al (ed.), *Tracking Nuclear Proliferation*, 163 ff.; Mohammed Abdelsalam, "Working Paper", 77.

[32]See Rodney W. Jones et al (ed.), Tracking Nuclear Proliferation, 3.

[33]President Mubarak said in a recent interview with the *Al-Hayat* newspaper the following: "For the time being, Egypt does not consider entering the nuclear club. But if the time comes where we are needing this weapon, and if we are forced, we shall not hesitate, because this is the last thing we think of." *Al-Hayat*, October 5, 1998, p. 1.

[34]It is not easy to determine the popular demand regarding nuclear weapons in the absence of popular surveys on this issue in Arab countries. Accounts of Arab and Iranian intellectuals and arms control specialists may remedy to a limited degree the absence of popular survey. The credibility of their accounts, or their ability to reflect social roaring is a function of the extent of the regime manipulation of their work, or their dependence on the regime.

external threats all need to be taken into consideration to measure the country's propensity to pursue a nuclear option. Social opprobrium, or disgrace, appear of little importance when compared with reasons of prestige or when evaluated by the populace. Following the second Gulf war, details about the extent of the Iraqi program became known. As to the others, talk of their programs remained the hostage of unilateral intelligence accounts, official denials, IAEA conformity certificates and renewal of the official commitment, of those States, for nuclear non-proliferation as a step towards nuclear disarmament.

Indeed the rhetorical commitment of Arab states and Iran for nuclear non-proliferation, remained steady. This however, did not prevent many of the key Arab states from adopting a position on chemical and biological weapons similar to the Israeli stance on nuclear weapons. Arab states like Egypt, Iraq or Syria, who are not parties to the Chemical Weapons Convention refuse to ratify the treaty as long as Israel do not become party to the NPT[35]. They conceive of their refusal to adhere, as a deterrent measure against the Israeli policy of nuclear ambiguity. Their ambiguity about the existence of any development, production or stockpiling of chemical weapons was devised to counter the threat posed by the Israeli ambiguous posture on nuclear weapons[36]. By so doing they remain consistent from a legal

---

[35] On the Egyptian position see Mahmoud Karem, "Some Light on the Egyptian Position Regarding the Treaty on the Non-Proliferation of Nuclear Weapons," in Arabic, *Al-Siassa Al-Dawlia*, (April, 1995), 76-85, 82.

[36] Recently the Egyptian representative to the First Committee of the General Assembly has had to respond to earlier Israeli charges that Egypt is not a party to the Chemical Weapons Convention by saying: "After citing long security arguments in an attempt to justify why (Israel) had not joined the NPT and placed its nuclear arsenals under IAEA safeguards, the Israeli representative chose to note that Egypt was one of the Arab states that had not signed the Chemical Weapons Convention. It was as if he was saying that it was only Israel's right to keep ambiguous nuclear policies to protect its security and all other Arab countries, in particular Egypt, should forgo their security concerns and ratify the Chemical and Biological Weapons conventions. Such a state was unacceptable and would not lead anywhere.", (First Committee, 14, Press Release GA/DIS/3116 11th Meeting (PM) 20 October 1998).

perspective, and offer a credible and cost-effective deterrent to face the Israeli nuclear threat. In some instances, particular regime perception of the internal and external threats also encourage the adoption of such a posture on chemical weapons. During the first Gulf war, chemical weapons were used, mainly by Iraq against Iran and its own Kurdish civilian population[37]. Nonetheless, Iraq exercised restraint during the second Gulf war. Reports repeatedly surface on the development, production and stockpiling of chemical and biological weapons by States parties to the Chemical or Biological Weapons Conventions such as Iran, in violation of those treaties. However, such information could not be verified, and most probably could not be ruled out neither, due to the relative accessibility of the production technology and the relative ease with which such weapons can be developed and covertly stockpiled[38].

The CTBT did attract some of the key Arab states such as Algeria and Egypt as well as Iran, who signed the instrument but did not ratify it as yet[39]. As the treaty awaits to enter into force, its signing by those states and its possible ratification appears to be a reaffirmation of their commitment not to proliferate. Indeed any endeavor to indigenously develop nuclear weapons, with mostly rudimentary technology that lacks the capability for lab-simulated tests, would require indispensable underground tests, which would be prohibited under the terms of the treaty if ratified and entered into force. As of this writing, none of those countries has taken the further step of ratification, a procedure that represents the culmination of

---

[37]See UN Secretary General Reports S/20060 & Add. 1, S/20063/Add.1, S/20134, and Security Council resolutions S/RES/612 (1988), of 9 May 1988, S/RES/612 of 26 August 1988.

[38]During the First Committee's deliberations Iran has had to respond to charges about its military capabilities by saying: "Iran, like others in the region, could not remain idle against the threat posed by Israel's mass destruction capabilities. Iran is a party to all conventions concerning weapons of mass destruction, without exception, and it considers its missile technology to be a legitimate conventional means of defense. Moreover, its missile technology serves the sole purpose of self defense." (First Committee, 15, Press Release GA/DIS/3116 11th Meeting (PM) 20 October 1998).

[39]The list of ratifications of the CTBT relied upon in the present chapter is the one retrieved on January 19, 1999 from the UN Treaties Department web site: http://www.un.org/Depts/Treaty/.

an acquiescing internal political consideration and legally indicates that the State becomes a full party. In addition, other important countries such as Libya, Iraq and Syria did not sign the CTBT. The reason for this, which both Syria and Libya shared, was that the treaty does not seem to further the cause of nuclear disarmament and may thus not be considered as a sufficient step forward in the right direction. Indeed, so they argued, despite the title, the treaty is not comprehensive, as it does not include laboratory tests, which can still be performed by the nuclear states to maintain and develop the readiness of their arsenals for the indefinite future[40]. Such states may have also reasoned that any further commitment in the nuclear realm could hinder their development of technology, if a nuclear option is to be revived to balance against any threatening changes in the Israeli nuclear policy.

The Advisory Opinion of the International Court of Justice on the legality of the threat or use of nuclear weapons, has offered an opportunity for almost all Arab states as well as Iran to voice their support for the Court's determination that states need to vigorously pursue negotiations in good faith for the achievement of nuclear disarmament[41]. Iraq has specifically stressed the Court's ruling to the effect that the threat or use of nuclear weapons is generally contrary to the requirement of

---

[40]See the Libyan statement before the First Committee of the General Assembly when the treaty was approved: "Regrettably, despite our prior support for the formulation of the CTBT, we did not find in the text of the current Treaty any convincing proof of its comprehensive nature. This has greatly disappointed us because although the Treaty bans explosive tests, it turns a blind eye to other technical methods for the qualitative development of nuclear weapons, such as laboratory and similar tests." (A/C.1/51/PV.10, October 21, 1996); see also the Syrian Statement: "That ban is not an end in itself but is merely one way to achieve nuclear disarmament. We should also ensure that the ban is comprehensive in the truest sense of the word. A treaty that does not ban all nuclear tests in all their forms, which does not put an end to qualitative improvements, in nuclear weapons, and which permits nuclear-weapons States to continue their nuclear weapons improvement programs through electronic means cannot be considered a comprehensive test-ban treaty." (A/C.1/51/PV.13 of October 24, 1996).
[41]See the statements before the First Committee of the UN General Assembly of Egypt (A/C.1/51/PV.4, p. 15), Algeria (A/C.1/51/PV.5, p. 10), Saudi Arabia (A/C.1/51/PV.10, p. 5), Libya (A/C.1/51/PV.10, p. 13), Yemen (A/C.1/51/PV.12, p. 13), Sudan (A/C.1/51/PV.12, p. 19), Oman (A/C.1/51/.12, p. 20), Iran (A/C.1/51/PV.13, p. 17).

international law applicable in armed conflict[42]. Earlier, Egypt and Qatar as well as Iran, had argued, orally and in writing before the Court for the illegality of any threat or use of nuclear weapons[43]. The Court's ambivalent conclusion on the question of the legality of the use of nuclear weapons in extreme circumstance of self-defense where the survival of the state is at stake may not be a source of support for those circles in the Arab or Iranian elites favorable to non-proliferation. The hesitation of the Court when faced with the survival question, while logically does not warrant a license for use, may well be relied upon in any Arab or Iranian effort to justify the quest to acquire a nuclear capability. Indeed, by positing the survival situation and declaring the absence of law on the matter, the Court is implicitly recognizing how the law may become simply irrelevant in an extreme case of self-defense. Such an interpretation already enhanced the Israeli possession in a manner that facilitates the possibility of its use against Arab countries. This legal boost implicitly granted to the Israeli nuclear option, might well be perceived by the Arab countries as an important elevation of the Israeli threat, one that would be capable of shaking the very survival of the regime/state. If the legality of the use of nuclear weapons in such an extreme case is not clear, the legality of its possession, so it may be argued, appears *a fortiori* also questionable despite the NPT. Indeed, a sceptic would not hesitate to conclude that the World Court opinion is as serious a blow for the NPT as those recently performed by India and Pakistan.

It is needless to dwell on the wide subscription by Arab countries and Iran to the principle of establishing a nuclear weapon free zone in the Middle East, as long as it leads to controlling Israel's nuclear capability. Indeed such a zone is originally an Arab and Iranian demand. It was Egypt and Iran who, in 1974, first introduced a

---

[42]See the Iraqi statement before the First Committee of the General Assembly (A/C.1/51/PV.13, p. 1).
[43]Legality of the Threat or Use of Nuclear Weapons, ICJ, Report, par. 5, 8; and the Oral Pleadings of Egypt, CR/95/23 on November 1, 1995; Iran CR/95/26 on November 6, 1995.

resolution to that effect in the General Assembly of the United Nations[44]. From the Arab perspective, it was an alternative worthy to pursue in view of the Arab non-possession of nuclear weapons. The reiteration each year of the call by the General Assembly for the establishment of such a zone has since been a rhetorical tool designed to put further pressures on Israel to sign the NPT. The resolutions carrying such a call have often been accompanied by other resolutions that usually denounced the Israeli possession of nuclear weapons. However, the repetition of the same resolution each year was also important in mobilizing and strengthening the little normative energy that General Assembly resolutions normally carry, in order to render the negotiation for the establishment of such a zone inevitable. The Arab countries seem also to have consented to an essentially Egyptian proposal, which called for the establishment of a weapon-of-mass-destruction free zone in the Middle East[45].

While a lot depends on negotiation for the realization of such proposals, it appears clear that the formal normative energy of law would be heavily relied upon to offer an authoritative framework of reference and a justification for appropriate procedures to verify compliance. However, with the Israeli rhetorical position in mind, it becomes obvious that all parties involved do not rely on such zone to change identities and interests but rather affirm that changes from the other side need to intervene prior to any meaningful negotiation on the establishment of any zone. The Israeli stance requiring the conclusion of peace treaties with all Arab states and Iran as a prerequisite for any discussion, resembles the Arab and Iranian demands that Israel must adhere to the NPT, as such a move is considered an important confidence-building measure that would show a genuine Israeli willingness to

---

[44]See *Yearbook of the United Nations*, Vol. 28, (1974), p. 18, and General Assembly Resolution 3263 (XXIX) of December 9, 1974.
[45]On the Egyptian proposal see Mohammed Shaker, "Prospects for Establishing a Zone Free of Weapons of mass destruction in the Middle East", *Director's Series on Proliferation*, (1994), 21-31.

renounce the nuclear option[46]. The role of the zone in enhancing mutual trust appears also as unlikely possibility. The Israeli distrust of the actions of Arab State and of the work of the IAEA drove it to demand an intrusive regional verification system, one that essentially allows for Israeli inspectors to directly control Arab compliance with the requirements of the zone. The Arab and Iranian distrust of the Israeli policies, supported by a record of Israeli resistance of international inspection, led them to conclude that the Israeli demands run on a one-way street. The objective verification mechanisms offered by the related international instruments are more reliable to make a zone free of nuclear and other weapons of mass destruction possible in the Middle East[47].

On the whole, the preceding brief overview shows, that the Arab and Iranian record of compliance with the law's demand to apply in the realm of nuclear weapons is significant. Their commitments helped render their inclinations to proliferate costly. Nevertheless, the Israeli reported nuclear capabilities have mainly fuelled the support for the Arab and Iranian quests to pursue a nuclear option. The dialectic of such an interchange have rendered the Arab positions contradictory. No sense about the understandings that influence such positions can be discerned. The commitment to the global agenda of nuclear non-proliferation cohabited with other positions envisaging to alter such an understating. As long as the reported Israeli nuclear capability remains unquestioned, the law on nuclear weapons will remain relegated to a secondary role for the Arab countries and the incentives to proliferate will generally gain greater influence. Against such confusing positions, it would be impossible to identify any useful trend, or to express any prediction as to what State has the greater incentive to defect and proliferate. Ultimately, proliferation depends on the content and intensity of the popular demands in each country, on the degree

---

[46]On this position see Abdulhay Sayed, "The Future of the Israeli Nuclear Force and the Middle East Peace Process", *Security Dialogue*, 28:1, (1997), 31-48, 41.
[47]See Mahmoud Karem, *A Nuclear-Weapon-Free Zone in the Middle East*, 129.

of the regimes' search for legitimacy and on the regimes' perception of the surrounding internal and external threats.

III

There remains to consider the positions of an influential actor in terms of both the global non-proliferation effort and Middle East politics, namely the United States. The heavy U.S. involvement in Middle Eastern affairs was explained by the special U.S. affinity towards Israel, the U.S. interest in the region's vital natural resources and the regional actors' "congenital" reliance on and defiance of the US. United States policies regarding nuclear weapons in the region are important, as its political weight is actively engaged in supporting the existing non-proliferation treaty, though only partially so in the Middle East.

The present account will not elaborate on the efforts made by the United States in support of non-proliferation. Suffice it to mention that the U.S. has actively sponsored the conclusion, the universalization, and the indefinite extension of the NPT. The U.S. has also been engaged in increasingly meaningful bilateral nuclear arms control efforts with the Soviet Union/Russian Federation aiming at reducing weapons stockpiles and halting further production. Domestically, the U.S. has also enacted several legislations and amendments to legislations in support of the global non-proliferation effort[48]. Of course, as a nuclear weapon state, the U.S. still retains a posture of nuclear deterrence, which in turn led the country to argue before the International Court of Justice for the legality of the threat or use of nuclear weapons in self-defense[49].

Nevertheless, the U.S. commitment to the principle of non-proliferation is the backbone of the NPT. This commitment is somewhat a generator of the

---

[48]See the Nuclear Non-Proliferation Act of 1978, United States Code, Title 22, § 3201.
[49]See the U.S. oral pleadings before the International Court of Justice, CR/95/34 on November 15, 1995.

normative energy carried by the treaty. The vigor of such a commitment remains indispensable to keep this energy radiating for purposes of realizing the universality of the treaty.

Yet, when it comes to dealing with Middle Eastern politics, the U.S. non-proliferation policy appears contradictory and selective. Historically and across all post-World-War II administrations, the U.S. has adopted a policy of "see no evil, hear no evil," in response to growing reports about the extent of the Israeli nuclear-weapon program[50]. Even administrations who made the nuclear nonproliferation issue a priority on their agendas deliberately turned a blind eye to the mounting of precision in reports about the Israeli nuclear capability. During the second Gulf war, the Bush administration went so far as nearly "endorsing the Israeli nuclear capability,"[51] when the Secretary of defense Dick Cheney responded to a journalist question about the likelihood that Israel might resort to the use of tactical nuclear weapons should Iraq escalates and use chemical warheads, by saying that "that decision the Israelis would have to make."[52] The Clinton administration did not press Israel to sign the NPT during the review conference of 1995, which approved the indefinite extension of the treaty. The administration expressed its understanding of the Israeli security concerns and merely requested that Israel declares that it is "ready to discuss this issue at some point in the future"[53]. Indeed all administrations have found much support in the U.S. congress for maintaining an Israeli exception to the application of the nuclear non-proliferation act. A unanimous opinion seems to have reigned across administrations, that the understandable existential threats Israel faces warrant its acquisition of nuclear weapons. Such an option is an

---

[50]On the U.S. policy see Shai Feldman, *Nuclear Weapons and Arms Control in the Middle East*, 175 ff.; see also Mohammed Abdelsalam, "Working Paper", 84, who speaks about the U.S. policy of "double standard."

[51]See Shai Feldman, *Nuclear Weapons and Arms Control in the Middle East*, 189

[52]CNN, Transcripts, Evans & Novak, February 2, 1991.

[53]Cited by Shai Feldman, *Nuclear Weapons and Arms Control in the Middle East*, 194.

indispensable deterrent, and a factor of stability in the Middle East. In addition, the .special affinity that exists between the U.S. and Israel, and the close ties the two countries maintain leave the American political elite confident of the Israeli wise and rationale use of such an option[54].

However, the U.S. has been considerably restrictive when dealing with reports about Arab or Iranian pursuit of a nuclear option. Indeed, the benefit of the doubt, which has been generously granted to Israel, has simply been denied to the other side. The U.S. heavily pressed the Arab countries to accept the indefinite extension of the NPT, and to give up their position linking their support with Israeli adherence to the treaty[55]. In addition, the U.S. closely monitors Arab and Iranian nuclear cooperation with other nuclear-weapons States such as China or Russia, and vigorously reacts to any reported intensifying of such action, despite assurances, by all parties involved that such assistance is for peaceful purposes and is set to be fully safeguarded. Iran has been at the forefront of States subject to U.S. sanctions, in response to reports about Iranian nuclear weapons development[56]. The U.S. has also pursued and is actively involved in a tough UN Security Council endeavor to disarm Iraq and destroy all human and material capabilities to pursue any weapons of mass destruction program. Such an objective has justified many U.S. and UK military strikes on Iraq, with and without Security Council mandate, when the special commission on disarmament faced or provoked reluctance from the Iraqis.

The contradictory U.S. attitude in approaching the question of proliferation of nuclear weapons in the Middle East, has fuelled bitter sentiments in Arab and Islamic countries. To be accurate, it is not the pursuit of a vigorous U.S. campaign

---

[54]Ibid., p. 191

[55]For a summary of events during the NPT review conference in 1995 see John Simpson, "The Nuclear Non-Proliferation Regime After the NPT Review and Extension Conference", *SIPRI Yearbook 1996*, 561-589, 567.

[56]See the Iran-Iraq Non-proliferation Act of 1992, United States Code, Title 50, § 1701, as amended by the Defense Authorization Act for Fiscal year 1996, P.L. 104-107, Sec. 1408 (Feb. 10, 1996).

in support of the NPT, which is at stake. It is rather the U.S. tolerance of the Israeli -nuclear capability in contradiction with the NPT, which is reproached. Indeed, Arab sources often argue that such a selectivity in approaching the nuclear question in the Middle East undermines the normative energy carried by the NPT. For those Arab countries, which are largely moved by deep sentiments of injustice from aggressive Israeli policies, the nuclear Non-Proliferation Treaty appears no longer credible and the quest to acquire nuclear weapons can no longer be reproached as unlawful. The pressure those streets exercise on the existing regimes and the extent to which those regimes are able to absorb or fuel the popular demands for proliferation, depend on the nature of internal politics in each country. A more balanced U.S. approach consistent with the nuclear non-proliferation promise, could have largely contributed in strengthening the treaty, and in mitigating the incentives to proliferate.

A contrary argument suggests that the U.S. tolerance of Israeli nuclear activities, is based on an understanding of the existential threats felt by Israel, and that once those threats are adequately addressed through the peace process, such tolerance would give way to more aggressive U.S. efforts for the establishment of a nuclear and other weapons of mass destruction free zone in the Middle East.

✳

Much of the global non-proliferation effort is generated by pacifist ideas that abhor war and abominate its nuclear manifestation. Such ideas call for nuclear disarmament as a step towards general and complete disarmament. They found in the normative energy that law normally carries, an important ally to further such an objective. Law embodied those ideals and, through its normative energy, attempted to provide the means for such ideas to materialize. Non-proliferation is regarded as an important step to be realized in this direction. Such a step is, indeed, indispensable for rendering nuclear disarmament possible. The comprehensive test-ban and the nuclear weapons-free zones are also additional steps in the same direction. With such objectives in mind, the law's normative energy has a pretense to force individual behaviors to conform with these intermediate goals.

The present chapter attempted to look at the question in the specific context of the Middle East. All along the previous development it appeared increasingly clear that it is difficult to identify any social structure regarding nuclear proliferation in the Middle East. Actors in the region dealt with the existing law on nuclear weapons in multivariate fashions, each being inspired by a combination of factors peculiar to its own situation. The difficulty in identifying any distinctive structure along the line of which regional actors actually operate, leaves research resigned to the universalizing theories circulating in the academia, which are ill-adapted to the regional specificity. The results that could be obtained from those theories, about the likelihood or the prospects of proliferation, would appear to be of limited value. Indeed, such theories (or what this chapter calls the "structures of shared knowledge") emphasize one facet of the social behavior and choose to consider complexity as secondary. It is as an effort to remind of this complexity that this chapter was written.

Chapter 16

The Denuclearization of South Africa

David Albright

South Africa made history by being the first country to abandon its nuclear weapons and join the Non-Proliferation Treaty (NPT). However, following its 1989 decision to abandon its program, it dismantled its weapons in secret without acknowledging that it had ever had them in the first place. Facing a growing controversy over its past activities, the government admitted in March 1993 that South Africa had six gun-type nuclear weapons and was finishing a seventh one at the time of the 1989 decision to curtail the program.

The History and Motivation of South Africa's Nuclear Weapons Program

Former South African nuclear weapon scientists trace the success of the nuclear weapons program to three main factors: (1) South Africa had the nuclear fuel cycle infrastructure, including supplies of natural uranium, to develop a reliable and plentiful supply of highly enriched uranium (HEU); (2) it had a sufficient scientific and industrial base to establish a nuclear weapons program; and (3) it had the conventional weapons capability to make a credible deliverable nuclear weapon.

Former members of the program usually stress two primary motivations for wanting nuclear weapons. The first was the political and military pressure created by international isolation and the perceived threat of military invasion by front line states and their supporters in the Soviet bloc. The second was that South Africa had the technical capability to make nuclear explosives.

The program itself can be divided into two periods. The first period, which lasted until about 1979, focussed on the development of the capability to make nuclear explosives. The second one, which ended in 1989 when the program was terminated, expanded that capability and developed a credible nuclear deterrent. During the first period, the program was under the authority of the scientific Atomic Energy Board (AEB), later replaced by the Atomic Energy Corporation (AEC). Afterwards, the program was transferred to the control of ARMSCOR, the state-owned Armaments Corporation and the military's procurement agency.

Early Period

Former members of the program have stated that initially the focus was on "peaceful" nuclear explosives. Tielman de Waal, managing director of ARMSCOR, said that in the 1960s "the idea to look into the feasibility of developing nuclear explosives for peaceful applications emerged as a scientific endeavor out of technological 'can-do' mentality."[57] During the 1970s, de Waal added that the nuclear explosive program also "coincided with the strengthening of South Africa's international isolation, which created a strong sense of showing the world that we can go it alone." The implication is that the program during the initial period was largely one of technology development and national prestige. One former member of the program said that in the 1970s the program was also a way to keep technically skilled people in prestige work.

Little documented information exists about this early period, particularly during the 1960s. Official accounts tend to emphasize civilian nuclear applications,

---

[1]Tielman de Waal, "South Africa's Past Nuclear Programme," paper presented at a press briefing in South Africa, April 6, 1995.

particularly the development of reactors for research and power production and enrichment plants for reactor fuel.[58] The motivations of the program's originators remain murky, and suspicions remain that nuclear weapons ambitions were the primary motivation. One fact is clear, however. Official accounts of that period show that these nuclear efforts had the full support of the top South Africa leadership.[59]

The principal technical challenge of the 1960s was the creation of uranium enrichment or plutonium production facilities that could make the basic material for both nuclear explosives and civilian reactors. Developing the capability to make fissile material is the most demanding part of acquiring nuclear explosives. The task of building the bomb itself is easier, although still challenging.

By the late 1960s, South Africa chose the uranium enrichment route and delayed its plutonium production plans. After several years of secret enrichment research, Prime Minister B. J. Vorster decided in February 1969 to approve the construction of a pilot uranium enrichment plant.[60]

In the same year, an internal committee of the AEB was appointed to investigate the economic and technical aspects of peaceful nuclear explosives with particular reference to South Africa's mining industry.[61] Although the AEB's interest in peaceful nuclear explosives (PNEs) was not secret, the actual work was highly classified.

Although the enrichment project had been shrouded in intense secrecy, the government decided that such a large construction project could not be hidden for

[2]See for example, Waldo Stumpf, Chief Executive Officer of the AEC, "South Africa's Limited Nuclear Deterrent Programme and the Dismantling Thereof Prior to South Africa's Accession to the NPT," Transcript of talk given at the South African Embassy, July 23, 1993.
[3]A. R. Newby-Fraser, *Chain Reaction* (Pretoria: Atomic Energy Board, 1979), pp. 97-102.
[4]Newby-Fraser, op. cit. p. 102.
[5]Report by the Director General, *The Denuclearization of Africa (GC(XXXVIIRESI'557),* GC(XY.XVII/1075, September 9,1993, p. 5.

long.[62] In July 1970 Vorster therefore announced in Parliament that South Africa intended to build a pilot enrichment plant. One purpose of the project was to sell enriched uranium overseas, and Vorster invited any noncommunist nation to collaborate in the exploiting of this new process for civilian purposes.

De Waal has speculated that if South Africa had been successful in obtaining international collaboration in the early 1970s, the development of a nuclear deterrent could have been obviated.[63] The government's apartheid policy, however, prevented such cooperation from happening.

In addition, international suspicions about the pilot-scale enrichment plant remained, particularly because South Africa refused to put the facility under International Atomic Energy Agency (IAEA) inspections or to reveal the plant's exact status and intended enrichment output. In particular, South Africa refused to admit that the plant was designed to make weapon-grade uranium.

Meanwhile, secret work on nuclear explosives continued at AEB, parallelling the construction of the enrichment plant. In March 1971, in accordance with the recommendations of this committee, the Minister of Mines gave approval to the AEB to commence secret research and development work on nuclear explosive devices.[64] In 1974, the first stage of the pilot plant was commissioned. During the same year, the AEB reported that the development of a nuclear explosive was feasible, and the Prime Minister approved a redefinition of the program to the limited development of a nuclear explosive capability to serve as a deterrent.[65] He also approved the construction of a nuclear test site in the Kalahari desert.

Nevertheless, the program remained with the AEB, and its emphasis continued to be the development of a nuclear explosive and not a nuclear arsenal.

---

[6]Newby-Fraser, op cit., p. 102.
[7]de Waal, op. cit., p. 2.
[8]*The Denuclearization of Africa*, op. cit., p. 5.
[9]*The Denuclearization of Africa,* op. cit., p. 5.

The decision to create a limited nuclear deterrent, however, likely reflected a shift in the primary purpose of the program at the most senior levels of government. If so, this shift was probably a response to the deterioration of South Africa's security situation. The Portuguese military seized power in Lisbon in April 1974 and decided to abandon its colonies, Angola and Mozambique, after more than a decade of trying to subdue indigenous guerrilla forces. The international effort against apartheid was also gaining momentum, further isolating South Africa.

Increasing Military Interest

Several events occurred from 1975 to 1978 that increased the interest of the military in the nuclear program, including the growing threat to apartheid South Africa from its neighbors, a change in the South African government, and diminished military confidence in the Atomic Energy Board's handling of the program.

Following Portugal's hasty departure from Mozambique and Angola in 1974-1975, Russia and Cuba intervened militarily in Angola and helped install a Marxist regime, which developed close relations with Mozambique, Zambia, and the anti-South African movements South West African People's Organization (SWAPO) and the African National Congress (ANC). Military intervention by South African forces in Angola encountered stiffer opposition than expected.

Regardless of the merits of South Africa's position at the time, its officials have often expressed bitterness and disillusionment with the actions of the U.S. government following the withdrawal of Portugal from Angola. According to Chester Crocker, former Assistant Secretary of State for African Affairs, "Pretoria blasted what it saw to be Western flakiness, if not perfidy, and pulled out of Angola [in 1976] after cutting a side deal" with Angola.[66] This Angolan episode, according

---

[10]Chester Crocker, *High Noon in Southern Africa* (W. W. Norton & Company: New York, 1992), p. 50.

to Crocker, had a traumatic effect in South Africa, prompting a "sentiment of revenge for past humiliation and an abiding suspicion of Western diplomacy."[67]

A former member of the South African nuclear weapons program said that the South African military felt strongly betrayed by the sudden halting of U.S. covert assistance during the Angola crisis. He said that this shift in U.S. policy against what South Africa viewed as a well-orchestrated communist threat strengthened the hand of those who believed that South Africa needed nuclear weapons to protect its security.

Another factor that contributed to a military nuclear program was the dramatic 1977 disclosure that South Africa was preparing to conduct a nuclear explosive test in the Kalahari desert. Although South Africa did not have enough fissile material for a nuclear explosive at that time, that shortage was the result of delays in the enrichment program that slowed the production of enough HEU for the first device until 1979. Nevertheless, the construction of the test site progressed according to earlier plans, which anticipated a test in 1977 or 1978. Upon its discovery the test site was closed, but not before an absolutely secret program had been exposed, according to a former member of the program.

The former member of the program added that AEB scientists wanted to conduct a test, and he believes that eventually they would have done so. Since any test would have been detected, however, he was unclear what the AEB scientists were thinking. Perhaps, the AEB believed that the world's reaction would have been no worse than its reaction to the 1974 Indian "peaceful" nuclear explosion. In any case, after this international fiasco, the people within the program argued that testing be avoided to prevent harsh and damaging international reactions.

---

[11]Crocker, op cit., p. 56.

After the Kalahari episode, the international community took additional steps to impose sanctions on South Africa because of its apartheid policies. In November 1977, the UN Security Council approved unanimously a mandatory military arms embargo on South Africa, which had been voluntary since 1963. In this resolution, the Council expressed "grave concern that South Africa is at the threshold of producing nuclear weapons" and decided that all states "shall refrain from any cooperation with South Africa in the manufacture and development of nuclear weapons."

In 1978, the UN General Assembly recommended that the Security Council impose an oil embargo on South Africa, which depends heavily on oil imports. The Security Council refused, although the General Assembly endorsed a voluntary oil embargo the next year. Nations also took steps to deny South Africa sensitive nuclear technology, and the IAEA removed South Africa from the Board of Governors.

Efforts to deny South Africa sensitive nuclear technology also contributed to its sense of isolation and bitterness. Since these actions were primarily motivated by opposition to apartheid, they reinforced the view within South Africa that it had little to gain from stopping its nuclear weapons program or joining the NPT, unless it first ended apartheid and made other fundamental domestic changes.

More importantly, according to de Waal, "These circumstances led to the conviction that in the event of a direct threat to its territorial integrity, the Government would not be able to rely on international assistance. The option of developing a nuclear deterrent became increasingly attractive."[68]

---

[12]de Waal, op. cit.

Cutoffs of nuclear aid, however, did not disrupt the nuclear explosive effort. South Africa produced enough HEU for its first device in 1979, and soon afterwards built a nuclear explosive device.

Meanwhile, in September 1978, Defense Minister Pieter Willem Botha became head of government. He had been the Defense Minister since 1966, and maintained that portfolio after becoming head of government. Botha was a proud nationalist who had presided over the buildup and modernization of the South African Defense Force and the growing ARMSCOR military-industrial complex which supported it.

Botha turned out to be a strong supporter of a nuclear weapons program. ARMSCOR officials stated that in October 1978, one month after taking office, Botha decided to implement the shift in emphasis from peaceful to possible military applications. Despite the 1974 decision to create a limited nuclear deterrent, ARMSCOR officials state that the program remained essentially a scientific exercise. For example, the AEB did not believe it had a mandate to weaponize the devices, according to a former member of the program. ARMSCOR's mission, according to a former member, was to turn the device into a weapon system. The AEB retained the task of providing the HEU, conducting theoretical nuclear weapon studies, and maintaining health physics expertise.

To build nuclear weapons, ARMSCOR built a new facility about 15 kilometers from Pelindaba. The facility was called the Circle facility. It built its first deliverable air-dropped bomb in 1982, suitable for delivery by the Buccaneer bomber (the AEB had manufactured a non-deliverable device in 1979). After several years of developing safety and security improvements in the weapon, it created by 1989 an arsenal of five certified bombs and a device suitable for underground testing. ARMSCOR was also finishing a new test device that incorporated many safety and security features absent in the other test device. Because the Buccaneers were fast approaching the end of their life and enemy states had improved their air defenses, the program was developing the ability to build a warhead for a ballistic missile when it was terminated.

Nuclear Weapon Strategy

Questions remain about the purpose of South Africa's nuclear weapons. However, the South African government has declared that its nuclear strategy was not aimed at war-fighting but it instead was a political strategy designed to force western powers, particularly the United States, to assist it against a threat to its territory.

The development of this strategy occurred in the early 1980s at ARMSCOR, and helped serve to define the program. The "deterrent" strategy was based on three phases. The ultimate aim of this strategy was to obtain western assistance in the case of an overwhelming military threat. The first phase was strategic uncertainty in which the nuclear capability was not acknowledged or denied. Phase two applied if the country was threatened militarily. At that time, the government would covertly acknowledge the existence of its nuclear weapons to leading western governments, particularly the United States. If phase two failed to persuade the international community to provide assistance against a military attack, the government would move to phase three and publicly acknowledge its capability or demonstrate it by an underground test.

Nuclear policies aimed at forcing support from a superpower, particularly the United States, are not new or unique to South Africa. Several countries, most notably South Korea, have threatened overtly or implicitly to develop nuclear weapons, if the United States withdrew its nuclear weapons umbrella. In the case of most western nations, the United States has remained a loyal ally, supplying conventional weapons and a nuclear umbrella. What is unique about South Africa's strategy is that it was developed while the United States was withdrawing its support.

Preconditions for the Decision to Rollback its Nuclear Arsenal

The end of the 1980s witnessed several events that significantly changed the fundamental security situation in Southern Africa and increased political support among white South Africans for an end to apartheid. At this point, the nuclear arsenal became irrelevant and, worse, a political liability.

By the beginning of 1989, white South Africa no longer feared a "communist onslaught." A comprehensive peace settlement in Southern Africa was brokered by the U.S. government. The end of the cold war was fast approaching. Some of the major events were:

South Africa, Cuba, and Angola established a *de.facto* cease fire in August 1988, followed by the complete withdrawal of South African troops from Angola by September 1, 1988.

On 22 December 1988, a tripartite agreement was signed at the United Nations among Cuba, South Africa, and Angola which provided for the independence of Namibia and the withdrawal of 50,000 Cuban troops from Angola.

The Cold War was coming to an end and developments leading to the destruction of the Berlin Wall and the break-up of the Soviet bloc had become the order of the day.

Settling these longstanding issues in Angola and Namibia raised expectations of South Africa moving away from a confrontational relationship with the international community in general, and with its neighbors in Africa, in particular, to one of cooperation and development. With Moscow removed as the major threat to Pretoria's existence, the South African government could now begin a more realistic reevaluation of South Africa's domestic situation. Since the ANC was viewed by Afrikaaners as a stalking horse for Moscow, these events meant that direct governmental negotiations with the African National Congress would no longer be seen as tantamount to national suicide.

Economic sanctions and the withdrawal of investments from South Africa combined with racial unrest had left South Africa by the late 1980s in its deepest financial crisis ever. Important members of the ruling National Party had begun to believe that apartheid was unworkable.

A growing number of South Africa's white elite began to believe in the ANC's moderation and the inevitability of its rise in power within South Africa. At the very least, many members of the National Party realized that the ANC and its political allies could not be defeated.

Although these changes were necessary for a nuclear rollback, they were not sufficient. In fact, in 1989 ARMSCOR had just finished a new set of facilities, and it was planning to modernize the nuclear arsenal. A change in political leadership was needed as well.

The most important patron of the nuclear weapons program, and opponent of efforts to end apartheid, was President Botha, whose well-known explosive temper and authoritarian manner earned him the nickname the "old crocodile." Although the Botha administration was committed to reforming the apartheid system, it was unwilling to sacrifice Afrikaaner power. Botha's reforms at best were token, and served mainly to inflame the black population. His efforts to suppress the black rebellion were ruthless, and intensified through the second half of the 1980s, leaving him increasingly autocratic and isolated.

Botha had also created a governing structure that hindered change, namely his revival of the State Security Council, which was composed of the so-called "securocrats," mostly Army, intelligence, and security officials, and a few of his closest ministers. Botha made this council the central instrument of control of the country, bypassing his own National Party and the Parliament.

The story of Botha's fall from power and replacement by F. W. de Klerk in 1989 has been extensively chronicled elsewhere. The political rise and transformation of F. W. de Klerk led to a radical change in South Africa, including freeing Nelson Mandela, demilitarizing the government's decision-making processes, and starting direct negotiations with the ANC. But parallelling these profound changes, de Klerk decided to secretly terminate the nuclear weapons program and dismantle the existing nuclear weapons.

The Decision to Rollback

When de Klerk became State President in September 1989, he already knew about the weapons program as a former Minister in charge of the Atomic Energy Corporation, although he had never been an "Insider" in Botha's government. When he became State President, he believed that South Africa's national interest lay in completely reversing its nuclear policy.

Waldo Stumpf, the head of the Atomic Energy Corporation, tells an anecdote that sheds some light on de Klerk's thinking when he came into office. Stumpf says that de Klerk called a meeting of a few key Ministers and experts including Stumpf one or two weeks after assuming office. According to Stumpf, President de Klerk said that he wanted to make South Africa a "respected member of the international community, and we'll have to turn around the politics and we'll have to terminate this programme, turn it around and accede to the NPT."[69] De Klerk recognized that the nuclear weapons program stood in the way of South Africa rejoining the international community, evidently a primary motivation for all of his actions.

---

[13]Transcript of Speech by Stumpf, op. cit.

Most observers believe that de Klerk and his advisors also worried about the fate of the nuclear arsenal. At least, the government doubted whether a future multi-party government could successfully share control over the arsenal. Eliminating the arsenal before launching major reforms prevented potential conflict among the major parties over the fate of the weapons and simultaneously created a regional and international policy against nuclear weapons. Because the ANC had opposed the South African nuclear weapons program, it would find it hard to oppose what de Klerk had done.

Although there is little evidence that de Klerk's thinking was dominated by concerns about a future ANC-led government inheriting nuclear weapons, Western intelligence agencies and right-wing military officials worried a great deal about the ANC's possible inheritance. To these groups, the potential of an ANC-controlled nuclear program that might have included stocks of nuclear weapons or highly enriched uranium was a major concern up to the time of the first democratic elections in April 1994. For example, a 1993 article in the London *Sunday Times* reported that western intelligence officials, who were concerned about the "unstable security situation in South Africa," had expressed "deep disquiet that a future ANC government might be tempted to start its own weapons-making program, or to sell the [highly enriched] uranium either to Libya, Iran, or the Palestine Liberation Organization, all of which gave the movement support during the years in exile."[70]

Dismantlement

On February 26, 1990, President de Klerk issued formal written instructions to terminate the nuclear weapons program and dismantle all existing weapons. The

---

[14]Richard Ellis, "Pretoria Seeks Haven for its Nuclear Stocks," *The Sunday Times,* August 15, 1993.

nuclear materials were to be melted down and returned to the AEC in preparation for South Africa's accession to the NPT.

In addition, he ordered the closure of the unsafeguarded enrichment plant at Pelindaba that had made the highly enriched uranium. It was closed in early 1990, and served as the first outward sign that the weapons program had ended.

The government, however, decided that it would not admit to the existence of the nuclear weapons program before accession to the NPT, a legally permissible action. According to Stumpf, the government feared that revelations about the nuclear arsenal could lead to the same type of confrontational inspections that were then occurring in Iraq. In addition, he said that the internal political situation mitigated against acknowledging the program. As a result, the dismantling project was classified top secret.

Dismantling started in July 1990. By September 6, 1991, all of the HEU had been removed from the weapons, melted down, and sent back to the AEC at Pelindaba for storage.

During the dismantlement process at Circle (which had been renamed Advena Central Laboratories in the late 1980s), the devices were removed from the vault where they were stored, taken apart, and the nuclear material removed. The HEU was melted and recast into ingots of a few kilograms each and returned to the vault. Criticality safe shelves were installed in one internal vault to safely store the recast HEU ingots. To ensure secrecy, the HEU was sent from the Circle building back to Pelindaba at night.

Soon after sending the last material to the AEC, the Circle building was completely decontaminated and the equipment that had been used for the re-melting and casting of HEU sent to the AEC. Machine tools which shaped natural uranium components were decontaminated, but remained at Circle. The main uranium processing section of Circle was carefully decontaminated. Walls were removed, and the concrete floor was jacked out.

Contamination was reduced to background levels. An ARMSCOR official said that they wanted the room clean enough so that they could plausibly deny the existence of the program. They personally did not believe that the program would ever be revealed.

Although this portion of the dismantlement work was not finished when South Africa acceded to the NPT on July 10, 1991, it was completed prior to entry into force of the safeguards agreement on September 16, 1991.

At this time, major non-nuclear components of the weapons, detailed design drawings, computer software, documents, and photos of components remained. Destruction of many of these items began in 1992 and continued into 1994.

Decision to Reveal the Existence of the Program

South Africa's lack of candor about its past nuclear weapons program finally erupted into a political controversy in late 1992 and early 1993. This controversy led President de Klerk to announce to the parliament the program's existence on March 24, 1993.

De Klerk gave as his reason that some countries and the media alleged that South Africa still had covert nuclear weapon aspirations and had not fully revealed its stockpile of highly enriched uranium. This suspicion was hurting South Africa's efforts to commercialize its nuclear infrastructure, particularly its efforts to export high-technology products. In addition, the ANC intended to make the secret nuclear weapons program an election issue, and this worried de Klerk's party.

U.S. officials had also urged South African officials to reveal fully its nuclear weapons program in order to reestablish South Africa's international credibility. Lacking such an admission, the U.S. intelligence community started seriously questioning South Africa's commitment to the NPT. A Bush Administration report, called the "Pell Report," that was sent to Congress on January 19, 1993, states: "The United States has serious questions about South Africa's compliance with its Article II and III obligations" under the NPT.

The Russian Foreign Intelligence Service expressed similar concerns. In an early 1993 report, it said that certain experts doubt that South Africa has declared all of its weapons or nuclear explosive materials.

To encourage more South African candour, U.S. officials told this author that members of the U.S. government leaked information about the program to the media. For example, on March 18, 1993, six days before de Kierk's announcement, the *Washington Post* published a long article titled "Tracking S. Africa's Elusive A-program." The article quoted U.S. officials saying they "strongly suspect South Africa has not accounted fully for all the bomb-grade uranium it produced or the other nuclear weapons components it amassed and [it] may still be hiding some nuclear bomb-related items." This article coincided with the visit of South Africa's Foreign Minister to Washington.

President de Klerk stated that his decision to reveal the program had been taken long before the *Washington Post* story, but he admitted that enough had leaked out that the government was getting press inquiries from "quite a number of sources."[71] He added that both countries and important commentators were expressing doubt that all the HEU had been disclosed, with the effect that trust in the government was eroded.

One major exception to the government's new openness was that it refused to reveal overseas sources of key items to the IAEA. It also refused to discuss details about its ballistic missile program.

---

[15]"De Klerk Holds News Conference on Speech," SABC TV I Network in English, 24 March 1993, transcript published in FBIS-AFR-93-056, 25 March 1993.

Conclusion

Despite some unanswered questions about the program, South Africa's nuclear weapons program has been dismantled and its HEU accounted for. This was the conclusion of the IAEA, which spent two years conducting a set of unprecedented inspections and verification activities in South Africa. Most of the effort was spent scrutinizing South Africa's declaration of its HEU at the time of signing the NPT to ensure it was complete. In response to concerns that it had not declared all its HEU, the government provided the IAEA with extensive historical production records for the pilot enrichment plant that made the HEU. In a September 1993 report, the IAEA concluded: "It is reasonable to conclude that the amounts of HEU which could have been produced by the pilot enrichment plant are consistent with the amounts declared in the initial report."[72]

Many have charged that the government hid away some HEU or exported indigenously produced enriched uranium. If this occurred in a significant way, then the IAEA should have detected it. If a significant amount of enriched material had been hidden or exported, the IAEA would have estimated an inventory that was significantly less than what the government declared. It did not do so, and it has concluded that such possibilities are remote.

After his March 1993 announcement, President de Klerk invited the IAEA to verify the government's statements about the production and dismantlement of its nuclear weapons. The IAEA did so through the spring and summer of 1993, and compiled a comprehensive understanding of the nuclear weapons program, particularly its timing and scope. It verified South Africa's statements that it dismantled its weapons.

---

[16]*The Denuclearization of Africa,* op. cit.

The HEU from South Africa's nuclear weapons and the knowledge to turn it into nuclear weapons remain in South Africa. Few question South Africa's commitment to non-proliferation or opposition to the resurrection of a nuclear weapons program. Nevertheless, many challenges lie ahead for the new government, including maintaining strict control over its nuclear explosive material and ensuring that its nuclear and missile technologies are not exported to countries that seek weapons of mass destruction.

Chapter 17

Non-Nuclear Became Beautiful:
The Sweden Case

Jan Prawitz

Introduction

Since the time of Hiroshima, various aspects of the nuclear weapon employment have been important issues in the politics of national security in Sweden. In the early days, the issue was when rather than if Sweden should acquire its own atomic bombs. Taking the risk of oversimplification, in the mid 1950s it was conventional wisdom that Sweden a decade later would be a nuclear weapon power – perhaps even before France. But the tide turned and in the mid 1960s, most Swedes took the opposite for granted: that Sweden should stay non-nuclear. In 1968, Sweden formally decided to stay non-nuclear and signed the Non-Proliferation Treaty.

The political process that eventually resulted in Sweden's abandoning the idea of becoming a nuclear weapon state was rather complex, long-lasting, and involved a number of factors. While discussed within the national security elite for some time, the issue got a high profile in 1954 and then played an important role in domestic politics and in party politics, sometimes in moralistic and emotional terms. Several political parties were split on the issue. A popular "ban-the-bomb movement" was organized which considered non-nuclear status a moral imperative rather than a security conclusion.

Internationally, flexible response succeeded massive retaliation as the prime strategic doctrine of the military blocs in Europe. Nuclear attack became unlikely but could not be ruled out as a secondary contingency. Conventional defense was an obvious necessity for neutral Sweden to deter conventional aggression assumed to be the most probable contingency. In addition, a nuclear strike force was economically out of reach. After all, Sweden was not as wealthy as France.

The "Nuclear Option" Period – up to 1968
The Early Military Discussion

In the early 1950s, nuclear weapons were generally considered just more powerful "conventional" weapons without special political meaning. Today´s hesitation to use nuclear weapons at all, was not so pronounced at the time. Therefore, it was argued, Sweden should as a modern and developed country with serious defense ambitions acquire atomic weapons in due time. It was also argued that Swedish soldiers should not be forced to fight with weapons inferior to those of an enemy.

In the tactical context, it was considered obvious that the ability of the Swedish armed forces to impede an invader would be much improved if equipped with nuclear weapons. A specific argument was that if Sweden had no tactical nuclear weapons of its own and was invaded by an enemy with such weapons, Sweden would be forced to spread out its military units to avoid their annihilation, while an enemy could create decisive advantages by concentrating his forces. Sweden´s defense planners at the time took it for granted that an invader having nuclear weapons would also use them if militarily convenient.[1]

---

[1]Most of the discussion within the defense community at the time is covered in R. Björnerstedt, L. Grape, (Eds), *Svenska Kärnvapenproblem* [Swedish Nuclear Weapon Problems, In Swedish], Aldus, Stockholm, 1965. This early monograph reflects important parts of a comprehensive top-secret (declassified today) report, *Kärnladdningsgruppens betänkande* [Report of the Nuclear Weapons Group], prepared under the auspices of the Commander-in-Chief of Sweden´s Armed Forces and completed in February 1962.

For many of those favouring acquisition of nuclear weapons for Sweden, the rational was as simple as that.

The policy of neutrality excluded sharing nuclear weapons with other nations or buying nuclear weapons from abroad. The latter was also excluded due to the determined attitudes of the nuclear weapon powers. Domestic manufacture of both nuclear explosive material and nuclear explosive devices had thus been the only way to acquire nuclear weapons.

Political actors arguing in favour of a Swedish nuclear force assumed that Sweden could afford one nuclear system only, and that that system would be a tactical nuclear force for the support of the defense against invasion across the land border or from the sea. Such a weapon system would not have required special means of delivery. Ordinary fighter-bombers of the type deployed by the Swedish air force at the time would have been adequate.

An independent strategic deterrence was also discussed but never seriously proposed, the prime reason being economic.

There is no doubt that Sweden at the time would have been able to manufacture a tactical nuclear force without assistance from abroad. The two basic requirements, domestic uranium and advanced nuclear technology, were available. It was clear that the Swedish atomic bomb would have to be based on plutonium produced in domestically-built nuclear reactors, as domestic production of weapon grade uranium would be out of question for economic reasons using the enrichment methods known at the time.

In addition, sites were sought and found where domestic testing of nuclear explosion devices both in the atmosphere and underground would have been possible without radioactive risks to the population. The available capacity for research and production would, however, have restricted a nuclear weapons programme to one type of warhead.

But it should be noted that going nuclear would have meant not only managing nuclear physics and fabricating bombs. It would also require the setting up of special military units for deployment of the new weapons, as well as special training for such personnel, special planning, command, control, communication, and intelligence activities for the nuclear weapons, special arrangements for their protection while in stock or deployed, special service and maintenance arrangements, etc, i.e. quite a sizeable operation. The bombs themselves would not have been the most expensive part of a nuclear force. All the same, a reasonable material basis for going nuclear did exist at the time.

Domestic Politics and Developments

The issue of acquiring nuclear weapons by Sweden was very controversial domestically. The official political debate in the Parliament as well as the debate in the media and generally in the public was very lively. Several political parties were internally split over the issue.[2]

An impressive number of arguments were raised for and against a Swedish nuclear force and covered issues of strategy, war-fighting and military tactics, foreign relations and arms control, costs, fabrication of nuclear explosive devices and accessibility of nuclear material, research and development, risks involved in test explosions, as well as pacifist and moral aspects.

As more and more data about the effects of nuclear explosions and the consequences of nuclear war in Europe became available, the attitudes of politicians

---

[2]The political debate on the nuclear weapon issue during the 1954-1960 period has been described by P. Ahlmark in *Den svenska atomvapendebatten* [The Swedish Atomic Weapon Debate, In Swedish], Aldus, Stockholm 1965. An appendix by H.-Å. Dhejne covers the 1960 - 1964 period, pp 135-145. Compare also S. Lindholm, L. Sjöberg, *Opinionsmätningar rörande svenska kärnvapen* [Opinion Polls Regarding Swedish Nuclear Weapons, In Swedish] in R. Björnerstedt, L. Grape, (Eds), *Svenska Kärnvapenproblem* [Swedish Nuclear Weapon Problems, In Swedish], Aldus, Stockholm 1965, pp 230-245.

and the public began to crystalize. In this period, it became increasingly clear that nuclear war on Swedish soil would be a national disaster. A study of the consequences of nation-wide nuclear strikes against Swedish cities showed that an attack with about 200 nuclear weapons with yields ranging from 20 to 200 kilotons would result in between 2 and 3 million fatal casualties or 30 to 40 percent of the population. 30 to 70 percent of Sweden's industry would also be destroyed while 60 percent of the industrial workers would be fatally injured. In case evacuation and other civil defense measures had been undertaken, the number of casualties would be reduced to between 200.000 and 300.000. This may be a worst case scenario and other examples have showed lower figures.[3]

Another factor influencing attitudes in Sweden at the time was the international negotiations on disarmament which discouraged the acquisition of nuclear weapons and of arms in general. In 1961, Sweden became a member state of the Geneva Disarmament Conference. At the time, the number one item on the disarmament agenda was "general and complete disarmament" which was taken seriously by many politicians including Swedish Cabinet members. Therefore, a political position at the time, held plausible by some people, was to start planning for drastically reduced military forces within a few years thus ruling out any new high-tech weapons.

The Social Democratic Party, forming the government at the time, was severely split over the atomic weapon issue. Among the politicians against nuclear weapons from the very beginning was the then Minister for Foreign Affairs, Dr Östen Undén, who wrote several analytical internal memoranda focussing on foreign policy

---

[3]This investigation was the basis for an unpublished paper by R. Björnerstedt, *Some Comments on the Effects of the Use of Nuclear Weapons* being a Swedish contribution to a UN expert study 1967 on nuclear weapons reported in UN document A/6858, *Effects of the possible use of nuclear weapons and security and economic implications for states of the acquisition and further development of these weapons* (UN Sales No. E.68.IX.1).

implications of going nuclear. Already in 1955, he argued that Swedish territory boosted by nuclear weapons would be perceived as a more dangerous neighbourhood by the Soviet Union, and that nuclear weapons would imply both a political disadvantage for Sweden in peacetime, and a military disadvantage in the early stages of a European war[4]. In 1959, he referred to the ongoing attempts to stop nuclear weapon proliferation and concluded that acquisition of nuclear weapons would go contrary to the international opinion and be a most severe foreign policy drawback for Sweden. He also concluded that in the nuclear age, reducing risks of war was more important than upgrading military defense[5].

The nature of such possible drawbacks referred to by Dr Undén could be subject to speculation only. It would be conceivable to assume, however, that the U.S. reaction upon a Swedish acquisition of nuclear weapons would have been similarly negative as demonstrated in the case of France. This could also, for instance, have jeopardized the considerable Swedish import of military equipment from the USA and other Western countries. In a U.S. National Security Council policy recommendation of 1960, it was stated that the USA should "be prepared to sell to Sweden military materiel, and to provide training to Sweden on a reimbursable basis", but that nuclear warheads should not be provided, and that Sweden should be "discouraged from producing its own nuclear weapons."[6]

---

[4]Undén, *P.M. om s. k. taktiska kärnvapen*, [Memo on s c tactical nuclear weapons, In Swedish] 1 August 1955. Memo top-secret at the time.
[5]Undén, Memo dated 15 April 1959. An edited version of the memo was published in Ö. Undén, *Tankar om utrikespolitik* [Thoughts on Foreign Policy, In Swedish]. Rabén & Sjögren. Stockholm. 1963. pp 77-149.
[6]NSC Document 6006/1 (Rev.), 10 November 1960, *U.S. Policy Toward Scandinavia (Denmark, Norway and Sweden)*, classified at the time. pt 35. a. The document also outlines possible preparations to support Sweden resisting a Soviet attack and recommends that the USA *"in event of communist domination of Finland"* should *"consider promoting Sweden's membership of NATO"*.

In the late fall of 1958, the Social Democratic Party set up an internal committee to investigate the nuclear weapon issue[7]. The resulting report suggested both that Sweden should not acquire nuclear weapons because of the ongoing disarmament negotiations among the major powers, and that Sweden should thus postpone its final decision on the issue. The report also suggested that research on protection against a possible nuclear attack should continue and be expanded[8]. The Swedish government decided accordingly.

In practical terms, this decision meant, at least for the time being, that there would be no crash-programme for the production of weapon-grade fissionable material (i.e. plutonium) and no research effort to design and test a deliverable warhead. Plutonium that could be used for warheads, could thus be produced only in the natural uranium heavy water power reactors of domestic design that were planned but not constructed at the time; a coordination of the civil and military programmes that would also have been motivated by economic factors.

Another implication was that the nuclear defense research programme was limited to a study of possible measures of protection against nuclear attack to Swedish territory including a general review of nuclear weapon design. The latter was considered necessary to make assessments of the types of nuclear weapons that might be deployed against Sweden. It was fully recognized and appreciated that know-how acquired by such research would also be valuable for a future design and manufacture of a Swedish nuclear weapon.

This "nuclear option policy" made possible a postponement of the final decision whether to go nuclear or not by several years until the civil nuclear power

---

[7]The Chairman of the committee was Prime Minister Tage Erlander. Dr Östen Undén was one of its members. Mr Olof Palme who in 1968 became Sweden's Prime Minster, served as the secretary of the committee.
[8]*Neutralitet - försvar - atomvapen. Rapport till Socialdemokratiska partistyrelsen* [Neutrality - Defense - Nuclear Weapons. Report to the Social Democratic Party Board, In Swedish]. Tiden. Stockholm. 1960. The report was released on 11 November 1959.

programme was further developed without losing time, if the final decision were to be positive, or money if the decision was negative.

In the late 1950s, the expected development of the nuclear power programme had indicated that by 1964 at the earliest, the decision to go nuclear had to be taken in order to achieve the earliest possible deployment[9]. As that time approached, however, it became clear that the whole basis for the "nuclear option policy" had been quietly changed for several reasons. The build-up of the nuclear power program was considerably delayed. Adapting to new energy market realities, the all-Swedish natural uranium heavy water reactor concept had been abandoned and replaced by a design using enriched uranium fuel and light water moderator. But enriched uranium was available only from abroad and only for peaceful use subject to safeguards. A reprocessing plant for plutonium extraction had been planned but was never built.

In the mid 1960s, it became clear that a Swedish nuclear weapon programme had to be a separate production programme without any link to the nuclear power industry. A number of economically motivated steps had made most of the civil nuclear power programme incompatible with military co-production and over the years almost added up to a "silent no" (*tyst nej*) to a Swedish nuclear force[10]. Instead of specifying a date for making a decision, Sweden thus maintained a constant estimated seven year[11] lead-time of research, development, and un-safeguarded plutonium production. Consequently, no decision was made. The first possible deployment had been postponed until the mid 1970s.

---

[9]M. Fehrm, T. Magnusson, *P.M. beträffande beslutsläget i atomvapenfrågan* [Memo on the situation regarding the nuclear weapon decision, In Swedish], 3 December 1957. This memo has been declassified in recent years. The authors were Director General and Director for Atomic Studies respectively at the Swedish Research Institute of National Defense.
[10]The "silent no" was first discussed in public by Dr R. Björnerstedt in *Sverige i kärnvapenfrågan* [Sweden and the Nuclear Weapon Issue, In Swedish], Försvar i Nutid, No. 5 1965. p 23.
[11]The seven years estimate was communicated to the author in 1967 by Dr Martin Fehrm, at the time Director General of the Swedish Defense Research Institute.

This development is not uniquely Swedish. As a result of the "Atoms-for-Peace"-initiative by U.S. President Eisenhower in 1953[12], many countries were granted "assistance" with nuclear fuel for developing their peaceful nuclear energy on the condition, however, that that assistance would not further any military purpose. In the end, only France turned out to be wealthy enough to be able to develop both a peaceful nuclear power programme and a nuclear weapon programme in parallel. But France had to pay the price in terms of reduced conventional forces.

International Politics

In the international arena, the issue of "the prohibition of the further proliferation of nuclear weapons" had entered the agenda of both the United Nations and the Disarmament Conference (the Eighteen Nation Disarmament Conference) in Geneva. The establishment of nuclear-weapon-free zones in various parts of Europe were proposed, including a zone in Northern Europe.

Sweden both maintained the "nuclear option policy" and pursued an active participation in the international negotiations on non-proliferation, thus preparing for both the nuclear and the non-nuclear options.

In 1961, Sweden proposed in the UN General Assembly that member states should be inquired as to what conditions "countries not possessing nuclear weapons might be willing to enter into specific undertakings to refrain from manufacturing or otherwise acquiring such weapons and to refuse to receive, in the future, nuclear weapons in their territories on behalf of any other country,"[13] or in short to join "a

---

[12]Statement by President Eisenhower at the 470th meeting of the UN General Assembly on 8 December 1953 (Department of State publication 5314/1953).
[13]UN document A/RES/1644 (XVI). 63 states responded to the inquiry, see UN documents DC/201 and Add. 1-3.

non-atomic club" (the Undén-plan)[14]. This initiative did not attract sufficient support and thus became a non-starter.

On 28 May 1963, the President of Finland, Dr Urho Kekkonen, proposed that the Nordic countries declare themselves a nuclear weapon free zone[15]. Dr Kekkonen argued that the proposed zone "would indisputably remove the Nordic countries from the sphere of speculation caused by the development of nuclear strategy, and ensure that this region will remain outside international tension." His concept of "Nordic countries" included Denmark, Finland, Norway, and Sweden.

The Swedish reaction to the Finnish proposal (the Kekkonen-plan) was cool, however, despite the fact that it was acknowledged that the Nordic countries were *de facto* nuclear weapon free[16].

In August 1963, the Partial Test Ban Treaty, just signed between the Soviet Union, the United Kingdom, and the United States, was opened for signature for all states. Sweden immediately signed as did a large number of other states yielding to international pressure and a desire to support arms control. It was understood at the time that this commitment would limit the possibilities for the development of a Swedish nuclear weapon, but not severely, because underground testing would still be a possibility, although impractical and more expensive.

---

[14]The non-nuclear club idea was called the "Undén-plan" after the Swedish Minister for Foreign Affairs at the time, Dr Östen Undén. Compare K. Brodin, *The Undén Proposal*, Cooperation and Conflict, Vol. I, 1966. pp 18ff.

[15]Statement by President Urho Kekkonen on 28 May 1963. For text, see U. Kekkonen, *Neutrality: The Finnish Position. Speeches 1943-1972*. Heinemann. London. 1973. pp.143-145. President Kekkonen made his zone proposal at a difficult point in time for European security: the Berlin Wall had been raised in August 1961; Finland had experienced a crisis with its superpower neighbor to the east, USSR, in November 1961 (the s. c. note-crisis); the Undén-plan of 1961 had failed; the Cuban crisis in October 1962 had brought the world to the brink of a nuclear war; and Finland's neighbor to the west, Sweden, pursued a nuclear option policy.

[16]Sweden reacted by a statement by Prime Minister Tage Erlander the next day, 29 May 1963. For text, see *Documents on Swedish Foreign Policy 1963*. Royal Ministry for Foreign Affairs. p.60. The cool attitude, as repeatedly expressed in the Parliament, prevailed for more than a decade.

Strategic Analysis Updated

One of the most important developments for the final assessment of the Swedish nuclear weapon issue was the military. In the early 1960s, the new military doctrine of "flexible response" was widely discussed in relation to the European theater. This doctrine was finally adopted by NATO in 1967 and later, by implication, also by the Warsaw Pact. The Soviet doctrine at the time was only vaguely known but the Soviets were widely assumed to adopt western doctrines with a time-lag of a few years. It was obvious, however, that the conventional forces of the Warsaw Pact more than equalled those of NATO, and were their main instruments of military force in Europe.

One feature of the new doctrine was that use of nuclear weapons in war could be authorized only by the political leader of the possessor state. It also implied that the nuclear weapon powers signaled in advance a great hesitation to escalate a conflict to nuclear levels, and that the threshold for escalation to nuclear war was elevated in order to make possible efforts to terminate a conflict before nuclear weapons would be considered. Conventional forces were allotted increased importance, while nuclear weapons became primarily "political weapons", although usable if necessary. This change influenced the defense environment even for the neutral Sweden and was interpreted to mean that a military conflict in Europe could be assumed to begin as a conventional conflict.

It was concluded that if Sweden, according to this scenario, would be invaded, it would most probably be an attack with conventional means. It was considered most unlikely that an aggressor, be it NATO or the Warsaw Pact, would escalate the conflict to a nuclear war in order primarily to support operations on the Swedish front, and by doing so risk a nuclear counter-attack from its main adversary on all fronts. If Sweden had allocated all defense resources to a conventional defense, it would be possible – such was the argument at the time – to deter a conventional attack and leave the aggressor with no alternative but to use nuclear weapons. An aggressor would then probably abstain from the attack rather than escalate.

If, on the other hand, Sweden had spent substantial resources on a tactical nuclear force and thus less on conventional forces, these conventional forces may not have been able to deter a conventional attack. If attacked by conventional forces, Sweden would then have had no choice but surrender or escalation. In the latter case, Sweden would itself have introduced nuclear weapons on the battlefield, thus inviting a nuclear counter-attack in contradiction to its basic security ambition to survive as a nation.

There was also the possible scenario that a European conflict would escalate to a nuclear war before Sweden became involved. The attacker could then use nuclear weapons against Sweden without risking further retaliation from his main adversary. Whether an enemy would do so or not, his main adversary could direct nuclear strikes against targets in Sweden. But nuclear strikes of the bloc forces could easily become orders of magnitude more powerful than any conceivable Swedish nuclear retaliation. A Swedish nuclear force would thus have little to add to such a situation.

The conclusion drawn from this analysis was that Sweden should not acquire a nuclear force. Assuming continued dominance of the two military blocs in Europe and also assuming their continued high nuclear threshold (flexible response) doctrine, a realistic defense planning dictated that a nuclear strike force in addition to the necessary conventional defense would not be possible within any conceivable peacetime level of Swedish defense expenditures[17]. This analysis prevailed and

---

[17]This analysis was first published by Karl Frithiofson, at the time Under-Secretary of State for Defense, in *Säkerhetspolitiska perspektiv på frågan om svenska kärnvapen* [The Swedish Nuclear Weapons Issue from a Security Perspective, In Swedish]. KKrVA Handlingar Vol. 170 (1966), p 303. The Swedish Government and the Minister of Defense, Mr Sven Andersson, had settled for this same analysis earlier but found it opportune not to go public until 1966 (K. Frithiofson, private communication 16 November 1993).

became the basis for the strategic decision in 1968 to assume an international commitment to go non-nuclear.

The only reservation to this policy was that possible long range developments making nuclear weapons standard equipment of ordinary states, might require a reconsideration of the conclusion. But such a development did not occur and seems now more unlikely than ever. The reservation has thus never been put to a test.

Crossing the Line

In March 1968, the Swedish government submitted a four year defense plan to the Parliament for approval in which it declared that "it is at present not a security interest of Sweden to acquire nuclear weapons". The Parliament confirmed that conclusion in May 1968[18], about a month before the NPT was opened for signature. Sweden signed the NPT on 19 August 1968 and deposited its instruments of ratification on 9 January 1970[19]. As a consequence of its policy of neutrality, Sweden declared itself not interested in the positive guarantees adopted by the UN Security Council[20] in support of the NPT[21]. This was a minor sacrifice, however, as all conceivable nuclear aggressors against Sweden were permanent members of the Security Council with a right of veto, making the guarantees redundant.

During the debate about the NPT in the Parliament, some members moved[22] that Sweden, when depositing its instruments of ratification, should also file a

---

[18]The principles and decisions referred to are reproduced in the official documents of the Parliament. (SOU 1968:10), Prop. 1968:110, SU 1968:122, rskr 1968:281 (All in Swedish).

[19]The documents of the Parliament on the ratification of the NPT are included in Prop. 1969:164, UU 1969:24, FK 1969:43 p 81ff, AK 1969:43 p 34ff, rskr. 374 (All in Swedish).

[20]UN resolution S 255 (1968).

[21]See for instance the Swedish statement in the Final Declaration of the First Review Conference of the Parties to the NPT, Document NPT/CONF/35/I, Annex II. According to the statement, "*the Swedish government has the view that should assistance to a country be contemplated under Security Council resolution 255 (1968), that country shall have the right to decide if and under what conditions assistance might be granted*".

[22]Documents of the Parliament M I 1969:1131 and M II 1969:1307

declaration that inadequate progress in nuclear disarmament at the time of the first review conference of the NPT in 1975 would constitute such an extraordinary event jeopardizing the supreme interests of the country that withdrawal from the treaty obligations would be legitimate. The proposal was intended to keep an option to return to the nuclear option. These motions did not pass, however.

With these formal steps Sweden became a permanent non-nuclear weapon state.

Non-nuclear Defense Against Nuclear Threat

Considering the military environment of Sweden at the time of entry into force of the NPT, the dominating contingencies for planning the Swedish defense were large scale invasions by conventional forces across the northern land border and from the sea. Possible use of nuclear weapons against targets in Sweden was considered unlikely because of the prevailing flexible response doctrine in the European theatre. But defense measures also had to be prepared against nuclear attack and threat of nuclear attack as secondary contingencies.

The continued existence of a nuclear threat meant that the nuclear weapon research programs within the defense sector had also to continue. The purpose was to acquire knowledge necessary for preparing protection against nuclear attack and for assessing the nature of nuclear arsenals available to possible enemies. This research effort was gradually reduced over the years along with the accumulation of knowledge but has been continued up to this day and will continue as long as a nuclear threat exists. The side effect of improving the understanding of nuclear weapon design will necessarily also continue although irrelevant for a non-nuclear weapon NPT party state.

Protection Strategy

It was assumed by the Swedish defense planners in the 1970s that an aggressor attacking Sweden would employ forces on a level to which the main conflict in Europe – an enemy's main preoccupation – had already escalated, but that he might attack on a lower level as well. An enemy might also be restricted by the tactical considerations of not counteracting his own operations once on Swedish territory. As a non-nuclear weapon state, Sweden could not itself play a role in an escalation game.

To meet explicit or tacit aggression involving a few nuclear explosions serving the purpose of threat or blackmail, reasonable protective measures were prepared so that those few explosions would not immediately stop essential functions of military defense and civilian society.

Adequate protection measures against the primary effects of nuclear explosions does hardly exist and were extremely difficult and expensive in the few cases attempted. But fortifications were designed to withstand collateral effects of nuclear explosions. Civil defense measures – primarily designed to protect against the effects of conventional war – were upgraded to protect against secondary nuclear explosion effects as well, if possible at a reasonable cost. In addition, passive measures such as dispersed deployment of military forces and evacuation of civilians from urban to rural areas could be undertaken with short notice if prepared for. Sweden is a sparsely populated country with only 19 persons per square kilometer.

The demonstrated willingness to undertake these measures was also intended to show any potential aggressor that the Swedish government would be determined to resist a threatened attack to a population center. This was intended to deter an enemy's intended blackmail, and make this type of aggression less attractive. In addition, the enemy's risk of unintentionally escalating the conflict with a main adversary would be increased.

Should Sweden on the other hand be subject to a large nuclear attack, the wisdom of continuing military defense – so the argument at the time went – would have to be judged in relation to the general possibilities of national survival. It would be impossible to give the population and the armed forces sufficient protection to permit them to survive permanently and thus to deter a large nuclear attack. However, the measures of protection undertaken to meet a "few bomb attack" were believed to permit both the military and the civil defense to function for a long enough time period to organize proper negotiations both with the aggressor and his main adversary. It should be observed that once Sweden had been attacked, the policy of neutrality had already failed, and it could be politically possible for Sweden to enter into agreement with an aggressor on permissible concessions and with its adversaries on military support and alignment.

Neighbourhood Nuclear Explosions

Also considered was the possible scenario that a nuclear war in Europe where Sweden is not involved would cause distant effects in Sweden and make protective efforts desirable. Such effects would primarily be radioactive fall out, but other effects such as Electro Magnetic Pulse black out from high altitude explosions, contamination of coastal waters from sunken nuclear propelled ships, and blast and heat effects from large explosions close to the national borders could also occur.

An idea discussed at the time was the possibility of closing the narrow straits leading into the Baltic Sea by means of 5 Megaton nuclear explosions on the seabed. The result would be underwater craters, the rims of which may even rise above the surface of the sea, and large tsunami waves severely hitting nearby coastal areas in addition to possible radioactive fog and rain.[23]

---

[23]The straits are mostly Danish (NATO) and partly Swedish (neutral) territory.

These possibilities were taken into account in the defense preparations to a reasonable extent.

The "Mini-Nuke" Challenge

The non-nuclear decision of 1968 with its reservation has never been subject to reconsideration, but it was in theory at least, challenged in 1972 by the proposal to introduce "mini-nukes" – subkiloton tactical nuclear weapons, with extreme delivery precision, and overlapping the power gap to conventional weapons – to be used by field commanders "under the threshold" in the European theater[24]. The express purpose of the proposed weapons was to replace the firepower of a substantial number of U.S. troops proposed to be withdrawn from Europe at the time.

The ramifications of these proposals, if implemented, would have been very unfortunate for the security of Sweden. Sweden had prepared a defense for deterring conventional attacks from one bloc, assumed to use the marginal forces it could afford to deploy in a direction towards Scandinavia, while being primarily occupied with a main adversary in Central Europe. But equipped with mini-nukes, such marginal forces could always be made strong enough to bring Sweden's conventional defense to a collapse. It was the proposed doctrine for use of the mini-nukes rather than the hardware that constituted the problem.

---

[24]The debate in Sweden was triggered by statements in support of a new generation of tactical nuclear weapons for the European theater in 1972 and 1973 by high Western officials including the U.S. Secretary of Defense, Melvin R. Laird, the NATO Supreme Allied Commander Europe, General Andrew J. Goodpaster, and the British Minister of State for Defense, Ian Gilmore. Published articles contributing were W. Beecher, *Under the Threshold,* Army (July 1972) p 17; W.C. Lyons, *On Deterrence in Depth,* Mimeographed (Nov. 1972); and W. S. Bennet, R. R. Sandoval, R. G. Schreffler, *A Credible Nuclear-Emphasis Defense for NATO,* Orbis (Vol XVII No. 2) 1973.

The government of Sweden, therefore, decided to try to discourage these ideas[25]. After a year of quiet and consorted diplomatic work among European states, all three nuclear weapon powers had formally declared that current treaties related to nuclear weapons and current doctrines for their use would treat all nuclear weapons equally whatever their explosion yield[26].

The Active NPT Support

The decision in 1968 to go non-nuclear and to sign the Non-Proliferation Treaty was based on the existing character of the military and political situation in Europe at the time. The endurance of the chosen doctrine would naturally depend on the continued relevance of the factors basing the original analysis as indicated in the reservation linked to the decision. For neutral Sweden, geographically situated in the militarized European environment, it thus became necessary to support, to defend and not to counteract those factors in order to ensure that the reservation would never be applicable. It was realized that the 1968 decision to go non-nuclear had to be an active policy and not a political museum piece. It became a national interest for Sweden – as for most other NPT parties – to contribute to the success of the treaty and the regime it defines.

---

[25]Statement by Minister of Disarmament Alva Myrdal on 9 August 1973 (Document CCD/PV. 620 pp 14-15).
[26]The official discussion about mini-nukes at the Geneva Disarmament Conference has been described together with extensive quotations from the formal declarations in J. Prawitz, *Mini-nukes and non-aligned defense. The Case of Sweden*, in the SIPRI monograph F. Barnaby (Ed.), *Tactical Nuclear Weapons: European Perspectives*, Taylor & Francis, Ltd. London. 1978. pp 247-261. A critical comment on the Swedish initiative is made by R. G. Schreffler in the same SIPRI monograph in his chapter *The New Nuclear Force* (Appendix I) pp 330-334. The Swedish Minister of Disarmament at the time, Mrs Alva Myrdal, has described the exchange of statements from a political point of view in her memoir book *The Game of Disarmament* (Revised and Updated), Pantheon. New York. 1982. pp 44-48.

Nuclear Disarmament Promotion Activities

A member of the Geneva Disarmament Conference since 1962, Sweden had concentrated much of its arms control efforts there as well as in the United Nations. As a party to the NPT, Sweden could participate in a number of international fora that this regime created.[27]

Swedish activity for promotion of the non-proliferation regime and for nuclear disarmament, as executed between 1968 and today, could be illustrated by a few examples:

- participation in the negotiations on a comprehensive nuclear test ban, active participation in research on seismic verification, running an advanced seismic array observatory with independent publication of detected underground nuclear explosions, operating a program for the sampling of airborne radioactivity with publication of detected atmospheric nuclear explosions as well as "vented" underground nuclear explosions[28], and after the comprehensive test ban treaty (CTBT) was adopted in September 1996, active participation in the establishment of the CTBT Organization in Vienna;

---

[27]The Conference on Security and Cooperation in Europe (CSCE, today OSCE), in which Sweden has been a participating state since 1972, turned out to be less important as a forum for nuclear issues as agreement was never explicitly reached to include nuclear weapons on the formal agenda of the CSCE (OSCE).

[28]The 1963 Partial Test Ban also prohibits nuclear explosions "*in any other environment* (i. e. underground) *if such explosion causes radioactive debris to be present outside the territorial limits of the State under whose jurisdiction or control such explosion is conducted*" (Art. I:1b). A few "technical" abrogations of the treaty occurred when underground nuclear explosions released radioactive debris into the atmosphere (so called "venting"). Several of these events were detected and identified in Sweden and became the basis for diplomatic inquiries to nuclear weapon powers.

- participation in international negotiations on nuclear disarmament measures[29], e. g. the removal of reliance of nuclear weapons from defense doctrines, promotion of the common security concept[30], the withdrawal of nuclear cruise missiles and other non-strategic nuclear weapons from warships at sea[31], the prohibition of radiological weapons[32], and other issues;

- participation in the negotiations on uniform and legally binding negative[33] nuclear security assurances that non-nuclear weapon states will not be subject to attack or threat of attack with nuclear weapons. As a neutral state, party to the NPT and with no nuclear weapons stationed on its territory, Sweden has several times insisted on being eligible for an automatic guarantee not to be attacked or threatened of attack with nuclear weapons. So far no binding commitment to that effect has been received from any of the nuclear weapon powers;

- participation in the guidelines for nuclear export of the Zangger Committee and the Nuclear Suppliers Group to avoid that sensitive material and equipment make their way to countries which are not truly committed to a

---

[29]During the years 1984-1989, the heads of government of Argentina, Greece, India, Mexico, Sweden, and Tanzania joined in the so called "Six-Nation Initiative", also called the "Five Continent Initiative", for the political promotion of nuclear arms control and disarmament, in particular a comprehensive nuclear test ban.

[30]The original concept of "common security" was presented in 1982 in a report by the "Independent Commission on Disarmament and Security Issues" or the Palme Commission named after its Chairman Olof Palme. *Common Security: A Blueprint for Survival,* Simon & Shuster, New York, 1982. UN document A/CN.10/38.

[31]In October 1985, Sweden's Chief Disarmament Negotiator, Ambassador Maj Britt Theorin, proposed in the UN General Assembly a number of naval arms control measures (UN document A/C. 1/40/PV. 4, pp 10-12), including four related to nuclear weapons.

[32]Since 1980, Sweden has actively pursued a proposal that an agreement on prohibition of radiological weapons should also include a prohibition on attacks on nuclear facilities containing large amounts of radioactive substances. A detailed proposal by Sweden was presented on 18 June 1984 (UN document CD/530). An outline of the Swedish position was presented on 7 April 1981 (UN document CD/PV. 122).

[33]"Negative" guarantees imply that the guarantor abstains from nuclear aggression as different from "positive" guarantees implying that the guarantor actively supports a victim of aggression.

non-nuclear weapon status, and establishing a related national export control system[34];

- participation in the preparation of three United Nations Expert Studies on Nuclear Weapons in 1968, 1980 (chairman), and 1990 (chairperson)[35] making extensive use of the research and study competence in nuclear matters built up at the Swedish Defense Research Establishment during the "nuclear option" years and maintained since.

Activities such as these, which share the Swedish experience with other states, also reflect a determined promotion of a message that "non-nuclear is beautiful."

The Nordic Nuclear-Weapon-Free Zone Proposals

As indicated above, Sweden had long maintained a cool attitude towards the original proposal by President Kekkonen of Finland in 1963 to establish a nuclear-weapon-free zone in the Nordic area (NWFZN). However in 1980, the political interest in the issue of a NWFZN began to grow explosively in all five Nordic countries. This interest, sparked by the Norwegian ambassador Jens Evensen in October 1980[36] and starting as a grassroots enthusiasm, soon modified the express attitudes of governments. Subsequent Swedish governments adopted a positive, though pragmatic, position implying: that the NWFZN concept should be considered "in its wider European context".

---

[34]L. van Dassen, *Sweden*, in H. Müller (Ed.), *Nuclear Export Controls in Europe*, European Inter-university Press, Brussels, 1995, pp 181-206.

[35]The reports of these study groups were published by the Unites Nations with Sales No. E.68.IX.1 (referred to in footnote No.), E.81.I.11, and E.91.IX.12 respectively.

[36]J. Evensen, Address at a trade union conference (Norsk Kemisk Arbeiderforbund) 3 October 1980. Compare also J. Evensen, *Norge i en farlig verden* [Norway in a Dangerous World, In Norwegian], in T. Jagland, S. B. Johansen, J. Nyhamar, A. Treholt, (Eds.), *Atomvåpen og usikkerhetspolitikk* [Nuclear Weapons and Insecurity Policy, In Norwegian]. Norsk Tiden Forlag. 1980.

In the early 1980s, all Nordic governments had expressed a positive attitude towards the idea of a Nordic nuclear-weapon-free zone. Real negotiations on the possible establishment of such a zone were never initiated, however, although in March 1987, the five Nordic governments agreed to appoint a joint group of senior officials to study the "prerequisites for a Nuclear-Weapon-Free Zone in the Nordic Area as part of efforts to achieve deténte and arms reduction in Europe". The group's report, which did not include any recommendations, was released in March 1991[37].

Today, almost all the proposed components of both NWFZN concepts have materialized as a consequence of other arms control measures adopted since 1988 following the end of the Cold War and the unilaterally declared withdrawal of non-strategic nuclear weapons from theaters of deployment and from ships[38]. Therefore, it can be safely concluded that these recent developments have achieved most objectives of the original NWFZN proposal.

Sweden's Policies Questioned

Despite the fact that Sweden's decision to adhere to the NPT and the active NPT promotion policies that followed have been well understood, sincerely respected and appreciated by the world community, suspicion was a few times expressed in the literature that some kind of nuclear option has in fact been maintained after 1968. Two such cases will be referred to here.

---

[37]*Nuclear-Weapon-Free Zone in the Nordic Area. Report from the Nordic Senior Officials Group.* Ministry of Foreign Affairs, Stockholm, March 1991. The group still exists dealing with the NWFZN and other security issues.
[38]Unilateral declarations by Presidents Bush of the USA and Gorbachev of the USSR, on 27 September and 5 October 1991 respectively. On 27 January 1992, Russian President Yeltsin confirmed the Gorbachev declaration. For the full text of the Bush, Gorbachev, and Yeltsin-statements, see e.g. *SIPRI Yearbook 1992*, Oxford University Press, 1992, pp 85-92.

In 1985, a Swedish weekly technical magazine, Ny Teknik [New Technology], published an article claiming that some Swedish scientists and military had been disloyal to the government's decision to adhere to the NPT, that they had carried out ten "tests" involving weapon grade plutonium in 1972, and that a neutron pulse generator suitable for initiation of fission explosions had been constructed[39].

The article triggered "sensationalism" in other media, in one case (CBS) even suggesting that Sweden had secretly stockpiled ten nuclear bombs since 1972. The Swedish government initiated an investigation into the allegations which were reported to be without basis[40]. The case has been researched and described by Mitchell Reiss[41].

Unfortunately, this information has taken on a life of its own and appears from time to time in the literature and in political writings.

On 25 November 1994, a front page article in Washington Post expressed the suspicion that Sweden maintained a mothballed option to fabricate nuclear weapons should a need emerge in an uncertain future[42]. The reasons stated for this conclusion was that the decommissioned Ågesta nuclear reactor[43] had not been completely demolished, the research report files from the nuclear weapon option years had not

---

[39]C. Larsson, *Svenska kärnvapen utvecklades fram till 1972!* (Swedish Nuclear Weapons were developed up to 1972!, In Swedish), Ny Teknik No. 17 April 25 1985, pp 54-83. A translation into English of this article has been made by the Research Service of the U.S. Congress. For a summary in English of the Christer Larsson articles, see T. B. Johansson, *Sweden's abortive nuclear weapons project*, Bulletin of the Atomic Scientists, Vol. 42, No. 3 March, 1986, pp 31-34.

[40]O. Forssberg, *Svensk Kärnvapen-forskning 1945 - 1972* (Swedish Nuclear Weapons Research 1945-1972, In Swedish), Ministry of Defense, Stockholm, 24 April 1987.

[41]M. Reiss, *The Politics of Nuclear Nonproliferation*. Columbia University Press. New York. 1988. Chapter 2, *Sweden* (Addendum). pp 73-77.

[42]S. Coll, *Neutral Sweden Quietly Keeps Nuclear Option Open*, Washington Post, 25 November 1994. A shorter version of the article was published in International Herald Tribune 26-27 November 1994.

[43]The Ågesta nuclear reactor was built underground in a southern Stockholm suburban beginning in 1961. It reached criticality for the first time in 1963 and was run with a thermal effect of 65 MWatts, later elevated to 80 MWatts. The reactor was decommissioned in 1974. The fuel was natural uranium, after 1971 also some low-enriched uranium. The moderator was heavy water supplied by Norway and the USA.

been destroyed, and that some nuclear weapon related research was still going on within the Swedish Defense Research Establishment. The Swedish government rejected the article's suggestions as ridiculous[44].

While the Post article did not make a flat suggestion that the Swedish government intentionally keeps a nuclear weapon option, it refers to the Swedish case as "an example of an emerging nuclear proliferation issue in the post-Cold War world" concerning "what specialists call 'virtual weaponization' programs by sophisticated, industrialized countries". The article also refers to Japan, Germany, Italy, Switzerland, Canada, South Korea, and Taiwan as countries in the same category. The message of the Post article has also taken on a life of its own and created exaggerated surprise worldwide.

This kind of publicity has been embarrassing enough for the Swedish government to motivate official reactions. But no one could seriously suspect that Sweden is a real nuclear threshold state. Instead, following the shortcomings of the NPT verification system in Iraq and elsewhere, the notion has been widely established that adherence to the NPT letter and acceptance of related IAEA safeguards would not alone be sufficient for credibly demonstrating compliance with the non-proliferation regime. More transparency and cooperation would be necessary.

---

[44] Mr Jan Eliasson – Under-Secretary of State for Foreign Affairs – two weeks later declared that *"Sweden does not keep a nuclear option - quietly or in any other way"* (Letter to the Editor, *Sweden's Nonexistent Nuclear Option*, Washington Post 14 December 1994).

Index

✳

SYMPOSIUM SERIES